JESUS

AMONG OTHER GODS

DELIVER US FROM EVIL

RAVI ZACHARIAS

THOMAS NELSON
Since 1798

NASHVILLE   DALLAS   MEXICO CITY   RIO DE JANEIRO   BEIJING

Published in Nashville, Tennessee, by Thomas Nelson. Thomas Nelson is a registered trademark of Thomas Nelson, Inc.

Thomas Nelson, Inc. titles may be purchased in bulk for educational, business, fund-raising, or sales promotional use. For information, please e-mail SpecialMarkets@ThomasNelson.com.

Unless otherwise noted, Scripture quotations are taken from the Holy Bible, New International Version®. © 1973, 1978, 1984 by International Bible Society. Used by permission of Zondervan Publishing House. All rights reserved.

Scripture quotations noted KJV are from the King James Version of the Holy Bible.

Excerpts from Peggy Noonan's essay, "You'd Cry Too If It Happened to You," in *Deliver Us from Evil*, chapter 10, are reprinted by permission of *Forbes* magazine © Forbes Inc., 1992.

ISBN 978-0-8499-4680-6 (Special Edition)

The Library of Congress has cataloged the earlier editions of these books as follows:

Zacharias, Ravi K.
    Jesus among other gods / Ravi Zacharias.
        p. cm.
    ISBN 978-0-8499-1437-9 (hardcover)
    ISBN 978-0-8499-4327-0 (trade paper)
    ISBN 978-0-8499-4263-1 (international edition)
    1. Apologetics. 2. Christianity and other religions. I. Title.
    BT1230 .Z33 2000
    239—dc21   00–039920

Zacharias, Ravi K.
    Deliver us from evil / Ravi Zacharias.
        p. cm.
    Includes bibliographical references.
    ISBN 978-0-8499-1395-2 (hardcover)
    ISBN 978-0-8499-3950-1 (trade paper)
    1. Christianity and culture—History—20th century.
    2. Moral conditions. 3. Apologetics. I. Title.
    br115.c8z33 1997
    270.182'2—dc20   96–34666

Printed in the United States of America

09 10 11 12 13 LBM 5 4 3 2 1

JESUS

Among Other Gods

To the memory of two very dear friends

Charles Kip Jordon
and
Robert Earl Fraley

Both had a share in this effort;
Kip greatly encouraged me to write the book.
Robert made sure I took the time to write it.

None of us knew how soon they would be with Him
Who is the focus of this work.

CONTENTS

ACKNOWLEDGMENTS

WITH THE SUPPORTIVE HELP OF MANY, THIS BOOK FINALLY TOOK SHAPE. I express my heartfelt gratitude to them all.

Danielle DuRant, as always, provided invaluable research support and took on the tedious task of tracking down sources.

Editors Jan Dennis and Jennifer Stair smoothed the bumps significantly.

Laura Kendall with W Publishing Group drew it together at the end. To the leadership at W Publishing Group—David Moberg, Joey Paul, Rob Birkhead, and others—I express my sincere thanks for their gracious words of encouragement.

Finally and most importantly, my thanks to my wife, Margie. She pored over every page with the utmost scrutiny to make her suggestions that make it more readable. I gladly allow her the last word.

This book comes as an expression of a heart grateful to God for all that He has done in my own life.

INTRODUCTION

WHEN I BEGAN WRITING THIS BOOK, I LITTLE DREAMED OF HOW difficult a task this was going to be.

The difficulty has really not been in knowing what to say, but in knowing what *not* to say. We are living in a time when sensitivities are at the surface, often vented with cutting words. Philosophically, you can believe anything, so long as you do not claim it to be true. Morally, you can practice anything, so long as you do not claim that it is a "better" way. Religiously, you can hold to anything, so long as you do not bring Jesus Christ into it. If a spiritual idea is eastern, it is granted critical immunity; if western, it is thoroughly criticized. Thus, a journalist can walk into a church and mock its carryings on, but he or she dare not do the same if the ceremony is from the eastern fold. Such is the mood at the end of the twentieth century.

A mood can be a dangerous state of mind, because it can crush reason under the weight of feeling. But that is precisely what I believe postmodernism best represents—a mood.

How does one in a mood such as this communicate the message of Jesus Christ, in which truth and absoluteness are not only assumed, but also sustained?

Well, for starters, let us be sure that Jesus was not western. In fact, some of His parables were so eastern that I think much of the West may not have entered into the rigor and humor of what He said. What has happened in the West is that His impact over the centuries has been so felt that the ethos and moral impetus of His message changed the course of western civilization. The western naturalist, in sheer arrogance, does not see this. Now, after technological progress, wealth and enterprise have so woven themselves around the message of Jesus that popular models of Christianity appear as nothing more than self and greed at the center, with strands of Christian thought at the periphery. This adulteration has rightly merited the severe rebuke of the critic. We would do well to remember, however, what Augustine said: We are never to judge a philosophy by its abuse. That aside, the way Jesus spoke, the proverbs and stories that He told, and the very context in which He addressed issues was steeped in an eastern idiom. Let us not forget that.

But if the western world has been guilty of adulterating His message beyond recognition, the eastern world has often forgotten that it has, by fault, left a mass of religious belief, sometimes bizarre, irresponsibly uncriticized. Take, for example, various forms of eastern worship and practice. During the writing of this book, I happened to be at several such settings. In one of these, devotees had a large number of hooks pierced into their bodies. Knives were pierced through their faces and small spears through their tongues. Sights like these terrify visitors and children. One has to ask, Why do the same thinkers who criticize any western forms of spirituality not take this to task?

Closer to home, we see the writings of Deepak Chopra, who teaches a doctrine of spirituality, success, and prosperity woven into Vedic teachings, karma, and self-deification. By contrast, we see millions devoted to that underlying world-view living in abject poverty. Have they somehow missed the mark? What is wrong with the picture here? One can readily see that every religion must face the responsibility of answering the questions posed to it.

Numerous other issues can be raised, but the point remains the same.

As a result of all this, serious distortions have come into vogue. Some proponents of other religious faiths talk about the "myth of Christian uniqueness." Others have demanded that propagation of one's faith is wrong and that "conversion" should be banned.

Such a mood brings a tyranny all its own.

The reality is that if religion is to be treated with intellectual respect, then it must stand the test of truth, regardless of the mood of the day. This book is a defense of the uniqueness of the Christian message.

As I have drawn it to a close, I wish I could have said more and argued more by contrast, but the current mood may not lend itself to any more than this.

The route I have followed is to present a clear difference between Jesus and any other claimant to divinity or prophetic status. I have taken six questions that Jesus answered in a way that none other would have answered. An opponent may disagree with His answers, but when those answers are all added up, antagonists will not be able to challenge His uniqueness. I believe every answer is fascinating, and I wish I could have done justice to them. As it stands, the chapters were becoming lengthier, as the subjects had to be adequately dealt with.

The difficulty in containing the length was exacerbated by the fact that I also needed to contrast the answers with those of other leading religions. By far, the most difficult one to deal with was the question posed to Jesus on pain and suffering. That chapter I have divided into three parts.

The final chapter is not a question posed to Jesus, but a question posed on His behalf, to His followers and to His doubters. It was only fitting to end it that way.

As you will soon note, I have not given His answers in distinction to every religion that offers answers on such matters. I have only dealt with those that still draw a large following around the world—Islam, Hinduism, and Buddhism.

I must say one other thing. I have covered thousands of miles during this writing, not only for the book, but also through invitations to speak in various parts of the world. I have walked through temples, mosques, and other religious sites. I have spoken to students at universities in which the predominant religion is not Christian. In the course of this, I have met some very fine and gracious people. By nature, I am a people person. I enjoy conversations, especially around a meal with newfound friends. One such person was the room attendant at a hotel where I was staying. He is a Muslim man. Every day when he came in to make up my room, he would also make me a cup of tea, and we would talk. On his off day, he took me sightseeing in his city, and we visited many places of worship. I will never forget him. I wish more people showed the kindness that he did and the courtesies he always offered.

And that is the point I wish to make. We can be world-views apart without anger and offense. What I believe, I believe very seriously. And it is because of this that I write the book. By equal measure, anything to the contrary, I must question.

My earnest prayer is that when you read this, you will make your judgment of the Christian message based on truth, not the mood of our times. Moods change. Truth does not.

Chapter One

CLIMBING A MASSIVE WALL

I BEGIN WITH AN INCIDENT IN MY LIFE THAT CAUSES STORMS OF emotion to well up within me. Some memories are easy to relive. Others, even with the passage of time, when recalled again, throb like a reinjured wound. For that reason alone I find this, of all my past memories, very difficult to retell. It is only because the intervening years have helped me to look beyond the earlier hurts that I am able to bring this long-past moment into the present. But more than that, this sad happening, alongside a handful of others, may well have begun my journey toward God by bringing me to a screeching halt and forcing me to ask myself some hard questions.

I was sixteen years old and a student in a community college because it provided a shortcut to finishing high school. One day after classes normally ended, I was cycling back home, little suspecting what lay ahead of me. It had been a routine day from my point of view, as normal as any other. But this one was going to end differently.

As I turned into our backyard, I saw a sight that was most unusual. Normally my father would not even be home at this time, but there he was, standing at the door with his arms stretched across the open doorway as if to block my entry into the house. I greeted him with a furtive glance, and he made no reply. I felt his eyes bearing down on me, which spelled terror into my heart.

My relationship with my father left a lot to be desired, and my aimless life was a cause of immense frustration to him. I can candidly say that I feared him in ways that to this day I am not sure I fully understand. This was a moment I will never forget.

"How was school?" he asked.

It was a question he had never asked before. My report card usually answered that question, giving rise to the resulting tense discussions. I should have known he had a reason for asking this day, but without any suspicion I answered, "Fine."

His exact language that followed would be hard to repeat, but the torrent of anger he unleashed on me and the thrashing I received left me trembling and sobbing. Had my mother not intervened, I could have been seriously hurt. My charade was over. A game I had foolishly played had come to a very bitter end, with no one the winner.

The truth is that I had not been at school that day. In fact, I had not been there for some time. I had spent my days wandering the streets on my bicycle in search of a cricket match I could watch or even perhaps take part in. Absent from classes, I would show up for the exams and squeak through. How I expected to get away with this ruse I will never know. But wrong-doing has a way of robbing one even of common sense.

Why had all this happened in the first place? One might think the whole episode merely indicated a passionate dislike for school. But there was far more than just that. No one who knew me would have ever suspected the depths of emptiness within me. I was one of those teenagers who struggled with much on the inside but did not know where to turn for answers. For that matter, I did not know if answers to my deepest hungers actually even existed. Was everyone I met in life facing the same degree of questioning and just masking it better? Or was skepticism the realm of just a hapless few? Putting it plainly, life, to me, just did not make sense. All the pent-up longings put together added up to nothing but a wish that had no possibility of fulfillment. Jean Paul Sartre's description of life as a useless passion seemed perfectly appropriate. That confrontation with my dad probably summed up all that was tearing me apart on the inside.

That night, I stood punished and facing a wall. It may well have been a fitting metaphor of my life. My most pressing struggles had imprisoned me, and in those hours, laden with remorse, I wondered how I would ever break free to breathe the fresh air of a life unshackled.

Oscar Wilde's poem "The Ballad of Reading Gaol," which was written from prison, says it well:

I never saw sad men who looked
With such a wistful eye
Upon that little tent of blue
We prisoners call the sky,
And at every careless cloud that passed
In happy freedom by.

I was one of those "sad men," although I never showed it. I had that wistful yearning to be free. Thus, as grim as that evening was, it put in perspective the walls that seemed immovable. I had to look reality in the face if I was ever to find a way to understand it.

The intense soul search that began that night was ultimately to lead me to the person of Jesus Christ. How that happened in a culture that is rigorously pantheistic and (at least on paper) religiously all-encompassing is a miracle in itself. I would like to trace some of those steps for you.

SEEING MILESTONES IN RETROSPECT

Selecting defining moments is not an easy task. In a rigorous effort to be both fair and realistic, I have looked at some of the road marks I have crossed and wish to bring you to the starting point of my reasoning. From a chronological perspective, one might misconstrue the sequence as an experience that led to an argument. But looking back down the road years later, I can see that logically, the argument preceded, and with time, was sustained by the experience. This opening chapter, therefore, begins with my story, but the following chapters will stand on the argument.

The purpose of this book is to lay out for you, the reader, why I firmly believe Jesus Christ to be who He claimed to be—the Son of the living God, the One who came to seek and to save a lost humanity. At a time in our cultural history when the West is looking more like the East and the East is covertly trying to emulate the West, this is much needed. Religions are making a revival, but often as a hybrid of western marketing techniques and eastern mythology—a devastating combination of seduction through media and mysticism. The first casualty in such a mix is truth, and, consequently, the person of God.

Yet if the human spirit is to survive and every legitimate discipline to find fruitful expression, truth cannot be sacrificed at the altar of a pretended tolerance. All religions, plainly and simply, cannot be true. Some beliefs are false, and we know them to be false. So it does no good to put a halo on the notion of tolerance as if everything could be equally true. To deem all beliefs equally true is sheer nonsense for the simple reason that to deny that statement would also, then, be true. But if the denial of the statement is also true, then all religions are not true.

In the real-life struggles between right and wrong, justice and injustice, life and death, we all realize that truth does matter. Jesus Christ repeatedly talked about the supreme value of truth. While His life has been scrutinized more than any other's, it is remarkable that even skeptics have granted and recognized His unparalleled life and impact. Here, for example, is an opinion from a highly respected scholar, the famed historian W. E. H. Lecky:

> The character of Jesus has not only been the highest pattern of virtue, but the strongest incentive in its practice, and has exerted so deep an influence, that it may be truly said that the simple record of three years of active life has done more to regenerate and to soften mankind than all the disquisitions of philosophers and all the exhortations of moralists.[1]

Historians, poets, philosophers—and a host of others—have regarded Him as the centerpiece of history. He Himself made a statement that was very dramatic and daring when He said to the apostle Thomas, "I am the way and the truth and the life. No one comes to the Father except through me" (John 14:6). Every word of that statement challenges the fundamental beliefs of the Indian culture from which I come, and in reality, actually stands against an entire world today.

Just look at the implicit claims in that statement. First and foremost, He asserted that there is only one way to God. That shocks postmodern moods and mind-sets. Hinduism and Bahaism have long challenged the concept of a single way to God. The Hindu religion, with its multifaceted belief system, vociferously attacks such exclusivity.

Jesus also unequivocally stated that God is the Author of life and that meaning in life lies in coming to Him. This assertion would be categorically denied by Buddhism, which is a nontheistic if not atheistic religion.

Jesus revealed Himself as the Son of God who led the way to the Father. Islam considers that claim to be blasphemous. How can God have a Son?

Jesus claimed that we can personally know God and the absolute nature of His truth. Agnostics deny that possibility.

One can go down the line and see that every claim that Jesus made of Himself challenged my culture's most basic assumptions about life and meaning. (It is important to remember, of course, that these basic religions within the Indian framework are also not in concert with each other. Buddha was a Hindu before he rejected some of Hinduism's fundamental doctrines and conceived in their place the Buddhist way. Islam radically differs from Hinduism.)

Ironically, it was that same apostle, Thomas, to whom Jesus spoke these words, who took the exclusive claims of Christ to India and paid for the gospel message with his life.

Was Jesus who He claimed to be? Is the Christian claim to uniqueness a myth? Can one study the life of Christ and demonstrate conclusively that He was and is the way, the truth, and the life? That is the question I propose to answer in this book. I believe there is overwhelming evidence to support Jesus' claims. I begin with my personal story only to put into context how my own journey began and how I arrived at the conclusion that Jesus is who He said He is.

A PERILOUS GLANCE

There is, understandably, in these preliminary thoughts a personal uncertainty. How do I say what I want to say without bringing hurt to anyone else or, for that matter, to any culture? This is hard. Home and culture are the treasured cradles in which one is nurtured. I find myself torn out of love for the truth and the cost of candor.

The hazard in such an undertaking struck me some months ago as I read the powerful book *Into Thin Air* by Jon Krakauer. The author recounts the ascent to Mount Everest by a team of climbers of which he was a part. I noted with empathy his anguished apology at the end of the book to many of the family members of those who lost their lives in the ascent, prompted by the errors he had made in some of his first stated recollections. Writing so soon after the tragedy found him erroneously recalling details that he later had to retract or correct. He conceded that had he waited before penning his account, he would have been less prone to such mistakes.

But there was more, and therein lay the rub. Some of what he had said reflected poorly not just on him, but on the character or efforts of others. For that he was truly sorry. This latter mistake is very serious, for one's own life may be laid bare at personal cost, but not at the cost of someone else's sacred trust. To that caution I shall pay close heed, and if I have failed, it is only because to suppress the incidents would be to distort the truth of my struggle.

I can now enjoy the benefit of time's distant view. The Jesus I know and love today I encountered at the age of seventeen. But His name and His tug in my life mean infinitely more now than they did when I first surrendered my life to Him. I came to Him because I did not know which way to turn. I have remained with Him because there is no other way I wish to turn. I came to Him longing for something I did not have. I remain with Him because I have something I will not trade. I came to Him as a stranger. I remain with Him in the most intimate of friendships. I came to Him unsure about the future. I remain with Him certain about my destiny. I came amid the thunderous cries of a culture that has three hundred and thirty million deities. I remain with Him knowing that truth cannot be all-inclusive. Truth by definition excludes.

You hear it a thousand times and more growing up in the East—"We all come through different routes and end up in the same place." But I say to you, God is not a place or an experience or a feeling. Pluralistic cultures are beguiled by the cosmetically courteous idea that sincerity or privilege of birth is all that counts and that truth is subject to the beholder. In no other discipline of life can one be so naive as to claim inherited belief or insistent belief as the sole determiner of truth. Why, then, do we make the catastrophic error of thinking that all religions are right and that it does not matter whether the claims they make are objectively true?

All religions are not the same. All religions do not point to God. All religions *do not say* that all religions are the same. At the heart of *every* religion is an uncompromising commitment to a particular way of defining who God is or is not and accordingly, of defining life's purpose.

Anyone who claims that all religions are the same betrays not only an ignorance of all religions but also a caricatured view of even the best-known ones. Every religion at its core is exclusive.

But the concept of "many ways" was absorbed subliminally in my life as a youngster. I was conditioned into that way of thinking before I found out its smuggled prejudices. It took years to find out that the cry for openness is never what it purports to be. What the person means by saying, "You must be open to everything" is really, "You must be open to everything that I am open to, and anything that I disagree with, you must disagree with too."

Indian culture has that veneer of openness, but it is highly critical of anything that hints at a challenge to it. It is no accident that within that so-called tolerant culture was birthed the caste system. All-inclusive philosophies can only come at the cost of truth. And no religion denies its core beliefs.

Within such systemic relativism, one tends to drift and float with the cultural tide and give no thought to the unforgiving nature of reality. That is how life is lived out in pantheistic cultures. No doubt, there is a wealth of thought that has built an impressive culture for more than one billion people, a culture that has defied economic privation, political turmoil, and religious hostilities, existing in the words of its people as "Mother India."

One does not have the advantage of choosing where one is born. Yet the words of the poet—"Breathes there the man with soul so dead, Who never to himself has said, 'This is my own, my native land'"[2]—ring wrenchingly true. In that cultural air, my life, my language, and my values were shaped and tested. I will ever be grateful for that privilege and for the treasured gifts it bestowed on me. The songs, the language, and the dreams it lodged in me I hope I never outlive. But a search for the one true God in a land full of gods is a very daunting task. Religion has a checkered history, and some of it is reprehensible.

An inheritor of the complexity of this culture, I grew up with walls of quiet desperation gradually building within me that moved me moment by moment to a point of personal crisis. I have heard it said that every weakness in a capable person is generally a strength abused. The same applies to culture. In the context of my upbringing, the abuses of those strengths of culture confirmed that adage.

VULNERABILITY IN STRENGTH

First and foremost is the strength of the nuclear family. As I knew it, the culture is strong and commendably reverential of the immediate family. The bonds of the household are wrapped tightly in India. But that strength becomes easily vulnerable to abuse. Many parents seem to seek to relive their lives through their children, and the success of the children socially elevates the family. Individuality is swallowed up by the clan. Every day, hundreds of advertisements are printed across the newspapers of the land in what is called the matrimonial section—parents looking for spouses for their children. Every prospective bride and groom is advertised as being from "a good home" and searching for someone from "a good home." "My son is an engineer." "My daughter is a doctor." "My son stood first in his class." "My daughter won a scholarship abroad." So run the boasts at social gatherings. Everything is done to keep the family as a single unit, with reverence for the parents' wishes on everything from jobs to marriage.

For me, the strength of the home was also the soil for the seeds of loneliness growing within. It centered on a vitally important fact—a highly successful and influential father who could not come to grips with an undisciplined son who flirted with failure in numerous directions. The father reached great heights of power. What would become of the son?

The second dimension, aside from the glue of the family, is the social reality of intense academic competition. Everything that defines an individual and his or her future is shaped by his or her performance in school. Every student wants to stand first in his or her class. It is not enough to do well. You must be at the top of your class or close to it. Intellect is worshiped.

When I was in school, every student's grades and position in the class were printed in the leading newspapers for all to see. Success or failure was reason for public pride or shame. One of my closest friends toyed with suicide after his high-school exams because he did not stand first in the entire city of New Delhi. Another one of my classmates in college actually burned himself to death because he did not make the grade.

Such distortion that has hurt so many still pervades many cultures. It is plainly wrong, but it is cherished with a passion.

This combination of the standard at home and the standard in society became a volatile mix in my life. I showed early signs that I would not be the boast of a powerful dad. This was not deliberate; it was just either the lack of capacity or capacity in search of a purpose. Life crept along while the long arm of cultural pressure was gradually creeping up on me, and I knew I would not pass the test.

Every morning, we would awaken to men and women standing outside our home, waiting for just one minute of my father's time. He held the keys to numerous jobs and contacts. With folded hands, they would plead for a chance at a job. On his way to the car, he would nod to them as if to say, "Leave it with me." And the truth is that many were helped by his connections. Scores of people revered his name because of such power. Could I not also have benefited someday from his influence? But too much lurked behind the scenes to offer a simplistic explanation.

In addition, my father had a foreboding side. With his enormous position in life, he battled a volatile temper. My lack of focus made it a situation awaiting crisis. That combination was to bring him and me into a relationship that I now regret. I am ever grateful to God that it did not end the way it began.

As committed as he was to a brilliant career for me, I was just as desirous of living for the sports field—a love of my life in which he had no interest. He had a point. Every boy growing up wanted to become a cricketer and play for India, just as every youngster in New York wants to play for the Yankees. But I did show some promise. I played for many teams at my college—cricket, hockey, tennis, and table tennis—yet never once did my dad come to see me play, even in any big game. We were marching to different drumbeats.

Throughout these years, I never lost respect for him. To this day, I believe my father was a good man, indeed, even a great man, but he did not know how to get close to a hurting, struggling child. I, for my part, pondered within and lived with my own private pain. Over the years I have come to believe that these things matter more than ordinary people may realize, but perhaps less than extremists would lead us to believe. Somehow we learn to cope, except that it places us near the edge of self-rejection and renders us more vulnerable when dreams are shattered.

Let me illustrate this point.

A few years ago, a former Olympic athlete came to visit me. He was looking for some direction in his life. He was a strong and solidly built man. It was a privilege to be around him—just in the hopes that muscles were contagious!

He told me of the time he was representing his country at the Olympics. It was a story of dreams that had struggled against a potential nightmare. From the age of twelve, the Olympics had been all he labored for. He had put every penny he earned and every purchase he made into someday becoming a gold medalist in the event he loved. He was totally focused. This is what he wanted. But he had a very turbulent relationship with his father, who had no interest in this dream of his, and, therefore, he had funded every penny himself.

When he was only seventeen, he filmed the world champion in the event for which he was training and broke down his every stride, frame by frame, to study his technique. He then had himself filmed in the same distance and matched it, stride for stride. By precisely piecing together where he was losing the precious seconds to the world champion, he determined to bridge the gap. Through sheer willpower, discipline, and courage, his goal was within reach.

He made the cut for his country's team, and life was suddenly like being atop a floating cloud. He won every heat and was emerging as the surprise and potential winner when the finals came. Was this a dream or was it real? No, it was real, he reminded himself.

He was at the starting point for the finals, and his nation was watching. Millions were cheering for him, and hearts were racing, expecting this "country-boy-makes-it-big" story to hit the headlines the next day. In fact, I remember watching the event. The gun was about to go off, signaling the start. This was the moment he had waited for most of his life. But the mind with all its tenacity and resoluteness is also a storehouse of unuttered yearnings.

"From out of nowhere," he said, "an unexpected thought suddenly flooded my mind—*I wonder if my father is watching me.*"

That unanticipated thought momentarily overcame him and may have added a fraction of a second to his first two strides, robbing him of the gold. With great credit, he still won the bronze. The third fastest in the world is no mean accomplishment. Yet, to him, the victory on the track lost its luster when measured against the deeper yearnings of life—the approval of the ones you love. Little did this Olympian know how my heart was beating as he shared this story with me. I understood him well.

Young dreams may be wild ones, but they are never corrected by ridiculing them. They must be steered by a loving voice that has earned the right to be heard, not one enforced by means of power. This is a very difficult lesson for parents to learn. And as cultures lose their restraining power, there will be greater need for mutual love and respect between parents and children if a relationship of trust is to be built, rather than banking on authority because of position.

Probably the most wrenching words I ever heard my father say to me were, "You will never make anything of your life!" And frankly, it seemed he was right. He was trying only to jolt me into reality. My mother's comfort could only carry me so far. In that sense, that fateful day when I cycled home was a critical point at which we ought to have sat down and talked. But I suppose the freedom to talk does not emerge in a vacuum. The moment of opportunity is built on hours of preparation.

WHERE DO I SEEK THAT I MIGHT FIND?

Our strained relationship was only made worse by a foundational, self-perpetuating thought. If life had no purpose, why try to work it out anyway? When I talk about purpose and meaning, I do not just mean some sense of existential peace. I mean a direction to life that upholds both reason and emotion. This is very critical to understand.

Now as I have moved to the West, I find that although many young people here identify with the problem, it is unexplainably ignored in the adult world. Why do I say this?

In the corporate world, every major company formulates a mission statement. That, in turn, is invoked when measuring achievements and failures. If a company does not know why it exists, then it will never know if it is failing or succeeding. How indicting, then, it is to all of us who will labor for hours to establish a mission statement for a company to sell toothpicks or tombstones but never pause long enough to write one out for our individual lives.

At the very point of writing, I have read an article interviewing one of Australia's great cricketers. He is in the midst of the world cup of cricket, representing his country. Rather teary in his otherwise "no-holds-barred" posture to life, he muttered a regret. Even as he is playing these matches, his wife is minutes away from delivering their second child, thousands of miles away. "I was gone for the first one and now am absent for the second. I have concluded that cricket is important to my life, but it isn't everything."

But that invokes a question, does it not? What is everything? Is anything everything? Why are we so eager to prove to the world that we are the best at what we do and care not for why or who we are?

How I wish there had been answers for me to such questions. Maybe there were, but I could not discern them amid the deluge of voices in a religious land. Purpose is to life what the skeleton is to the body. The muscle may have strength, but it needs support and attachment. All my pursuits had no supporting structure. Life drifted with affections and sports, but without ultimate purpose.

Just think of the alternatives our cultures have given to us. Pleasure, wealth, power, fame, fate, charity, peace, education, ethnicity—the list goes on endlessly. And when none of these work, some amalgam of spirituality and pragmatism is embraced. But these pursuits do not tell us why we are here in the first place. These may be ways of ordering one's life, but is life to be defined by what I pursue, or must my pursuit be defined by what life was meant to be?

In a culture where the academic is the ultimate and my life was not measuring up, a culture where philosophy is abundant but purpose is never imparted, where could I turn? The ultimate loss is the loss of face when failure attends. This thing we call shame is deeply embedded in the Hindi language, so much so that when one fails, part of the scolding is to be branded a shameless individual. That night it seemed as if I had lost face forever, and my punishment was both a metaphor and a reality.

THE SEEKER FINDS OUT HE IS SOUGHT

Somewhere in the midst of all this turmoil, the Hound of Heaven was on my trail. His footprints are everywhere as I look over my shoulder now. He was, indeed, nearer than I thought. I can see now, in hindsight, the trail that is evident, even in the grimmest moments. When you live in a small, two-bedroom home with four siblings and two parents, you cannot run for a hiding place. Yet it is utterly amazing how one can hide within oneself.

But the work of God had long begun. From out of the blue, one day my sister was invited to a youth event that would feature music and a speaker. She invited me to attend this meeting with her. On this occasion the visiting speaker was a man who, though a total stranger to me, was a well-respected Christian leader internationally.[3] My memory of it is too blurred to recall exactly all that transpired. But this I know. He spoke on a text that is probably the best-known text in the Bible: "For God so loved the world, that he gave his only begotten Son, that whosoever believeth in him should not perish, but have everlasting life" (John 3:16 KJV).

Even more powerful than what he said was his demeanor, and his heart came through in his words. There were both tenderness and power. Unaccustomed to being at such an event, I found myself walking conspicuously alone to the front at his invitation to trust in Jesus Christ as my Lord and my Savior. Although I had been raised in a church, I held out such little hope that its message had anything to do with life that I grasped only a portion of what he said. None of these things meant anything to me. To this vocabulary I was a stranger. I only knew that my life was wrong and that I needed somebody to make it right. I wanted new hungers, new longings, new disciplines, and new loves. I knew God had to matter. I just did not know how to find Him.

I left that night with a hint in my mind that there was something so right about the message, even though I had not got it all together. My confusion notwithstanding, a very important context was put into place. As the weeks went by, I continued to attend all of the popular Hindu festivals and to enjoy watching dramatic presentations of their mythology. I had an ardent Hindu friend who worked very hard at getting me to embrace the Hindu view of life.

Then a very significant event took place. I was cycling past a cremation site and stopped to ask the Hindu priest where that person, whose body was nothing more than a pile of ashes, was now.

"Young man," he said, "that is a question you will be asking all your life, and you will never find a certain answer."

If that is the best a priest can do, I thought, *what hope is there for a novice like me?*

As the months went by, without the further explanation that I needed, the continued loss of meaning led me to a tragic moment. Had I read the atheistic philosopher Jean Paul Sartre at that stage of my life, he would have confirmed every sense of isolation that I felt. Two of his best-selling books, *Nausea* and *No Exit*, exactly described my state. Sartre went so far as to say that the only question he could not answer was why he did not commit suicide. Is it not amazing that when life seems meaningless, the poets and artists are unafraid to plead guilty while the rationalists denounce that posture and wax eloquent with little reason?

My decision was firm but calm. A quiet exit would save my family and me any further failure. I put my plan into action. As a result, I found myself on a hospital bed, having been rushed there in the throes of an attempted suicide. In that hospital room, a Bible was brought to me, and in the desolation of my condition, a passage of Scripture was read to me. The speaker's message from that youth event still rang in my ears. I needed it as a base on which to build. He had preached from the third chapter of the Gospel according to John about God's love. Now in the hospital, I was being read the fourteenth chapter of John about God's purpose.

The words in that chapter were spoken to the apostle Thomas, who, as I said, came to India. His memorial exists to this day, just a few miles away from where I was born. Remember that Jesus had said to him, "I am the way and the truth and the life. No man comes to the Father except through Me." But my attention was captured by a few words farther along, when Jesus said to His disciples, "Because I live, you shall live also." Again, I was not sure of all that it meant. I knew it meant more than just biological life. Piecing together God's love in Christ, the way that was provided because of Christ, and the promise of life through Him, on that hospital bed I made my commitment to give my life and my pursuits into His hands. The struggles of my relationships, my origin, and my destiny were all addressed in that conversation Jesus had with His disciples two thousand years ago. My commitment stands now as the most wonderful transaction I ever made. I turned my life completely over to Jesus Christ.

In the same poem I quoted earlier, Oscar Wilde said:

And all the woe that moved him so
That gave that bitter cry,
And the wild regrets and bloody sweats,
None knew so well as I:
For he who lives more lives than one
More deaths than one must die . . .
And every human heart that breaks
In prison-cell or yard,
Is as that broken box that gave
Its treasure to the Lord,
And filled the unclean leper's house
With the scent of costliest nard.
Ah! Happy day they whose hearts can break
And peace and pardon win!
How else may man make straight his plan
And cleanse his soul from Sin?
How else but through a broken heart
May Lord Christ enter in?

I walked out of that hospital room a new man. The Lord Christ had entered in. The transformation was as dramatic as I could have ever imagined. There is no other way to describe it. From then on, my longings, my hopes, my dreams, and my every effort has been to live for Him who rescued me, to study for Him who gave me this mind, to serve Him who fashioned my will, and to speak for Him who gave me a voice.

The passion for learning, the recognition of the value of study, and the need to understand great thinkers and their thoughts—all were gradually put into their legitimate place. Our intellect is not intended to be an end in itself, but only a means to the very mind of God. Books, which were once a curse, became a gold mine.

The Hebrews had a motif by which they symbolized the ideal: "Every man under his own fig tree." If the Lord were to allow me a metaphor today, it would be, "Every man in his own library." The very pursuits that at one time brought so much inner heartache are now for me the transcending delight of my heart. Little did I know the long academic journey that lay ahead of me. I have loved it.

So much has transpired since that day that it would fill volumes. God has given me the privilege of speaking for Him on every continent and in dozens of cities, presenting a defense of the Christian faith in some of the finest institutions of the world. I am privileged beyond measure. I am as much at home in New Delhi as I am in Atlanta or Toronto. I love the peoples of this world, each with their accents and cuisines and idiosyncrasies. I have truly enjoyed the challenge and privilege that being a Christian apologist has brought my way. Christian apologetics is the task of presenting a defense of the person and the message of Jesus Christ. Over the years, I have become more convinced than ever that He is exactly who He claimed to be—God incarnate, who came to give us life to the fullest and to point us to the beauty and freedom of truth. The thrill of seeing thousands of lives transformed is a thrill I cannot deny.

THE PATTERN UNFOLDS

As I bring this chapter to a close, I would like to share how a purposeful design emerges when God weaves a pattern from what, to us, may often seem disparate threads.

Some years ago, I was visiting a place where some of the most beautiful saris are made. The sari, of course, is the garment worn by Indian women. It is usually about six yards long. Wedding saris are a work of art; they are rich in gold and silver threads, resplendent with an array of colors.

The place I was visiting was known for making the best wedding saris in the world. I expected to see some elaborate system of machines and designs that would boggle the mind. Not so! Each sari was being made individually by a father-and-son team. The father sat above on a platform two to three feet higher than the son, surrounded by several spools of thread, some dark, some shining. The son did just one thing. At a nod from his father, he would move the shuttle from one side to the other and back again. The father would gather some threads in his fingers, nod once more, and the son would move the shuttle again. This would be repeated for hundreds of hours, till you would begin to see a magnificent pattern emerging.

The son had the easy task—just to move at the father's nod. All along, the father had the design in his mind and brought the right threads together.

The more I reflect on my own life and study the lives of others, I am fascinated to see the design God has for each one of us, individually, if we would only respond to Him. Little reminders come my way to show the threads He has woven into this life. The following story is a small pointer to that end.

Almost thirty years to the day after my surrender to Christ, my wife and I were visiting India and decided to visit my grandmother's grave. I had only vague recollections of her funeral, the first funeral I had ever attended. I had a challenge trying to tell the cemetery manager the year of her death. We finally arrived at the year—as I recalled I was probably nine or ten when it might have happened. After thumbing through old registers that were bigger than his desk, we eventually found her name. With the help of a gardener, we walked through the accumulated weeds and dirt and rubble in the cemetery until we found the large slab of stone marking her grave.

No one had visited her grave for almost thirty years. With his little bucket of water and a small brush, the gardener cleared off the caked-on dirt and, to our utter surprise, under her name, a verse gradually appeared. My wife clasped my hand and said, "Look at the verse!" It read, "Because I live, you shall live also." As I said, He was on my trail long before I knew it.

As the years have gone by, we have made a study of when the gospel first made inroads into our family. On both my mother's and my father's sides, five and six generations ago, the first believers came from the highest caste of the Hindu priesthood. The first to come to the Lord was a woman. She was intrigued by the message brought to her village by missionaries and continued to seek them out, in spite of her family's terrible displeasure. But one day, as she was about to leave the missionary compound in order to be home before her family found out where she had been, the doors of the compound were shut because a cholera epidemic had broken out in the village. She had to remain with the missionaries for several weeks until the time of quarantine was past. By that time, she had committed her life to the Lord. The walls of a closed compound were the means of bringing her face to face with Jesus Christ.

All walls are not barriers. They may be there for a purpose. As I look back upon the journey, there is one image and two poets who come to mind. In the New Testament, we are told of the conversion of Saul of Tarsus. He, of course, was a terrorist to the Christians. God graciously tracked him down with His love to make him one of His choice apostles. Those who were once his friends now threatened his life. The disciples put him in a basket and lowered him over a city wall that he might escape his tormentors.

For me, the torment was within. God planted the feet of some who lifted me in a basket of love and persuasion and lowered me over the walls I could not scale on my own. Such is the grace of Christ who meets us where we are.

Readers of English poetry will recall the turbulent life of Francis Thompson. His father longed for him to study at Oxford, but Francis lost his way in drugs and failed to make the grade on more than one occasion. Those who knew him knew that inside was a slumbering genius, if only his life could be rescued.

When Francis Thompson finally succumbed to the pursuing Christ, he penned his immortal "Hound of Heaven," describing the years behind the moment of transaction:

> I fled Him down the nights and down the days.
> I fled Him down the arches of the years,
> I fled Him down the labyrinthine ways
> of my own mind: And in the mist of tears
> I hid from Him, and under running laughter
> Up vistaed hopes I sped;
> Down titanic glooms of chasmed fears
> From those strong feet that followed, that followed after
> For though I knew His love that followed
> Yet I was sore adread
> Lest having Him I have naught else beside.

All that I took from thee I did but take
Not for thy harms
But just that thou might'st seek it in my arms.
All which thy child's mistake fancies are lost
I have stored for thee at home:
"Rise, clasp my hand, and come."
Halts by me that footfall:
is my gloom after all,
shade of His hand, outstretched caressingly.
Ah, fondest, blindest, weakest,
I am he whom thou seekest!
Thou dravest love from thee, that dravest me.

What a wonderful day it was when I stopped running and, by His strength, let the embrace of His love envelop me. The words of a famous hymn by Charles Wesley reflect that triumph and my story:

Long my imprisoned spirit lay,
Fast bound in sin and nature's night.
Thine eye diffused a quickening ray,
I woke, the dungeon flamed with light.
My chains fell off, my heart was free,
I rose, went forth and followed thee.[4]

Only one thing need be added. I was twenty years old when my family moved to Canada. There, my mom and dad made their commitments to Christ too. It was a new day for all of us. My dad worked hard at recovering the lost years. In 1974, I was in my twenties, young in the ministry, and I was in Cambodia, preaching in some very fearsome circumstances. My father sent a letter with me that he wanted me to read after I left. In it he reflected upon the days when all seemed lost to me and to him in our relationship. It was a beautiful letter. I read it, lying in my bed in Phnom Penh.

One line summed it up when he said, "I thank God that He considered our family in calling as one of His servants, one of my children."

He passed away in 1979 at the age of sixty-seven. I do miss him in these wonderful years of ministry. He would have been such an encouragement. God's grace is beyond description. He lifted all of us over the walls of our own imprisonment.

So much for the story. Now to the argument.

Chapter Two

ADDRESSING A HEAVENLY HOME

ONE OF THE GREATEST OPPORTUNITIES EVER ACCORDED A MEMBER of our family took place when Queen Elizabeth and Prince Philip visited India in the late fifties.

My younger brother, who happened to be seven or eight years old and the youngest member of the choir at the Delhi Cathedral, was to be formally introduced to the queen following a Sunday service. He certainly never lacked for counsel on how to prepare for this extraordinary meeting. We ceaselessly coached him, repeatedly reminding him to address her as "Your Majesty" and not "Auntie," the latter being a typical way of showing respect in India. The moment came, and he passed with flying colors.

Unknown to us, his meeting with the queen was carried on television back in England as part of a news clip, prompting calls to the television station to inquire whether "that cute little boy" was available for adoption. Since that day, at any hint of his misbehavior, we siblings have never missed the opportunity to suggest that we should have taken the English up on their offer! Four decades have gone by since that wonderful memory of bowing before the queen, and he never misses the opportunity to remind us of his greater privilege.

Meeting historic figures is not a humdrum experience. Lines are rehearsed, questions are debated, and protocol is practiced long before the event. I have no doubt that the more elaborate the pomp and pageantry accompanying the occasion, the greater the fear of saying or doing something improper.

One can only imagine a conversation in the home of Andrew and Simon Peter, the earliest followers of Jesus, when Andrew first informed their family that he believed he had met the long-awaited Messiah. This redeemer figure was the only hope for a nation languishing under the scourge of successive foreign rulers. Any good Israelite had prayed for the coming of the One who would free His people. A cynic at the evening meal probably choked on his food when the announcement was made by Andrew that he and Simon had just come back from meeting the prophesied deliverer. Many barbs were probably withstood while the brothers insisted they were not out of their minds. They had talked to Him, spent hours with Him, and Andrew had even been given the opportunity to ask Him any question he desired.

Out of sheer curiosity, one at the table may have muttered, "And what, perchance, did you ask Him?"

"I asked Him where He lived," came the confident reply.

Can we not hear it? Silence around the table.

"That was the best you could do, Andrew? To ask Him *where He lived*?"

Could there not have been a better question that would have put Jesus' claim to the test? At least that is how we, in our time, might have remonstrated. Why did Andrew, face to face with Him who claimed such unique status, not pose a greater challenge than a simple query, "Where do You live?" Malcolm Muggeridge, the English journalist, remarks in his autobiography on the opportunities he had to interview noted dignitaries around the world. Being an incurable cynic and iconoclast, and just for the sake of playing to the readership, he would ask a deliberately absurd and belittling question, for example, asking a bishop, at a most poignant moment and before a highly reverential audience, "Are bishops really necessary?" He did that, he conceded, because he leveraged his profession as a journalist to live off shock value, at the cost of substance.

Was this some kind of "shock" question, a trivializing gibe from Andrew so that they could find out the street address of the Messiah and then heap scorn upon the claimant? Was he playing to the audience too? The more I have thought of it, the more I am convinced that the would-be disciple had sound reasons for asking what he did. His serious investigation into the person of Jesus had begun. Was this truly the Christ, the Anointed One? For nearly two thousand years, the prophets had told of His coming. Was this that fulfillment? Let us take a hard look at what prompted so basic a question for so monumental a claim.

A Provocative Introduction

The setting of the disciple's question is given to us in John's Gospel, the first chapter. Immediately one is struck by the casualness with which Jesus made His entry. There is no drumbeat, no great tumult, no parade to herald the One whose name was to be on the lips of humanity in a way no other name had ever been. There was no time given for rehearsals.

John the Baptizer was given the honor of making the unadorned announcement. John, draped in strange attire and living off even stranger food, was gaining a huge following. In the eyes of the devout, he was a prophet of supreme honor. And in truth, before his birth, the angel had spoken of his privileged and purposeful God-given calling. His assigned place in history was to be the one who introduced Jesus to the world. Of all the fanfare that he could have mustered for his declaration, he chose instead a simple utterance. This was so bereft of regal accompaniment that no "king-maker" would have conceived such modesty for so world-changing an announcement. And especially not in the East.

Yet, on a given day and at a divinely appointed moment, Jesus came to John to be baptized. Awe-stricken by this privilege, John stuttered out his own unworthiness of such an honor, declaring that he was not even fit to untie the shoes of his Lord. How could he dare to baptize Him? The scene is memorialized to this day by the dove that descended upon Jesus. As this heavenly affirmation was given, John looked at two of his own disciples and said, "Look, the Lamb of God."

It is hard to resist the sobering portent behind the designation. The average Jewish family grew up with lambs and sacrifices. The temple probably reeked of animals and their slaughter, especially on the Day of Atonement. The exterior grandeur of the temple housed only a rather grim and messy-looking altar. Every lamb sacrificed was from the possessions of the petitioner and was thus, a lamb of men offered to God. In fact, it was not even a representative from *among* men, an equal. It was a lamb *owned* by men, a dumb, unsuspecting animal brought into the temple, never to return.

Now, in this appointed moment in history, an offering came from God Himself and was given *by* God on behalf of humanity. This was the Lamb of God. But how could such a thing be? One born for the designed purpose of being sacrificed on the altar someday? Would not that have provoked a different question from those wanting to become His disciples, especially since that was the jolting introduction chosen by John?

Someone well versed in the Scriptures would have probably harked back immediately to the narrative in Genesis 22, in which Abraham was called upon to offer up his long-awaited son, Isaac. As father and son walked toward the mountain, Isaac asked the obvious question, "The fire and the wood are here, but where is the lamb?" As the story unfolds, Isaac himself was laid upon the altar and readied as a sacrifice.

At the last moment, as Abraham's hand holding the blade descended upon Isaac, God exclaimed, "Stop! There is another I will provide." God, who had planned this all along to test Abraham, providentially trapped a ram in the thicket to serve as a substitute for Isaac, even as it represented a different lamb that would come on a different day.

John's announcement, in effect, said, "Here He is—the Lamb of God who was promised long ago." The day was approaching when there would be another hill and another altar, and this time the hand of the Father would not stop the slaying.

The disciples of John who heard his pronouncement of Jesus as the Lamb of God turned from him to follow Jesus. The first question Jesus put to them had deliberate and reasoned bluntness: "What do you want?" They had no real understanding at this point that they were following One who was on a one-way journey that would ultimately end at an altar.

I wonder if any of us would have asked what they did in that momentous encounter. A better question might have been, "What does John mean when he calls You the Lamb of God? Are You headed for a gruesome end?" Instead, they were interested in His beginnings, asking the astounding question, "Where do You live?" I made the assertion earlier that in the East, the home is the defining cultural indicator. Everything that determines who you are and what your future bodes is tied into your heritage and your social standing. Absolutely everything.

The first time I returned to speak in India after an eleven-year absence, my wife (who is from Canada) witnessed firsthand the esteem conferred by one's family. At a reception that was held in our honor in Bombay at which I was to speak, her astonishment lay in the way I was introduced. The very long and formal introduction I was given was filled with superlatives. Yet, in its entirety, absolutely nothing was said about me. Instead, it was a lavish description of my father's credentials and accomplishments. It was one of those moments when you wanted to look around and identify this highly decorated individual. Then the last line was tagged on—"and this is his son, who is to speak to us." That was the only line that referred to me.

My immediate response was to laugh on the inside. But it suddenly dawned on me that I was representing somebody bigger than myself—my father. Because of him, I was given a hearing. I knew I was in the East. An introduction in the West, particularly in North America, is all about what *I* have or have not accomplished. The credentials are individual, almost as if an individual owes even his beginning to himself. There is little or no mention of family. But in India, the country of my father's birth, my father's credentials, my mother's birth, and my roots become very important to the audience.

I notice this significant difference to this very day. In the West, it does not take long for a stranger to ask, "Where do you work?" or "What is your business?" The questioner's thoughts are forming a picture, to determine your financial profile and corporate influence so that the conversation can follow that trail. In the East, the question comes with equal deliberateness, "Which was your home city when you lived here?" "Which part of town did you live in?" "What did your father do?" Names, addresses, and family background are very defining. East or West, the goal may be the same, to place you in society's assigned place. Only the routing is different.

You see, in a stratified society, your home address gives the inquirer literally a wealth of information about you. The privilege of birth opens doors. It is not at all surprising that Nathanael's response when he was first told about Jesus was, "Can anything good come out of Nazareth?" That is followed some verses later by, "Is this not the son of Joseph, the carpenter?" How in the name of reason could the answer to the hopes and dreams of Israel, in search of the Messiah, come from a city of such low esteem and from a family of such modest professional status? The best way for them to find out whether He could really be who John described Him to be was to follow Him to His house—to the earthly address of the One who claimed to be the Son of God.

Jesus' answer builds the intrigue. He did not give a street name or a house's identification. He simply said, "Come and see." They went with Him to see where He was staying and evidently spent the night there. Andrew returned to tell his brother Simon that they had found the Messiah, that is, the Christ, and invited him to come and see also.

The next day, Philip, who was also from the same city, invited Nathanael to join them by saying, "We have found the one Moses wrote about in the Law, and about whom the prophets also wrote—Jesus of Nazareth, the son of Joseph." There you have it—the city and the parentage. Nathanael is predictably cynical and is given the same challenge: "Come and see."

A MEMORABLE ENCOUNTER

The Scriptures remain silent on numerous issues. Matters in which we would be greatly interested are left without description. What kind of home did Jesus live in? What kind of carpentry did He do, if any? How was His home furnished? What wealth or poverty did it bespeak? I have often thought that instead of the space given to ponderous genealogies, some other details of Jesus' life would have been of greater interest to the reader. How much did He earn? What kind of clothes did He wear? What did He look like?

But maybe this is where God's vision of reality seeks to lift us from the enslavement and distortion of our earth-driven view. Historic figures have homes to visit for posterity; the Lord of history left no home. Luminaries leave libraries and write their memoirs; He left one book, penned by ordinary people. Deliverers speak of winning through might and conquest; He spoke of a place in the heart.

Would it have been that difficult to preserve an article of clothing or a piece of furniture, just so we could put it in a museum for the world to see? One can go into little towns today and see excavations of homes from Jesus' time. Why was not His own home preserved? In a museum in Turkey, one can see the sword of Mohammed and what are claimed to be strands from his beard. Recently we have been informed that a tooth of Gautama, the Buddha, has been found. We can go back across time and see extraordinary collections of artifacts connected to monarchs and heroes from even before the time of Christ.

He who owns the cattle on a thousand hills left no such information. Of Christ we are told that He did not have a place to lay His head. The same Gospel writer forthrightly states this: "In the beginning was the Word, and the Word was with God, and the Word was God. . . . [And] the Word became flesh and made his dwelling among us" (John 1:1, 14). John's "In the beginning" has a striking parallel with the first words of the Scriptures, "In the beginning God. . . ."

As important as His earthly parentage was, His home address was not an earthly one—for in a very real sense, He had no beginning. Amid the "where" and "when" questions that plague our finitude, there is no such encumbrance for the eternal and infinite One. To lift them beyond the here and now was the task ahead of Jesus when He said to them, "Come and see." I suspect there were going to be shock and a need of much explanation. Andrew had a reason for asking the question, and Jesus was offering a journey of thought as His answer. We will take that journey. At this point, put yourself in Andrew's sandals. He had been invited to the home of the One identified by a recognized prophet as the Lamb of God. Andrew went. What was he anticipating? Would he be disappointed?

Billy Graham tells of the time he was at a crusade in Pittsburgh. He had just entered the hotel lobby where he was staying for the week and, with a couple of his teammates, walked into the elevator where a handful of businessmen were in conversation. As the elevator began to lift, one of the businessmen said, "I hear Billy Graham is in this hotel." One of the others who recognized Dr. Graham smiled, looked at the one who had made the comment, pointed to Billy Graham, and said, "That's he." The startled businessman paused, looked again at Billy Graham, and said, "What an anticlimax!" Being the humble man that he is, Dr. Graham fully sympathized with the person's disappointment and admitted that this was all there was to him.

What was this man really expecting? Some haloed and winged figure who did not need an elevator and who would only be seen praying and rising on air? In our human imagination, we so often perceive our heroes to be something larger than life. We exalt them in ways that do them disservice. We make them to be almost plastic in our imaginations. And when they bleed or grow old or stumble, we either cast them aside or find some way to perpetuate the myth. To sustain this illusion in our minds, we build statues and erect monuments, and artists paint them with haloes to establish their surreal personae. We convince ourselves that they are or were something essentially different from the rest of us.

This one time in history this person *was* essentially different from all of us. But, from Nazareth? The son of a carpenter? Even the temple that was erected as God's dwelling place had beauty and wealth expended beyond imagination. Now that God had come in the flesh, His home was so paltry by comparison. To help sort it out, Nathanael is brought into the picture. He was one of those who was so committed to the truth that when he was invited to come and meet Jesus, he agreed to go along, probably in the hope of dispelling this "deception" that had been manufactured in the minds of his friends. But when he came within range of Jesus' voice, Jesus spoke those carefully chosen words: "Here is a true Israelite, in whom there is nothing false."

There lay the first surprise. There are few things as disquieting to a person as having his or her inner thoughts laid bare by the words of a stranger.

He had come to "check out" this person and instead, his own character was revealed for what it really was. "How do You know me?" demanded Nathanael. And Jesus replied, "I saw you under the fig tree, before Philip called you."

What did this mean to Nathanael?

Was he pondering something when under the fig tree? Did he have a premonition while under that tree that a life-defining moment was around the corner? Was it a private moment of which he thought no one else was aware? Something in Jesus' disclosure made Nathanael react impulsively, almost rashly, and he uttered these life-changing words: "Rabbi, you are the Son of God; you are the King of Israel" (John 1:49). I believe Jesus jarred Nathanael's skepticism by a gentle uncovering of the thoughts and intents of Nathanael's own heart.

It was at this very point that Andrew's question—"Where do You live?"—met a most incredible answer. Jesus had seen Nathanael when Nathanael did not know he was being watched. He identified the determination with which Nathanael pursued reality, which certainly gained his attention. In one of his psalms, King David confessed that he could not flee from God's presence, for God knew him in his inmost being—"Wherever I go, You are there" (see Ps. 139:7–10). Nathanael had just realized the same truth.

Jesus also knew that Nathanael did not think very much of Nazareth. Recognizing what was in his heart, Jesus challenged his impulsive declaration and said, "You believe because I told you I saw you under the fig tree. You shall see greater things than that. . . . I tell you the truth, you shall see heaven open, and the angels of God ascending and descending on the Son of Man" (John 1:50–51).

Jesus, in short, said, "You are shocked because I revealed you to yourself? Wait until you see the full disclosure of who I am and from whence I come." He took Nathanael from explaining the puzzlement of lesser things to a destination of glorious insights.

The description He gave of angels ascending and descending on the Son of Man was not tossed out in a vacuum. It pointed to Jesus' "parentage." Peter, Andrew, and Nathanael all knew the story of the father of their nation, Jacob, which really provided the backdrop for Jesus' answer.

The Old Testament carefully records that incident. As a young man, Jacob had cheated his brother, Esau, and was on the run to flee from his wrath. On his journey to distant parts, he thought he was alone, far from the eye of anyone else. He had been raised in a home in which the altar, as the center of the family's worship of God, played a significant part. His grandfather, Abraham, was known as "the man of the tent and the man of the altar." Abraham saw his home as temporary but his worship as permanent. Now, on the run, Jacob was homeless and altarless. When he reached a place called Luz, he slept with a stone for a pillow. Even for a desert dweller, that was rough.

And while he slept, the Lord came to him in a dream in which he saw a stairway that reached from the earth to heaven. Angels ascended and descended the stairway. And there above it stood the Lord, who said, "I am the LORD, the God of your father Abraham and the God of Isaac" (Gen. 28:13). When Jacob awoke from his sleep, he thought to himself, "Surely the LORD is in this place, and I was not aware of it. . . . How awesome is this place! This is none other than the house of God; this is the gate of heaven" (vv. 16–17). Jacob took the stone pillow and left it as a marker in the place he was now going to call Bethel—meaning, "the house of God."

Whether the disciples fully understood it or not, a thundering message was given when Jesus spoke those words to Nathanael. He staked a claim. Were they aware that the Lord who fashioned the heavens and the earth was standing beside them? Angelic hosts attended His abode. Even at that, we struggle to word it precisely. The word *abode* immediately brings to mind the concepts of residing and of boundaries, neither of which is a fitting term for One who is without beginning and is omnipresent. Jacob found out that God's presence to bless could transform any location into the house of God. Now the disciples learned the same. They were inclined to judge Jesus by His earthly father, Joseph the carpenter. They were trying to measure His worth by His earthly home, Nazareth. He opened up to them the truth that any earthly setting at which He is present becomes the gateway to heaven. What comfort this must have brought them.

But, more than that, they rightly inferred from what Jesus said that He had come from His heavenly Father, who was the God of Abraham, Isaac, and Jacob. He took them farther back than their own understanding and lifted them to further heights to show them that the word *home* was at best only an analogical representation of living with God. The disciples were clearly overwhelmed by that initial impact. They did not fully comprehend all that this encounter was going to mean to them. Their lives would change beyond their wildest dreams, so that the day would come when they would leave their own homes to tell the world of Jesus of Nazareth. "If you marvel at what I have shown you of yourself, Nathanael, this is only the beginning of what awaits you when I disclose My glory to you." *That*, He assured them, would be no anticlimax.

GLIMPSES OF ANOTHER HOME

Jesus broached some very significant truths in this simple interaction—truths that lift our thoughts to the limit emerge from this first conversation. Let us engage these thoughts one at a time.

The primary and unique indicator here, literally and figuratively, is Jesus' revelation of the realm of His existence. To ask for the "where" of Jesus' home is the same as asking the "when" of God's beginning. Such categories are necessary in our finite existence, because there was a time when we were not. But God transcends such categories. Jesus' references to a heavenly dwelling and to the angels ascending and descending in His service point to the fact that He is the Lord of heaven and earth who exists eternally and necessarily. His existence precedes every spatial metaphor. Just as it is impossible for Him not to be, so it is not necessary for Him to have a *place* to live. That is precisely what He said to David, who wanted to build a temple where God could "dwell" (2 Sam. 7:5). It is more sensible to ask where He has promised to *bless* us than to ask where His locus of existence is.

Such transcending categories seem so beyond our reach, and yet they intimate our ultimate destiny. Even now, we realize that concepts such as time, space, and motion are so bound up into the limited dimensions of our understanding of the nature of reality that for most of us, they seem the domain of geniuses. Yet the deeper we penetrate into such mysteries, the more inexorably we are drawn to the lowest common denominator of what makes life the way it is. We look for the minutest part of reality in the physical world so that we can, in the words of the scientist, arrive at a theory of everything.

Jesus reversed the process. He told us that the only way we could understand who we are is to cast our gaze not on the equation that binds it all together, but on the relationship toward which we move in the sum total of our being. It is the assemblage of an object that gives it its purpose, not the reduction of it. In the words of Jesus to Nathanael, our amazement will know no bounds when we understand all that the realm of God's existence means.

No other claimant to divine or prophetic status would ever have answered this question of his home in this manner. Even John the Baptizer took great pains to remind his followers of this difference: "A man can receive only what is given him from heaven. . . . The one who comes from above is above all; the one who is from the earth belongs to the earth, and speaks as one from the earth. The one who comes from heaven is above all. He testifies to what He has seen and heard" (John 3:27, 31–32).

Even if they are teaching truth, all others who have claimed or been accorded prophetic status are still at best human beings on whom this call from God was bestowed. Their assignment is a given one; they are the human receptors. Jesus, in distinction, is the Supreme Giver Himself. He is "from above," say the Gospel writers.

In another conversation, Jesus stated that His ascent into heaven was preceded by His descent from heaven (see John 3:13). Implicit in that claim is the assertion that His knowledge of everything is perfect and complete. That alone sets Him apart. His vision of reality, His explanation of life, His opening up of mysteries, and His glimpses into what matters and what does not matter proceed out of His being in the eternal. And that is the point. His earthly sojourn was not an origination, but a visitation.

Every other person who is at the heart of any religion has had his or her *beginning* either in fancy or in fact. But nevertheless, there is a beginning. Jesus' birth in Bethlehem was a moment preceded by eternity. His being neither originated in time nor came about by the will of humanity. The Author of time, who lived in the eternal, was made incarnate in time that we might live with the eternal in view. In that sense, the message of Christ was not the introduction of a religion, but an introduction to truth about reality as God alone knows it. To deny Jesus' message while pursuing spirituality is to conjure an imaginary religion in an attempt to see heaven while sight is confined to the earth. That is precisely what Jesus challenged when He said, "I have come that [you] may have life" (John 10:10). His life spells living. Your life or my life, apart from Him, spells death.

POSITIONED BY TRANSCENDENCE

"Where do You live?" asked the curious disciple.

"With My heavenly Father," was the answer.

For Nathanael, new vistas of being and of time suddenly brushed into his consciousness. But an obvious question arises: How could Jesus sustain such a claim? To claim to have no beginning is one thing; to make it reasonable is another. If heaven is the point of reference for all of reality, then two major ramifications were entailed for the disciples, and therefore, also are for us. The first is that of position with reference to Him and the second, that of position with reference to us. The second logically follows from the first.

What do I mean by position? I mean the very vantage point from which I may now view life because of Him.

Have you ever experienced the confusion of a seemingly senseless configuration on a poster that appears to be random shapes or dots? As you continue to stare at it and tilt your head one way or the other, a word or a picture suddenly leaps out from that cluttered pattern. We call it a cryptogram.

Something fascinating happens once you have seen that the dots or shading were just masking the real message. You start tilting your head in various positions in an attempt to lose the ordered pattern and to regain the initial disorder. The latter exercise comes into play only because you start wondering how it was possible in the first place to miss the word. When the eye has captured the image, it interprets the message for what it is. When the eye loses the message, disarray dominates.

May I suggest that the challenge of Jesus' earthly ministry was to enable us to see the message so that the picture could be understood. Staring at life's cryptogram, we either see His name unmistakably resplendent or we see the confusion of religions with no single message, just garbled beliefs that plague our existence, each justified by the voice of culture. That may be the tragedy of the beguiling sentiment we call tolerance, which has become a euphemism for contradiction. The result is treacherous.

Jesus Christ came to challenge every culture on the face of the earth so that we might gain a perspective from higher ground. But how does one reach that higher ground? We can see the hint of our predicament even from our lower vantage point. In spite of the limitations of our earthbound perspective, we still recognize wickedness. We still talk of witnessing evil. Maybe, there is a reason.

C. S. Lewis helps us here:

> Heaven understands hell and hell does not understand heaven. . . . To project ourselves into a wicked character, we have only to stop doing something and something we are already tired of doing; to project ourselves into a good one we have to do what we cannot and become what we are not.[1]

"To do what we cannot and to become what we are not." Those limitations separate purity from evil. To change this, heaven's eyes must be planted in us. That is what Jesus offers the one who comes to Him—to be what in ourselves we cannot be and to do what by ourselves we cannot do.

As a young lad, I remember reading a story about Sir Isaac Newton that left a profound impression on me. He had worked for hours on his scientific inquiries into the very core of the physical universe, exhaustedly laboring by candlelight. By his side over the weeks sat his beloved dog.

On one occasion when Newton left the room for a moment, the dog jumped up to follow him and inadvertently bumped into the side of the desk, knocking over the candle and setting the papers ablaze. All that seminal work was reduced in moments to a pile of ashes.

When Newton returned to his study to see what remained of his work, his heart was broken beyond repair. Rescuing what little was left of the room, he sat down and wept with his face in his hands. Gently stroking the dog, he said, "You will never, never know what you have done."

Even if it were possible for the dog to grasp that something tragic had happened, it was impossible for the creature to know the *kind* of tragedy, not just the degree of what had been done.

By analogy, that kind of essential distance is what makes our situation so manifestly impossible. Living in an evil world makes it much easier for me to understand my own wickedness than to think in the crystal-clear terms of perfect purity. In his biography of Mother Teresa, Christopher Hitchens set out as his goal to find something that would mar her character. He said of Mother Teresa, "She is the great white whale for the atheist in me."[2] So he had to play Ahab and bleed her.

How revealing that is of human nature. We resent the indictment purity brings. Is it any wonder that we cannot understand God? This gap is not only one of morality; it is one of capacity. It is easier for me to think in terms of time than for me to think in terms of eternity. How can I ever explain the dwelling of a perfect Being in eternity when my being is so locked into imperfection and time? How can I understand the supernatural when I am so bound by the natural?

There is a German term that separates existence from life: *dasein ohne leben*—"existence without life." Jesus came to remind us that we who are bound to the temporal subsist without life's blueprint. Though we continue to exist, we miss life for what it was meant to be. He wants us to see what it means to live through the lens of the eternal. That takes place when He makes our lives His home. There, He has promised to bless us.

Jesus once said to someone who questioned Him, "I have spoken to you of earthly things and you do not believe; how then will you believe if I speak of heavenly things?" (John 3:12).

Is this distinctive of Christ's heavenly dwelling a unique factor in world religions? Indeed it is. Perhaps this unequaled credential of Jesus may be in the minds of Muslim scholars when they attempt to attribute to Mohammed a momentary excursion into heaven. Islam claims that at one point in his life, on one particular night, Mohammed was transported to heaven on a single journey, to be given a glimpse of what heaven is like.[3] Regardless of all the confusing arguments over this claim, it does establish that even if the text is taken at face value, what warranted the heavenward journey for a night was that heaven was foreign to Mohammed. And that is the point of difference.

With such a unique difference, the skeptic may ask a legitimate question. Is there any evidence that can be adduced to support Jesus' claim of origin?

CONCEPTION WITHOUT CONSUMMATION

If Jesus had no beginning, then His very birth must explain how He could be "born" and yet not have a beginning. The virgin birth of Jesus most certainly addresses that.

When one is searching for evidence to confirm a startling claim, it is necessary to look for some other source that gives credence to it, even though it would not be in its own best interests to do so. The virgin birth is certainly in that realm, both for those who experienced it and for those inimical to the gospel. For Mary herself to claim such an outlandish conception would have been to not only risk her own life, but also to have put Jesus' life at risk.

Though I have quoted this numerous times before, I would like to repeat it here. The popular talk-show host Larry King was once asked whom he would choose, if he had the choice to interview one person across history. Larry King replied that he would like to interview Jesus Christ and that he would ask Him just one question: "Are You indeed virgin born?" "The answer to that question," said King, "would explain history for me."[4]

Larry King is right. The virgin birth at the very least points to a world unbound by sheer naturalism. The claim is lofty, but think it through even in its original and early context. Jesus' virgin birth was claimed while giving it the clear possibility of being verified along many lines.

Of any influential life that you have witnessed or studied, ask yourself how this person would justify a virgin birth and an eternal existence, if such an assertion were being made. This would be a particularly significant question if it had been predicted before the person was born. How do you perfectly fit together prophecy—in fact, hundreds of prophecies—and its fulfillment? For Jesus' antagonists, it would have been easy to measure, generation by generation, whether this claim to be the Messiah could possibly have withstood the scholars' scrutiny and the Scriptures' test. That is why the genealogies were far more important for the early disciples than the furniture in the house.

Apart from Mary and Joseph, consider the testimonies of Zacharias the priest and his wife, Elizabeth (the parents of John the Baptizer), for whom it would have been natural not to want their son to play "second fiddle" to a cousin, especially a younger cousin. In a culture rife with power and position, where the home bespoke volumes, shame would not be the path of choice for anyone. Had the virgin birth not been true, to assert its truth was the path of cultural ostracism, if not suicide, for all of them. For Elizabeth to lose her son, John, to the sword of Herod and for Mary to be told by the angel that a sword would pierce through her heart would not have been desired by any mother. Mary, Joseph, Zacharias, Elizabeth, John, and then the disciples risked everything for this truth.

But even beyond the Hebrew disposition and the family's claim, possibly the most astounding affirmation of the virgin birth comes from one religion that for centuries has attempted to stand against the Christian gospel, Islam. Even the Koran, written six hundred years after Jesus, affirmed His virgin birth (see Surah 19.19–21). This would serve Islam no self-glorifying purpose.

Here, then, is the man from Nazareth, who claimed that His origin was from heaven and that His Father is none other than God Himself—a Son not born out of physical consummation nor out of a need for communion, but the consummate expression of God in the flesh, in eternal communion with the Father.

His birth was not by natural means. This cannot be said of Mohammed, Krishna, or Buddha. Islam, while defending the virgin birth, denies that Jesus was the Son of God. It has, therefore, never been able to break free from a contradiction of its own making on the matter of Jesus' sonship. Its assertion that it is blasphemous to suggest that God could have a Son is based on their notion that sexual union is necessary for a child to be born, and of course, that would demean God. So there is a half-truth here, with an ironic twist for a religion whose founding prophet had numerous sexual unions, all, they claim, instigated by God. But that aside, if they have already granted the virgin birth, then they have acknowledged that God, in His infinite power, can initiate life without sexual union. In the beginning, communion and the power to give life existed in God Himself. In His infinite being, relationship was intrinsic, without the fleshly prerequisite of physical consummation. God, who is Spirit, is, in fact, Being-in-relationship. In Christ, the Word *became* flesh. He alone, who dwelt in eternity, could consecrate the flesh while differentiating between the inherent power of creation and the bestowed power of procreation, even as He transcended the means by which we are bound.

A LIFE WITHOUT BLEMISH

But there was a second way in which Jesus proved His absolute and eternal existence. His life has always been regarded as the purest that has ever been lived. On numerous occasions, His antagonists were challenged to bring some contrary proof against Him. They were never able to besmirch His pristine life. He challenged His adversaries to lay any charge of sin at His feet. As we progress in this book, we will see how hard they tried.

By contrast, no other individual has ever elicited such accolades. By their own admission, this includes Mohammed, Buddha, and Krishna. Their lives and their struggles are recorded within their own scriptures. Throughout the Muslim world today the belief is held that all of the prophets were sinless. One marvels at this doctrine, as it was never a view of the prophets presented in the Old Testament nor is it evident in their own scriptures. The shortcomings of two of the most renowned and respected prophets in Islam, Abraham and Moses, are plainly stated in the Koran. For example in Surah 28,16 Moses asked for forgiveness after slaying the Egyptian. In Surah 26,82 Abraham asked for forgiveness on the Day of Judgment. The word used here, which Muslims translate as "fault" rather than "sin," is the same word that in other contexts they translate as "sin."

In Surahs 47 and 48, Mohammed himself was told to ask for forgiveness for sin, once again translated as "faults" rather than "sin." Again, the word that is used in Surah 47,19 is the same word that is translated as "sin" in

Surah 12,29, where it is applied to Potiphar's wife in her attempted seduction of Joseph. Numerous linguists see this attempt to bypass what is really being said as nothing short of the development of a tradition so that Mohammed's life did not suffer in contrast to Jesus'.

There is great diversity in the attempts to explain this away. But what is a "fault" that needs forgiving? Is it something that ought to be a certain way but is not? Is it a thought that was entertained in error?

There is much more that can be said by way of contrast between the lives of Mohammed and Jesus. Mohammed's marriages to eleven wives have been a fascinating subject for Muslim scholars to explain. Whatever else a marriage does or does not prove, it clearly establishes the gradual need to die to one's self so that the two can become one. It is a process of failing and picking up, never one of perfection. But even if one were to grant all of the strained explanations for Mohammed's practices, included in which is the embarrassing Koranic description of heaven as "wine and women" (Surah 78.32ff, which Muslims dismiss as metaphorical), there is never even a hint in the life of Jesus that He was ever driven by sensuality or needed to seek forgiveness for anything. Jesus alone emerges as the spotless One, untainted by any error of omission or commission.

It should also be noted that this contrast is not only evident in the way Jesus and Mohammed lived, but also in the way they understood their call. So different is this sense of origin and call that, by Islam's own accounts, when Mohammed first claimed to have received revelations, he was confused and not sure what it meant. It was others who told him that this could be the voice of God speaking to him. Jesus, on the other hand, knew exactly who He was and from whence He came.

Hinduism is not exempt from this scrutiny. The playfulness of Krishna and his exploits with the milkmaids in the Bhagavad-Gita is frankly an embarrassment to many Hindu scholars.

How does Buddha measure up against the standard of personal purity that Jesus set? The very fact that he endured rebirths implies a series of imperfect lives. When he left his home in the palace, turning his back on his wife and son, it was in search of an answer. He did not start with the answer. His

"Enlightenment" was an attainment. Even taken at face value, it was a *path* to purity, not purity per se.

Jesus did not begin His mission by leaving more comfortable surroundings in order to gain enlightenment so that He would find the answer to life's mysteries. That was the origin of Buddhism.

He did not come to give a certain group of people ethnic worth so that they, too, could have an identity as others around them did; Islam had its beginnings for such reasons.[5]

He did not give any people a reason to boast of particular privilege because of the age of their culture or the perceived strength of their society's cohesion; virtually all pantheistic cultures pride themselves on how long they have been in existence.

He did not come to affirm a people who boasted in the strength of their military power, as the citizens of Rome did in claiming their city to be the eternal city.

He did not come to compliment the Greeks for their intellectual prowess.

In fact, He did not even come to exalt a culture because it was the recipient of God's moral law, a boast the Hebrews delighted in.

His strong and unequivocal claim was that heaven was His dwelling and earth was His footstool. There never was a time when He was not. There never will be a time when He will not be. His was a positing of truth from an eternal perspective that uniquely positioned Him.

CHANGING OUR ADDRESS

I said earlier that not only was our position of vision affected, but our very place in life was redefined. If the privilege of Jesus' position gives us His unique vantage point, sustained by His supernatural birth, then one very necessary application follows if we are to apply His truth to our homes.

The implication was clearly a surprise to Nathanael, for whom nothing good could come out of Nazareth. Nazareth was hardly on the map. It took scholars years even to pinpoint Nazareth. Of all the places on earth, why would the Lord of heaven and earth choose Nazareth? Is it possible that since heaven was His abode and earth was His footstool, He chose the foot of the footstool so that those of us who pride ourselves on our birth may take note that our heavenly Father has better credentials for us than our earthly roots?

Our world has strayed so far from God's will for us that we have made ourselves wretched by measuring ourselves in terms of race or power or progress or learning. The flames of prejudice of every kind have burned through twenty centuries. The politicization and absolutizing of culture may well be the cause of our next worldwide conflagration. All of the privileges of birth and possession become destructive when they are unhinged from our Creator's moorings.

The words of Jesus are a stirring reminder to all of us that the pride of birth carried to extreme can be a vortex that sucks us into destructive ways of thinking and living. The rising voice of nationalism has unleashed horrors too numerous to mention. In years of travel, I have been to many places in the world where people think they are superior because of their culture, places like China, the Middle East, Europe, and America. One way or the other, we all think we are the center of the universe because of our place in life. We had absolutely nothing to do with our birth. Jesus did, and He chose a most unlikely city to call home. He was not ensnared by the flimsy and fickle attachments of nationalism.

But if culture or birth must never give way to prejudice, neither must wealth become a means of measuring essential worth. I find the silence of Scripture on Jesus' economic conditions at home to be very instructive. In a culture where location and city meant so much, the only hint we are given as it applies to Jesus is that He came from unexpected economic ranks. I believe it is a solemn reminder not to make our goal in life one of sheer material pursuit. The allurement is great, and the disappointments are proportionate.

I recall reading, in one of New York's leading newspapers, an interview with the wife of a New York Yankees ballplayer who had just signed an $89 million contract. He had held out for a long while before signing, hoping that the management would match the $91 million offer of another team. The Yankees did not budge. His wife later said, "When I saw him walk in the house, I immediately knew that he had not succeeded in persuading them to move up from eighty-nine to ninety-one million. He felt so rejected. It was one of the saddest days of our lives."

Such, alas, are the vagaries of the human mind.

Most of us will never have our hearts broken because we were offered a paltry eighty-nine million instead of the ninety-one million we wanted. But many of us do lose our way within our own material contexts. It is not the size of the check that messes us up; it is our priorities. I do not believe for a moment that the Scriptures are against wealth. But the warning to those who make wealth their pursuit is a stern reality. Wealth must be processed through a philosophy of life that is greater than wealth itself. If not, it shapes the mind for bitter disappointments. Over the years, God has given me the privilege of being with some who are naturally gifted in multiplying what has been entrusted to them. Many have admitted to me that learning to walk with wealth is a very difficult discipline.

Nikos Kazantzakis was thoroughly wrong about Jesus in his book *The Last Temptation of Christ.* He presented a scene in which Satan passed before Jesus' imagination what He could have had if He had resisted the cross—a home in Bethany, the enthrallment of a wife in Mary or Martha, or both! Kazantzakis was wrong. Dead wrong. He never paused to reflect that a home in Bethany would not exactly be an allurement to One whose dwelling was in heaven.

I bring this chapter and its lessons to a close with a personal memory. Some years ago, we were spending Christmas in the home of my wife's parents. It was not a happy day in the household. Much had gone wrong during the preceding weeks, and a weight of sadness hung over the home. Yet, in the midst of all that, my mother-in-law kept her routine habit of asking people who would likely have no place to go at Christmas to share Christmas dinner with us.

That year she invited a man who was, by everyone's estimation, somewhat of an odd person, quite eccentric in his demeanor. Not much was known about him at the church except that he came regularly, sat alone, and left without much conversation. He obviously lived alone and was quite a sorry-looking, solitary figure. He was our Christmas guest.

Because of other happenings in the house, not the least of which was that one daughter was taken to the hospital for the birth of her first child, everything was confusion. All of our emotions were on edge. It fell upon me, in turn, to entertain this gentleman. I must confess that I did not appreciate it. Owing to a heavy life of travel year-round, I have jealously guarded my Christmases to be with my family. This was not going to be such a privilege, and I was not happy. As I sat in the living room, entertaining him while others were busy, I thought to myself, *This is going to go down as one of the most miserable Christmases of my life.*

But somehow we got through the evening. He evidently loved the meal, the fire crackling in the background, the snow outside, the Christmas carols playing, and a rather weighty theological discussion in which he and I were engaged—at his instigation, I might add. He was a very well-read man and, as I found out, loved to grapple with heavy theological themes. I do, too, but frankly, not during an evening that has been set aside to enjoy life's quiet moments, not someone's polemical mind.

At the end of the night when he bade us all good-bye, he reached out and took the hand of each of us, one by one, and said, "Thank you for the best Christmas of my life. I will never forget it." He walked out into the dark, snowy night, back into his solitary existence.

My heart sank in self-indictment at those tender words of his. I had to draw on every nerve in my being to keep from breaking down with tears. Just a few short years later, relatively young, and therefore to our surprise, he passed away. I have relived that Christmas many times in my memory.

The Lord taught me a lesson. The primary purpose of a home is to reflect and to distribute the love of Christ. Anything that usurps that is idolatrous. Having been lifted beyond the prejudice of culture, Jesus repositioned for the disciples the place of wealth. So staggering was the impact that many of them in the years to come would leave their own homes to go to distant parts of the world in order to proclaim the heaven-sent message that redefined their earthly homes. Eleven of them paid for that message with their lives.

The first time I walked through the noisy streets of Bethlehem and endured its smells, I gained a whole new sense of the difference between our Christmas carols, glamorizing the sweetness of the "little town of Bethlehem," and the harsh reality of God becoming flesh and dwelling among us. Ah! But is it not part of the wonder of God's disclosure of reality that He points to what we live with to show us what true living is meant to be?

For the disciples, Jesus' answer to their simple question—"Where do You live?"—was to lift them beyond race and culture, beyond wealth and power, beyond time and distance to make them true citizens of the world, informed by the world to come. He brought them into a dramatically different way of living and thinking from the one to which they were accustomed. He showed them the inclusiveness of His love for the whole world. But implicit in that was the exclusivity of His truth, for which they were willing to give their lives. We have reversed Jesus' order. We have made truth relative and culture supreme and have been left with a world in which wickedness reigns.

Jesus brought truth to light and a different world to His message. In Him my heart finds its true home.

G. K. Chesterton has captured the wonder in how Jesus' earthly address changes ours, as only he can do.

> A child in a foul stable,
> Where the beasts feed and foam;
> Only where He was homeless
> Are you and I at home:
> We have hands that fashion and heads that know,
> But our hearts we lost—how long ago!
> In a place no chart nor ship can show
> Under the sky's dome.
> To an open house in the evening
> Home shall men come,
> To an older place than Eden
> And a taller town than Rome.
> To the end of the way of the wandering star,
> To the things that cannot be and that are,
> To the place where God was homeless
> And all men are at home.[6]

Where does Jesus live? Come to Christ and see what it means to live.

Chapter Three

THE ANATOMY OF FAITH
AND THE QUEST FOR REASON

THE NOTED ATHEISTIC PHILOSOPHER BERTRAND RUSSELL WAS ONCE asked, "If you meet God after you die, what will you say to Him to justify your unbelief?"

"I will tell Him that He did not give me enough evidence," Russell snapped.

Bertrand Russell may have been an unusually hostile voice against all religious belief, and Christianity in particular, but his thirst for evidence or his demand for proof is not unique.

For my part, I confess that I wonder more about those who seek no such support for the things they believe than about those who do. There are hundreds, if not thousands, whose paths I have crossed in my journeys who have not only "theoretically believed" in some divine entity, but have also made their commitment with heartfelt devotion. "Gods" and "goddesses" with ghastly features and attributes are venerated by millions bringing their offerings and prostrating themselves in worship. I am confounded by such unquestioning commitment, practiced because of a feeling that is engendered or is the bequest of their culture.

On the other hand, I also grant that finding a hard-nosed rational justification for belief can be a tedious and sometimes hazardous pursuit. But if truth is the motive for the search, when reasonably pursued, it has its rewards. There is an old adage that says, "It is better to debate a question before settling it than to settle a question before debating it." My own intellectual battles were rather necessary in a land filled with as many "gods" as people.

Unfortunately, for reasons justifiable and unjustifiable, individuals hostile to belief in God often malign faith in Him as the lure of emotion clinging to an idea with the mind disengaged. They do not believe that faith can sustain the weight of both the emotions and the mind.

I realize we are all built with different capacities for thinking on such matters. However, that will not serve as reason enough to support one view over another. We cannot evade the questions that opponents have posed to those who "live by faith." They are justified in wanting to know what distinguishes faith from foolishness or irrationality, when no coherent logic is ever offered for one's "faith."

My mother, in great frustration, on one occasion asked me, "From where do you come up with all these questions? Must there be an explanation for everything?" I envied her simplicity. But our idiosyncrasies aside, I have to raise the counterpoint in a world plagued with contradicting ways of defining ultimate reality. To commit one's life, habits, thoughts, goals, priorities—everything—to a certain world-view with no questions asked is, from the antagonist's point of view, to build one's life upon a very questionable foundation.

In this encounter with Jesus, we will deal with a hard question that was asked of Him, and we will see as a result both the anatomy of faith and the quest for reason. Indeed, Jesus warned the seekers of signs in very serious terms. But He also justified His claims in extraordinary ways. There is a balance, and we must find it.

Some years ago, while in the Philippines speaking at some meetings, I was staying at a small, family-run hotel. The woman who managed the place had a graduate degree in philosophy and struck up quite a conversation with me on the rationality or irrationality of belief in God. During the conversation, she asked me if I had met a particular family staying in that hotel, who had come from Australia to have their son cured of cancer by a "faith healer."

Eventually, one evening I found myself in the room of this couple, with their young son. I cannot at this point recall his exact age, but I believe he was somewhere between ten and twelve years old. He lay in his narrow bed, emaciated, motionless, and pitiful, almost lifeless. His face, ashen gray, was drawn with the look of death. His parents and I talked in low tones in that small room. By his side was a night table, on which was a jar with some murky liquid and a frightful-looking purple fleshy mass that sprouted hairy roots.

The boy's mother pointed to it and asked me, "Do you see what is in that jar?"

I nodded.

"That is the cancer that the faith healer removed without surgery. It is like magic. We are sure that our son is now healed."

I just stared at them with heaviness of heart, thinking of their terrible pain. At the same time it was extremely difficult to be face to face with such credulity, looking into the eyes of those who were willing to put the life of their child into the hands of such claimants to the miraculous, many of whom are known charlatans. There, against all outward signs, two educated and well-to-do people boasted a cure from one who muttered an incantation and supposedly, without making any incision, extracted this fist-sized thing that was "causing the cancer" in their son. How does one explain this extreme form of "faith"? The human capacity to believe the bizarre, especially in the face of dire need, is limitless.

I have no doubt that in the Scriptures God often intervened in the healing of the body many times and that He continues to do so today. But this episode was a far cry from that, for here the mercenary and cultic elements were too obvious to miss.

Before I left, I explained to them that my work took me into many parts of the world and that it would really help me to know if the power of that healer were real or devious. "I would greatly appreciate you doing me the favor of writing to me within a month or two and telling me if your son has been truly healed," I said. They took my address and promised they would write. That was more than a decade ago. I have never heard anything from them.

If isolated instances demand that we not risk our lives on the preposterous claims of some self-styled demagogue, how much more important it is that we not risk the very destiny of humanity on someone who insists that He is the only true answer to life's purpose and destiny—unless that claim can be thoroughly tested and justified. Interestingly enough, to those like Bertrand Russell who contend that there is a paucity of evidence, the Bible makes a staggering counterpoint. The Scriptures categorically state that the problem with such people is not the absence of evidence; it is, rather, the *suppression* of it. The message of Jesus Christ shifts the charge of insufficiency from the volume of evidence to the intent of one's will.

Was Jesus implying that belief is nothing more than a blind commitment of the will? I think not. But He did say, in effect, that if you test His claims by the same measure that you legitimately substantiate other facts, you will find Him and His teaching thoroughly trustworthy. The evidence is already there. The denial of Christ has less to do with facts and more to do with the bent of what a person is prejudiced to conclude. After years of wrestling with such issues in academia, I have seen this proven time and again.

Notice, for example, the words of Thomas Nagel, professor of philosophy at New York University. This is how he explains his deep-seated antipathy toward religion:

> In speaking of the fear of religion, I don't mean to refer to the entirely reasonable hostility toward certain established religions . . . in virtue of their objectionable moral doctrines, social policies, and political influence. Nor am I referring to the association of many religious beliefs with superstition and the acceptance of evident empirical falsehoods. I am talking about something much deeper—namely the fear of religion itself. . . . I want atheism to be true and am made uneasy by the fact that some of the most intelligent and well-informed people I know are religious believers. It isn't just that I don't believe in God and naturally, hope there is no God! I don't want there to be a God; I don't want the universe to be like that.[1]

That is unabashed, committed unbelief. "I don't want there to be a God." While Bertrand Russell's skepticism may be represented as the honest search of reason, we had better be sure that it is not actually the wanton unbelief of Thomas Nagel that lurks beneath that intellectual quest. That kind of skepticism is the distortion of reason, masquerading as candor. To such a disposition, nothing would serve as sufficient evidence. We will find that as we study this theme of reason and faith and the place of the sign, God has much more to say about it than we realize.

Nothing New in the Demand

Long before our modern skeptics demanded evidence, the most religiously minded of their day came to Jesus and asked, "What miraculous sign can you show us to prove your authority to do all this?" (John 2:18).

They were not the Russells and Nagels of their day, lambasting the supernatural. In fact, they were a vital part of the life of the temple, which was at once the religious and mercenary ocean into which all of their efforts flowed. Tables were set up within its grounds from which to sell and profit from the people's desire to be right with God. From sacrificial lambs to trinkets, the exploiters and the exploited kept it a busy place, humming and buzzing with the sounds of eternal and temporal fears. The physically deprived and disabled would come as close as they were permitted to, in search of healing and restoration. Keepers of the moral law, the ceremonial law, and laws of their own invention found the temple to be their salvation.

Of all the enterprises in which the human heart engages, none lends itself more to abuse and manipulation than the activities of religion. For here, sacrifice and greed can meet in the most trusting and exploiting context. The much-respected scholar and one-time missionary Stephen Neill once said, "I am inclined to think that ambition in any ordinary sense of the term is nearly always sinful in ordinary men. I am certain that in the Christian it is always sinful, and that it is most inexcusable of all in the ordained minister."[2]

I believe that Neill was right. From Voltaire to Einstein, thinkers have heaped grave suspicion on institutional religion because of its checkered past. It is a tragedy that the history of religion, Christianity included, is filled with so much abuse that skeptics are very often justified in their "rational rejection" of the message. Jesus bore the brunt of the anger of the ecclesiastical authorities when He reminded them that their duplicity was the cause of unbelief in the masses.

It was in such a confrontation between Jesus and the guardians of the temple that the demand for a sign came. On a given day and at an appointed time, Jesus walked into the temple and flipped over the tables of the peddlers of religious paraphernalia and drove them out of there. "Get these out of here! How dare you turn my Father's house into a market!" (John 2:16). They had transformed a place of worship into a hangout for crooks.

In a certain part of the world that I have visited often, right outside the hotel is a little shrine. I have watched every morning, as thousands walked by. Most would pause, bow, fold their hands, or make some kind of a reverential sign to honor the deity and then move on. Many of those who ceremoniously carried out that ritual would then walk a few paces and "lie in wait" to see which tourists they could hoodwink that morning. From unfurling nude pictures or offering the services of a prostitute, to selling fake Rolex watches for twenty dollars, their day was spent in the illegal and the immoral. They were zealous and aggressive in leading the gullible astray.

As I have pondered this, I have tried to put together their habits of worship and their scandalous business. I have come to the conclusion that *hypocrite* is a very innocuous word to describe such a life. Their activities, both sacred and perverse, were not hidden—they were all done in the open. I believe that what has actually happened is a cutting of the nerve of spirituality at the neck, so that it never filters down to the heart, hands, and feet. Life is lived out in self-contained compartments with nothing to connect them. Their bowing recognizes the sacred. Their exploiting grants the material. In living, they desecrate others without a twinge of conscience. Yet if anyone were to hint at desecrating that shrine, his life would be in peril. Such is the amputation of religion that pays homage to God but would be the most surprised if God were ever to show up.

To such a band of thugs, Jesus came. It was an unprecedented confrontation. To borrow current-day jargon—"Politically incorrect" would be a lamblike description for a lionlike act. To run afoul of the powerbrokers and to refer to the temple as His Father's house? Both the deed and the words were shocking to the observers. This event was to burn itself into the memories of the onlookers and sealed His adversaries in their determination to do away with Him. As the disciples watched the entire episode, they were terribly nervous. But the account tells us that a voice from the past pierced their consciences. They suddenly remembered a passage of Scripture penned by King David one thousand years earlier: "I am a stranger to my brothers, an alien to my own mother's sons; for zeal for your house consumes me, and the insults of those who insult you fall on me" (Ps. 69:8–9). Jesus, they took note, embodied that prediction.

His antagonists could not contain their rage and demanded that Jesus give them a sign to justify His daring action. He only annoyed them further by countering that their question was anything but a quest for truth. But He did not end there. In His answer, He offered proof that no other claimant to Messianic or divine office has ever fulfilled. For so great a challenge, it was going to take an unparalleled demonstration of power.

A New Response

"Destroy this temple, and I will raise it again in three days" (John 2:19).

"What?" they countered. "It has taken forty-six years to build this temple, and you are going to raise it in three days?" (v. 20).

The Gospel writer adds, "The temple he had spoken of was his body. After he was raised from the dead, his disciples recalled what he had said. Then they believed the Scripture and the words that Jesus had spoken" (vv. 21–22).

There are so many different ways in which He could have shown His authority. He chose one particular point of reference—the temple. But He incorporated into that metaphor a meaning that would address both the skeptic and the religious person alike. For in the human body lie opposite possibilities: our propensities for the sensate and the willingness even to disfigure the body for the sake of the spiritual. Jesus could not have chosen a better illustration to justify His authority than His reference to the body in connection with the temple.

There are at least three distinct facets to His answer.

To see the first facet, we need to look at the *pretext* that the skeptic brought to the verbal exchange. "What sign do You offer for Your authority?" In this challenge, we will see the conflict of faith and reason.

The second is the *text* with which Jesus responded: "Destroy this temple and in three days I will raise it up." In time, this was going to be the single greatest proof of His claim. Centuries of determination to try to prove Him spurious have only strengthened His proof.

The last facet of Jesus' answer is the *context* within which He wanted the implication of His message understood. He offered the ultimate miracle by taking that which posed the greatest threat to spiritual inclination and translating it into the center of spirituality. In time, they would recognize that His answer was unique and was sustained in history.

THE SEDUCTION AND DEDUCTION OF A SIGN

Let us first grapple with the *pretext* of the skeptic.

One may be surprised to hear that history does not have a long list of serious claimants to divine status. What has resulted, however, is the gradual manufacturing of divinity by human choice. That list is ponderous.

On one occasion I stood by the side of a road, watching the golden statue of a "god" being transported from one temple to another. Thousands clamored to give an offering and to receive a blessing. The priests accompanying the god had incense and ash in their hands and generously distributed the goodwill of the deity upon any fruit or piece of clothing placed before them. The sight was extraordinary. Rich, poor, young, and old stretched their hands up as this chariot went by at a snail's pace. I asked a woman who had just received her "blessing" if this god actually existed or if he was just an expression of some inner hunger. She looked very hesitant and then said, "If you think in your heart that he exists, then he does."

"What if you believe he does not exist?" I asked.

"Then he doesn't exist," she softly said. That possibly summarizes the major personages to whom divinity is ascribed today. Some will attempt to prove their beliefs; others just quietly carry them in their hearts, creating deities whom they then try to appease.

Common sense dictates that in asserting a conviction of belief, we do more than offer a heart's desire or present some isolated strands of the claimant's credentials with which to leap to grandiose conclusions. A true defense of any claim must also deal with the evidences that challenge or contradict it. In other words, truth is not only a matter of offense, in that it makes certain assertions. It is also a matter of defense, in that it must be able to make a cogent and sensible response to the counterpoints that are raised.

And here something very important surfaces. Sometimes the choice is not between that which is manifestly contradictory and that which is consistently coherent. To contrast the former cult leader Jim Jones with Jesus Christ is not difficult. The challenge emerges when a claimant to deity may have some unique features that attract, while covering up a multitude of contradictory teachings or a contradicting lifestyle.

Unsuspecting people make a fatal mistake when they give their allegiance to a system of thought by focusing on its benefits while they ignore its systemic contradictions. The entire life of anyone making prophetic or divine claims must be observed in concert with the teaching offered. Numerous historical and philosophical matters come into play when one seriously evaluates such claims.

This is precisely what makes Jesus so unique. The whole range of both His life and His teaching can be subjected to the test of truth. Each aspect of His teaching is a link in the greater whole. Each facet is like the face of a diamond, catching the light as it is gently turned.

We assume, at this time in the history of thought, that the ancients were more gullible than we and that we have come of age when, in truth, some of the credulity we have displayed would have rightly made them squirm. If anyone denies that reality, just ask those in the marketing industry whether it is form or substance that sells. Several times in the Gospels someone in the audience challenged Jesus to give a sign in order to prove His claims. They were not a naive bunch. It is telling that in virtually every instance, the challenge came on the heels of a miraculous act that Jesus had just performed. They were not even satisfied merely to see the miraculous. They wanted something more.

For example, in John 6:30, the demand for a sign follows His feeding of five thousand people from a handful of loaves and fishes. Immediately after the miracle the skeptics in the group reminded Jesus that Moses had fed the masses with manna. "What miraculous sign then will *you* give that we may see it and believe you?" (emphasis added). In Matthew's Gospel, the demand for a sign came after the healing of a blind and mute man (12:22–45).

These give us clues to what Jesus was up against and why He responded the way He did. When the Pharisees and the teachers of the law demanded a sign of Him in Matthew 12, He replied with some rather pointed words:

> A wicked and adulterous generation asks for a miraculous sign! But none will be given it except the sign of the prophet Jonah. . . . The men of Nineveh will stand up at the judgment with this generation and condemn it; for they repented at the preaching of Jonah, and now one greater than Jonah is here. The Queen of the South will rise at the judgment with this generation and condemn it; for she came from the ends of the earth to listen to Solomon's wisdom, and now one greater than Solomon is here. (vv. 39, 41–42)

Jesus is charging that the very motivation that impelled them to demand a sign revealed not only that they were not genuinely seeking the truth; their resistance to truth, though they were religious, made the hardened pagan look better than they. In other words, it was not the absence of a sign that troubled them. It was the *message* behind the signs that provoked their discomfort. If Jesus could sustain who He was, the ramifications for them were cataclysmic. Everything they pursued and owned, every vestige of inordinate power they enjoyed, was dependent on their being the determiners of other people's destinies. Sometimes religion can be the greatest roadblock to true spirituality.

The bitter tip of Jesus' verbal arrow struck a raw nerve in them when He said that even a murderous people like the Ninevites were more honest than they were. Why? Because Jonah's preaching to the Ninevites resulted in a national repentance on such a scale that it made history. And Solomon's wisdom was so widely recognized that it brought people from distant lands just to listen to him.

In brief, Jesus is saying that a message in itself won the hearts of the pagans, but those who claimed spiritual fervor were fleeing from the implications of what they already knew to be true. He demonstrated more authenticating signs and persuasions than Jonah, more beauty and wisdom in thought than Solomon. Jonah was not the author of the miraculous. Jesus was. Solomon was not the source of His wisdom. Jesus was. Yet that difference counted as nothing to them.

From then on, all the way to His death on the cross at their hands, Jesus proved that it was not evidence they were looking for, but control of their enterprises, even at the cost of truth.

I would venture to suggest that the skepticism of some in our time may well come from the same motivation. A major difference for the average person of our day from the context of Jesus' day is that He was trying to establish Himself as Messiah to an audience that at least believed in the existence of God. In our day, we must first establish the existence of God. Only then can we present the evidence that Jesus is God incarnate.

To the religiously minded, the challenge is more complex. How do we establish that Jesus is the only way to God? Where do we find the common ground on which to begin?

FAITH AND REASON

Faith has not always been as suspect a category as it has now come to be. Both the Hebrews and the Greeks had an understanding of faith. True, there were some differences, but faith still had legitimacy. Today, if faith is admitted at all, it is seen as the faith to have faith. It is packaged as a private matter and banned from intellectual credence.

"Everyone has to have some faith," we quip.

"If it were not for my faith, I would never have hung in there," we may hear someone else say.

Faith in what, one might ask? In such a faith, the focus is often on anything but truth and on everything that signals pragmatism—"It worked for me, whether it's true or not." Such glib pronouncements have made us vulnerable to the faith marketers of our time. It is time to do some "temple cleansing" of the mind and face this reality head-on.

First, let us clearly understand what faith is not before establishing what it is. The faith that the Bible speaks of is not antithetical to reason. It is not just a will to believe, everything to the contrary notwithstanding. It is not a predisposition to force every piece of information to fit into the mold of one's desires. Faith in the biblical sense is substantive, based on the knowledge that the One in whom that faith is placed has proven that He is worthy of that trust. In its essence, *faith is a confidence in the person of Jesus Christ and in His power, so that even when His power does not serve my end, my confidence in Him remains because of who He is.* Faith for the Christian is the response of trust based on who Jesus Christ claimed to be, and it results in a life that brings both mind and heart in a commitment of love to Him. Is this an irrational or unreasonable response based on all that Christ demonstrated Himself to be?

Each individual who comes into this kind of faith in the one true God does so through a different struggle. In the Old Testament, Moses was the classic example of how faith was built into someone for whom the implications of trust were not easy. Repeatedly and protractedly, God pursued Moses until Moses understood that the God he served expected his trust and that He would prove Himself, both before and after the trust had been followed through. God gave him just enough, along his journey, to demonstrate who He was but saved the climactic proof for the end of Moses' journey of faith.

On the other hand, Abraham is shown to us as one who so hungered after God that he was willing, with minimal outward proof, to leave his home and to build for posterity a community of faith in the living God. But even in his case, every step in his faith-building process was met with the affirmation of God. God deals with both kinds of us, those of us who long for more evidence and those of us for whom a little evidence will do. But He works always in concert with a revelation of His character.

But notice that there are twin angles here. The first is that of trust. Jesus claimed to be the consummate expression of God. The true believer trusts Him to be speaking the truth. Everything He said and did sustains that claim, and contrarily, nothing He said or did challenges that claim. It has been said that human nature abhors a vacuum, and that must be true of our faith too. None of us lives comfortably with a vacuous faith. There ought to be both substance to our faith and an object of our faith.

But there is a second common misunderstanding about faith. We often assume that it is a crutch for those who are hurting or are in need of some kind of transcendent intervention in a situation from which they cannot rescue themselves. How often we hear testimonies of faith from the sick and the dying or the injured and bleeding. That, we assume, is the grandest expression of faith. Without doubt, a faith that stays strong in the storms of life is a faith that must be envied.

May I suggest, however, that in reality this kind of situation is more often the realizing or the *testing* of one's faith. An equally viable faith is demonstrated when dependence upon God is shown in the midst of success, when everything is going right. That kind of faith knows that every moment and every success in life is a gift from God.

I could illustrate this in two contrasting ways. Some years ago, I had the privilege of meeting a couple by the name of Mark and Gladys Bliss, who for fourteen years were missionaries in Iran. We were together at a gathering of Iranian Christians. As the evening progressed, our Iranian host took me aside and began to tell me the Blisses' story.

In 1969, he said, Mark and Gladys were driving with their children and some friends to visit a new church some miles from Teheran. In fact, said this gentleman, "I was a young lad, and they had come to my house to pick me up for this trip. But I couldn't go." On their journey late at night, they met with a terrible accident in which all three Bliss children—thirteen-year-old Karen, eleven-year-old Debbie, and three-year-old Mark—were killed. The other couple with them in the car lost their six-month-old baby in that awful tragedy. (On a side note, it was the father of that six-month-old who, twenty-five years later, was martyred. Haik Hovsepian was stabbed to death because of his love and service for Jesus Christ. Evidently, early tragedy had not diminished his faith.)

As I heard this story, I glanced toward Mark and Gladys Bliss, and my heart sank. How was it possible to look so at peace when you have buried your three children at the tender ages of protective need? An ache such as that seems too large to contain within the heart. "Their testimony became a shining light in our community," said this Iranian man. "Only their faith in God carried them through."

Contrast this with the following. Some years ago, I was invited to the Orient by a businessman to address a gathering of people called "diamond-collared" executives. He himself is known to be one of the wealthiest men in his country. In fact, I subsequently realized that he is listed by those who make such lists as one of the ten wealthiest people in the world. When I arrived there, I asked him what had brought him to place his trust in Jesus Christ.

"Oh," he said, "about eighteen months ago, I said to my wife, 'I have everything in life, but I am still so empty. I do not know where to turn. I believe I need God.'" His wife supported that yearning. With that they began their search and found their way to Jesus Christ. Nothing dramatic. No big crusade. Just a regular attendance at a weekly Bible study group, and they were now in tune with the wealth of a newfound relationship with Jesus Christ.

Was the faith of the one any less than the faith of the other? It may be true that perhaps one has been tested more than the other. But certainly, to turn to God when all your earthly needs are already met is to express in no uncertain terms that faith in God is to trust Him even when other supports are within reach. Jesus said that for a rich man to make such a commitment was almost impossible. But thankfully He went on to say that with God it was possible.

You see, that is the way God has designed us. One of the most startling things about life is that it does not start with reason and end with faith. It starts in childhood with faith and is sustained either by reasoning through that faith or by blindly leaving the reason for faith unaddressed. The child's mind has a very limited capacity to inform it of the reason for its trust. But whether she nestles on her mother's shoulder, nurses at her mother's breast, or runs into her father's arms, she does so because of an implicit trust that those shoulders will bear her, that her food will sustain her, and that those arms will hold her. If over time that trust is tested, it will be the character of the parent that will either prove that trust wise or foolish. Faith is not bereft of reason.

FAITH AND UNREASON

There is another side. Jesus reminded His followers that the commitment of the will is a fickle thing when it comes up against the beckoning arms of God. The tendency of the human heart is so defiant that every generation will find ways to challenge that which God proclaims. This point is critical in order to understand that whatever proof is offered at any time in history, we will always demand something else. In Luke 7:31–35, Jesus said:

> To what, then, can I compare the people of this generation? What are they like?
> They are like children sitting in the marketplace and calling out to each other:

> > "We played the flute for you,
> > and you did not dance;
> > we sang a dirge,
> > and you did not cry."

> For John the Baptist came neither eating bread nor drinking wine, and you say, "He has a demon." The Son of Man came eating and drinking, and you say, "Here is a glutton and a drunkard, a friend of tax collectors and 'sinners.'" But wisdom is proved right by all her children.

By this Jesus powerfully exposed the bent of the human will. When John warned them of the severity of the law, they called him demon-possessed because they wanted more liberty. When Jesus came and mingled with the outcasts of society, they called Him a hedonist because they wanted a tighter reign over the law. But Jesus declared that wisdom reveals itself by what it produces. It does not take more than one look at our society to see the utter absence of wisdom, and it is because we understand neither law nor grace. To such a mind-set, faith will always be caricatured as a symptom of credulity. Jesus was not hesitant to call their bluff, as He does ours.

But He turned the tables on them and reminded them that their faithlessness to what they knew to be true said more about their own character than it did about the evidence. This, I believe, is the essential component that is often missing from a discussion of faith. Yes, there is the component of content that speaks to the truth. Yes, there is the component of love that speaks to the blending of the emotion and commitment. But there is also the component of honesty that speaks to the truthfulness or the integrity of the individual. It is here that the battle lines are publicly drawn. It is here that the real truth about reason is revealed.

THE REAL CONFLICT

A recent article in the *Times* in England titled "The Rage of Reason," penned by Matthew Parris, is fairly typical of a thinker who claims to be a lover of reason over against the irrationality of religion. He punctuates his plea with a wish for the Bertrand Russells, Thomas Paines, and David Humes of the past to return and deliver us from the scourge of the "religious nonsense" around. I cannot engage all of what he says in this space, but let me respond to at least one of his invocations.

Echoing the words of Blake in calling for Milton—"Oh Milton, thou shouldest be living at this hour, England hath need of thee!"—Parris entreats, "Oh David Hume, thou shouldest be living at this hour, we have need of thee."[3]

David Hume, who lived in the eighteenth century, was one of the most vocal philosophers to contend for the factual nature of science against what he termed the irrationality of religion. He was a thoroughgoing skeptic, and his philosophical attack upon the nature of religious belief is echoed in academic halls to this day. Hume roundly denounced the very possibility of miracles.

The writer of the *Times* article, Parris, quotes these famous lines from Hume, lines that many skeptics have repeatedly used without having pondered them carefully: "The Christian religion not only was at first attended with miracles, but even at this day cannot be believed by any reasonable person without one." So said Hume, and so far, so good.

But now note what Hume says must be the test for anything meaningful:

If we take in our hand any volume: of divinity or school of metaphysics, for instance; let us ask, *Does it contain any abstract reasoning concerning quantity or number?* No. *Does it contain any experimental reasoning concerning matter of fact and existence?* No. Commit it then to the flames; For it can contain nothing but sophistry and illusion.[4]

Quoting these lines with an air of triumph, Parris seems to think that a devastating, knockout punch has been delivered to religion so that it now lies unconscious before the stupendous stature of science. All religion has been stigmatized as nothing but "sophistry and illusion" because its "volume of divinity" does not stand the test of either mathematics or science. Unless a statement fits into either of these categories, it must be "tossed into the flames."

The only problem with Mr. Parris's test for meaning, quoting Hume, is that *the test itself does not pass the test.* David Hume's grand statement is neither scientific nor mathematical. If, in order to be meaningful, a statement must be either mathematically sustained or scientifically verifiable, then David Hume's statement itself is meaningless. It is a philosophical solvent that dissolves itself. The emperor has no clothes, while boasting the finest threads.

What unmitigated arrogance to so narrow reason when, in truth, it is this kind of unreason that has lost sight of itself! The Bible, in fact, speaks of such a person, who looks in the mirror and then walks away, forgetting what he looks like. Writers like Parris, who brag that they live in the bright sunlight of reason and wish to deliver this world from the darkness of every religious belief, abound today. They are only outwardly more sophisticated than the woman on the side of the road who said, "If you want to believe he exists, then he exists." Their hollow reasoning is no less self-serving. I dealt with this critique of Hume at Oxford University recently, and one student came at the end and said "OK, we are unreasonable, so what!" Our subsequent conversation could fit into either tragedy or comedy, depending on one's mood.

How tragic that so many are living in the darkness of unreason, clinging to their absolute skepticism. The prophecies, person, and work of Christ, His resurrection from the dead, and numerous other affirmations do have points of verification in history. What does the naturalist do with them? No, the Christian's faith is not a leap into the dark; it is a well-placed trust in the light—the Light of the World, who is Jesus.

But that is only one-half of the naturalist's problem. Some years ago, I was having dinner with a few scholars, most of whom were scientists. They were a fine group of people, and I was honored to be in their company. At one point, our discussion veered into the conflict between naturalism's starting point— nature and nature alone—and supernaturalism's starting point, which is that God is the only sufficient explanation for our origin.

I asked them a couple of questions. "If the Big Bang were indeed where it all began [which one can fairly well grant, at least to this point in science's thinking], may I ask what preceded the Big Bang?" Their answer, which I had anticipated, was that the universe was shrunk down to a singularity.

I pursued, "But isn't it correct that a singularity as defined by science is a point at which all the laws of physics break down?"

"That is correct," was the answer.

"Then, technically, your starting point is not scientific either."

There was silence, and their expressions betrayed the scurrying mental searches for an escape hatch. But I had yet another question.

I asked if they agreed that when a mechanistic view of the universe had held sway, thinkers like Hume had chided philosophers for taking the principle of causality and applying it to a philosophical argument for the existence of God. Causality, he warned, could not be extrapolated from science to philosophy.

"Now," I added, "when quantum theory holds sway, randomness in the subatomic world is made a basis for randomness in life. Are you not making the very same extrapolation that you warned us against?"

Again there was silence and then one man said with a self-deprecating smile, "We scientists do seem to retain selective sovereignty over what we allow to be transferred to philosophy and what we don't."

There is the truth in cold, hard terms. The person who demands a sign and at the same time has already determined that anything that cannot be explained scientifically is meaningless is not merely stacking the deck; he is losing at his own game.

THE MIND BEHIND THE QUESTIONER

There remains yet one thing that needs to be said about the demand for a sign. Is that demand not a sign in itself? After all, the reason a sign is demanded is because we are intelligent beings. We seek evidence because we think, and thinking cannot but be the result of a mind. But our minds cannot justify our propensity for reason if there were no ultimate reason and no mind behind the existence of our minds, because the framing of our minds is the result of complex information. We must marvel not only at what the mind seeks, but at what the mind is. Lewis Thomas makes this comment in *Medusa and the Snail* about the information-rich blueprint in the human gene.

> The mere existence of that cell should be one of the greatest astonishments of the earth. People ought to be walking around all day, all through their waking hours, calling to each other in endless wonderment, talking of nothing except that cell. . . . If anyone does succeed in explaining it, within my lifetime I will charter a skywriting airplane, maybe a whole fleet of them, and send them aloft to write one great exclamation point after another, around the whole sky, until all my money runs out.[5]

Writing about this same human cell, Chandra Wickramasinghe, professor of applied mathematics at the University of Cardiff, Wales, reminded his readers that the statistical probability of forming even a single enzyme, the building block of the gene, which is in turn the building block of the cell, is 1 in $10^{40,000}$. The translation of that figure is that it would require more attempts for the formation of one enzyme than there are atoms in all the stars of all the galaxies in the entire known universe. Though a Buddhist, Dr. Wickramasinghe concedes this supernatural notion.[6]

So "impossible" is this event that Francis Crick, the Nobel Prize–winning scientist who helped crack the code of human DNA, said it is "almost a miracle."[7]

In short, both David Hume's own test and Bertrand Russell's plea for evidence force one to wonder who has to have more faith. Is it the Christian who uses his mind to trust in God, or is it the one who, without any attempt to explain how his mind came to be, nevertheless uses that mind to demand a sign and disbelieves in God? When Russell was asked to explain the existence of the universe, he said, "It's just there." That is not an explanation. That is an explaining away. King David said long ago in his psalms of praise to God, "I am fearfully and wonderfully made" (Ps. 139:14).

Years ago, I read an episode of the cartoon strip "Born Loser." Brutus Thornapple was seen lounging beside a magnificent stretch of beach. He turned to a stranger next to him and confided, "I was able to afford this trip because of a ten-thousand-dollar insurance claim on a fire in my house."

The man replied, "I am here because of a twenty-thousand-dollar insurance claim on a flood that destroyed my house."

Brutus looked utterly defeated and then turned to face the man, whispering, "How does one start a flood?"

Little fires and little floods are easy to start if you have matches and water. How does a universe, which itself developed from nothing, impart into every human strand of DNA enough specific information to cover six hundred thousand pages of information from nothing? Intelligence is intrinsic to our makeup. Jesus warned against taking what is intrinsic and manipulating it into a scenario that excludes other equally intrinsic facets that drive us to God.

In summary, therefore, faith in Jesus Christ is a cognitive, passionate, and moral commitment to that which stands up under the scrutiny of the mind, the heart, and the conscience. It is not an escapist grasp that comes to the rescue when life is out of control. It is recasting every threat and possibility that life presents into the design of God.

This is why Jesus challenged the notion that more evidence would have generated more faith. George Macdonald said years ago that to give truth to him who does not love the truth is to only give more reasons for misinterpretation.

THE GREATEST PROOF OF ALL

Now Jesus places the *text* of His answer against the ultimate test of His claim: "Destroy this temple, and in three days I will raise it up."

What greater proof could He offer than to rise from the dead? Naturalism is compelled to believe that death is the cessation of life, the irreversible ceasing of one's brain activity. There is a sense of finality about death that centuries of discussion have not been able to dissipate. The philosopher Albert Camus said wryly, "Death is philosophy's only problem." If somehow death could be conquered, life could be redefined.

Jesus gave the greatest proof of His authority by accurately predicting His death and the time of His bodily resurrection. Of all people, the temple authorities should have been alert to His promise, but they never dreamed that it would actually come to be. They were sure it was an empty boast. The fulfillment of that prediction reveals the uniqueness of Jesus above all contenders.

It is important to note that Jesus did not predict merely a spiritual resurrection. That would have been an easy way out. He predicted a *physical*, verifiable resurrection. After He was laid in the tomb, the temple authorities needed only to produce His body to disprove His claim. But they could not. He proved precisely what He said He would.

The hope that He brings is in the demonstration that death has been conquered. Paul, recognizing the Christian claim, said that if the hope that comes from Christ being raised from the dead is not true, "we are of all men most miserable" (1 Cor. 15:19 KJV). It was the encounter with the resurrected Jesus that turned this obstinate individual, a murderer named Saul of Tarsus, into the apostle Paul.

But the uniqueness of His resurrection is not left as a "futuristic" hope. It is tied into present privileges and responsibilities. This is where Jesus moved beyond their pretext and His text to the larger context for all of us.

WHEN BODIES DO NOT MATTER

At the beginning of this chapter, I stated that there was a reason Jesus used the concept of the body to talk about the temple. His words truly carried a double edge for both the skeptic and the religious person. The Bible says that those who heard Him say these words did not know that He was speaking of the temple of the body, which He called "the temple of God." That is the context within which He gave His answer. He lifted their sights beyond stones and mortar to the place where He seeks to dwell—within every human being. Your body and my body are His temple.

This is an extraordinary conferral of sanctity upon what it means to be human. It means that this body is deemed worthy of respect and reverence. Not only is the proof of Jesus' authority different from any other claimant to deity, its application and implication present a world of difference.

Please take very careful note of what I am saying now. In all pantheistic religions and in New Age thinking, the body is seen as an extension or continuation of the universe. Popular speaker and writer Deepak Chopra is a classic example of this. He is an exponent on the themes of spirituality, wealth, and success, and he is representative of a world-view that in essence is pantheistic and prides itself on its blend of naturalism with the spiritual. Chopra makes a case for our material commonality with every part of the universe. He further argues that, in its randomness, the subatomic world provides the basis for all of life. From this randomness and cosmic oneness we find our being, our common values, and spiritual goals. This is how he explains it in his book *The Seven Spiritual Laws of Success:*

> On the material level, both you and [a] tree are made up of the same recycled elements: mostly carbon, hydrogen, oxygen, nitrogen, and other elements in minute amounts. You could buy these elements in a hardware store for a couple of dollars. . . . The real difference between the two of you is in the energy and in the information. . . . Your body is not separate from the body of the universe, because at quantum mechanical levels there are no well-defined edges. You are like a wiggle, a wave, a fluctuation, a convolution, a whirlpool, a localized disturbance in the larger quantum field. The larger quantum field—the universe—is your extended body.[8]

One must wonder how such thinking can actually retain logical integrity. In effect, it violates the disciplines of both science and of religion. *It reduces my being to sheer matter while spiritualizing it and exalts the mind to spiritual supremacy while naturalizing it.* To base an entire philosophy of life on the impersonal subatomic world while espousing both randomness and absoluteness is to give the impression of doing magic with words. Chopra makes philosophical extrapolations that are quantum leaps in themselves. One might as well argue that if his deductions are true, his philosophizing is nothing more than a wiggle or a wave or a localized disturbance. Such is the seduction and reduction of this kind of thinking, supposedly done in the name of wisdom and success. Chopra's world of human essence and Jesus' description of human worth are at opposite poles.

A truth gleaned from Shakespeare's *The Merchant of Venice* provides an illustration here. This is basically the story of a man who had loaned some money to the friend of a friend. The moneylender, Shylock, held his friend, Antonio, responsible for the debt until it was repaid. If the debt was not repaid, according to the deal, Shylock was owed a pound of flesh from Antonio's side. Predictably, Antonio's ships were lost at sea, and when the debt became due, he did not have the wherewithal to pay Shylock. With glee, Shylock demanded his pound of flesh, as was his due according to the law. But the judge, not to be outdone, declared, "You can have your pound of flesh, but if even one drop of blood is spilled in the process, you will have to pay with your own blood." All of a sudden, Shylock had lost at his own game.

It is no more possible to take a pound of live flesh without the shedding of blood than it is possible to make the body inviolable while reducing it to sheer matter. Naturalists cannot have their pound of flesh without bleeding the life out of it. Through the substance of human flesh flows life. Life is more than matter. Religions that attempt to keep the body sacred while denying the Creator's hand are in the same boat as skeptics who try to protect life while saying it is nothing more than matter.

All the desacralizing that has engulfed our culture lies in this very struggle to understand the place and sacredness of the body. The right of every individual life, even the one still in its mother's womb; the pleasure and consummation of sexual delights, reserved for the sanctity of marriage; the injunction against suicide; the care and protection of one's health; the injunction against killing; and the command to love others more than we love ourselves and to work for their good—all of these flow from the fact that this body becomes the dwelling place of God. Our world would be a different place if we comprehended this sobering privilege.

Having lost this truth, what are we left with? Pornography and the cruel degradation of men, women, and children; death in the womb in the name of personal rights; the breakdown of the family for myriad reasons; the profanation of sex in our entertainment industry; violence in unprecedented proportions. One can only weep for the bleeding and the loss. In losing the high value that God has placed on the body, we are in a free fall, at the mercy of greed, cruelty, and lust.

During my travels in one particular part of the world, I found myself sitting next to a woman who worked for an international agency that cared for children. As we talked, she confessed to me that after all she had seen in her work, it was very difficult to remain optimistic about the future of this world. Why, I asked her, had she become so cynical? She paused and began a narration of heartbreaking stories. She named a particular city where she had been recently and described the horror of all that went on there. In a section in that city called "Snake Alley," men come at night and drink a combination of snake's blood and alcohol. When they are under its influence, they are taken into a back room where children are offered to them for their sexual pleasure. This woman told me that the youngest one they rescued from this terrible state was only eleven months old. Many, of course, are used this way and then killed, often in the act itself. "Where are the city fathers of a city such as that?" I asked. "They are on the take," was her sad reply.

How is it possible for something like that to be given legitimacy? Or is it just easier to pretend it does not happen? The scourge of violence and vileness is the offspring of a mind that has lost respect for the body while the body has lost its sanctity.

Nearer home, though the stories are different, the rationale is the same. In March 1998, two boys ages eleven and thirteen went on a shooting rampage in their school in Jonesboro, Arkansas, killing four girls and a teacher and injuring ten others. That tragedy at Westside Middle School was at the time the largest school massacre in America. On the night of the shootings, many were being counseled in small groups in the hospital waiting room. Friends and relatives were waiting for word of the victims. The whole scene was one of desolation and horror.

In one corner sat a woman alone, looking dazed and helpless. A counselor went to her to see if she needed any assistance and discovered that she was the mother of one of the girls who had been killed. She had no husband, no friends, and no family. "I just came to find out how to get my little girl's body back," she said. But the body had been taken to Little Rock, one hundred miles away, for an autopsy.[9]

"I just came to get my little girl's body back."

She did not come to pick up a wiggle or a wave or a fluctuation. She came to pick up the body of her daughter, not just an extension of the universe. What a grim reminder that is to the rest of us. We trivialize the body in our indulgences. We treat it as a means to other ends. But when death comes, we grasp at it and cling to it because it is all we have left.

Jesus made it clear that the body is not just informationally different from other quantities; it is purposefully different. That is why the resurrection is a physical one at its core. The body matters in the eternal sense, not just the temporal.

A REMARKABLE COMPLIMENT

The final ramification of Jesus' words to all of us is gratifying, for if our bodies are His dwelling place, worship rises above a location. In no other religious world-view is this connection made between the body and the temple. In fact, in every other world-view the body is distinct from the temple. Rules are laid out for the body before it can enter the temple. A litany of prerequisites surrounds entry into so-called "holy places" of worship.

During the course of writing this book, I had the privilege of witnessing in one country a festival called Thaipusam. As I walked in the midst of teeming masses and saw all that was going on in a desire to worship, my mind was in a constant state of shock. Devotees involved in this ceremony demonstrate the terrifying extent to which they are willing to go in order to gain the favor of their god. Iron spears are pierced into their bodies, and large skewers are forced from one side of their faces through to the other. Another skewer is pierced through their tongues, and the devotees parade for miles and for hours with this apparatus on them. In fact, trailing each one is a helper, who holds reins on the hooks and pulls in the opposite direction, compelling the devotee to strain against the force as he walks the long trek. At the end of the journey, he mounts one hundred steps to the temple of Lord Murugan, the second son of the Hindu god, Shiva.

One is surprised to see that the flesh does not rip and the blood flow is minimal, if any. Each devotee is in a trance. The temple is busy as each participant arrives and is unhooked from the weight he has been laboring under, and the ceremony continues. The ashen mark on his forehead at the end of the day is ash from burned and "purified" cow dung. All this is to win the blessing of the one he worships in the "sanctity" of the temple, *the place of encounter with his god,* and to be blessed at the hands of the priest. How did such strange beliefs come to pass?

Readers will remember the assassination of India's prime minister, Indira Gandhi. The murder was prompted by revenge because she had sent the military into the Sikh Temple, where weapons were being stored. She was murdered in order to preserve a temple. Jesus would have told them that they had actually destroyed what was intended to be His temple in order to preserve a place.

More recently, Hindus and Muslims engaged in bombings and killings over the sacred birthplace of a Hindu deity, upon which a mosque had been built. This anger, ironically, is the logical outworking of a belief that exalts places into exclusive venues where God is met or encountered. Muslims will never allow a church in their country to have a steeple taller than a mosque. In fact, where there is already an existing church, it is not uncommon for Muslims to build a mosque next to it that is taller.

Islam ridicules Christianity for profaning God's name, calling Jesus' incarnation blasphemous. But in His incarnation He exalts the body, first by being conceived in the womb of a virgin, then by taking on human form and giving it the glorious expression of God in the flesh.

The history of Christendom is not free from perversions. But Jesus sent a message loud and clear. *We* are His temple. We do not turn in a certain direction to pray. We are not bound by having to go into a building so that we can commune with God. There are no unique postures and times and limitations that restrict our access to God. My relationship with God is intimate and personal. The Christian does not go to the temple to worship. The Christian takes the temple with him or her. Jesus lifts us beyond the building and pays the human body the highest compliment by making it His dwelling place, the place where He meets with us. Even today He would overturn the tables of those who make it a marketplace for their own lust, greed, and wealth.

Was this not the stunning truth behind the woman's expression as she poured the alabaster ointment on Jesus, as described in Luke 7? On one hand it was to prepare for His death, but on the other hand something greater had taken place. She was a woman of ill repute. Her life's living was possibly earned through prostitution. Now Jesus welcomed her and restored the worth of the human body to her. In her soiled earthly temple, she came to give an offering to Him whose dwelling place it would be. Jesus said of her that wherever the gospel story would be told, the story of what this woman had done for Him would also be told. It was the ultimate transaction between her corruption and His purity. It represented the changed relationship between the dwelling and its occupant. "Christ in you," said the apostle Paul, is "the hope of glory" (Col. 1:27). What more glorious news than to find out that He seeks to live within you?

"What sign do You give us?" they cried.

"Destroy this body and in three days I will raise it up."

They did not know He spoke of the temple of the body. Why? Because in their greed and love of power, they were focused on a temple made of stone. How much they lost in exploiting other people, other temples—and indeed themselves—within which God wanted to dwell. No other claimant would have answered it Jesus' way.

Chapter Four

A TASTE FOR THE SOUL

"TRUTH IS STRANGER THAN FICTION," IT IS SAID.

G. K. Chesterton, with his ever-ready wit, told us why that is so: "It is because we have made fiction to suit ourselves." Modern-day techniques have only enhanced the capacity to mass-produce lies. With that combination of propensity and facility, we live with the reality that sometimes the truth seems impossible to believe.

Some years ago, my family and I were visiting the city of Bedford, England, a little west of where we were living in Cambridge. In the heart of Bedford stands a larger-than-life statue of the famed seventeenth-century author John Bunyan. In fact, so imposing is the size of that sculpture that some prankster has painted bold, gigantic white footsteps from the edifice all the way to the public toilets. The message implied, sarcastically or otherwise, is that Bunyan still lives.

Any reader of literature knows that though Bunyan has long been dead, his brilliant work, *Pilgrim's Progress,* does indeed live on. That book has been translated into more languages than any other book in history, with the exception of the Bible. We wandered through the museum built to his memory, where there was exhibited a copy of the book in every language in which it has been printed. We were quite impressed by the people of various nationalities engrossed in the display, walking from room to room, studying the exhibits.

As I was leaving, I commented to the woman at the front desk, "Isn't it amazing that a simple little book from the hands of a mender of pots and pans has won such worldwide acclaim?"

She paused and said, "I suppose that is true, but I must confess that I haven't read it."

If there hadn't been a hard floor beneath me, I would have voluntarily fainted. Unable to help myself, I asked her, "Why not?"

"I found it too difficult, I suppose," came the very dispassionate reply.

If shock were to be measured along a scale, at this point, I was nearly off the chart. What does one say to the person who sells tickets to a museum, the existence of which is owed to one book, while she herself has left the work unread? I recommended that for the sake of sheer curiosity, if not propriety, she might at least try the children's version so she could get a mild taste of what the interest was all about.

What a remarkable illustration of self-inflicted poverty! It is possible to hold a treasure in your hand but be ignorant of it and go for the wrapping instead. This proximity to truth and distance from its worth is repeated innumerable times in our lives. In Chesterton's words, we hold the dust and let the gold go free.

No one saw this tragedy lived out more than Jesus did. The masses came to Him frequently and left embracing lesser things while forfeiting the real treasure He was offering them. He often expressed surprise at their shallowness in being unable to look beyond the surface.

One of the most dramatic illustrations of this failing was illustrated in their encounter with a truth at once so captivating and so dramatic. The lingering tragedy throughout history is that millions have made the same mistake and left these words of Jesus either unread or shamefully distorted.

I faced its implication once in a public challenge. I had just finished a talk before a somewhat hostile audience in India. During the question-and-answer time, a man abruptly shouted from the back of the tent, "Christians are cannibals! Jesus promoted cannibalism!"

There was absolutely no logical or thematic connection between what I had spoken on and his outburst. His attack only revealed his animosity toward the message of the Christian faith. In my experience, while I never get used to such attacks, I certainly have learned to anticipate them. The natural inclination is to fight back and to dish out exactly what you are facing— derision for derision, blow for blow, gibe for gibe.

But that is not the answer to an angry questioner. In fact, such a response would only diminish the effectiveness of any answer. The truth is that as I stood there, I had a fairly good idea why this man was insinuating what he did, although most of the audience gasped at his assertion.

My response was a simple counter. "Why do you say that, and what is your source?"

He had none. He assured me that if I gave him time to run back to his home and check the book in which he had read it he could sustain his charge.

He really did not need to go searching for his book. I could have pretty much named the philosopher he had read and on what page he had made that allegation. Antitheistic philosophers have not spared their scorn in their eagerness to mock this, of all Jesus' sayings. So I knew precisely what this student had in mind. I did offer him the platform to come up and debate the point, but he turned down the offer.

"Christians are cannibals!"

What on earth was he talking about? Had he ever read the Bible? Did he ever seek an explanation for what he read? Or was this the way he wanted it to read?

For those who have grown up in a Christian home or who have been raised with an active church life such a bizarre thought may have never been entertained. But for one who comes to Christ from outside a Christian environment, or for the skeptic in search of an argument, a particular passage does leap out of the Scriptures with discomforting coarseness. The words are unadorned to impress sensitivities.

"This is My body. . . . Take and eat." "This is My blood. . . . Drink all of it."

These words of Jesus prompted such shock when He spoke them that I cannot completely fault the student for his reaction. I well remember as a young lad hearing those poignant lines intoned in a ministerial pitch, Sunday after Sunday, at the church to which I was reluctantly dragged. But what I recall most is that I dreaded the length of the service and had no idea what those words portended—in fact, I never even gave them a thought. I did see people walking up the aisle, kneeling at the altar with palms cupped, receiving something that they would put into their mouths. For my part, I had it all timed. I knew that when those words were uttered we were about twenty minutes away from the end of the service, and I was an hour away from being on the cricket field or in the movie theater.

I was so close to one of the most sublime truths and transactions ever taught and demonstrated by Jesus, yet I was oblivious to its meaning. Like the clerk at Bunyan's home, I had left those words unread. Now I know that for someone who truly seeks to understand what all this means, its depth is immeasurable.

Once again, if we are to follow the path to understanding we must lay hold of the sequence to Jesus' assertions. First, the simple, then, the profound. His utterance, I believe, offers an element of the gospel that stands in brilliant and unarguably unique contrast to other faiths.

PROPELLED BY THE SENSATIONAL

> Earth's crammed with heaven,
> And every common bush afire with God;
> But only he who sees takes off his shoes;
> The rest sit round it and pluck blackberries.[1]

So said the poet Elizabeth Barrett Browning. Her lament takes us back to that spellbinding encounter when God appeared to Moses in the burning bush and issued a call to him that he might lead His people out of slavery into a land flowing with milk and honey. That epiphany, as Browning points out, was not for Moses' culinary delight. No more, I might add, than the thunder and lightning on Sinai were so that the people could enjoy the glow on the landscape.

The dazzling, almost fearsome accompaniment of the elements in both these defining moments for His people pointed beyond the portents to the One who controlled those elements. God's inexhaustible presence graced those occasions with brilliant and awesome splendor. How inconceivable was the loss for the people when the signs became the ends in themselves and the One signified became the means. The special effects became the attraction, and the central figure was obscured. The world of humanity has lived with such blindness, and the mistake has been repeated in virtually every life.

And so it was that, centuries after the event, people were still locked into that blindness. The crowd in Jesus' ministry followed Him and intruded upon His time alone. They came with a one-upmanship challenge to Him to match the manna from heaven that Moses gave his people. They were not expecting an answer anywhere near as jarring as His. Talking about bread was the easier part. What followed was staggering to them. By the time He had finished, many left Him, asking, "How can we accept such a hard saying?"

The truth, in this instance, *was* beyond belief because the mind was unwilling to ponder the provision and, of course, the implication. Between their expectation and His offer was a wide chasm, and they started to leave without seeking an explanation. Jesus then looked at His disciples and asked if they were going to leave Him too. Was this all too much for them to comprehend?

After His death, they would relive those moments and remember what He had said. Millennia later, while the Church repeats those words in virtually every language, many have found the teaching too difficult and still leave these words unstudied.

MISREADING THE SCRIPT

When Jesus said, "Take and eat; this is my body. . . . Drink from it, all of you. This is my blood of the covenant" (Matt. 26:26–28), He was not speaking in a cultural vacuum to consign His followers to cannibalism. Rather, His words were intended to lift the listeners from their barren, food-dominated existence to the recognition of the supreme hunger of life that could only be filled by different bread. It was in that very journey under Moses that He had first told them that physical bread had limited sustenance. He wanted to meet a greater hunger.

To a culture with such specific instruction on their spiritual need, to say nothing of their strict dietary laws, only ignorance would manufacture the notion that Jesus was prescribing the consumption of human flesh. Their charge that it was "a hard saying" betrayed a serious misunderstanding. It is just that response that leaves every human being bereft of life's real meaning.

The longer I have pondered these words, the more profoundly I am moved to realize why our hunger for something transcendent is so rooted in our very being, yes, even in our physical craving. That may be why we cannot shrug it off, however hard we try.

It is, therefore, a significant loss that a teaching so great has been met with an understanding so shallow. Unfortunately, like the questioning student in India, rather than getting to the truth that Jesus is revealing, many "sit round it" instead, as philosophers or critics, and "eat blackberries."

What is the context we have? What preceded this demand by the crowd to bring down food from heaven?

Before his record of this conversation, John had already described several miracles that Jesus had done. The first was the conversion of water into wine, in which Jesus revealed His power over the elements. Then John narrated two episodes of healing, in which Jesus showed His power over sickness. Following that, he relates Jesus' multiplication of a young lad's lunch to feed five thousand people—His power over all provision. Finally, he pens the well-known story of Jesus walking on water—His power over natural law.

An incredible history of response has followed these stories, ranging from the reverential to the ridiculous, from the artistic to the philosophical. Capturing the beauty of the conversion of the water into wine, the poet Alexander Pope said, "The conscious water saw its Master and blushed." That sublime description could be reworked to explain each one of these miracles. Was it any different in principle for a broken body to mend at the command of its Maker? Was it far-fetched for the Creator of the universe, who fashioned matter out of nothing, to multiply bread for the crowd? Was it not within the power of the One who called all the molecules into existence to interlock them that they might bear His footsteps? Why were they not making that connection?

But is this not the very impertinence that grasps the gift and ignores the giver? Naturalism by its purpose engineers the displacement of the miracle and puts in its place explanations that defy reason. Those who smirk at His walking on water have forgotten the miracle He has already performed in the very composition of water.

Think of this for a moment. In eighteen milliliters of water (about two swallows full), there are 6×10^{23} molecules of H_2O. How much is 6×10^{23}? A good computer can carry out ten million counts per second. It would take that computer two billion years to count to 6×10^{23}.

Look at it another way. A stack of five hundred sheets of paper is two to three inches high. How high would the stack be if it had 6×10^{23} sheets? That stack would reach from the earth to the sun, not once, but more than one million times.[2]

Yet, in about two gulps of water, God has packed that many molecules. The miracle of walking on water is small for Him who created it in the first place. The multiplication of bread was but a simple command for Him when the very earth was brought forth at His command. (C. S. Lewis commented that a slow miracle is no easier to perform than an instant one.) The skeptic, of course, will challenge such credulity that accepts wholesale such stories, not realizing that what they swallow in a glass of water is a miracle in and of itself!

The people and the disciples who saw Jesus performing the miracle of feeding the multitude followed Him with deliberate intentions. They sought the very power that they assumed would make life more delectable—to ensure a full stomach and a limitless supply of bread. Who could fault them? I heard recently of a man who had won an enormous sum in a lottery. "What is the biggest difference in your life?" asked an interviewer. "I eat out more often," came the matter-of-fact answer.

Food and power distracted the mind from the need of nourishment for the soul. The generosity of God, incidental to the miracles, became a stumbling block because the eyewitnesses lost sight of the purpose of the deed and longed only to replicate the capacity in themselves. They wanted to know how a little boy's lunch could feed several thousand people and still have baskets full of crumbs left over. How could a paralytic of nearly four decades suddenly walk again? Is this power transferable? Can it be bought?

It is crucial to note that Jesus' response to their demand is in stark contrast to the self-aggrandizement that would-be messiahs covet. Rather than bask in the accolades of a feigning crowd and soak in their praise or enlarge His following, Jesus slipped away from their clamoring midst. In fact, He wept over their self-deception. He knew the motives and the misconceptions with which they lived. And when they somehow tracked Him down, they burst upon Him with a question, "Our fathers ate manna in the desert. . . . Why don't You give us the same?"

This is where He began His answer that was to lead them farther than they had ever planned on going. But He first tried to lead them away from their error before He could bring them to His truth.

IGNORING THE AUTHOR

It is not surprising that the first temptation Jesus faced in the wilderness was to change stones into bread. "Do this," said Satan, "and the world will follow You."

Anyone who has been in countries where hunger is publicly exposed as a means for eliciting pity and a handout can easily understand the emotional tug of such a temptation. I myself was raised in a land where there was never a shortage of hungry people. How can food sit comfortably in your stomach when someone else's hurts for the lack of it? This was, therefore, not a soft temptation thrust upon Jesus. The tempter knew, precisely, the force of his taunt. How much more relevant could God be than to be a provider of food for life? What good is religion if it cannot feed the hungry? Satan was perilously and painfully close to a truth. But it was a half-truth, and a half-truth gets so interwoven with a lie that it becomes deadlier by the mix.

Ask yourself this question: What kind of a following would result if the sole reason for the affection toward the leader is that he provides his followers with bread? Both motives would be wrong—for the provider and the receiver. These are the terms of reward and punishment that are mercenarily tainted and have diminishing returns, at best engendering compliance, but not love. Their appeal, too, is soon lost when offered as enticements or when withheld to engender fears. Dependence without commitment will ever look for ways to break the stranglehold.

The temptation Satan posed to Jesus stalked Him throughout His ministry, even as the crowd was increasing with its demand for a limitless supply of bread. Politics of power through abundance is not a new invention.

That is the way demagogues have controlled the masses. Jesus took pains to show them that their preoccupation with bread as the primary purpose and expression of enjoyment of life had seriously displaced both what bread was meant to do and what life was meant to be.

In our high-paced living, this truth does not sink in with any greater ease than it did in ancient Palestine. With all our ingesting and consumption, our hungers are still many and our fulfillments are few. Must we not think about that? Is that not in itself an indicator that our hungers are displaced?

In his play *Our Town,* Thornton Wilder tells the story of life as it is lived out in the mundane and amid the hassles of daily living. The details are specific, but the lesson is like a mirror held out to all of us. We see the routine in all its monotony—the milk arrives, breakfast is eaten, working people go to their jobs, homemakers tidy their homes, handymen work in the yards—each day reflecting the previous one. In the story, the turning point comes when Emily Gibbs, in her youthful prime, dies giving birth to her baby, and the routine is suddenly broken.

From the realm of the dead, Emily was given a chance to return to earth for a day of her choice as it was actually lived out when she was on earth. Only now, from her otherworldly existence, she viewed it with nostalgic eyes. She watched the harried activity and busyness in celebration of her twelfth birthday. As she well remembered, the household was preoccupied with presents and food and chatter. The party buzzed with activity.

But now in this irreversible state, Emily noticed the complete loss of any personal attention, though her heart craved it. The focus, instead, was on the things that needed to be done, rather than the people for whom it was done. She was aghast at such blindness to all of their real needs. From the unseen, she pleaded, "Just for a moment we're happy. Let's look at one another." But her plaintive cry was unheeded. They could not hear her because they were trapped by the superficial. The party had to go on, another birthday would come, and the moments dissipated into activity. As she bid her final farewell, she cried, "Oh, Earth, you're too wonderful for anyone to realize you!"

Then she turns to the stage manager, who serves as the narrator, and asks this remorse-filled question: "Do any human beings ever realize life while they live it—every, every moment?"

The answer comes, "No. The saints and poets, maybe—they do some."

"Do any human beings ever realize life while they live it?" The only way one can realize life while one lives it is if he or she realizes that life is not a matter of nutrition alone but of the greater hunger that is beyond words and food. We do not live so that we can eat, nor do we just eat so that we can live. Life is worth living in and of itself. Life cannot be satisfied when it is lived out as a consuming entity. When it is filled by that which satisfies a hunger that is both physical *and* spiritual in a mutuality that sustains both without violation of either, only then can life be truly fulfilling. Authenticity and continuity are the offspring of the true and the eternal. For the millions who live out their lives day to day with the pursuit of bread dominating their dreams and actions, life, as it was meant to be, passes them by, and their unsatisfied hungers continue to scream out at them.

"The saints and poets, maybe—they do some," because they slow down and think and look beyond the activities to their longings and somehow broach the possibility of meaning that transcends their actions. In short, if we are to truly understand who we are, we must understand what bread can and cannot do.

Jesus has a similarly striking question for His audience, as He does for all of us. Does any one of us live every minute of life, knowing its essential worth? To realize the full impact of Jesus' patience with them, we must remember that this was not the first time the topic of food and hunger had surfaced in a conversation between Jesus and His followers. He had previously tried to bring this point home in an effort to thwart this "religion-for-bread" pursuit.

The most extended discussion had actually taken place a while before in an event that surprised the disciples—a conversation with a Samaritan woman (see John 4:1–42). In that dialogue, Jesus had tried to open up the understanding of their minds to what made up the form of life and what constituted its substance. In fact, He had a brilliant lead-in, had they but listened. Evidently the disciples missed His point.

They had their lunchbags in their hands and so were completely preoccupied. He was talking to a socially ostracized and desperate woman whose life had been used and abused till she had no sense of self-worth left. They chided Him for talking to this outcast. "You must be hungry," they said. "Is it not time to eat?"

"I have food to eat that you know nothing about. My food is to do the will of My Father."

There is the first remarkable pointer. If I am to be fulfilled, I must pursue a will that is greater than mine—a fulfilled life is one that has the will of God as its focus, not the appetite of the flesh.

He went on to say: "Open your eyes and look at the fields! They are ripe for harvest" (see John 4:32–35).

Here is our next clue. Maintaining the metaphor of food, He pointed to a hunger that was universal and that went beyond bread and water—a distinctive hunger of universal proportion. Every sentence of His response had food in it, but of a different kind. There was hunger everywhere, He said, and food enough for all. But it was not wheat or water. It was Christ Himself, the Bread of Life and the spring of living water. The Samaritan woman grasped what He said with a fervor that came from an awareness of her real need.

The transaction was fascinating. She had come with a bucket. He sent her back with a spring of living water.

She had come as a reject. He sent her back being accepted by God Himself.

She came wounded. He sent her back whole.

She came laden with questions. He sent her back as a source for answers.

She came living a life of quiet desperation. She ran back overflowing with hope.

The disciples missed it all. It was lunchtime for them.

Interestingly enough, it was only a short while after this conversation with the Samaritan woman that Jesus performed the miracle of feeding the thousands. So bread and food were not absent from His mind. He was moving them from the more difficult to the easier to perform; from the eternal to the temporal; from the soul's need to the body's hunger. But they were stuck on their desire for more food. They did not get it the first time around.

RAISING THE CURTAIN

So here it comes again in the sixth chapter of John. But this time Jesus added a very dramatic element. Hunger now takes on a wider scope, as it eventually had to if it were to be indicative of life.

If we were to enumerate all our hungers, we might be surprised at how many legitimate hungers there are. The hunger for truth, the hunger for love, the hunger for knowledge, the hunger to belong, the hunger to express, the hunger for justice, the hunger of the imagination, the hunger of the mind, and the hunger for significance. We could name more. Vast psychological theories have emerged in recognition of these hungers, or needs.

Here is the point. Some of our individual pursuits may meet some of these hungers. Education may bring knowledge. Romance may bring a sense of belonging. Accomplishments may bring significance. Wealth brings some things within reach. The message of Jesus affirms that no one thing will meet *all* of these hungers. And furthermore, none can help us know whether the way we fulfill them is legitimate or illegitimate until we feed on the bread of life that Jesus offers. That nourishment defines the legitimacy of all else.

Not only do we remain unfulfilled when we pursue these hungers, but in their very pursuit comes a disorientation that misrepresents and misunderstands where the real satisfaction comes from. This is very, very important to know.

As I mentioned previously, Jon Krakauer's book *Into Thin Air* relates the hazards that plagued the climbers in their expedition to Mount Everest during the spring of 1996. That year, the attempt to reach the summit resulted in a great loss of life. Some circumstances were out of their control, but fundamental mistakes cost them dearly. And some of those were unfortunately made while still within reach of solutions.

One of those whose life was lost was Andy Harris, one of the expedition leaders. Harris had stayed at the peak past the deadline that the leaders themselves had set. On his descent, he became in dire need of oxygen. Harris radioed his predicament to the base camp, telling them of his need and that he had come upon a cache of oxygen canisters left by other climbers, all empty. Those who had already passed by the canisters on their own return from the summit knew that they were not empty, but full. Even as they pleaded with him on the radio to make use of them, it was to no avail. Already starved for oxygen, Harris continued to argue that the canisters were empty.[3]

The problem was that the lack of what he needed so disoriented his mind that though he was surrounded by a restoring supply he continued to complain of its absence. The very thing he held in his hand was absent in his brain and ravaged his capacity to recognize what he was clutching in his grasp.

What oxygen is to the body, the Bread of Life is to the soul. Without that bread, all other hungers will be improperly perceived. In fact, in like manner, the absence of that bread over a prolonged period makes the bread itself seem worthless. Life is meant to be lived with the fulfillment of the one need that defines all other means of fulfillment and the one love that defines all other loves.

By His miracles, Jesus demonstrated from the greater to the lesser. In His answers, He moved them from the lesser to the greater. He reminded them in His words of Communion that the physical and the spiritual meet. Here the now and the forever converge. Here life and death co-mingle. Implicit in these verses is the climactic direction toward which Jesus was headed and to which He was to come back, moments before His death.

The people ought to have grasped more than they did. You see, to the Middle Eastern mind-set, bread is not just a source of nourishment. It is the bearer of so much more. Food is the means of fellowship. Jesus says, in Revelation 3:20, that He stands at the door and knocks; if anyone opens that door, He will come in and eat with him. What a beautiful expression that is of friendship. Food is the means of celebration. The return of the prodigal was celebrated by the killing of the fatted calf, which signaled that the feast had begun. Food is also a medium of pleasure. Solomon's palace thrived on such offerings. To this day, food is a big thing in eastern culture. As well as providing nourishment, it is the means of friendship, celebration, and pleasure.

We are not much different, East or West, and we know this. Yet, with all our nurture and friendships, our celebrations and pleasures, there come those crossroad moments in our lives when no food can sustain life, no friendship can overcome certain eventualities, no celebration can be endless, and no pleasure can be perfect. The body ages and weakens, and it is not within the capacity of food to ultimately restore the strength or lost youth. It moves inexorably toward a diminishing return. In short, there are two built-in limitations with food. The first is obvious. The body weakens and someday dies.

I have a friend whose life has enriched mine over the years. There came a time when his wife was stricken with cancer. I will never forget his example to me. The one word that comes to my mind is how he *cherished* her. By nature he is a busy, high-paced individual. One could get tired just watching him. Yet, when he knew her days were numbered, he dropped everything else to attend to her needs.

During the weeks and months, life ground down to one purpose, taking care of the one he loved. He sat by her side, loving her in the midst of her dissipating life. Nothing was good enough for her but fresh juices from only organically grown vegetables, processed only through a certain type of juicer. No country was too far to go to find a cure. No expense was too great to bring back her health.

But the end did finally come when her body was too far gone for any nourishment to sustain her. No bond was strong enough to hold on to her permanently. The problem was not with the nourishment or with the absence of his desire to prolong her life. The problem was that a destructive cell had so taken over her body that the best of nourishment could not restore to life what was dying.

That break comes for all of us, at different times and in different ways. The nourishment of food, the bonds of friendship, the occasions for celebration, and the delights of legitimate pleasure end in a matter of a moment for each life and each relationship.

It is to this vulnerability of living that Jesus points His finger. The poet puts it in these words:

Our life contains a thousand springs
and dies if one be gone;
Strange that a harp of a thousand strings
can stay in tune so long.

There is an old adage that says you can give a hungry man a fish, or better still, you can teach him how to fish. Jesus would add that you can teach a person how to fish, but the most successful fisherman has hungers fish will not satisfy.

GETTING BEHIND THE SCENES

There is a second but not so obvious truth. "I am the Bread of Life," said Jesus. "He who comes to Me will never go hungry, and he who believes in Me will never be thirsty." Notice the power implicit in the claim.

At the heart of every major religion is a leading exponent. As the exposition is studied, something very significant emerges. There comes a bifurcation, or a distinction, between the person and the teaching. Mohammed, to the Koran. Buddha, to the Noble Path. Krishna, to his philosophizing. Zoroaster, to his ethics.

Whatever we may make of their claims, one reality is inescapable. They are teachers who point to their teaching or show some particular way. In all of these, there emerges an instruction, a way of living. It is not Zoroaster to whom you turn. It is Zoroaster to whom you *listen*. It is not Buddha who delivers you; it is his Noble Truths that instruct you. It is not Mohammed who transforms you; it is the beauty of the Koran that woos you.

By contrast, Jesus did not only teach or expound His message. *He was identical with His message.* "In Him," say the Scriptures, "dwelt the fullness of the Godhead bodily." He did not just proclaim the truth. He said, "I *am* the truth." He did not just show a way. He said, "I *am* the Way." He did not just open up vistas. He said, "I *am* the door." "I *am* the Good Shepherd." "I *am* the resurrection and the life." "I *am* the I AM."

In Him is not just an offer of life's bread. He *is* the bread. That is why being a Christian is not just a way of feeding and living. Following Christ begins with a way of relating and being.

Let us use Buddhism as a specific example. It is a system that is gaining a following among many in Hollywood. It is often very simplistically defined as a religion of compassion and ethics. The truth is that there is probably no system of belief more complex than Buddhism. While it starts off with the four noble truths on suffering and its cessation, it then moves to the eightfold path on how to end suffering. But as one enters the eightfold path, there emerge hundreds upon hundreds of other rules to deal with contingencies.

From a simple base of four offenses that result in a loss of one's discipleship status is built an incredible edifice of ways to restoration. Those who follow Buddha's teachings are given thirty rules on how to ward off those pitfalls. But before one even deals with those, there are ninety-two rules that apply to just one of the offenses. There are seventy-five rules for those entering the order. There are rules of discipline to be applied—two hundred and twenty-seven for men, three hundred and eleven for women. (Readers of Buddhism know that Buddha had to be persuaded before women were even permitted into a disciple's status. After much pleading and cajoling by one of his disciples, he finally acceded to the request but laid down extra rules for them.)

Whatever one may make of all of this, we must be clear that in a nontheistic system, which Buddhism is, ethics become central and rules are added ad infinitum. Buddha and his followers are the originators of these rules. The most common prayer for forgiveness in Buddhism, from the Buddhist Common Prayer, reflects this numerical maze:

> I beg leave! I beg leave, I beg leave. . . . May I be freed at all times from the four states of Woe, the Three Scourges, the Eight Wrong Circumstances, the Five Enemies, the Four Deficiencies, the Five Misfortunes, and quickly attain the Path, the Fruition, and the Noble Law of Nirvana, Lord.[4]

Teaching at best beckons us to morality, but it is not in itself efficacious. Teaching is like a mirror. It can show you if your face is dirty, but the mirror will not wash your face. To truly understand this complicated theory, one would almost need a graduate-level understanding in philosophy and psychology.

By contrast, in a very simple way Jesus drew the real need of His audience to that hunger which is spiritual in nature, a hunger that is shared by every human, so that we are not human livings or human doings but human *beings*. We are not in need merely of a superior ethic, we are in need of a transformed heart and will that seek to do the will of God.

Jesus also taught and held up a mirror, but by His person He transforms our will to seek His. It is our being that Jesus wants to feed. Christ warns that there are depths to our hungers that the physical does not plumb. There are heights to existential aspirations that our activities cannot attain. There are breadths of need that the natural cannot span.

In summary, He reminds us that bread cannot sustain interminably. He is the Bread of Life that eternally sustains. And He does it as no other has ever done.

EXPLAINING THE PLOT

Having made His point of the limitations of bread and that He was the eternal Bread of Life, Jesus now comes to the thought that they needed to carefully consider. No one will deny the uniqueness of the thought here. There is nothing in any other religion that would even come close to this profound teaching.

Our greatest hunger, as Jesus described it, is for a consummate relationship that combines the physical and the spiritual, that engenders both awe and love, and that is expressed in celebration and commitment.

In other words, that hunger is for worship. But worship is not accomplished only by a transaction uttered in a prayer or a wish. *Worship is a posture of life that takes as its primary purpose the understanding of what it really means to love and revere God.* It is the most sacred intimacy of all. This is where the broken piece of bread provides the means of expression and transaction.

On my first visit to the kingdom of Jordan, my family and I were hosted to a very special meal on the eve of our departure. They called it Mensef. The guests stood around a large platter of rice, beautifully garnished with succulent delicacies, flavored with aromatic spices and a gravy that gave it a mouthwatering taste. But then came the fun part. We all rolled up our sleeves and together enjoyed the meal directly from the tray, eating it with our bare hands. That was Middle Eastern food with all of its purposes and at its best. For one of Indian descent, which is my birthright, it was like coming home and more.

There is a symbolism to that way of eating. The enjoyment of a delightful combination of food, the fellowship one with the other, the touch of the hand into the same platter, the celebration of life and its purpose—all signifying trust and closeness and the memories of days we had spent together. Every detail was an invitation, saying, "Welcome to our home and become one of us." We were greeted with a kiss and bidden good-bye with a kiss. We had gathered as friends and left with an intimate trust of a deeper friendship.

That, may I add, is only an inkling of what Jesus was offering to His followers—communion with Him. Even atheistic religions like Buddhism and pantheistic religions like Hinduism, though they deny a personal, absolute God, still smuggle in ways of worship in which a personal being is addressed, only because the isolation within drives the self to a transcendent personal other.

The reason for this is that we are more than just in search of ritual. We are, in fact, broken. We have broken away from God; we are broken in relation to our fellow human beings. And the most elusive reality is that we are broken even from ourselves. We do not connect our own proclivities. Life is a story of brokenness.

This is at the core of the gospel. We have come apart from within. And to this brokenness, Jesus brings the real answer, not just a simplistic "come and get fed."

I am the living bread that came down from heaven. If anyone eats of this bread, he will live forever. This bread is my flesh, which I will give for the life of this world. . . . I tell you the truth, unless you eat the flesh of the Son of Man and drink his blood, you have no life in you. (John 6:51–53)

Upon hearing it, many of His disciples said, "This is a hard teaching. Who can accept it?" But Jesus said to them, "Does this offend you? What if you see the Son of Man ascend to where he was before! The Spirit gives life; the flesh counts for nothing. The words I have spoken to you are spirit and they are life. Yet there are some of you who do not believe" (John 6:60–64).

If this were all Jesus had said on the subject, I have no doubt it would have been the supreme puzzle of His teaching. The bluntness of the way it translates into our language is bound to leave the reader befuddled. But like many of Jesus' discourses, He gave them piecemeal until the final moment. Then the disciples harked back to the first instance when He hinted at the truth. This is clearly the hint. The fulfillment was to follow just days before His death and be finally understood only after His death.

Let us track the event that explained this puzzle.

First of all, it is patently obvious that He could not have meant a literal eating of His physical flesh and His physical blood because He was there in the flesh giving them a piece of bread, not a piece of His flesh.

Second, if He meant His actual flesh and blood, it would be tantamount to saying that only a small number could have shared in that life He offered. It would be restricted to the finite number of pieces a human body could be broken into.

Third, it would be chronologically restrictive. That body would soon decay and the blood would no longer bear life. Only those present at His physical death would have been able to share in that consumption.

Fourth, He had already said that He would raise up that body after it was killed, so that the body itself could not be referred to without making the whole process a masquerade.

Fifth, He commanded the Church to repeat what He was doing across history as a throwback to that moment. That would be impossible with His literal body.

Sixth, He said that His words were Spirit and not flesh.

And finally, when the actual moment of His sacrifice came as He had predicted it would, He explained what it meant. He sat down for the Passover meal with His disciples. The food that sustained, the fellowship this provided, the celebration it encompassed, and the pleasure of God's provision were enjoyed. Only now, there was a heaviness in their hearts. For that heaviness, manna alone would not help. This was a time to face life's supreme worth. An offering of such worth was in the making. The sacrificial Lamb of God was blessing the meal even as He was to be sacrificed. He took the bread, gave thanks, and gave it to His disciples, saying, "Take and eat. This is My body given for you; do this in remembrance of Me." He took the cup, gave thanks, and said, "This cup is the new covenant in My blood, which is poured out for many for the forgiveness of sins." They tasted, touched, smelled, knew, and felt the dimensions of their salvation. He was physically present as He offered the elements.

Then He went on to say, "I tell you, I will not drink of this fruit of the vine from now until that day when I drink it anew with you in My Father's kingdom."

There you have it. This broken piece of bread *represented* what was about to happen. He was going to be physically and emotionally battered in a way that would draw the attention of friend and foe alike. Yet, in that actual brokenness, a mending would ensue. We ourselves would have the way provided to reconnect with God, with our fellow human beings and with ourselves. We would have access to a new relationship, which is part of a larger body, individually and corporately, because of His body broken for us. We could be part of an unbreakable fellowship because He would come and dwell within us. We could take part in an eternal celebration when we would be in the presence of God forever. We could know pleasure at His right hand because worship would be its climactic expression. These symbols of His body broken for ours, His binding for our dismemberment—these are given a tangible expression in the elements when we gather together for worship.

Although by remembering Jesus' past teaching the disciples had a partial understanding of what was happening that night, they were still unclear about all that it meant. That clarity was attained in a significant moment after the resurrection. The day Christ died had been a day they could not understand or appreciate. They saw His body broken, and their lives were devastated. They had questions galore and no one to ask them of.

After Jesus' crucifixion, some of the disciples were returning to their homes, and as they walked on the road toward the town of Emmaus, a stranger came alongside them. Much had happened during those few days, and they were in deep discussion, trying to understand it all. The stranger, listening in, asked why they were so despondent. They told him of the tragic happenings in the death of Jesus three days previous and added, "Are you the only one in Israel who does not know what has happened?"

The truth is that He was the only one in Israel who *did* know what had happened. But they did not yet know who He was. He began to expound all of history and how it tied into that day and its events. They were wonderstruck at the way everything connected. They still did not know who He was and pleaded with Him to stay and have the evening meal with them.

As they sat down to eat, the defining moment came. He broke some bread. And the Bible says that as He did that, their eyes were suddenly opened, and they knew it was Jesus Himself. There has not been a simpler act in history with more profound transhistorical memory attached. What a moment! What a meal! What a message! What a transcendence!

Indeed, to this very day, the Christian sits down with his or her fellow believers and shares in the broken bread and the cup. In that simple transaction, all of history finds its meaning in the person of Christ. Jesus' death in the past is remembered in the present and points to the future when we will break bread with Him in eternity. Every sense is brought into play—touching, tasting, smelling, hearing, and seeing. In that act, every barrier is broken—the barrier of sin between us and God, the barrier between body and soul as the physical and the spiritual connect, the barrier between life and death, the barrier of race and prejudice—for we all stand before Him at the same meal. It is the "Mensef of God." Can there be a greater reason to celebrate? Now life can be realized with every moment that it is lived.

In his book *Life After God,* Douglas Coupland tells a fascinating story. He was out on a walk in a beautiful park when he came upon a group of blind women, picnicking for the day. When they heard him walking by, they asked him if he would take a picture of them. He gladly consented, and they all snuggled close to get into the picture. But after he left, he pondered, "What on earth would a group of people devoid of sight want a picture for?"[5]

May I suggest that in the way God has fashioned us, He enables us to enjoy the capacity of someone else so that we might share in a benefit even without the ability to experience it. The pictures were probably shown to those with sight, who could add to the insight of these women who, in their memories, could relive the occasion, transcending the way they had lived it the first time.

In this unique moment in history, by offering a broken piece of bread, God brings both sight and insight to the participant through the life of the One whose body was broken and who can therefore lift him or her into a sacred memory. And in that simple act, He refashions him into a new wholeness. That broken bread bridges every humanly unbridgeable chasm in millions of lives. We see in a way nothing else could have imparted—through His eyes, with His presence.

TRANSLATING INTO LIFE

In the practice of the Christian faith, this sharing of the bread and of the cup has been aptly called Communion. God has come near, and we enjoy the indwelling of His presence in us. The contrast here from every other faith is as diametric as one can imagine.

Hinduism at its heart and in its goals teaches us that we are to seek union with the divine. Why union? Because the Hindu claims that we are part and parcel of this divine universe. The goal of the individual is, therefore, to discover that divinity and live it out.

Listen again to the words of Deepak Chopra on this purpose of life. He makes this assertion in the early part of his book: "In reality, we are divinity in disguise, and the gods and goddesses in embryo that are contained within us seek to be fully materialized. True success is therefore the experience of the miraculous. It is the unfolding of the divinity within us."[6]

Later in his book, Chopra makes a statement that forms the basis of his philosophy: "We must find out for ourselves that inside us is a god or goddess in embryo that wants to be born so that we can express our divinity."[7]

I cannot resist asking, Who are the we? Who is the god? Who is the self? Are these different entities with which we are cohabiting? Is there a god who needs me (which me?) to bring him (which him, if it is actually me?) to birth so that my deluded self will cease to be deluded and will emerge divine as the real self? How did this god end up in embryonic form while I became full grown, so that I will give him the privilege of birth and lose my humanity to find my divinity? At the risk of being frivolous, this is the ultimate version of "Who's on first."

Toward the end of his book, Chopra asks us to make a commitment to the beliefs he has espoused in these words:

> Today I will lovingly nurture the god or goddess in embryo that lies deep within my soul. I will pay attention to the spirit within me that animates both my body and my mind. I will awaken myself to this deep stillness within my heart. I will carry the consciousness of timeless, eternal Being in the midst of time-bound experience.[8]

This is the heart of philosophical Hinduism—self-deification. One of India's premier philosophers stated as forthrightly as one could, "Man is God in a temporary state of self-forgetfulness."

How can it be that we are the outworking of the quantum world but at the same time, gods? Is this what a few thousand years of human history have taught us? We are lonely and confused gods who have lost our way? This is the reason the "you" disappears in Hinduism and the meditative process is enjoined, so that we can as individuals merge with the one impersonal absolute—the capital "I," because there is no significant other.[9]

Union with the impersonal absolute defies language, reason, and existential realities. It does not satisfy the longing for communion. However much one may respect the intent of such teaching, we deceive ourselves if we believe that it is philosophically coherent. It is not. That is why some of the most respected Hindu philosophers and thinkers have brandished it as one of the most contradictory systems of life's purpose ever espoused.[10] Not only that, Hinduism could not survive the sterility of this kind of self-deification. Personal deities are erupted by the millions, and the temples are crowded with people seeking to worship. No, the suggestion of inward divinity is psychologically imprisoning and the individual breaks away to find another.

While Hinduism goes to one extreme—the deification of the self—Islam is at the other extreme. In Islam, the distance between God and humanity is so vast that the "I" never gets close to the "Him" in God. And because this distance between the two is impossible to cross, worship takes on an incredible clutter of activity, designed to bring the worshiper close. Repetition and submission take the place of the warmth of a relationship. One need only glimpse a Muslim at worship to see the difference. With all that he observes and all the rules he keeps, there is never a certainty of heaven for the common person in Islam. It is all in the "will of God," they say. One's destiny is left at the mercy of an unknown will. When relationship is swallowed up by rules, political power and enforcement become the means of containment.

One day a Muslim friend and I were out for the day together. I had forgotten that the Fast of Ramadan had just begun and suggested that we step into a restaurant for a cup of coffee. "I will spend years in jail for that cup of coffee," he said, so of course I apologized for the suggestion. Then in low tones he admitted that his fast was restricted to public view and that he did not practice it in private. "I cannot work ten hours a day without eating," he said. There was an awkward silence, and he muttered these words: "I don't think God is the enforcer of these rules." As anyone knows who has asked any Muslim, they will admit with a smile upon their faces that during the month of the Fast of Ramadan more food is sold than during any other month of the year. But its consumption takes place from dusk to dawn rather than from dawn to dusk. Legalism always breeds compliance over purpose.

In the Christian message, the God who is distinct and distant came close so that we who are weak may be made strong and may be drawn close in communion with God Himself, even as our identity is retained as we are. That simple act of communion encapsulated life's purpose. The individual retains his individuality while dwelling in community. The physical retains its physicality but is transcended by the spiritual. The elements retain their distinctness but become bearers of truth that point beyond themselves to a spiritual fellowship that our spirits long for.

Just as the consummate act of love between a man and his wife concretely expresses all that the moral and spiritual relationship embraces, so the simple act of taking the broken bread and the cup encompasses the actual reality of the intermeshing of God's presence in the life of the individual. It is an act of worship that represents a life that is full of meaning. The ramifications are profound.

THE REALITY EXPERIENCED

Let me take you to a unique place at the tip of a desert. I have been there, and my heart has been spoken to in ways beyond description. Walk into a Sunday morning worship service, and this is what you will see. There sit two women missionaries, surrounded by a group of people who, when they smile, look pitiful. When they come closer, you feel a lump in your throat. But they are wonderful people who love Christ. This is a home for people with leprosy. There in that room, the moment of Communion has come. The elements are passed, and the object lesson is staggering.

Beyond the heinousness of the disease emerges a glorious message of oneness and hope. His body is broken for all of us so that His nourishment, His friendship, His celebration, and His pleasure bind us together as one. One day those bodies will all be made new when we drink from that cup and eat from that bread with our heavenly Father.

This brings us to a most staggering conclusion on what *worship* means. Food and health may be a relevant branch to which we hold. But the trunk that is rooted in the sacred call of God to worship is based on a reversal of that relevance. It is not that God needs to be relevant to us. It is the very counterperspective of God that beckons *us* to become relevant to *Him*. What do I mean?

In his book *The Integrity of Worship,* Paul Waitman Hoon includes a chapter called "The Irrelevance of Worship." His whole point is summarized in one paragraph in which he reminds us that the experience of worship can sometimes call us to look beyond our need to what God is calling us toward:

How often have we craved light on our life in the world, only to be summoned to ponder our destiny in eternity. How often have we been preoccupied with the church local, and instead found our vision turned to the Church triumphant and universal. And how often have we asked that worship bless our souls with peace, only to hear the lesson for the day calling us to a holy warfare. How often have we desired strength to overcome the world, only to learn that we are to be stoned and sawn asunder in the world. How often have we sought comfort to our sorrows, and instead found the sorrows of the world added to our own. Such reversals may be strange to men. But only such contradiction answers to realities both relevant and irrelevant that are at the heart of the Church's worship.[11]

This was the reversal the disciples did not expect. They came to Jesus asking for the abundance of bread so their stomachs could be full. They discovered that there was bread of a different kind broken for them because of a deeper emptiness than they had imagined. They had bought their lunch at a nearby restaurant. But they were being invited to a different table. With their purchase, they would soon be hungry again. Jesus was offering them eternal fulfillment with moment-by-moment freshness. That is why the task of the Church is not so much to make God relevant to the people as much as it is to make people relevant to God.

There is a magnificent woodcarving in Worms, Germany, called "The Altar of Blood." It is a depiction of the Lord breaking the bread for the disciples. I stared at that masterpiece, which took years of a craftsman's life to complete, and found it beyond my capability to describe. It is the heart of what God calls us to. It is in that exchange that He sobers the mind, quiets the heart, and bridges every barrier.

Is our God so small that He cannot impart life without cannibalizing? Those who understand the depth of what Communion means understand the fulfillment of worship. Those who don't understand leave hungry and cannibalize their own souls. The songwriter rightly pleads for all of us, so that our deepest hunger may be sated.

> Break Thou the Bread of Life,
> Dear Lord to me,
> As thou didst break the loaves

Beside the sea;
Beyond the sacred page
I seek thee, Lord;
My spirit pants for thee,
O living Word.

Thou art the bread of life,
To me, to me,
Thy holy Word, the truth
That saveth me;
Give me to eat and live
With thee above,
Teach me to love Thy truth
For Thou art love.

Oh, send Thy Spirit, Lord,
Now unto me,
That He may touch my eyes
And make me see;
Show me the truth concealed
Within thy Word,
And in Thy Book revealed,
I see Thee Lord.[12]

Chapter Five

IS GOD THE SOURCE
OF MY SUFFERING?

I WOULD LIKE TO BEGIN THIS CHAPTER BY RESPECTFULLY QUOTING, with the permission of the writer, portions of one of the most heartbreaking letters I have ever received. I truly admire the courage, the candor, and the teachability of the man who wrote it. It is obviously not easy to bare one's soul. My heart aches for him and his family in this terribly painful experience.

This letter, though specific and immediate in the writer's context, represents a question asked of Jesus two thousand years ago, in a similar situation. In fact, for all of us, if we are honest, behind this question lies possibly one of the greatest barriers to belief in God.

Dear Mr. Zacharias,

I need your help desperately. I'm not asking for money or anything like that. . . . I seek your counsel.

Please take time to read this letter. It is extremely personal and heartbreaking. My situation is serious, and I am now well into my second year of torment and fear. I thought I would be able to figure out all the "answers" I would need to find peace in my soul but have continually run into the proverbial brick wall. Or perhaps the answer was there all the time and it is just too grim for me to accept. I don't know. Quite simply I am confused and frightened. And I need your help.

On August 4, 1997, at 3:15 P.M., my son, Adam Mark Triplett, died in an airplane accident. It happened in the town of New Richmond, Wisconsin. Adam was a flight instructor for a local flight school in St. Paul, Minnesota. Adam was a respected student, fine musician, professional pilot, devoted friend, and dedicated Christian man. He was also a delightful brother, husband, and son. My only son. Adam died at the age of 23, after only three months of marriage. I can't imagine life without him. . . .

A few years ago my wife and I purchased a new computer. Little did I know how much danger it would bring into my life. One day, casually exploring the Internet with my newfound friend of technology, I was surprised to discover an e-mail message sent to me anonymously. To my shock and surprise, I found myself looking at a picture of perversion and hard-core pornography.

I became angered by this vulgar intrusion and set out to find out more of where it came from. I continued my search, thinking I could become a crusader of sorts for the cause of decency. But I fell victim to the wiles and devices of the devil himself and soon became trapped in a pattern of personal viewing.

If I had a "bad day" at work or the car broke down (any excuse would do), I would settle the score as it were by balancing the scales with a bit of "personal viewing." By now I justified my "personal viewing" as not harmful. . . . I wasn't intruding on or hurting anyone else. I paid no attention to what I was doing to myself.

One day at church I found myself in "personal viewing" in my mind, not paying attention to the pastor's message. Fear jumped into my heart, and I began to try to do away with this evil practice. No success. The downward spiral continued, affecting my business and family relationships, to say nothing of my responsibilities as a leader in my church.

On August 4, I dropped my son off at the airport. His next student was waiting for him. As he walked away from the car he turned and smiled and gave me a "thumbs-up" sign (our personal sign of approval). As I drove away, looking in the rearview mirror . . . I had a strange and faint realization that it would be the last time I would ever see him on earth. I shook it off as a random thought. I discarded it. Forgot it completely. I went back to work.

By the end of the day I was in a steep rage over God only knows what . . . [and I decided that] I would just go home and do some "personal viewing." At least I could find some satisfaction there, I thought.

[As I was driving,] very quietly, almost in a whisperlike tone, soft and gentle, in a pleading voice I felt God saying to me, "Mark, please, I don't want you to do that."

My response was harsh and direct, "Oh, You don't want me to. Big deal! You don't want me to do anything, do You? I always have to be perfect, don't I? Well, not today!" The Lord then spoke a bit louder and more serious, "I'm asking you not to behave this way." Again I responded with arrogance, "How are You going to stop me? What will You do, kill my son?"

A third time the Lord God spoke to me. But this time His tone was more forceful, strict, and authoritative, "Mark, you don't understand. I'm telling you that I do NOT want you behaving this way."

By now, my ego was in full swing. My response was deliberate and direct. I heard no more from the Lord regarding the issue.

I arrived home at about 5:30. My wife was cooking on the grill in the backyard. She asked me if I had heard of a plane crash that day. I said no. She seemed unnerved and suspicious and afraid. I "felt" something was wrong. . . .

Then the sheriff arrived. Katrina (Adam's sister) screamed. Linda wept uncontrollably. I was completely numb but felt a presence of strength take over my body and mind. I believe it was God's Holy Spirit. . . .

In the weeks that followed Adam's death, I began recalling the events of that day. I became consumed with the guilt of my sin against God that day. I became acutely aware of my wretchedness and the need to fall at His feet and seek forgiveness. . . . Was I to blame for this horror? Oh, dear God, let it not be so.[1]

As you can well imagine, this letter stopped my day. As I read it, with each paragraph the anguish intensified, as blood flooding into emptied arteries. My heart throbbed, beating out sensations of self-examination. Everything else faded into secondary importance. I put myself in this man's shoes and imagined the horror.

How much more painful can life be than to carry such enormous guilt, laden on top of such tragedy? When the wording was narrowed down, the sharp question remained, "Did God take my son's life? Was He making me pay for going against His wishes?"

This double-pronged search for an answer—"Is God the author of pain?" "Is my pain because of my sin?"—has disturbed both skeptic and believer alike. Every thinking person attempting to make sense of a world enriched with good but convulsing with evil tries to think this through, yet finds no easy solution, especially when something as dramatic as this happens. After centuries of debate, to find an adequate response remains a daunting task. It is a question worthy of our greatest attention. At the same time, I am convinced that there is no more comprehensive answer to the problem of suffering and evil than the one that the Christian faith affords.

The Bible does not avoid raising this struggle. Jesus faced this question head-on. Sometimes it came to Him in subtle forms, sometimes in direct tones. The most striking incident in which He faced this challenge is recorded in the ninth chapter of John's Gospel. The discussion ensues on the heels of one of the lengthiest reports of any miracle that He performed. There is more than normal dialogue that precedes and succeeds this particular healing, and the reason is because an explanation is sought for a person's physical deformity.

As Jesus was walking along with His disciples, a man who was blind crossed their path. The disciples, in this instance, were not content just to witness the miracle of sight restored. They went for the jugular, aiming quite clearly at the role of God in a tragic situation. One of the disciples asked Jesus rather abruptly, "Who sinned, this man or his parents, that he was born blind?"

Is he responsible for his plight, or is someone else the cause?

Jesus completely surprised them with His response that it was neither the young man nor his parents who were responsible for the man's deformity. "This happened so that the work of God might be displayed in his life. As long as it is day, we must do the work of Him who sent Me. Night is coming when no man can work. While I am in the world, I am the Light of the World."

What did He mean, "That the work of God might be displayed in his life"?

As He tried to unfold the answer, bear in mind that He was up against four groups of people, each with its own reason for questioning Him. The first were the disciples themselves. They wanted this question answered because they sought an explanation of individual suffering. But then there were the neighbors. They knew a miracle had taken place and were puzzled at the "how" of it all. How could He give sight to the blind? The skeptics in the group literally saw the effect but did not want to admit the "Who" behind it. They did not like where Jesus' answer led them because it compelled them to decide whether or not they had the honesty to repudiate their pride and follow Him. And finally, there was the blind man himself. He had personally experienced the transformation and was somewhat overwhelmed by all of the implications—especially, facing the critics. A personal conversation with Jesus left him without doubt that He was not merely a healer of the eyes; He was the transformer of the heart.

It is obvious that Jesus' answer in this passage goes beyond the agonies of parents who have lost children or of those who have graciously borne much pain. He recognized immediately that there was a question behind the question.

The answer, therefore, goes deeper, not only to touch the pain of the human heart but to understand the breadth of evil, pain, and suffering. If we are to go as deep, the answer necessarily will take us through a long journey. The question simply cannot be answered while ignoring possible challenges to the answer at every stage. Those who stay with it will see that the biblical world-view is the only one that accepts the reality of evil and suffering while giving both the cause and the purpose, while offering God-given strength and sustenance in the midst of it. Those who refuse to accept these truths that Jesus presents will continue to find this a barrier to God and, I dare suggest, a barrier to reason itself.

Years ago, there was a lighthearted story making the rounds. It was the story of a breakdown in a power plant that sent the city into confusion. For a long time, no engineer could be found who was able to fix the problem. Finally a man came along who, by the push of a button, restarted the system. He billed the city for a million and one dollars. Surprised at the number, somebody asked him why it was a million and one, and not just a million. His answer was that one dollar was for pushing the button. The one million dollars was for knowing where to push.

At first glance, Jesus' response to their question seems rather meager. It consists of a few simple statements. But those brief lines are weighted with comprehension on a larger scale. That is why the incredible depth in Jesus' answer can only be appreciated if the world-view behind it is understood. To just take hold of these few lines and miss the context of His total message is to do violence to a very important theme. To avoid that peril, I will take the question back to its underlying challenge and face the hard but real struggle of evil and pain in a world to which a loving God lays claim. Once we have comprehended the broader Christian perspective, we will understand that Christ readily answers the immediate question in light of the bigger question behind it.

A Universal Anguish

At the outset, let us remember that *every* world-view—not just Christianity's—must give an explanation or an answer for evil and suffering. Either evil categorically proves that God does not exist, as the atheist avows, or evil is "not ultimately real evil," as the pantheist claims, or evil is most coherently explained by the Christian view of God and His purpose in creation. In short, this is not a problem distinctive to Christianity. It will not do for the challenger just to raise the question. This problem of evil is one to which we all must offer an answer, regardless of the belief system to which we subscribe.

Among the discoveries I have made as I have studied this subject is that every writer who attempts to answer this question has one thing in common with all others and one fundamental assumption. The common factor is that each one begins with a litany of horrors and atrocities. It is not just one person born blind, or one baby innocently killed. The list seems interminable. It is as if we ourselves need reminders of how emotionally charged this problem is, defying any reasonable solution. Horrors of unimaginable proportions are cataloged. I found that in itself instructive, and this approach has a lesson that I will address later.

But then there emerges a second component, and that is the determination of a starting point. Much is assumed or concealed right at the beginning. For the skeptic, the question ties him or her up, immediately. That confusion ought to pay heed to the Irish farmer who, when asked for directions by a lost tourist, said, "If that is where you want to go, this is not where I would begin." You see, most skeptics begin their challenge to God's existence with the problem of evil or at least reserve their greatest emotion for that discussion. But in doing so, they dig a deeper pit than the one they are trying to get out of, because raising the problem of evil without God runs the risk of failing to justify the question. But many do begin here and get wrongheaded. As this discussion proceeds, I will point out why this is not a logically sound starting point for one who seeks to disprove the existence of God.

POSITIONING THE PROBLEM

The Christian world-view suggests that evil is better posed as a mystery than as a problem. Now, before the antagonist jumps up and cries, "Foul!" thinking that by branding it a mystery I am attempting to evade a solution, let me calm that fear. To call it a mystery is not to avoid the necessity of realizing a solution. Problems seek answers, but mysteries demand more—they merit explanation. This means that there will need to be converging lines of argument, not just a single answer signed off with Q.E.D.

But there is a very important reason to brand evil a mystery. Gabriel Marcel defined a mystery as a problem that encroaches on its own data. By that he meant that the questioner unwittingly becomes the object of the question. We are not merely observers to the reality of evil. We are involved in it beyond any mere academic discussion. Peter Kreeft, professor of philosophy at Boston College, comments, "Getting to Mars is a problem. Falling in love is a mystery."[2] Evil, like love, is not a problem. It is a mystery.

One cannot address the problem of evil without ending up as a focus of that problem. Skeptics calmly bypass this reality and proceed as if they were spectators observing a phenomenon, when in reality, they are part of the phenomenon. Let us position the challenge to Christian theism in the words of the renowned thinker David Hume, and we will quickly see how the question carries the questioner with it. This is how he words it:

Were a stranger to drop on a sudden into this world, I would show him, as a specimen of its ills, a hospital full of diseases, a prison crowded with malefactors and debtors, a field of battle strewn with carcasses, a fleet floundering in the ocean, a nation languishing under tyranny, famine, or pestilence. To turn the gay side of life to him, and give him a notion of its pleasures; whither should I conduct him? to a ball, to an opera, to court? He might justly think that I was only showing him a diversity of distress and sorrow.[3]

Hume complains elsewhere that it is impossible to square such a world with an ultimate purpose of love. This is possibly better posed than Hume even realized, for he hinted at an explanation even in the question. The thrust of his question is forthright. The problem of pain and suffering is real and individually felt. That is why every group got involved with Jesus on this matter.

Not only is the problem real and felt, it is also universal. No religion attempts to explain this more than Buddhism. Buddha's entire pilgrimage toward "Enlightenment" began because of his absorption with the mystery of evil and suffering. The universality of it was what set him on his course.

But if there is the reality of it and the universality of it, there is also the complexity of it. Evil is questioned from at least three sides: the metaphysical problem (What is the source of it?), the physical problem (How do natural disasters, etc., fit into the discussion?), and the moral problem (How can it be justified?).

The third of these is at the heart of the issue: How does a good God allow so much suffering? Immediately we enter into a very serious dilemma. How do you respond to the intellectual side of the question without losing the existential side of it? How do you answer the Mark Tripletts of this world without drowning it all in philosophy?

Those who feel the pain of the question most, often shudder at how theoretical philosophical answers are. We do not like to work through the intellectual side of the question because we do not see where logic and philosophy fit into the problem of pain. If you have just buried a son or a daughter, or have witnessed brutality firsthand, this portion of the argument may bring more anger than comfort. Who wants logic when the heart is broken? Who wants a physiological treatise on the calcium component of the bone when the shoulder has come out of its socket? At such a time we are looking for comfort. We want a painkiller.

But to focus only on the result without paying due heed to the process may only temporarily kill the pain, leaving the joint still out of order.

Somewhere and at some point, logic must stand on its own. Comfort will follow if the reasoning is surefooted.

And to you, the reader, I plead: Even if this first portion seems tedious, please stay with it, because it is here that we study the question, before proceeding to the answer. We must not allow the anguish of the heart to bypass the reasoning of the mind. The explanation must meet both the intellectual and the emotional demands of the question. Answering the questions of the mind while ignoring shredded emotions seems heartless. Binding the emotional wounds while ignoring the struggle of the intellect seems mindless.

What, then, is the starting point? Since the crux of the problem is first and foremost moral questioning, how can there be moral justification for evil? An analogy from C. S. Lewis may be of help. He reminded us that when a ship is on the high seas, at least three questions must be answered. Question number one, How do we keep the ship from sinking? Number two, How do we keep it from bumping into other ships? These two may be obvious but behind them lurks the most important one, number three, Why is the ship out there in the first place? The first of the questions deals with personal ethics. The second addresses social ethics. The third one wrestles with normative ethics.

Our cultures at best deal with the first and the second questions. They ignore a rational defense of the very purpose of life and do not know where to turn for guidance. If one does not know one's purpose, any destination will do. And when the ship starts to sink or bumps into another ship, how does one safely reach the harbor without any instruments?

Let us be certain that no ethical imperative can be established and no moral pronouncements can be made without first establishing life's imperative and knowing how to measure progress. Why do we exist, anyway? And it is here that the skeptic flounders on the high seas of life. If we are here purely by accident and we navigate purely by whim, how does one determine whether any journey is in the right or wrong direction? Why be in one place rather than anywhere else?

Now we shall see why the question itself defeats the skeptic who at the same time wants to deny that any purpose for life actually exists.

LIVING WITH CONTRADICTION

Let me present two doors through which the person who has raised the question of God's existence tries to escape from the entailments of disbelief with the semblance of a reason. I am afraid, however, that those doors are marked "No Exit."

The first escape route in the problem of evil is propounded by those who protest that God cannot exist because there is too much evil evident in life. They see no logical contradiction within their system since they do not have to prove that evil coexists with a good Creator. Evil exists; therefore, the Creator does not. That is categorically stated.

But here, Christianity provides a counterchallenge to remind them that they have not escaped the problem of contradiction. If evil exists, then one must assume that good exists in order to know the difference. If good exists, one must assume that a moral law exists by which to measure good and evil. But if a moral law exists, must not one posit an ultimate source of moral law, or at least an objective basis for a moral law? By an objective basis, I mean something that is transcendingly true at all times, regardless of whether I believe it or not.

This argument is very compelling and must be given due consideration by anyone who denies the existence of God but accepts the presence of evil. In contrast to the Christian's assertion that God is necessary in order to posit the notions of good and evil, the skeptic responds by asking, "Why cannot evolution explain our moral sense? Why do we need God?"

This is the latest approach by antitheistic thinkers who seek to explain good and evil apart from God. Over the years naturalists first denied causality as an argument to prove God's existence: Why do we have to have a cause? Why can't the universe just be? Then they denied design as an argument for God's existence: Why do we need a designer? Why could it not have all just come together with the appearance of design? Now they deny morality as an argument for God's existence: Why do we need to posit a moral law or a moral law source? Why can't it just be a pragmatic reality? This I find fascinating! They want a *cause* for suffering or a *design* for suffering, but they have already denied that either of these is necessary to account for every effect.

This attempt to deny God because of the presence of evil is so fraught with the illogical that one marvels at its acceptance. Not one proponent of evolutionary ethics has explained how an impersonal, amoral first cause through a nonmoral process has produced a moral basis of life, while at the same time denying any objective moral basis for good and evil. Does it not seem odd that of all the permutations and combinations that a random universe might afford we should end up with the notions of the true, the good, and the beautiful? In reality, why call anything good or evil? Why not call it orange or purple? That way, we settle it as different preferences. By the way, Bertrand Russell tried that latter approach and looked quite pathetic at it.

The truth is that we cannot escape the existential rub by running from a moral law. Objective moral values exist only if God exists. Is it all right, for example, to mutilate babies for entertainment? Every reasonable person will say no. We know that objective moral values do exist. Therefore God must exist. Examining those premises and their validity presents a very strong argument. In fact, J. L. Mackie, one of the most vociferous atheists who challenged the existence of God on the basis of the reality of evil, granted at least this logical connection when he said:

> We might well argue . . . that objective intrinsically prescriptive features, supervenient upon natural ones, constitute so odd a cluster of qualities and relations that they are most unlikely to have arisen in the ordinary course of events, without an all-powerful God to create them.[4]

Therefore, the conclusion must be agreed upon that nothing can be intrinsically, prescriptively good unless there also exists a God who has fashioned the universe thus. But that is the very Being skeptics want to deny because of the existence of evil.

The first exit door to flee from God is opened, and the sight is terrifying. Only one option is left, and that is to try to alter the shape of the door. Recognizing that if evil is admitted then an objective moral law might need to be invoked, the skeptic tries a new tack. Listen to this incredible explanation by one of atheism's champions, Richard Dawkins, of Oxford:

In a universe of blind physical forces and genetic replication, some people are going to get hurt, other people are going to get lucky, and you won't find any rhyme or reason in it, nor any justice. The universe we observe has precisely the properties we should expect if there is, at the bottom, no design, no purpose, no evil and no other good. Nothing but blind, pitiless indifference. DNA neither knows nor cares. DNA just is. And we dance to its music.[5]

Do you see what has happened? The skeptic started by presenting a long list of horrific things, saying, "These are immoral, therefore there is no God." But to raise these issues as moral issues is to assume a state of affairs that evolution cannot afford. There is just no way to arrive at a morally compelling ought, given the assumptions of naturalism. What then does the skeptic do? He denies objective moral values because to accept such a reality would be to allow for the possibility of God's existence. He concludes then that there really isn't such a thing as evil after all.

This is supposed to be an answer? If DNA neither knows nor cares, what is it that prompts *our* knowing and *our* caring? Are we just embodied computers, overvaluing our senses? If our feelings have no bearing at all on the reality of this question then maybe *ours* is the artificial intelligence and the computer's is the genuine one, for it has no feeling; it has only information. Computers do not "care" and do not "grieve over evil," and are, therefore, closer to reality.

Is this what we have come to? We must be warned that there are no brakes on this slippery slope once we step onto it. The denial of an objective moral law, based on the compulsion to deny the existence of God, results ultimately in the denial of evil itself. Can you imagine telling a raped woman that the rapist merely danced to his DNA? Tell the father of young Adam Triplett that he is merely dancing to his DNA. Tell the victims of Auschwitz that their tormentors merely danced to their DNA, and tell the loved ones of those cannibalized by Jeffrey Dahmer that he merely danced to his DNA. So dance along!

How repugnant! This is not a dance! This is the escapist's foot on the throat of reason, gasping for rationality while denying that logical points of reference exist. In effect, while seeking an answer to the question of evil, he ends up denying the question. In fact, I put this theory to the test with some students at Oxford University. I asked a group of skeptics if I took a baby and sliced it to pieces before them, would I have done anything wrong? They had just denied that objective moral values exist. At my question, there was silence, and then the lead voice in the group said, "I would not like it, but no, I could not say you have done anything wrong." My! What an aesthete. He would not like it. My! What irrationality—he could not brand it wrong. I only had to ask him what then remains of the original question, if evil is denied?

Dawkins could have helped him even further. In his 1992 lectures to the British Humanist Association, he made an astounding assertion. Having debunked the notion of God in his numerous writings and explained away evil as DNA's dance, what then must we make of the sense of morality that we find in the human experience? Why do we even pose such questions about good and evil?

Dawkins has the answer. Viruses. A virus scrambles the data within the human gene and spits out this misinformation. Somehow if we can expunge the virus that led us to think this way, we will be purified and rid of this bedeviling notion of God, good, and evil.[6]

In Dawkins-speak, those who asked Jesus the question needed an antivirus program. In fact, Jesus Himself would need reprogramming. And I suppose, one who moralizes on the Holocaust needs new antivirus protection. That way the question of evil would not even surface. One would like to ask Dawkins if we are morally bound to remove that virus. Let us not forget that he himself is, of course, free from the virus and can therefore input our moral data.

The problem has encroached upon itself. In an attempt to escape what they call the contradiction between a good God and a world of evil, skeptics exorcise the mind of theistic notions, only to be entered and overcome by contradictions sevenfold.

Though I have often quoted G. K. Chesterton in his criticism of this kind of thinking, no one says it better, so I would like to quote him again:

All denunciation implies a moral doctrine of some kind and the modern skeptic doubts not only the institution he denounces, but the doctrine by which he denounces it. Thus he writes one book complaining that imperial oppression insults the purity of women, and then writes another book, a novel in which he insults it himself. As a politician he will cry out that war is a waste of life, and then as a philosopher that all of life is waste of time. A Russian pessimist will denounce a policeman for killing a peasant, and then prove by the highest philosophical principles that the peasant ought to have killed himself. A man denounces marriage as a lie and then denounces aristocratic profligates for treating it as a lie.

The man of this school goes first to a political meeting where he complains that savages are treated as if they were beasts. Then he takes his hat and umbrella and goes on to a scientific meeting where he proves that they practically are beasts. In short, the modern revolutionist, being an infinite skeptic, is forever engaged in undermining his own mines. in his book on politics he attacks men for trampling on morality; in his book on ethics he attacks morality for trampling on men. Therefore the modern man in revolt becomes practically useless for all purposes of revolt. By rebelling against everything he has lost his right to rebel against anything.[7]

Let me illustrate Chesterton's point with something more contemporary. In pathetic ways, we saw this exemplified when America was caught in the throes of the Clinton-Lewinsky scandal. In our moral contradiction, an amazing cultural mood was uncovered. The president's famous line that "it all depends on what the definition of 'is' is," sent reporters scampering onto the streets with the question of the century: "Do words have a fixed meaning, or may we give them any meaning we choose?" (What could encroach upon itself more than purveyors of words inquiring if words have any meaning, while using words to ask the question?)

To the utter "surprise" of the surveyors, most people seemed to agree that words can sometimes mean different things to different people, assuming, of course, that there was no equivocation in meaning as the question was posed and the answer given.

That prompted the next question: "Is morality an absolute or a private matter?" The overwhelming response came back that morality is a private matter.

These two questions became the lead-in on a CNN news report. First, that words only have personal meaning. Second, that morality is a private matter. Ironically, the third item on the news was that the United States had just issued a stern warning to Saddam Hussein that if he did not stop playing word games with the nuclear inspection teams we would start bombing Iraq.

Suddenly, words did matter. We would not let Saddam dance to *his* DNA. We would not let him write *his* own dictionary. We would not let him live by *his* own ethic, but we could let each of *our* citizens determine the meaning of the words they used and insist that our morality is no one else's business.

This is precisely the world to which Dawkins and those of similar philosophy must be logically driven. It is a world of systemic contradiction. If morality is nothing more than evolution's climb, there is no way to measure when we have reached the top. By their own admission, there was no prevision in the random collocation of atoms. In the end, such a philosophy of evil makes life unlivable in a community. Dawkins cannot explain evil by denying an objective moral law, and he cannot deny evil without losing his challenge for the existence of God. This door for the skeptic is marked "No Exit," even as his ship sinks.

ASKING GOD TO BE CONTRADICTORY

The second door seems, at first, to be a certain way out. The skeptic asks why God could not have made us to always choose good. Philosophers of note have raised this as the sharpest edge of their challenge to Christianity. But here, too, the challenge violates reason.

Alvin Plantinga of the University of Notre Dame, who is considered by many to be the most respected Protestant philosopher of our time, has made a strong and compelling argument against this challenge of the skeptic. He argues that this option bears a false view of what God's omnipotence means. We must realize that God cannot do that which is mutually exclusive and logically impossible. God cannot make square circles. The terms are mutually exclusive.

Plantinga is right. I might add that if God *can* do anything at all, even that which is mutually exclusive, then He can also contradict His character, which would by implication render the problem of evil moot, needing no defense. The very reason we raise the question is because we seek coherence. In a world where love is the supreme ethic, freedom must be built in. A love that is programmed or compelled is not love; it is merely a conditioned response or self-serving.

Once again, even thinkers hostile to Christianity inadvertently assert truths that agree with Christian thought. For example, Jean Paul Sartre, in *Being and Nothingness,* says:

> The man who wants to be loved does not desire the enslavement of the beloved. He is not bent on becoming the object of passion, which flows forth mechanically. He does not want to possess an automaton, and if we want to humiliate him, we need try to only persuade him that the beloved's passion is the result of a psychological determinism. The lover will then feel that both his love and his being are cheapened. . . . If the beloved is transformed into an automaton, the lover finds himself alone.[8]

How insightful! Love compelled is a precursor to loneliness. Having the freedom to love when you may choose not to love is to give love legitimate meaning. This is why I said earlier that David Hume had more of an answer in his question on the problem of pain than he may have known. Is not an ultimate purpose of love the only way you *can* square the problem of pain? To ask that we be denied freedom and only choose good is to ask not for love, but for compulsion and for something other than humanity.

Both doors of escape for the skeptic are shut tight. You cannot posit evil without a transcendent moral law, which macroevolution cannot sustain. And you cannot gain the highest ethic without the possibility of freedom. The first sends us into lives of contradiction. The second demands a contradiction of God.

In brief, for the naturalist, the man born blind was dancing to his DNA. As to the question behind the question, the naturalist not only fails to answer it, he fails even to justify it.

How would other religions answer the disciples' question, and the question behind the question?

As I have stated, pantheistic religions have attempted extensive answers, and sometimes those answers are terribly confusing. The difficulty with Hinduism is that it has no monolithic answer to the problem of suffering. By declaring everything in the physical world to be nonreal, illusory, changing, transitory, it ends up with philosophical problems beyond measure. And, of course, one is compelled to ask, What has brought on this "illusion" of evil, if everything is part and parcel of the divine reality? They do try to answer that.

There is a classic passage in the Bhagavad-Gita in which Krishna counsels young Arjuna, who is on the battlefield, facing the possibility of killing his own half brothers. He struggles and cannot bring himself to do this. Krishna, who comes as his chariot-driver, talks to him about his duty. This was his duty, to fulfill his caste's responsibility as a warrior. This is the way life moves on. But he told Arjuna not to fear to do his duty, for all good and evil are fused in the one ultimate reality, Brahman. In Brahman, says Krishna, the distinction breaks down. That which appears evil is only the lesser reality. In the end, all life, all good, all evil, flow from God and back to Him or it. "Go to war and do your job." This convergence of everything into one absolute reality forms the hub of the answer to the question behind the question. One can see how a sense of fatalism dominates when all reality is inexorably and inevitably unfolding.

There is a humorous story told of India's leading philosopher, Shankara. He had just finished lecturing the king on the deception of the mind and its delusion of material reality. The next day, the king let loose an elephant that went on a rampage, and Shankara ran up a tree to find safety. When the king asked him why he ran if the elephant was nonreal, Shankara, not to be outdone, said, "What the king actually saw was a nonreal me climbing up a nonreal tree!" One might add, "That is a nonreal answer."

While these are seen as fables, there is no way for classical Hinduism to deal with the problem of evil. To deny that evil is real does not diminish wickedness, nor does it daunt the heart's desire to seek purity. So much of

Hindu worship is steeped in purification rites. That is why the entire corpus of popular Hinduism is filled with the forms of worship, fear of punishment, means of obtaining God's favor, etc.

But why are these hungers themselves seen as real? In fact, one of Hinduism's strongest criticisms of Christianity and the reason given for refusing its validity is the Hindu's reference to the days of the British Raj and to the evil of the exploitation of the subjugated. One cannot have it both ways; evil cannot be both illusory and concrete.

Hinduism explains this perception of evil as induced by ignorance. But that only pushes the question one step further. If all is one, and plurality is an illusion born out of ignorance, then who is the source of the ignorance but the one? And if the one is the source of the ignorance, then the impersonal absolute in the one is an absolute that lacks true knowledge. But here we face Hinduism's real answer to the question of the man who was blind from birth.

Reincarnation is a central feature of Hindu philosophy. In fact, some eastern thinkers have leaped upon this particular passage of the blind man as proof that the Bible teaches reincarnation. How else could the man have sinned before birth? Let us be assured that it is both a misrepresentation of the passage and an avoidance of facing up to what their doctrine of reincarnation actually espouses.

First, this section hardly "teaches" reincarnation. It is merely a question asked. The Bible's teaching is that "it is appointed unto men *once* to die, but after this the judgment" (Heb. 9:27 KJV; emphasis added). In fact, in this very context Jesus states that there was no direct connection between any previous act and the man's condition, and that the opportunity to choose to believe God's message is brief, after which there is no recourse. By contrast and by definition, reincarnation is a recurring cycle of cause and effect, till all infractions have been paid for and the absolute attained. Jesus clearly denies that possibility. "Night is coming when no man can work," He said. Opportunity ends.

Rather than hearing my thoughts on what reincarnation in Hinduism means, listen instead, to the words of the Upanishads on this matter:

Accordingly, those who are of pleasant conduct here—the prospect is, indeed, that they will enter a pleasant womb, either the womb of a Brahman [the priestly class], or the womb of a Kshatriya [the warrior or royal class], or the womb of a Vaisya [the working or professional class]. But those who are of stinking conduct here—the prospect is, indeed, that they will enter a stinking womb of a dog, or the womb of a swine, or the womb of an outcast. (Chandogya Upanishad, 5.10.8)

There are other passages of descriptions that go into further detail, ideas that one cannot read with indifference. Hinduism here conveys an inherited sense of wrong, which is lived out in the next life, in vegetable, animal, or human form. This doctrine is nonnegotiable in Hindu philosophy. There are passages in the Upanishads that are rather jolting, when one reads them.

Buddhism also invokes the doctrine of karma and reincarnation. The opening lines of the Buddhist scriptures say that every individual is the sum total of what he or she thought in his or her past life. One of the collections of Buddha's discourses is called the Anguttara Nikaya. Here are some thoughts:

My *kamma* [past and present actions] is my only property, *kamma* is my only heritage, *kamma* is the only cause of my being, *kamma* is my only kin, my only protection. Whatever actions I do, good or bad, I shall become their heir.[9]

(Take note that the Pali language of the Buddhist scriptures has a different sound to some words that have become common in English from Hinduism. *Kamma*, for example, carries the meaning of *karma*.)

So, for Buddhism, too, the answer to the disciples' question regarding the blind man's predicament—"Who sinned, this man or his parents?"—would be, "Both this man and his parents have sinned." The suffering of the blind man is the inheritance of his past life's sin, and it is the lot of the parents to inherit this situation.

They do have a difference, though. Hinduism argued by saying that behind the world of the transitory or nonreal lies what is ultimately real. Buddhism reversed that by saying that behind the real world is actually impermanence. Thus, the reason for all our cravings is that because we think there is permanence, we have cravings. Once we know there is nothing permanent, not even the self, then we stop craving. In the state of "Enlightenment," the self is extinguished and all desire, and therefore, suffering, is gone. That is the goal of Buddhism.

How can we end suffering? According to Buddhist teaching, if we can obliterate desire we will obliterate evil. In fact, the very word *nirvana* means the negation of the jungle of desire to which our rebirths have condemned us.

Can one resist asking, How does a world-view that considers everything to be impermanent even explain the origin of impermanence and the seduction of the mind to see these as permanent? What, then, is this self if it doesn't even exist, except as an illusion? The answer of Buddha is that he himself lived under the illusion of permanence until through multiple reincarnations he discovered the impermanence of all reality. Then he announced that this would be his last existence, since he had obtained complete desirelessness. In that last incarnation, of course, he corrected his disciples in their erroneous views. He challenged several Hindu teachings.

But above all, Buddhism faces a truly insurmountable problem. If life is cyclical and there is no beginning to the incarnations, why is there an end? How does one have an infinite regress of causes, if there is a final incarnation?

Philosopher William Lane Craig reminds us that an infinite regress of causes is like trying to jump out of a bottomless pit. How do you start if you never reach the bottom? On the other hand, one might well ask, if every birth is a rebirth, what *kamma* was paid for in his first birth? One might also ask that if desirelessness is the ultimate *nirvana,* would it then be safe to say that in that state there is not even the desire to see evil come to an end?

The incredible aspect of this teaching is that the more painful one's existence, the more certain that the previous life is successfully paying its dues. So that when one picks up the body of a little child, deformed from birth, *kamma* is in operation. One might not wish to admit this, but that is the existential reality of this teaching.

Some years ago, I was told of a group of missionaries and their families who had been killed in a bus accident near a village in a Buddhist country. Within minutes, the bus was ransacked and the bodies pillaged for loot. The reason—those who died were only receiving their *kamma,* and there is nothing wrong in taking what is left from one who is paying his or her dues.

If every life is a payment for a previous life, one also wonders why Buddha was so reluctant to allow women into the sacred order and decreed that the rules for governing them be far greater. In fact, even a woman who had been in the order for years owed greater reverence to a man who was just an initiate. If *kamma* is in operation, why were these rules superimposed, assuming a virtue of higher order placed upon some? Unless of course, a woman, by virtue of being a woman, inherited a greater *kamma.*

What becomes evident is that the pantheistic ship comes apart on the reef of evil. One cannot affirm the absence of a self while individualizing *nirvana,* and one cannot talk about the cessation of suffering without also giving the origin of the first wrong thought. Buddhism has an intricate set of rules and regulations because it needs them. As a nontheistic path, it is a road strewn with *kamma.* It recognizes evil and then, fatalistically, shuts its eyes to it, seeking escape.

In striking contrast, the Christian message recognizes the horror of evil and seeks to offer a morally justifiable reason for God to allow suffering. Let us turn to the Christian response, so that we may see the difference.

THE GIVER OF LIFE

When all that the Scriptures have said is pulled together, there are six elements that combine to give an explanation that is coherent and unique. No escape is sought, either in the denial of the question or in the implications of the answer.

First, the God of the Bible reveals Himself as the Author of life and as the Being in whom all goodness dwells. The chasm between the skeptic and the Christian is huge, right from the start. God is not merely good. This means that with reference to God we are dealing with more than moral issues of right and wrong, pleasure or pain. *We are dealing with a transcendent source of goodness that is opted for, not because it is "better" in a hierarchy of options, but because it is the very basis from which all differences are made.* Moral categories, for us, often move in comparisons and hierarchies. We talk in terms of judging or feeling that one thing is better than another. Our culture is more advanced morally than someone else's culture, at least so we may think. God's existence changes those varying categories and moves us not into comparative categories but into a presentation of the very essence of what the word *goodness* is based upon.

God is holy. This difference is what makes the argument almost impossible for a skeptic to grasp. Holiness is not merely goodness. "Why did God not create us to choose only good?" "Why do bad things happen to good people?" The reality is that the opposite of evil, in degree, may be goodness. But the opposite of absolute evil, in kind, is absolute holiness. In the biblical context, the idea of holiness is the tremendous "otherness" of God Himself. God does not just reveal Himself as good; He reveals Himself as holy.

In the play *Phantom of the Opera*, there is a song called "The Music of the Night." It is sung by the half-sinister figure of the Phantom, who woos the woman he loves. He soothes her with his voice and entices her into his world, telling her that the darkness of the night sharpens each sensation and heightens the imagination. He pleads with her to abandon her defenses and yield to the tug of the senses, even as night blankets the eyes of truth.

Then comes this line: "Turn your face away from the garish light of day," because in the darkness, one can change the "oughts" of the conscience to the pleasure of one's passions. The melody is haunting, the words are seductive, and the will is taunted. To such a way of thinking, light *is* garish because it exposes the wickedness that is shrouded by the darkness.

The holiness of God is like light in a dark world. Just as the coming of dawn exposes the thoughts or deeds of the night before and often leaves a sickening feeling of wrong, so holiness discloses what light itself is—the source of discovering and liberating what the lie has ensnared. The Old Testament prophet Isaiah described his awe-stricken state when God revealed Himself to him. Isaiah, a morally good man, nevertheless fell on his face and immediately sensed that he was unfit to be in God's presence. He was not just in the presence of someone better than he was. He was in the presence of the One by whom and because of whom all purity finds its point of reference. That is why he was speechless.

Here, Islam and Christianity do find a partially common perspective. God is transcendent, not only in His being, but in His nature.

God's holiness, in turn, conveys an intrinsic sanctity to our lives. We are His offspring. This is not a culturally conferred sacredness or a legally determined sacredness. Every person has intrinsic value. That value is one's birthright with God as his or her heavenly Father. Was it not that recognition that prompted the question in the first place? If my birth is sacred, then what wrong merited my blindness?

THE SOURCE OF THE STORY

Second, from this authorship flows a deduction. If God is the Author of life, there must be a script. We are not, in Jean Paul Sartre's terms, empty bubbles floating on the sea of nothingness. We are not on a cruise with no purpose or destination or instruments.

It is not that the world is a stage and we can pick and choose different scripts. The lines that are given tell us that this is not a play, but real life that directs the story in every act and thought. The individual subplot must gain its direction from the larger story of God's purpose for our lives.

The blind man, the disciples, and the neighbors all knew the story. In the beginning, God created the heavens and the earth. God was sovereign over every life. How did this man's blindness fit into the story? The particular was seeking an explanation in the larger context. If the larger plot were fully understood, the smaller story would make sense.

There is a very simple way to illustrate this. I referred earlier to a song from Andrew Lloyd Webber's *The Phantom of the Opera,* which has been one of the most successful musicals on Broadway. The music is superb, and the story line is riveting. I recall that when I first heard some of the music over the radio, I was surprised that portions of it seemed discordant, sometimes even shrill. How could the same composer orchestrate both the delightful and the jarring? I could not blend the two until I finally saw the play. Then, it all fit together— the magnificent and the pathetic, the harmony and the discord, the hideous and the beautiful. Why? Because there was a script to explain it.

When one comes to grips with the story of God's plan and purpose born out of His holy and pure character, both good and evil speak within its context. Without God, there is no story, and nothing makes sense.

I once had the privilege to attend a lecture at Cambridge University when Stephen Hawking was speaking. His goal was to examine the question "Is man determined or free?" Hawking went through his material meticulously and then came his long-awaited conclusion: "Is man determined? Yes. But since we do not know what has been determined, we may as well not be."

(I could not resist wondering if he had himself risen above determinism in order to make such a pronouncement, or was the pronouncement part of the determinism he espoused? Had the data encroached upon itself?)

The audience all but groaned. There were actual audible sounds of disappointment. You see, there is no way to understand design without a pattern. There is no right way to live out life if there is no script. In fact, not only do we lose the story, we also lose all commonality of reference for meaning.

During the First World War, something fascinating took place one Christmas Eve. In the midst of an uneasy silence of the guns at night, suddenly a lone voice began to sing a Christmas carol. Irresistibly, another voice joined in, and before one knew it, there was a wave of music because of Bethlehem, cascading across enemy lines, as both sides joined in reading the same script. The story of the babe in a manger, the Prince of Peace, was able to bring communion between warring factions, even for a few hours. This is how a songwriter tells that story. Unfortunately, I can quote only a few stanzas here:

> Oh, my name is Francis Tolliver,
> I come from Liverpool.
> Two years ago the war was waiting
> For me after school,
> From Belgium and to Flanders,
> Germany to here,
> I fought for King and country I love dear.

'Twas Christmas in the trenches
And the frost so bitter hung,
The frozen fields of France were still,
No sounds of peace were sung,
Our families back in England
Were toasting us that day,
Their brave and glorious lads so far away.

I was lying with me mess-mates
On the cold and rocky ground,
When across the lines of battle came
A most peculiar sound.
Says I, "Now listen up, me boys,"
Each soldier strained to hear
As one young German voice rang out so clear.

"He's singing very well, you know,"
My partner says to me.
Soon one by one each German voice joined in the harmony.
The canons rested silent
And the gas cloud rolled no more,
As Christmas brought us respite from the war.

As soon as they were finished
And a reverent pause was spent,
"God Rest Ye Merry Gentlemen"
Struck up some lads from Kent.
The next they sang was "Stille Nacht,"
"'Tis 'Silent Night,'" says I,
And in two tongues one song filled up the sky.[10]

You see, two languages can proclaim the same meaning when the message is known to both. When even the thought of God's presence could stop the killing on that night, how much greater impact would the commitment to His entire script have? Goodness can endure a few moments; holiness is life-defining.

God has a script. He has spoken of it in His Scriptures. Finding the script moves us closer to solving the mystery.

THE POINT OF THE STORY

Third, if there is a story, what is at the heart of it? Not only is God holy, but He also reveals to us the *sacred* nature of love, to which He beckons us. And from this sacredness of His love must flow all other loves.

The important aspect of this logical flow is that intrinsic sanctity provides both the reason and the parameters of love. The inability to understand the mystery of evil leads to an inability to understand the sacredness of love. A deadly mistake that I believe our cultures make in the pursuit of meaning is this illusion that love devoid of the sacred, a naked love, is all we need to carry us through life's tests and passions.

Such a love cannot sustain us. Millions of lives are hurt every day in the name of love. Millions of betrayals have been made every day because of love. Love may make the world go round, but it does not keep life straight. In fact, love by itself will make evil more painful. Love can only be what it was meant to be when it is wedded first to the sacred. Sacredness means separateness. Holiness beckons not just to love but moves in increments till it is climaxed in worship.

What does all this have to do with suffering? Everything. You see, when the skeptic asks why God did not fashion us so that we would only choose good, he or she completely misses—drastically misses—what goodness is in God's eyes. Goodness is not an effect. If an effect is all that is important, of course God could make us that way. There is nothing logically contradictory about making us as automatons. But if life is born out of sacredness, neither goodness nor love alone is the goal. It is reverence, and it must be chosen even when it is hard and costly. This kind of love is a choice to let the sanctity of life dictate the commitment of the will. This kind of reverential love can look upon suffering and see it beyond the clutches of time and through the victory of eternity.

Dr. J. Robertson McQuilkin was formerly the president of Columbia Bible College and Seminary. He is one of the most remarkable people in our world. He is a conference speaker and author of note. But none of those credentials exceed his exemplary and heart-gripping love for his ailing wife, Muriel. She has walked down the grim and lonely world of Alzheimer's disease for the last twenty years. Dr. McQuilkin gave up his presidency and numerous other responsibilities to care for her and to love her. He has penned his emotional journey in one of the most magnificent little books ever written. At one point in the book he recounts this incident:

> Once our flight was delayed in Atlanta, and we had to wait a couple of hours. Now that's a challenge. Every few minutes, the same questions, the same answers about what we're doing here, when are we going home? And every few minutes we'd take a fast paced walk down the terminal in earnest search of—what? Muriel had always been a speed walker. I had to jog to keep up with her!
>
> An attractive woman sat across from us, working diligently on her computer. Once, when we returned from an excursion, she said something, without looking up from her papers. Since no one spoke to me or at least mumbled in protest of our constant activity, "Pardon?" I asked.
>
> "Oh," she said, "I was just asking myself, 'Will I ever find a man to love me like that?'"[11]

What a testimony that is to a great love and to a great hunger. Will any one of us find a love, a selfless love like that? We all recognize a sacred love when we see it, and we long for it. Sacred love is not without boundaries. There are lines that commitment will not cross, because when they are crossed it ceases to be love.

Interestingly enough, in the old English usage of words in the wedding ceremony of the Church of England, each spouse standing before the altar pledged to the other, "With my body, I thee worship." That was a remarkable pledge. It meant that there was an exclusivity and reverence physically expressed that gave a language to that love. Until we understand that kind of love we will never understand why it cannot be programmed. Nor, for that matter, will we ever grasp the true nature of evil. From worship flows this love.

That is why God did not make us choose good. It is not goodness we are called to, but worship. Jesus did not just say, "You shall love the Lord your God." He described it as a posture that incorporates mind and heart and soul. When that kind of love is expressed to God, every other love finds its cue.

Robertson McQuilkin ended his book with these words:

> Yet, in her silent world Muriel is so content, so lovable, I sometimes pray, "Please Lord, could you let me keep her a little longer?" If Jesus took her home, how I would miss her gentle sweet presence. Oh yes, there are times when I get irritated, but not often. It doesn't make sense. And besides, I love to care for her. She's my precious.[12]

The book is magnificently titled, *A Promise Kept*. You see, there is a script, and only when that script is etched upon the heart is life truly livable.

Douglas Coupland gives a sobering reflection of a generation, himself included, that wandered in the wilderness of life without God. He cuts through the hype and the velvety veneer of absolute freedom and at the end of his book writes a surprising postscript:

> Now, here is my secret: I tell you with an openness of heart that I doubt I shall ever achieve again, so I pray that you are in a quiet room as you hear these words. My secret is that I need God, that I am sick and can no longer make it alone. I need God to help me give, because I no longer seem to be capable of giving; to help me be kind, as I no longer seem capable of kindness; to help me love, as I seem beyond being able to love.[13]

Only when holiness and worship meet can evil be conquered. For that, only the Christian message has the answer.

THE CENTERPIECE OF THE STORY

This brings us to the fourth step. How is it possible for the sacred to acknowledge the reality of evil and still be able to offer a morally justifiable explanation?

The core of the Christian message posits a way that by all estimates has been a unique and matchless expression in the face of evil. Jesus described His journey to the cross as the very purpose for which He came. His death in that manner brings a message with double force. It demonstrates the destructiveness of evil, which is the cause of suffering and, in Jesus' example, the ability to withstand suffering even though it is undeserved.

Suffering and pain did not spare the very Son of God. Looking at Him on the cross were the very ones who sang songs of joy at His birth. Surely, for Mary, this had to be an utterly traumatic moment. The One who was conceived of God was now at the mercy of man. But I suspect she knew in her heart that something had yet to be completed in the script.

Looking at the cross, evil becomes a mirror of fearsome reality. But by carefully looking *into* the cross, we discover that it is not opaque but translucent, and we are able to glimpse true evil *through* it. The suffering of Jesus is a study in the anatomy of pain. At its core, evil is a challenge of moral proportions against a holy God. It is not merely a struggle with our discomfort. Here, two staggering truths emerge.

Remember what I said as we began, that every exponent seemed to begin with a long list of horrible tragedies or atrocities. Here is the first entailment. The more intense the moral dilemma, the less the skeptic is able to justify it as evil. Alvin Plantinga very cogently points this out for us:

> What is genuinely appalling is not suffering as much as human wickedness. But can there be any such thing as horrifying wickedness if naturalism were true? I don't see how. There can be such a thing only if there is a way rational creatures are supposed to live, obliged to live, and the force of normativity is such that appalling and horrifying nature of genuine wickedness is its inverse. Naturalism can perhaps handle foolishness and irrationality, acting contrary to what are your own interests. It can't accommodate appalling wickedness.[14]

The more grim the reality we face, the more obvious is the measuring stick. Though secular thinkers persist in hiding from this truth, we cannot explain appalling wickedness without seeing through it for what it really is.

A few years ago, a rap group recorded a song that became an instant hit. If I were to quote the words here, shock, revulsion, and horror would be the common response. The dehumanizing cruelty, inordinate sadism, and the celebration of violent rape took vulgarity to a new depth of depravity. Yet, within days of its release millions of copies had been bought by anxious fans.

How does one respond to this? Or more to the point, how does one explain it? Was it not witnessing the sadistic delight of the audience in a movie theater as they cheered for cruelty that led the poet William Auden to begin his own search for God? Unvarnished evil bore a terrifying reflection. He was compelled to find an explanation for it.

Where does one look for the explanation? With compelling measure, the cross of Jesus Christ brings into focus evil's assault upon innocence so that we can see both a mirror and a window. How this comes about, I can make but a feeble attempt to explain as we lisp toward clarity. It is here that the second staggering truth emerges.

Eleonore Stump, professor of philosophy at the University of St. Louis, has written an outstanding essay titled, "The Mirror of Evil." Unfolding her own personal journey toward God, she has brought a fascinating argument to the forefront. In the beginning, she recounts Philip Hallie's struggle on the same issue, as he described it in his book *Lest Innocent Blood Be Shed*. Hallie was struggling to work through human depravity. The appalling wickedness that changed his whole life was in coming to terms with the unmitigated brutality in the Nazi death camps. His despair reached its limit when he wrote:

> My study of evil incarnate had become a prison whose bars were my bitterness toward the violent, and whose walls were my horrified indifference to mass murder. Between the bars and the walls I revolved like a madman. . . . Over the years I had dug myself into hell.[15]

As he became immersed in this man-made hell, Hallie noticed a hardening in his own heart. He ceased to feel the horror of evil. But as a prisoner to his own indifference, something happened. He came across the heart-gripping work of the people in a small French village, Le Chambon, and found himself responding to their supererogatory acts—acts of extraordinary kindness in the face of evil. Undaunted by the cruelty around them, the Chambonnais repeatedly risked their own lives to rescue those most directly under the Nazi scourge and to alleviate their suffering.

As Hallie read of their deeds of mercy, he found himself almost unconsciously wiping away a tear, then two, then three, till his face was covered with tears. Surprised by such an uncorking of emotion from a heart he thought had died to the schemes of men, he stopped himself and asked, "Why am I crying?"

Had something released him from behind the bars of bitterness and indifference? Had the translucent mirror of evil let through just enough light from the other side that he could see not only the face of wickedness, but also a faint possibility beyond the mirror, the countenance of God? Had some light shone forth from the darkest corner of the world and directed the path of this one, trapped by fear?

On the verge of seeing himself stripped of all feeling in the pit of wickedness, the merciful had opened up a spring of tears. The Chambonnais became a symbol of all that was contrary to the hell unleashed by the Third Reich. There was no more perplexity for him. There was only one antidote. He saw through the wickedness, and Hallie wrote:

> We are living in a time, perhaps like every other time, when there are many who, in the words of the prophet Amos, "turn judgment to wormwood." Many are not content to live with the simplicities of the prophet of the ethical plumb line, Amos, when he says in the fifth chapter of his Book, "Seek good, and not evil, that ye may live: and so the Lord, the God of Hosts, shall be with you.". . . . We are afraid to be "taken in," afraid to be credulous, and we are not afraid of the darkness of unbelief about important matters. . . .
>
> But perplexity is a luxury in which I cannot indulge. . . . For me, as for my family, there is the same kind of urgency as far as making ethical judgments is concerned as there were for the Chambonnais when they were making their ethical

judgments upon the laws of the Vichy and the Nazis. . . . For me the awareness
of the standard of goodness is my awareness of God. I live with the same sentence
in my mind that many of the victims of the concentration camps uttered as they
walked to their deaths: "Shema Israel, Adonai Elohenu, Adonai Echod." "Hear O
Israel, The Lord your God is one."[16]

Borrowing that lesson from Hallie, and thinking of the tear in response to
goodness, Eleonore Stump then applies it in her own way. She proves Hallie's
point by giving another illustration.

A woman imprisoned for life without parole for killing her husband had her
sentence unexpectedly commuted by the governor, and she wept when she
heard the news. Why did she cry? Because the news was good, and she had been
so used to hearing only bad. But why cry at good news? Perhaps because if most
of your news is bad, you need to harden your heart to it. So you become accustomed to bad news, and to one extent or another, you learn to protect yourself
against it, maybe by not minding so much. And then good news cracks your
heart. It makes it feel keenly again all the evils to which it had become dull. It
also opens it up to longing and hope, and hope is painful, because what is hoped
for is not yet there. . . .

So, in an odd sort of way, the mirror of evil can also lead us to God. A loathing
focus on the evils of our world and ourselves prepares us to be the more startled
by the taste of true goodness when we find it and the more determined to follow
where it leads. And where it leads is to the truest goodness of all—the goodness
of God.[17]

I found this to be surprisingly true in my own life. Just some days ago, I
happened to be in Calcutta. It is a city that shows its wounds in public. Some
estimates claim up to two million people living on the streets—the old, the
young, infants—by the millions, hurting. The pain is so evident and so per-
vasive that its effect is to anesthetize you against it. Then, with some friends,
we visited an orphanage operated by the order founded by Mother Teresa. As
we walked in, children rose to their feet in their tiny little beds, and shouts

of "Uncle!" came from different parts of the room, as little arms were raised. Our hearts melted, and tears flooded our eyes. Goodness in the face of evil is magnificent, because it is more than goodness; it is the touch of God.

Is this possibly what Malcolm Muggeridge meant when he said:

> Contrary to what might be expected, I look back on experiences that at the time seemed especially desolating and painful, with particular satisfaction. Indeed, I can say with complete truthfulness that everything I have learned in my seventy five years in this world, everything that has truly enhanced and enlightened my existence, has been through affliction and not through happiness, whether pursued or attained. . . . This, of course is what the Cross signifies. And it is the Cross, more than anything else, that has called me inexorably to Christ.[18]

Nobel Laureate Elie Wiesel relates in one of his essays an experience he had when he was a prisoner in Auschwitz. A Jewish prisoner was being executed while the rest of the camp were forced to watch. As the prisoner hung on the gallows—kicking and struggling in the throes of death, refusing to die—an onlooker was heard to mutter under his breath with increasing desperation, "Where is God? Where is He?"

From out of nowhere, Wiesel says, a voice within him spoke to his own heart, saying, "Right there on the gallows; where else?"[19]

Theologian Jurgen Moltmann, commenting on Wiesel's story, astutely observed that any other answer would have been blasphemous.

Is there a more concrete illustration than the death of Christ to substantiate God's presence, right in the midst of pain? He bore the brunt of the pain inflicted by the wickedness of His persecutors—and showed us the heart of God. He displayed in His own suffering what the work of God is all about in changing our hearts from evil to holiness.

In fact, one of the most forgotten realities emerges from the Scriptures. Jesus struggled with the burden of having to be separated from His Father in that momentary event of His crucifixion, as He bore the brunt of evil. He cried out, "My God, My God, why have You forsaken Me?" *The incredible truth was that at the very moment His Father seemed farthest from Him, He was in the center of His Father's will.* That is precisely what an understanding of the cross means. Only when one comes to the cross and sees both in it and beyond it can evil be put in perspective.

What emerges from all of these thoughts is that God conquers *not in spite of the dark mystery of evil, but through it.*

Mahatma Gandhi made the comment that of all the truths of the Christian faith, the one that stood supreme to him was the cross of Jesus. He granted that it was without parallel. It was the innocent dying for the guilty, the pure exchanged for the impure. This evil cannot be understood through the eyes of the ones who crucified Him, but only through the eyes of the Crucified One. *It is the woman who has been raped who understands what rape is, not the rapist. It is the one who has been slandered who understands what slander is, not the slanderer. It is only the One who died for our sin who can explain to us what evil is, not the skeptics.* The cross points the way to a full explanation.

This leads to the "how" of it all.

THE SHOCK OF THE STORY

Fifth, if all that has preceded this is true, then the focus of evil should shift dramatically. Evil is more than an exterior reality that engenders universal suffering; it is an internal reality from which we run.

I recall talking to a very successful and very wealthy businessman who throughout the conversation repeatedly raised this question, "But what about all the evil in this world?" Finally, the friend sitting next to me said to him, "I hear you constantly expressing a desire to see a solution to the problem of evil around you. Are you as troubled by the problem of evil within you?" In the pin-drop silence that followed, the man's face showed his duplicity.

The longer I have encountered this question about evil, the more convinced I am of the disingenuousness of many a questioner. During a forum that I took part in on the subject of evil and suffering, an atheist asked me, "If you found out that God did not exist after all, what would you immediately do that you are not doing now out of fear of Him?"

That, alone, tells you the mind-set. There is a kind of antinomianism—an antilaw state of mind. "If God would get off my back, I could do many more things." One may as well ask, "If there were no policemen to look out for, what kind of speed would you drive?" or, "If there were no criminal justice systems, what kind of crimes would you commit?" or, "If nobody would ever find out, what wickedness would you engage in?" In short, it is a failure to see that the unguarded heart actually makes a prison for everyone—a prison where there are no rules.

Evil is to life what contradiction is to reason. If an argument is contradictory, reasoning breaks down. If life is consumed by evil, life breaks down. The problem of evil begins with me. One of the shortest letters written to an editor was by G. K. Chesterton. It read, "Dear Sir: In response to your article, 'What's wrong with the world'—I am. Yours truly, G. K. Chesterton."

ADMITTING THE SURPRISE

This brings us to our final point in the process of sustaining the Christian world view regarding evil. The surest evidence that evil is not the enemy of meaning is this inescapable existential reality: that meaninglessness does not come from being weary of pain but from being weary of pleasure. This obvious truth is conspicuously absent in the arguments of skeptics. It is not pain that has driven the West into emptiness; it has been the drowning of meaning in the oceans of our pleasures. Pleasure gone wrong is a greater curse than physical blindness. The blindness to the sacred is the cause of all evil.

This is where Jesus' answer to the question of the blind man comes through with extraordinary power and relevance. When He says that the man's blindness was due neither to the sin of the man nor of his parents but so that the glory of God might be displayed, the lesson is drastic because the message is profound. The restoration of his spiritual sight was indispensable to his understanding of the horror of sin's blindness. Darkness is devastating, and Jesus offers light and life. His cure was to help them see what they were really blind to, yet refused to see.

The problem of evil has ultimately one source. It is the resistance to God's holiness that blanketed all of creation. It is a mystery because we are engulfed in it—spiritual blindness. And there is ultimately only one antidote, the glorious display of God at work within a human soul, bringing about His work of restoration. That transformation tenderizes the heart to become part of the solution and not part of the problem. Such a transformation begins at the cross.

But like the skeptics of Jesus' day, some want to find a reason to deny who Christ is and the healing He can bring. Like the neighbors, the curious masses wish to know how it happened. Like the parents, those who come into close contact will witness the transformation that Christ brings. And like the blind man, those who have personally experienced Christ's power to transform their lives will understand the greater blindness from which they have been rescued.

This may be the real-life illustration in the struggle of which Mark Triplett wrote with such candor. The truth is not that his suffering and pain were brought about by the death of his son and his fear that he had caused it. As he himself had realized, by the terrible scourge of profaning the sacred, he had already brought about a separation from God and suffering to his own soul. He recognized what it had done to him—he had betrayed his wife, betrayed his family, and betrayed his God. The purveyors of sensual pleasure knew full well that his insatiable involvement with their offerings would take him down the road to financial waste and the potential death of his marriage. In the name of pleasure, they had inflicted the ultimate pain. Everything of worth was lost.

Here, at least, one man was stopped in his tracks to understand the cause and effect in a way that the skeptic never seems to understand. Whether or not the father's sin had taken the son's life is not the real point. In fact, the truth is that when Mark uttered those angry words to God, Adam was already dead. What is now pertinent is that through the loss of his son's life, the father has been brought face to face with what was killing him on the inside. But in the midst of that tragedy, the work of God was displayed. He procured pleasures of infinitely greater value than the profane pleasures of excitement without worth and without promise. The embrace of a forgiving wife, the lasting impact of a departed son, the fresh commitment to life's sacred trusts—these are the real treasures of life. That which had snared him was suddenly nauseating and repugnant to him. That to which he is now freed is to tell the world that life's real worth is to be found only in God.

When God restores our spiritual sight through the mystery of evil, we are then able to see the work of God displayed within the framework of our most difficult question. With tears of joy we bend before Him.

In summary, for the Christian, evil is real, this world is real, and time is real. Jesus recognized all three realities with reference to the blind man. He pointed out that this world has built into it the component of time. And upon the anvil of time beats the hammer of eternity until time ultimately reflects the values of the eternal and will be shed as a shell, from within which ultimate truths will be freely embraced. When we enter that stage, we will find out that the real anvil was eternity, that time provided the hammers, and that God's glory and purpose will be what remains.

Chapter Six

WHEN GOD WAS SILENT

IN ROBERT BOLT'S PLAY BASED ON THE LIFE OF SIR THOMAS MORE,
A Man for All Seasons, there is an incredibly poignant moment when More
is brought before a makeshift court. The judge and jury are enraged because
he will not side with their spineless scheme to support the king in his
immoral decision.

Mounting the threat of death, they pressure More to join their ranks. But
he stands quietly before them, refusing to acquiesce. They know very well the
reason for his wordless response, but they continue to ply and bully, all in an
effort to make him break his silence and speak. Still, More says nothing.

At one point, one of the judges says to him, "Your silence must then be
construed as a denial of the affirmation we seek, because that is what the
people will take it to mean."

Sir Thomas More, in measured words, replies, "The world must construe
according to its wits. This court must construe according to the law."

They finally give up. They cannot break him. But he pays for his commitment to truth with his life.

It is with good reason that some of the finest novelists and playwrights
have dug their narrative spades into the soil of injustice. Philosophers from
the time of Socrates and Plato have placed supreme value in the virtue of justice in any civilized society. Aristotle went so far as to say that justice was the
cornerstone of all ethics. Why? Because justice is the handmaiden of truth,
and when truth dies, justice is buried with it. The silence that attends such

a tragedy may well be the silence accorded the perpetrators, a haunting moment of truth.

Thomas More probably saw his precedent in Jesus, who stood before a similar court as He was being charged with, among other things, treason against the king. As Jesus stood before Pontius Pilate and those who accused Him, His demeanor was fascinating. His silence was nerve-racking to His questioners. They were hoping that in a war of words they could subdue Him. It was not by accident that their conversation, supposedly dealing with justice, actually ended up in a discussion of truth.

The sequence of events that brought Jesus before Pilate shows how organized crime also has an ancient legacy. Cowardice, treachery, falsehood, scheming, murder—all the passions that authors of fiction draw upon in their suspense novels—spring to life in the harsh reality of the most historic display of injustice in history, when truth was on trial.

The religious leaders wanted Jesus out of their way. But they were torn between two systems of law—their own and the laws of Rome. Try as they would, they could engineer no moral grounds on which to kill Jesus. But even if they could have constructed some scenario of moral justification, they did not have the authority to execute Him, which was their intended goal. It often happens that when the moral law protects the innocent, a ceremonial law is invoked to accomplish immoral ends.

Jesus committed an unpardonable offense in their eyes when He claimed to be equal with God. That, of course, carried no weight in a Roman court, as long as He did not pose a threat to Caesar. In the Greco-Roman world, it is said, to the popular mind all religions were considered to be equally true; to the philosophers, they were equally false; and to the magistrates, they were equally useful.

In short, Rome was no friend to Hebrew religion. The only hope of the high priest and his party, therefore, was to argue their case by representing Jesus' crime as a challenge to Caesar and a crime of treason. They no more cared for Caesar's well-being than Caesar cared for theirs. But the ploy helped their case.

Caught in the middle of all this was the weak-kneed Roman governor,

Pontius Pilate. Old Testament scholar Dennis Kinlaw has astutely noted that poor old Mrs. Pilate never envisioned that her son's name would make it across history—etched into the Christian creeds. No doubt, he, himself, never gave thought to the momentous trial that would be permanently scripted into the story of civilization.

With all that Jesus said to Pilate, Pilate marveled most at His silence. The Bible says, "The chief priests accused him of many things. So again Pilate asked him, 'Aren't you going to answer? See how many things they are accusing you of.' But Jesus still made no reply, and Pilate was amazed" (Mark 15:3–5).

The interaction between them gives us a critical look at how Jesus handled the skeptic's taunt and the religious person's anger at Him. Jesus had already been through an exhausting series of events. First, He had been arrested when Judas sold out for a meager sum of money and took Him to Annas, the father-in-law of the high priest, Caiaphas. After questioning Him, Annas sent Him on to Caiaphas, who shrewdly sought to justify a crucifixion by quoting Scripture, that it was imperative that "one die for the many."

Caiaphas, in turn, sent him to Pilate who, unknown to the priest, had been warned by his wife not to incriminate himself in this horrible plot. Discovering that Jesus was a Galilean, Pilate wrested an excuse to avoid making a judgment and sent Him to King Herod. But Pilate could not avoid his appointment with destiny. For Herod, after taunting Jesus, sent Him back to Pilate.

Jesus became an object flung from one set of hands to the other, as words and intentions were woven together to subvert the truth, all in the name of morality. When Pilate finished examining Him, he said to the religious authorities, "You brought me this man as one who was inciting the people to rebellion. I have examined him in your presence and have found no basis for your charges against him. Neither has Herod, for he sent him back to us; as you can see, he has done nothing to deserve death. Therefore, I will punish him and then release him" (Luke 23:14–16). And Pilate had Him flogged, in an attempt to somehow appease the crowd.

This was the moment the leaders of the synagogue had awaited, and in the will of God, this was the moment toward which all of history had been moving and by which history would be forevermore defined. There is much that can be said here, but it is Jesus' conversation with Pilate that occupies our attention.

THE OPENING LINES

The text, as we study it, does not begin with Jesus' silence. It begins with a brief interchange between Jesus and Pilate before Jesus refused to answer some of Pilate's questions. We would be prudent, therefore, if we first look at the answers He did give, because His silence is understood in the light of the words He spoke.

The first question Pilate asked Jesus was very straightforward: "Are You the king of the Jews?"

This was a specifically worded question. Pilate would have preferred to keep it an internal affair between the Jews. That way, he might possibly have been able to avoid any responsibility in the matter. The priests, on the other hand, knew they would have to drag Rome into the problem if they were to have the legal authority to execute Jesus. With these cross-purposes, the trial began.

To the question from Pilate about His kingship, Jesus countered with a question of His own: "Is that your own idea, or did others talk to you about Me?"

Pilate snapped back, "Am I a Jew? It was *Your* people and *Your* chief priests who handed You over to me. What is it You have done?" (see John 18:33–35).

Pilate was evidently irritated by Jesus' question, but he had obviously missed the point. What Jesus wanted to expose to Pilate was the concealed disingenuousness that lay behind his question—mere ceremonial curiosity. To answer a question for which an answer is not genuinely sought is only to prolong the charade. Jesus was closing in on Pilate to show him that he was really no different from those who were bringing the accusation against Him. The significance of this question is that the confrontation did not pertain only to one nation of people. This implicated the whole world. His accusers were willfully deaf to His answers, even as Pilate was performing a function of his office with complete disregard for truth behind his judgments. God was on the witness stand; humanity was playing its courtroom shenanigans.

An immediate lesson surfaces. We hear so much criticism from skeptics about what they often brand as "secondhand faith." It is implied that many people believe in God only because of the context of their birth or family or determined conditions. If the criticism is justified, and undoubtedly it sometimes is, why do we not show the same distrust of secondhand doubt? If it is possible for a person's belief to be merely an echo of someone else's faith, are there not hypocrites in doubt also?

Was this a genuine search on the part of this Roman governor, or was it the pretense of a procedure, reflecting no real will to listen? That was Jesus' point.

I have, on numerous occasions, heard some valiant questioner pile argument upon argument to challenge the Christian faith. The arguments begin to sound hollow when you recognize by the very wording that they are the expressions of another's voice or borrowed from some notable thinker. This is not to suggest the validity or the invalidity of the question or of the argument. This is only to assert that, many times, so-called reasons for rejecting the truth are so blended with individual prejudice that it is hard to differentiate between the question and the wanton desire of the questioner.

Some time ago, I was lecturing at a university on the assigned subject, "Ethics and the Invasion of Cyberspace." I was told that I was invited as the token theist so that there would be at least one speaker who would propose a transcendent basis for ethical judgments! It was a fascinating conference.

After the lecture, we sat down together for a lunch hosted by faculty members and student leaders. During the lunch, one of the faculty members said something like this: "All this philosophizing about an objective morality seems so highbrow and philosophically weighty. The basic question I have is very simple: How do we keep students from cheating?"

As I answered her question, I also reminded her that she was still dealing with the symptoms and ignoring the cause.

At the end of the lunch, a handful of students surrounded me with a flurry of questions. One of them, in low tones, said, "I really have a problem. I was asked by my professor to come and take in your lecture and to critique what you said. But the truth is that after hearing your arguments, I find myself agreeing with you."

"Well, then," I asked, "why don't you say that in your paper?"

"Oh no! I will be definitely docked in my grades if I concur with your reasoning. The professor had been certain that I would disagree with you and wanted me to offer a scathing rebuttal. I am a straight-A student, and I cannot afford to drop my grade."

"Are you sure your professor will penalize you just for agreeing with this position on ethics?" I asked her.

"I am positive," she said.

"Was your professor here at the luncheon?" I asked.

"Yes," came the obviously hesitant response.

"Who was it?"

There was an awkward silence and then an even more uncomfortable admission. "The one who asked you how she could keep students from cheating."

So much for the genuine hunger for truthfulness. I seriously had to wonder if a teacher such as that really wanted her students to learn not to cheat or only to learn to think as she did, even if it meant an entire life of pretense—secondhand doubt.

I am convinced that there are tens of thousands of students turned out of our universities whose minds have been trained to disbelieve in God, any contrary argument or evidence notwithstanding. The father of modern rationalism is the French philosopher Rene Descartes. His dictum—"I think, therefore I am"—resonates in the halls of philosophy. From that fundamentally rationalistic approach to existence, skeptics have extrapolated their own dictum—"I doubt, therefore I am an intellectual." For many, such doubting actually follows a particular intellectual, rather than squarely facing the questions of the intellect.

A DIFFERENT KING

Jesus was well aware of the contagion of doubt. That, in part, was His reason for remaining quiet. Pilate, of course, quickly dismissed any personal involvement in the proceedings by insisting that it was an internal matter within the Jewish community that had started the whole problem in the first place. Jesus then proceeded to pursue Pilate to the point that he would realize that it indeed *was* Pilate's concern, because Jesus' kingship did not have anything to do with the governance of a nation or of a culture, but had *everything* to do with the rule of the heart.

Jesus said, "My kingdom is not of this world. If it were, my servants would fight to prevent my arrest by the Jews. But now my kingdom is from another place" (John 18:36).

Pilate, somewhat taken aback, exclaimed, "You are a king, then!"

This was when the defining answer came. "You are right in saying I am a king. In fact, for this reason I was born, and for this I came into the world, to testify to the truth. Everyone on the side of truth listens to me" (v. 37).

Immediately, we notice that three dramatic assertions have been made.

First, that Jesus' kingdom was of such a nature that it was not procured by military might or power. Its rule is neither territorial nor political. If history has proven anything, it is that the spread of the gospel by the sword or by coercion has done nothing but misrepresent the message and bring disrepute to the gospel.

To be sure, Jesus was not talking here about pacifism or warfare. He was making a definite difference between the way His kingdom grows and the way earthly nations establish control. He was making a significant point to a prosecutor with political motives. His kingship cannot and will not be established by force or threat. This fact alone would have given Pilate reason enough to go beyond the surface of what was going on. It was really the nations of this world that were on the witness stand, and God who was doing the judging. Pilate ought to have known immediately that this was no Caesar standing in front of him. This was someone with a drastically different kind of authority.

At the risk of repetition, at this point I would like to recount an instance I have shared in some of my other writings. I do so now because I wish to carry this a step further.

Some years ago, a military general in Russia invited me to speak at a round-table discussion with seven members of the faculty who chaired different departments at the Center for Geo-Political Strategy in Moscow. From the beginning, the atmosphere in the room was cold and antagonistic and the expressions upon their faces hard. One by one, their attacks came upon religion in general, and upon Christianity in particular with its history stained with bloodshed. I attempted to defuse one question after another but I could tell that the discussion was progressing nowhere because they kept reverting to Christendom's checkered past.

We suddenly came to a very tense moment. One of the officers, with great passion and antagonism in his voice, leaned toward me and said, "I remember as a child seeing a German soldier come into my home and shoot my grandmother to death. On his belt buckle were the words, 'God is for us.' *That* is what religion has done for our country!" he charged.

He was right. Perhaps he did not remember, or even know, that those buckles were not thus inscribed by the Nazis, but were remnant paraphernalia from the days of the Kaiser. As the Nazi war machine ground down into a serious lack of equipment, they had begun to use these remnants from a bygone era. That aside, from the days of Constantine, the symbol of the cross has been so repeatedly emblazoned on weapons of hatred and war that the message of Christ has been apprehended by what Nietzsche called "the will to power."

I paused and admitted to him that I partially agreed with what he had said.

That surprised him, and he cautiously lowered his guard. Then I said this: "But you know, General, Jesus never came to establish a government upon the people by force. He did not even talk about political systems. He came to rule in the hearts of people, and not by the establishment of political power. He asks to live in *you*, not to control your state."

With that, I went on to share my own personal testimony with them. I was on the verge of quoting what Aleksander Solzhenitsyn once said, that the thin line between good and evil does not run through states or ideologies, but through the heart of every man and woman. But I resisted, fearing that even that reference may have stirred political passion.

The officers were very quiet when I finished, some looking introspective and others reluctantly nodding their heads in agreement. The general who had invited me had a look of calm triumph over his face, as if to say, "There, gentlemen, is the answer you and I never thought of."

I then went on to ask them what seventy years of Marxism had done for their people. I reminded them of the emptiness in the lives of their youth, who were now living in one of the most lawless countries on earth.

As suddenly as the subject had been introduced in the first place, so dramatically did the tenor of the conversation change. It is ironic, I think, that the city of Moscow bears the scars of the brutality of both Nazism and Napoleon's exploits. There are reminders of what the Nazis did and markers of how far Napoleon came in his attempt to defeat Russia. Their names symbolize terror and war to the huge Soviet Empire. The still-vivid memories of their savageries make the Russian people ever skeptical of any power that threatens.

Yet, in an extraordinarily staggering statement about Jesus Christ, Napoleon said something that is almost unexcelled by any political leader. I quote it at length because of its incredible insight. I only wish I had had it with me when I met with these generals. Napoleon expressed these thoughts while he was exiled on the rock of St. Helena. There, the conqueror of civilized Europe had time to reflect on the measure of his accomplishments. He called Count Montholon to his side and asked him, "Can you tell me who Jesus Christ was?" The count declined to respond. Napoleon countered:

Well then, I will tell you. Alexander, Caesar, Charlemagne and I myself have founded great empires; but upon what did these creations of our genius depend? Upon force. Jesus alone founded His empire upon love, and to this very day millions will die for Him. . . . I think I understand something of human nature; and I tell you, all these were men, and I am a man: none else is like Him; Jesus Christ was more than man. . . . I have inspired multitudes with such an enthusiastic devotion that they would have died for me . . . but to do this it was necessary that I should be visibly present with the electric influence of my looks, my words, of my voice. When I saw men and spoke to them, I lighted up the flame of self-devotion in their hearts. . . . Christ alone has succeeded in so raising the mind of man toward the unseen, that it becomes insensible to the barriers of time and space. Across a chasm of eighteen hundred years, Jesus Christ makes a demand which is beyond all others difficult to satisfy; He asks for that which a philosopher may often seek in vain at the hands of his friends, or a father of his children, or a bride of her spouse, or a man of his brother. He asks for the human heart; He will have it entirely to Himself. He demands it unconditionally; and forthwith His demand is granted. Wonderful! In defiance of time and space, the soul of man, with all its powers and faculties, becomes an annexation to the empire of Christ. All who sincerely believe in Him, experience that remarkable, supernatural love toward Him. This phenomenon is unaccountable; it is altogether beyond the scope of man's creative powers. Time, the great destroyer, is powerless to extinguish this sacred flame; time can neither exhaust its strength nor put a limit to its range. This is it, which strikes me most; I have often thought of it. This it is which proves to me quite convincingly the Divinity of Jesus Christ.[1]

Whatever else one may say in response, it is difficult to explain this away as mere eloquence. In fact, it was to counter mere eloquence and such artificial power that Napoleon said what he did. With unbelievable insight, he saw how Jesus Christ conquered. It was not by force, but by winning the heart.

Napoleon understood Jesus better than Pilate did. Pilate probably had no clue what Jesus meant when He said, "My kingdom is not of this world," or how far into the future this Christ would conquer—and that, without the methods by which empires are normally expanded, of which Rome was a prime example.

A Different Cause

Having given the first part of His answer, Jesus moves to the second. "For this reason I was born, and for this I came into the world, to testify to the truth. Everyone on the side of truth listens to me" (John 18:37).

This is one of the most defining statements Jesus ever made, both for His mission and for our ultimate condition. His purpose in coming was to testify to the truth. He already knew who He was. His testimony was to reveal to us who *we* are. His answers would not change under any pressure His accusers could apply. Whenever He spoke, He spoke the truth. His word was truth.

This conversation could have placed Pilate in a very unique place in history, on the side of that which was right, had he only asked his question and waited for the answer. Instead, in dramatic fashion, he responded to Jesus' statement that anyone who is on the side of truth listens to Him with an impatient dismissal, "What is truth?" and walked away. He did not wait for the answer and so proved Jesus' point that he was not really looking for the truth.

Pilate walked out of the hall abruptly and tried to set Jesus free. He just wanted out of the whole situation. He offered the crowd a choice. He would free a prisoner of their choosing, any prisoner, because it was Passover time. He hoped and probably felt sure that they would opt for the release of Jesus. But he was out of step with the determination of the religious leaders. Instead of calling for Jesus' release they cried for Barabbas, who had been imprisoned because of his part in a political rebellion. That itself showed that it was not Jesus' rebellion against Rome that prompted their motive; rather, it was their rebellion against God that was impelling their passions. This is how the Bible tells the story, as recorded in John 19:4–7:

> Once more Pilate came out and said to the Jews, "Look, I am bringing him out to you to let you know that I find no basis for a charge against him." When Jesus came out wearing the crown of thorns and the purple robe, Pilate said to them, "Here is the man!"
>
> As soon as the chief priests and their officials saw him, they shouted, "Crucify! Crucify!"
>
> But Pilate answered, "You take him and crucify him. As for me, I find no basis for a charge against him."
>
> The Jews insisted, "We have a law, and according to that law he must die, because he claimed to be the Son of God."

The Bible then adds this:

> When Pilate heard this, he was even more afraid, and he went back inside the palace. "Where do you come from?" he asked Jesus, but Jesus gave him no answer. "Do you refuse to speak to me?" Pilate said. "Don't you realize I have power either to free you or to crucify you?"
>
> Jesus answered, "You would have no power over me if it were not given to you

from above. Therefore the one who handed me over to you is guilty of a greater sin." (John 19:8–11)

Finally, Pilate handed Him over to be crucified.

In many ways Pilate is a most pitiable character, for he lived in fear on every side. He feared Caesar, if perchance he conveyed that he did not deal with someone who was a threat to Rome. He feared the implications of what he was doing, because his wife had warned him that she had had a dream about Jesus and that he should not have a share in punishing that innocent man. He feared Jesus Himself, not quite sure who he was dealing with.

Pilate may well be the quintessential example of what politics has come to mean. He knew what was right but succumbed to the seduction of his position. In life's most severe tests of motives, there is a politician in each and every one of us. While Pilate was ignorant of the role he was playing, the priests justified their heinous deed, quoting Scripture in support of their cause. Divine purpose, political maneuvering, and religious fervor met in the plan of redemption.

It was to be God's Passover Lamb that Jesus came into the world in the first place. The world wanted to explain Him away by its own wits. He stood at the bar of God's grace and spoke mercy. It was at this point that the Lamb of God began to move to the moment of death.

There are four distinct references to Jesus' silence along this trail to His death. Let us probe them.

The first occurs when He is standing before the Sanhedrin, as narrated in Mark 14:60. Conflicting testimony was given by false witnesses. Their charges did not add up, yet Jesus remained silent. Contradiction itself ought to be self-indicting. When it is not, either truth or truthfulness has died.

The second silence occurred when, in the presence of Pilate, the high priests repeated their charges of treason, and Jesus remained silent. He knew that they were determined to crucify Him. It is difficult to bring a defense against religion without truth, especially when it is galvanized by a crowd. Any words of self-defense on Jesus' part would have been pointless.

I believe that Jesus' demeanor here is profoundly exemplary. It was the silence of truth in the midst of the noise of prejudice and hate. I have personally experienced situations like this and have witnessed others in a similar position. The one who stands silently in the face of mocking and hate-filled people exposes the scandalous capacity of hatred and, in his silence, speaks volumes of God's character.

The third moment of silence is in front of Herod and his band of mockers. They wanted a show. The Bible says this:

> When Herod saw Jesus, he was greatly pleased, because for a long time he had been wanting to see him. From what he had heard about him, he hoped to see him perform some miracle. He plied him with many questions, but Jesus gave him no answer. . . .
>
> Then Herod and his soldiers ridiculed and mocked him. Dressing him in an elegant robe, they sent him back to Pilate. That day Herod and Pilate became friends—before this they had been enemies. (Luke 23:8–9, 11–12)

This passage tells a fearsome tale. There are many who want Jesus to be nothing more than a miracle worker or an entertainer. And how ironic it is that enemies became friends out of a common desire to be rid of Him. Has anything changed since then?

The fourth time Jesus was silent was when Pilate became fearful, hearing that He claimed to be the Son of God. "Where do You come from?" he asked. But Jesus remained silent. He had already told Pilate where He came from. But Pilate did not have the courage to deal with His answer.

In the mix of these silent responses, there is a wealth of thought from God to us.

A DIFFERENT POWER

First, there is the silence of *goodness* in the face of orchestrated evil. The entire episode before the Sanhedrin was an effort to frame Him. They knew their power. He knew their weakness. They knew the letter of the law. He knew the spirit of the moral code. They did not know Him. He knew them.

Anytime evil becomes organized, its ferocity breathes the air of hell. There is nothing that can quench that fury. It cannot be stopped until it has accomplished its purpose. That is why hell is unending. Its nature is to burn on the inside, and no outward consolation or influence can change wickedness that is inflamed by numbers.

The second silence is the silence of *perception*. When evil justifies itself by posturing as morality, God becomes the devil and the devil, God. That exchange makes one impervious to reason. Certainly, the high priests represented that lot. Nothing, absolutely nothing that Jesus could have said would have convinced them of who He really was or caused them even to care. Their capacity to hate and their love for ceremonial law far exceeded any desire to know truth and goodness.

Jesus knew that their love for the law was nothing more than a desire to find ways to manipulate the law to serve their own immoral ends. Anytime Scripture is quoted for the express purpose of advancing one's selfish aims, light is turned into darkness.

In all of literature, there are very few passages that are as gripping and penetrating in insight as Dostoevsky's portrayal of the Grand Inquisitor in his book *Brothers Karamazov*. In a conversation with his younger brother, Alyosha, who was far more spiritually minded than he, Ivan, an atheist, is relating of a time when he, too, thought on spiritual matters. In fact, he had even penned a poem that he called "The Grand Inquisitor." It was the title Ivan had given to an aged chief cardinal heading the Spanish Inquisition. Alyosha asked Ivan to tell him about the poem, and Ivan narrated it as prose. It was based on events during the 1500s, in the Spanish town of Seville, when the Church was burning "heretics" at the stake. After giving the historical backdrop, Ivan began his story.

On a certain day that a large number of heretics had been tortured and burned under the complete and angry command of the Grand Inquisitor, suddenly, in the midst of all the appalling sounds and sights of torture, a figure quietly and gently appeared and walked among the suffering.

He came softly, unobserved, and yet, strange to say, everyone recognized Him. . . . The people are irresistibly drawn to Him, they surround Him, they flock about Him, follow Him. The sun of love burns in His heart, light and power shine from His eyes, and their radiance, shed on people, stirs their hearts with responsive love.

It is obvious that in Ivan's narration this figure is Jesus Christ, walking in simple guise among the people. Suddenly, the Grand Inquisitor came along in his carriage and saw Him. Recognizing who He was, he immediately had Him arrested and thrown into prison. That night, lantern in hand, in his coarse cassock, he came to visit his prisoner. The conversation is profound:

> "Is it Thou? Thou?" But receiving no answer, he added at once, "Don't answer, be silent. What canst Thou say, indeed? I know too well what Thou wouldst say. And Thou hast no right to add anything to what Thou hadst said of old. Why, then, art Thou come to hinder us? For Thou hast come to hinder us, and Thou knowest that. But dost Thou know what will be tomorrow? . . . I shall condemn Thee and burn Thee at the stake as the worst of heretics. And the very people who have kissed Thy feet, to-morrow at the faintest sign from me will rush to heap up the embers of Thy fire. . . ."
>
> When the inquisitor ceased speaking he waited some time for his prisoner to answer him. His silence weighed down upon him. He saw that the prisoner had listened intently all the time, looking gently in his face and evidently not wishing to reply. The old man longed for Him to say something, however bitter and terrible. But He suddenly approached the old man in silence and softly kissed him on his bloodless lips. That was all His answer. The old man shuddered. His lips moved. He went to the door, opened it, and said to Him: "Go, and come no more. . . . Come not at all, never, never!" And he let Him out into the dark alleys of town.[2]

Dostoevsky's genius reveals a brilliant understanding of the power of miracle, mystery, and authority. The Inquisitor lives in many a religious person's mind even today. We scream at Jesus but want no answer that will add to the claims He has already made. We want Him to leave and come no more.

Such was the mind-set of the religious authorities. Jesus' silence was purposeful. He knew what His questioners were about.

But His silence was not only one of character and perception, it was also the silence of *consistency*. By His silence He taught us how to fight slander. His behavior was in keeping with His teaching. This, over the years, has come home to me as possibly one of the most easily missed examples that Jesus set for us in the face of so much that was reprehensible in human behavior. His silence is a lesson that answers are not always the way to reason. To give in to the temptation to try to fight slander with words in most instances dirties both the slanderer and the one who has been slandered. Escaping from slander, therefore, is a hazardous task when the very accusation can become valid not because of the truth, but because of the lack of composure with which one seeks to defend oneself. Jesus made no such mistake.

I have been told of an incident that occurred some years ago. As I was not present, I was not privy to the details. But the same descriptions of the event came to me from several different sources. A Christian leader was being subjected to the haranguing and bullying of some in the church who wanted him out. There was no big killer argument that could be mounted. So petty and ridiculous charges were made with unmasked fury, leveled one after another.

To a person, the identical report came back that the most eloquent expression of the entire occasion was the example of the leader, who sat silently before his accusers with tears staining his face. He had nothing to say and yet, everything was communicated. The outbursts and the tirades of the attackers were nothing less than the poisonous venom of misguided lives. Such scenarios ought to be instructive of true power. The man who was the one accused looked like Christ in the midst of his enemies.

But finally, we must understand that the silence of Jesus was the silence of *fulfilled mission*. His silence before those who were to take His life was predicted by the prophet Isaiah, eight hundred years before it took place: "He was oppressed and afflicted, yet he did not open his mouth; he was led like a lamb to the slaughter, and as a sheep before her shearers is silent, so he did not open his mouth" (Isa. 53:7).

It is a natural reaction to speak in our own defense, even when we are in the wrong. He remained silent, though He was innocent of the charges. His silence was for our sake, because He stands before the Father on our behalf.

At the heart of this entire episode is a truth that God had given from before the foundation of the world.

In *The Lion, the Witch and the Wardrobe*, C. S. Lewis wrote a magnificent passage illustrating this. Aslan, the lion, is a figure of Christ. One of the children, Edmond, had betrayed Aslan and endangered his siblings by selling out to the wicked witch, the Queen of Narnia, who had seduced him by offering him a taste of turkish delight. By the terms of the law, that betrayal merited Edmond's death. There was only one way to save Edmund: Aslan must be delivered into the hands of the queen, which had been the real objective in her scheme all along.

Quietly and without resistance, the more powerful Aslan submits to the queen's demands. After he was humiliated, he was bound to a table of stone, which represented the law, and killed. Edmond's sisters, Lucy and Susan, were totally despondent as they grieved over their friend. Suddenly, Aslan appeared before them, triumphant over death. "What does it all mean?" they wondered.

Lewis, at this point in the story, makes this brilliant observation.

"It means," said Aslan, "that though the Witch knew the Deep Magic, there is a magic deeper still which she did not know. Her knowledge only goes back to the dawn of Time. But if she could have looked a little further back, into the stillness and the darkness before Time dawned, she would have read there a different incantation. She would have known that when a willing victim who had committed no treachery was killed in a traitor's stead, the Table would crack and Death itself would start working backwards."[3]

That incantation that Lewis speaks of is the prior will of God, that He who knew no sin would willingly lay down His life to pay the price of sin. The Word of God, as promised, was fulfilled.

A Different Way

Does Jesus' silence, with all of the implications that we have drawn, reveal a contrast to others in similar situations who have claimed divine or prophetic status?

Yes, it does. Dramatically so. He came with a message and a method that address three very significant differences on individuality and society. I speak of conversion, compulsion, and revelation. How is the Christian faith unique?

First is the issue of conversion. Jesus' message reveals that every individual, whether Jew or Greek or Roman or from any other civilization, comes to know God not by virtue of birth, but by a conscious choice to let Him have His rule in his or her individual life. Jesus' kingdom is not of this world, neither is our inheritance in His kingdom a world into which we enter by physical birth.

This is very important to understand. We are living in a time when angry voices demand with increasing insistence that we ought not to propagate the gospel, that we ought not to consider anyone "lost" just because they are not "Christians." "We are all born into different beliefs, and therefore, we should leave it that way"—so goes the tolerant "wisdom" of our time. Mahatma Gandhi, for example, strongly spoke out against the idea of conversion. When people make such statements, they forget or don't know that *nobody* is born a Christian. All Christians are such by virtue of conversion. To ask the Christian not to reach out to anyone else who is from another faith is to ask that Christian to deny his own faith.

One of India's leading "saints," Sri Ramakrishna, is said to have been for a little while a Muslim, for a little while a Christian, and then finally, a Hindu again, because he came to the conclusion that they are all the same. If they are all the same, why did he revert to Hinduism? It is just not true that all religions are the same. Even Hinduism is not the same within itself. Thus, to deny the Christian the privilege of propagation is to propagate to him or her the fundamental beliefs of another religion.

If conversion is individual and not by virtue of birth, this leads us to the next issue of compulsion. The teaching of Jesus is clear. No one ought to be compelled to become a Christian. This sets the Christian faith drastically apart from Islam. In no country where the Christian faith is the faith of the majority is it illegal to propagate another faith. There is no country in the world that I know of where the renunciation of one's Christian faith puts one in danger of being hunted down by the powers of state. Yet, there are numerous Islamic countries where it is against the law to publicly proclaim the gospel of Jesus

Christ, and where a Muslim who renounces his or her belief in Islam to believe in anything else risks death. Freedom to critique the text of the Koran and the person of Mohammed are prohibited by the laws of blasphemy, and the result is torturous punishment. One must respect the concern of a culture to protect what it deems sacred, but to compel a belief in Jesus Christ is foreign to the gospel, and that is a vital difference. The contrast is all too clear.

It is in this matter of conversion and compulsion that political theory emerges. As I stated earlier, the gospel is not to be spread at the point of a sword. When Christendom has resorted to such methods, it was not the gospel of Jesus Christ that was propagated, but a political theory that used the gospel for the benefit of power-seeking institutions and individuals. People are justifiably fearful when they think of religion in tandem with political control. Jesus' method was to touch the heart of the individual so that he or she responded to Him out of love for Him, rather than from compulsion or control.

Contrast this with the practice of Mohammed. However one might wish to interpret it, the sword and warfare are an intrinsic part of the Islamic faith. Even the best of apologists for Islam acknowledge the use of the sword in Islam but will mitigate it by saying that in each instance it was for defensive purposes. I suggest that the reader read the Koran and the history of Islam for himself to determine whether this was so.

As for the executions that were carried out at Mohammed's behest, his apologists argue that they were not so much ordered by him as carried out on his behalf. Here again, I would recommend reading the narrative to see if this defense is in keeping with the historic record.

But even the best of Muslim apologists is hard-pressed to navigate around Mohammed's own injunction to kill, illustrated in a verse from the Koran known as the *ayatus-saif,* or "the verse of the sword."

> But when the forbidden months are past, then fight and slay the idolaters wherever ye find them, and take them, and prepare for them each ambush. But if they repent and establish worship and pay the poor due, then leave their way free. (Surah 9.5)

One Islamic scholar takes off on this passage and makes this comment:

And a traitor guilty of high treason is an outlaw and may be killed by anyone without any special authority. May God guide us all to the Truth and spread peace and unity amongst mankind![4]

I shall say no more on this very difficult and divisive issue here because any comment would breed hard feelings, and that is not my desire. What it clearly boils down to is this. Where Islam and Christianity do agree is that truth is supreme; however, they see truth finally revealed in different persons—in Islam through Mohammed, and in Christianity through Jesus Christ. This is why a comparison between the two persons is necessary.

This brings us to the final matter. At the heart of all this lies one issue. Jesus' silence does not mean He does not speak. He reminds us that He has already spoken in His Word, the Scriptures. Here, the final source of authority is truly divergent from other faiths.

The Muslim sees the Koran as the perfect and final revelation of Allah. Allah was the revealer, and Mohammed was the receptor. The very words were dictated to him. He, to them, is the last and the greatest prophet. The proof of his supremacy is the beauty of the Koran. It is the *book* that is considered to be the ultimate expression of perfection and the repository of truth.

The difficulty here is manifold. How does one sustain that this written text is perfect? Let us consider just one troublesome aspect, the grammatical flaws that have been demonstrated. Ali Dashti, an Iranian author and a committed Muslim, commented that the errors in the Koran were so many that the grammatical rules had to be altered in order to fit the claim that the Koran was flawless. He gives numerous examples of these in his book, *Twenty-Three Years: The Life of the Prophet Mohammed*. (The only precaution he took before publishing this book was to direct that it be published posthumously.)

A further problem facing the early compilers of the Koran was the number of variant readings of some of the important texts. Now, in recent times, scholars have begun to look at the Koran and have raised some very serious questions regarding its origin and compilation. This has sent many Islamic scholars scrambling for a response.[5]

What one does need to grant is that the poetry and the style are beautiful. The postmodern, visually controlled mind has much to learn about the place of beauty in speech. But the question before us is whether this book can be considered to be the word of God. Also, considering that Islam claims Mohammed to be a prophet to the world, the "miracle" is limited to one language, a significant portion of which is considered incomprehensible, even to those who know the language. In other words, to truly see the miracle, one has not only to speak Arabic, but also to be highly sophisticated in it. Rather narrow and highly restrictive is a claim such as that.

As for truth and the Hindus, the terrain gets very rocky. Gandhi, for example, said, "God is truth and truth is God."[6] But what does that mean? It does not answer the more fundamental question of whether the existence of God is true or false. Shankara, one of the principal exponents of Hinduism, evaded that question by saying that while a person *may* worship God, it is only an inferior way of expressing truth. Ultimately, the worshiper moves to the supreme truth that he is identical with God. The bottom line is that the Hindus point to their scriptures as truth. Here, the challenge is very complex.

The Hindu scriptures actually fall into two broad categories—the Smriti and the Sruti. *Smriti* means, "That which is remembered." The authors are many and the assertions they make are diametrically different. In this corpus lie the speculations of Indian sages, ranging from the profound to the utterly bizarre, by their own admission. *Sruti*, on the other hand, means, "That which was revealed." This is the eternally true revelation of the devout Hindu.

If this revelation is eternally true, then the religion cannot claim that all ways are true for the simple reason that some religions deny the eternal veracity of the Vedas. Muslims, Buddhists, and Christians would deny such a claim. As a matter of fact, even some Hindu scholars would deny that claim. Either their denial is true, or the claim of the Hindu is true.

But, there is a deeper question. If "that which was revealed" is the eternal authority, then the logical question for pantheism, which claims that all is one, is, Who is doing the revealing? To even attempt to answer this would take a book by itself. Some words from Sri Ramakrishna will reveal the problem.

> God alone is, and it is He who has become this universe. . . . "As the snake I bite, as the healer I cure." God is the ignorant man and God is the enlightened man. God as the ignorant man remains deluded. Again, He as the guru gives enlightenment to God in the ignorant. [7]

We see the mind-boggling implications of such a view of God and revelation. If all that exists is God, then all that we know is either God in ignorance or God in enlightenment. The question arises, then, that when Buddha rejected the Vedas, was he God in ignorance or God in enlightenment? When Mohammed posited monotheism and the way of submission to Allah, was he God in ignorance or God in enlightenment? So run the sequence of questions when all that exists is God. The revealer and the receptor are the same, only in different stages of truth.

By dramatic contrast, the Christian view of revelation is given to us in the Scriptures. The claim of the writers is set forth clearly:

> Above all, you must understand that no prophecy of Scripture came about by the prophet's own interpretation. For prophecy never had its origin in the will of man, but men spoke from God as they were carried along by the Holy Spirit. (2 Pet. 1:20–21)

The Bible also says that "in the past God spoke to our forefathers through the prophets at many times and in various ways, but in these last days he has spoken to us by his Son" (Heb. 1:1–2).

What, then, is the difference? Is it only one of a claim? No. First of all, in contrast to the Koran, the Bible was written not by one author, but by several human authors. The Bible was written over a fifteen-hundred-year span, by writers from various backgrounds, times, and learning, who, under God's inspiration, wrote down the revelation. Over that vast span of time, their message is one—they point to the birth, the death, and the resurrection of God's Son, Jesus Christ. When you think about it, that is an incredible confluence of thought over nearly two millennia. The spread itself defies natural explanation. Long before all converged in the person of Jesus Christ, His coming was envisioned, foreshadowed, and described in detail. After His death, the written Scriptures spoke of the life so dramatically born, lived, crucified, and risen. In other words, God has spoken and given to us His Word. And the climax of that Word is the person of Jesus Christ. The written Word is complete. He is perfect. He reminded us that the Scriptures cannot be broken—His Word never falters.

Further, in the fulfillment of the prophecy, as He stood silent, He showed another aspect of scriptural authority. The Bible is not merely a self-referencing book, but a book in which history, geography, and the miraculous content of prophecy and other acts were subject to the principle of verification. Some of those supernatural elements we have already seen in the other chapters, claimed and defended.

Thus, when Jesus stood before His accusers in silence, He had already prophesied in His Word centuries before that He would be silent before them. They knew the Scriptures and were even spoken of in them, but they suppressed the truth to justify their unrighteous lives. Both attitudes converged in fulfillment. They who marveled at His silence lost the wonder of what He had said. By His words and His silence, and by their words and their deeds, we see that the trial was exactly as God's Word stated it would be. We see in that His regard for His Word and our disregard for it.

Are we willing yet to listen and to see ourselves portrayed in the Scriptures? In a world of noise, the silence of God can be terrifying. Martin Luther once cried out, "Bless us, Lord! Yea, even curse us. But please be not silent!" Thanks be to God, He is not silent toward us. That is why the apostle Paul said to young Timothy:

> But as for you, continue in what you have learned . . . and how from infancy you have known the holy Scriptures, which are able to make you wise for salvation through faith in Christ Jesus. All Scripture is God-breathed and is useful for

teaching, rebuking, correcting and training in righteousness, so that the man of God may be thoroughly equipped for every good work. (2 Tim. 3:14–17)

One more thing needs to be said. Just before Sir Thomas More went to his death, his daughter, Margaret, asked him why he couldn't just give verbal consent and mutter words of support to the king without having to really mean them. She justified that life-saving ploy by saying, "You are the one who told me that it is the thoughts that one looks at and not the words. Just say it. Don't mean it." More's response to her is brilliant.

It's a poor argument, Meg. When a man takes an oath, he's holding his own self in his own hands. Like water [he cups hands], and if he opens his fingers, then— he needn't hope to find himself again. Some men aren't capable of this, but I'd loathe to think your father one of them.[8]

The makeshift court and More's own family reasoned with him that he could say something without meaning it. More reminded them that the word of a person was only as good as he is. One's word was one's life.

This is an enormous truth. That is why Jesus did not fear His accusers. He was committed by His Word. He, above all, lived a life where the word and life were identical. Of no other life can this be said. Either there was a breakdown within one's word, or there was a breakdown between the life and the word. Jesus, by honoring His Word, offered them and us His life. He did not merely die for justice. He died in prophetic fulfillment, demonstrating that you cannot kill the truth. Therefore, in a real sense, they could not destroy Him either.

I once saw a poster on the wall in the office of a school principal. It simply said, "If you cannot understand me in my speech, how can you understand me in my silence?"

The world will try to interpret truth by its wits. The Christian interprets truth by His Word—and by His silence.

Chapter Seven

IS THERE A GARDENER?

"WHY ARE YOU CRYING? WHO IS IT YOU ARE LOOKING FOR?"

That was the question asked of Mary when she went to the garden where the body of Jesus had been laid in a tomb. During the few short years that the disciples had with Jesus, their conversations had abounded with questions. There is, therefore, a tender note of indictment when this question is asked of *them*. This actually has overtones of a question He had asked them on more than one occasion. To His earliest followers, He had asked, "What do you want?" He had asked the same of the disciples of John the Baptizer—"What did you go out to see?" One has to presume that He repeatedly stopped them to ask of themselves what it was that they wanted God to be in order to merit their approval.

During their years with Him, their inability to grasp so much of what He said wins both our sympathy and our bewilderment. Indeed, they were with One who was like no other, and therefore, their tentative posture every step of the way is understandable. But how much more specific did He have to be before they were clear as to who He was?

The trail to this question is actually one that spans the breadth of human existence and goes back across millennia to another setting, when the first man and woman were placed in a garden and the questions of life and death began. In brief, the story of Jesus of Nazareth could be succinctly told around the setting of four gardens. I have selected this as the framework in which I want to present some of the most convincing evidence of the uniqueness of Jesus Christ in history and in the religions of the world.

HIDING TO SEEK

Many years ago, philosophers Anthony Flew and John Wisdom drafted a parable, posing the question of God's existence in the following way:

> Once upon a time two explorers came upon a clearing in the jungle. In the clearing growing side by side were many flowers and many weeds. One of the explorers exclaimed, "Some gardener must tend this plot!" So they pitched their tents and set a watch.
>
> But though they waited several days no gardener was seen.
>
> "Perhaps he is an invisible gardener!" they thought. So they set up a barbed-wire fence and connected it to electricity. They even patrolled the garden with bloodhounds, for they remembered that H. G. Wells's "Invisible Man" could be both smelt and touched though he could not be seen. But no sounds ever suggested that someone had received an electric shock. No movements of the wire ever betrayed an invisible climber. The bloodhounds never alerted them to the presence of any other in the garden than themselves. Yet, still the believer between them was convinced that there was indeed a gardener.
>
> "There must be a gardener, invisible, intangible, insensible to electric shocks, a gardener who has no scent and makes no sound, a gardener who comes secretly to look after the garden which he loves."
>
> At last the skeptical explorer despaired, "But what remains of your original assertion? Just how does what you call an invisible, intangible, eternally elusive gardener differ from an imaginary gardener or even from no gardener at all?"[1]

The point of the parable is clear. How many times have we ourselves asked that we might see God, just to be assured that He is actually there? But with all of our waiting and watching, like the explorers looking for the gardener, we do not see Him, yet still we contend that He is there. The atheist looks pleadingly and says, "Show me God." Our answers seem evasive because we do not have any visible body to point to. Flew and Wisdom ask the question of us: What is the difference between an invisible, elusive gardener and no gardener at all? It is a question well taken.

Philosopher John Frame responded with a brilliant counterpoint. This is his parable.

Once upon a time, two explorers came upon a clearing in the jungle. A man was there, pulling weeds, applying fertilizer, and trimming branches. The man turned to the explorers and introduced himself as the royal gardener. One explorer shook his hand and exchanged pleasantries. The other ignored the gardener and turned away.

"There can be no gardener in this part of the jungle," he said. "This must be some trick. Someone is trying to discredit our secret findings."

They pitched camp. And every day the gardener arrived to tend the garden. Soon it was bursting with perfectly arranged blooms. But the skeptical explorer insisted, "He's only doing it because we are here—to fool us into thinking that this is a royal garden."

One day the gardener took them to the royal palace and introduced the explorers to a score of officials who verified the gardener's status. Then the skeptic tried a last resort, "Our senses are deceiving us. There is no gardener, no blooms, no palace, and no officials. It's all a hoax!"

Finally the believing explorer despaired, "But what remains of your original assertion? Just how does this mirage differ from a real gardener?"[2]

John Frame's point is equally well taken. There is so much intelligibility and specified complexity in this world that it seems willful and prejudiced to try to explain it away with no intelligence behind it. Can morality, personality, and reality be reasonably explained without a personal, moral first cause? How does one explain some of the features of a garden apart from there being a gardener? What kind of proof for a gardener will suffice anyway? What if the gardener did come and was seen and desires that our trust in his work not be dependent on only a direct sighting of him, because the essence of our relationship is not the constancy of sight and intervention, but the steadfastness of trust and sufficiency?

Between the taunt brought by Flew and Wisdom in their parable and the answer given by Frame in his parable, where are we left? Is the evidence for the existence of God merely a matter of perspective? Can each side just deride the other and leave it at that? Interestingly enough, the last question the disciples faced when they went looking for Jesus addresses the questions raised by these very parables. Is there a gardener in this combination of flowers and weeds that we call Planet Earth?

It is a bit of a winding path to follow. But when we get to the end, the reason for this journey might open up new vistas. The goal will be to see whether or not He has spoken to us and how Christ has revealed God to us.

It Began in a Garden

The biblical narrative opens with the words "In the beginning." The focus moves quickly to the world God created, the crowning point of which was the creation of man and woman. The context shows a world of relationship, purpose, and beauty, with natural law set in place and stewardship over creation entrusted to human beings.

Tragically, naturalism (in which all reality is explained in natural terms) and theism have collided in these opening verses of the Bible. Instead of understanding the intention and the context of those to whom the revelation was given, the naturalist mocks the Bible's description of God's act of creation as bereft of scientific sophistication. On the other extreme is the theist who tries to make the record of creation look like a cosmologist's dissertation and then struggles to defend it.

No portion of Scripture ever claims to be a piece of scientifically technical material, intended to satisfy a technician's mind. I have repeatedly heard popular iconoclasts ridicule the ancient belief that the earth was flat and the belief that the world was created in 4004 B.C., declaring these assertions to be taught in the Bible. They never pause to prove their point by showing you where they have read that in the Bible.

Since that historic and histrionic Scopes trial in 1925, any discussion between a theist and an atheist on the question of origins is treated as if only a fool would now hold that a supernatural origin to this world is plausible. As frequently as that landmark trial is dragged into the conversation, castigating the Christian view of origins, I have discovered that most who talk about it have never even read the script and the context surrounding the trial. (They have seen the movie, to be sure.)

In this closing chapter, it is not my intention to reopen that conflict because there are already superb works that bring this debate into modern-day dialogue. But that snub at the hands of capable challengers still hangs over us like a pall. I return to it for a brief moment only to point out the fallacy and prejudice embraced then and espoused even now. If the tables were turned and the method used then against the theist were used against the naturalist, the derision could be just as loud.

A PAGE FROM THE PAST

What was that fallacy? Let us start with the backdrop, which itself was a travesty. The trial took place in Dayton, Tennessee, in 1925. The emotions ran deep, as the media harnessed an event and tailored it to full entertainment value. Predictably, the larger points were missed. There were so many issues that were woven through the proceedings that one has to wonder whether the setting, the arguments, or the process had anything to do with the specifics of the case. If today one were to analyze the questioning by Clarence Darrow of William Jennings Bryan, it would be readily seen that Darrow's answers to an equally adept challenge would have been at least as unconvincing. His whole scheme was to persuade Bryan to take the stand in defense of the miraculous and then to destroy him. Bryan thought he was up to it, and for him, it was the equivalent of getting O. J. Simpson to try on the glove. The supernatural elements of the Scripture as caricatured by Darrow did not fit the "scientific" framework, and Bryan looked bedraggled and defeated.

But was that really the way to determine whether the Bible could be trusted as a document on origins? Herein is the fallacy. Can particulars of a world-view be defended without first defending the world-view itself? It defies logic that something so methodologically tendentious could be taken as compelling proof. Any brilliant lawyer can tell you that in most trials, when only selected facts are permitted into the courtroom, any adept wordsmith can construct a farce. The added component of the media only compounds the sham.

Think of this. One of the questions for which Mr. Darrow demanded an answer of William Jennings Bryan was where Cain got his wife. That could be a fair question if it were permitted that the Bible could first be defended in its intent and content, and if the assertion were also made that it contained every detail of how human reproduction began. But none of that was even given possibility. So let us reverse the questioning and challenge the naturalist to, in effect, answer the same question. How did the first *Homo sapiens* get "his" or "her" partner? Predictably, our entire values orientation is defined on answers to this. Could Mr. Darrow have sounded very persuasive here?

How did human sexuality and marriage emerge in the evolutionary scheme of things? I would like to have asked Mr. Darrow to explain how the "Big Bang" came to confer on sexuality the enormous combination of intimacy, pleasure, consummation, conception, gestation, nurture, and supererogatory expressions of care and love. All this came from the explosion of a singularity? In no other discipline would so much information density be swallowed up under the nomenclature of chance. In case Mr. Darrow was not forthcoming with an answer, I could help him even with the most modern research.

William Hamilton of Oxford has offered one theory (this is serious, by the way): "Sex is for combating parasites." You see, in warm and rich climates where microscopic parasites threaten the stable health of their hosts, the hosts mess up the attacking power of these foes through sex and procreation. That is the reason sex came to be: to stay ahead of the game![3]

My! How different prescriptions look today to ancient cures. Imagine what the late-night comedians could do with this material. The laughter could be even more hilarious than the derision afforded to Bryan.

The shredding of fine points bereft of a studied understanding of the base of truth on which it all stands is an illicit process in which anything can be made to look absolutely idiotic. You do not form a conclusion on the presence of a gardener by studying only one bush. There is much more.

And here we see in small print what really should be the larger point. A glance at the sidebars of the trial actually betrays where the real prejudice lay, as it does to this day. On the third day of the trial, the judge asked a minister present to open in prayer. The controversy engendered was almost a circus in itself. But in spite of Clarence Darrow's strong objection, the judge allowed the prayer to proceed. Darrow's team of attorneys then rounded up a group of ministers to sign a petition objecting to the prayer on the grounds that their particular theological persuasion was not represented in it. That objection was denied by the judge. Finally, they submitted another petition signed by two Unitarian ministers, one Congregationalist minister, and one rabbi. It stated that they believed that God had shown Himself as much in the wonders of the world as He had in the written Word, and hence, a prayer that did not reflect that was abhorrent to them.

One can only shake one's head in disbelief. How ironic that "the wonders of the world" were placed on equal footing with God's spoken Word, while all along the very case being argued was whether these wonders required natural or supernatural explanation. You see, the real issue was not the explicability of the material world. The real issue was whether God had spoken through language as well as through nature.

Eden surfaced again—"Did God really say that?" Is there only a garden to look at, or is there also a voice with which the gardener speaks?

In the same manner as that small-town trial, we bring this prejudice to Genesis and think that we are capable of deciding whether God acted in six days or through fifteen billion years. That was not the intention at all. The four major thoughts of the Genesis text have been lost in the volume of extraneous debate. The principal thrust in the opening pages of Genesis is that God is the Creator and that He is both personal and eternal—He is a living, communicating God. The second is that the world did not come by accident, but was designed with humanity in mind—man is an intelligent, spiritual being. The third thrust is that life could not be lived out alone but through companionship—man is a relational, dependent being. The fourth aspect is that man was fashioned as a moral entity with the privilege of self-determination—man is an accountable, rational being.

Three significant relationships entail: that of man toward God—the sanctity of worship; that of man toward his spouse and fellow human beings—

the sanctity of relationship; and that of man toward the created order—the sanctity of stewardship. Upon and from the first flow the other two.

If this order is contrasted with that of the naturalist, the following pattern emerges. The impersonal universe brought itself into being and just happened to strike upon the conditions in which life could arise—the elimination of any ultimate purpose. Somehow over time, in order to thwart disease and destruction and to survive, procreation brought multiplication—the materiality and amorality of sex. Codes were developed that were mutually beneficial—the cultural and relative nature of morality.

Every assertion in that paradigm flies in the face of reason and intuition. It is scientifically and existentially incoherent. Take just the first. Bare nothing has never been known to produce something. Can one scientifically explain how a state of absolute nothingness can bring about intelligent processes and results? However one wants to disagree on the processes, the fact is that this is an ontologically haunted universe. By that, I mean that the ultimate cause of our being and our very mode of thinking demand that what we are and how we came to be cannot just be dismissed as "it happened." There is intelligibility running through our veins, and from that we cannot run.

Every deduction of the naturalist can be readily countered, from our coming into being to the relationships we experience with others, to the moral imperatives in our lives. That is why, may I add, millions, indeed billions, in this world will never shrug off the supernatural no matter how high the naturalist raises his volume. Not because those billions are fools, but because plain intuitive certainty tells them that something with such spiritual and physical complexity just cannot come from nothing.

You see, in the Genesis account, the question is not whether the garden was by design or by accident. That was the most reasonable recognition. Rather, doubt was planted as to whether or not God had spoken and given the ground rules for life. The answer from the naturalist is a thunderous "No!" To accept that God has spoken is to surrender the first principles of naturalism. So the real debate is distracted by mockery and by name-calling. The difference between name-calling and calling one by name is world-views apart. I will explain this when the argument is unfolded. But at the outset, we see that the difference between a silent world and one in which God has spoken is the dramatic line of division between the theist and the naturalist.

A VOLUME OF SILENCE

Some time ago, I had to undergo an examination using magnetic resonance imaging to diagnose a disc herniation in my lower back. This was one of those experiences in which the examination seemed to be at least as distressing—if not more so—than the problem itself. I was laid on a movable table and slid into a narrow tunnel where the door was shut on me. The confines were so small and the darkness so grim that I am convinced that whoever designed it must have received his or her inspiration from studying Egyptian sarcophagi. Humor aside, it was a terrifying experience, especially for one who is claustrophobic, as I am. Moments after the door was shut, I was in a pitch-black, silent world. Long, fearsome seconds ticked away, and then at last the technician's voice crackled through an electronic speaker in the capsule, "Before I begin, do you have any questions?" he asked. Did I ever have questions! I nervously blurted back, "Sir! Will you be there the whole time that I am in here?" He answered, "I promise you, Mr. Zacharias, that I will be here through the entire length of the procedure."

Just recounting the incident sends a shiver through me. I want you to know that even a total stranger's voice was of immense comfort to me in this closed box that had me in its clasp. As I lay there, a horrifying thought suddenly came upon me. In the naturalistic scheme, humanity has been tossed into this closed system called the universe, and we are hurtling through space, with no voice out there to speak to us. There is nobody to ask us if we have any questions, and nobody to tell us that he is there for us. As one comedian put it, "We are in this together, alone." We are on our own. That is the world Darrow was, in effect, arguing for. And it is a world the Bible soundly rejects. God is, and God has spoken.

You see, if there is no voice from without, we are the cause and the keepers of the garden. All relationships may be legitimately redefined. We speak to ourselves. We define ourselves. We regulate ourselves. Free society mocks any self-regulating body, yet when it comes down to living in a community, that is precisely what we do. Notice the number of laws the free world must enact in order to keep us from destroying this garden because there is no gardener but us. The naturalist is merely looking for himself. There is no one to speak to us but ourselves.

God, by contrast, hung it all on one law—to love the Lord your God with all your heart and soul and mind, and to love your neighbor as yourself. That is not enscripted in the planets; it is written for us in His Word. By His grace, He has placed this law into our hearts. When we toss it out of our hearts, questioning if He has indeed spoken, innumerable laws must be written in the place of God's law, and countless agencies must be formed to enforce those laws.

There is yet a further point of inference. From this silent, lonely world within, there logically followed a disintegration of those very relationships that Genesis revealed as being sacred. Genesis did not tell us how Cain got his wife because in the world of which God is the Creator, that is a secondary concern. In fact, when God spoke to Adam and Eve of the priority of husband and wife over father and mother, there were not even fathers and mothers at that time. Genesis did tell us that a man and a wife were in a loving, binding relationship, blessed by God, and progenitors of the human race through the establishment of the home. The home and the family were God's idea, not ours. Cain rejected that, murdered his brother, and broke the hearts of his parents—and the family was ruptured. The garden became a jungle of fear and death.

Those same implications are with us today, as the following story illustrates. Some years ago, Edmund Gosse wrote a very powerful book entitled *Father and Son*. It is the gripping and true account of a son's struggle between the faith of his father and his own growing doubts of God's existence. His father was a marine biologist while he, the son, was a lecturer in English literature who later became the librarian at the British House of Lords. In the book he traced his journey into skepticism to the day when he finally told his father that he was through with God and could no longer bring himself to believe in His existence.

The father wrote back in the most heart-wrenching terms. Toward the end of the book, Gosse quotes that letter in its entirety, and says, "It buried itself like an arrow within my heart." Here are some excerpts from his father's letter.

My dear son,

When your mother died, she not only tenderly committed you to God, but left you as a solemn charge to me, to bring you up in the nurture and admonition of the Lord. That responsibility I have sought to keep before me. . . . Before your child-hood passed, there seemed God's manifest blessing on your care; for you seemed truly converted to Him. . . . All this filled my heart with thankfulness and joy. . . .

[But] when you came to us in the summer, the heavy blow fell upon me; and I discovered how very far you had departed from God. It was not that you had yielded to the strong tide of youthful blood . . . it was that which had already worked in your mind . . . sapping the very foundations of faith. Nothing seemed left to which I could appeal. We had, I found, no common ground. The Holy Scriptures had no longer any authority. . . . Any oracle of God that pressed you, you could easily explain away; even the very character of God you weighed in your balance of reason and fashioned it accordingly. You were thus sailing down the rapid tide towards eternity without a single authoritative guide (having cast your chart overboard), except what you might fashion and forge on your own anvil. . . .

It is with pain, not in anger that I [write] . . . hoping that you may be induced to review the whole course, of which this is only a stage, before God. If this grace were granted to you, oh! How joyfully should I bury all the past, and again have sweet and tender fellowship with my beloved son, as of old.[4]

So ended the letter. Edmund made his response, telling the reader that he had a choice, either "to retain his intelligence and reject God" or "to reject his intelligence and submit to God." This is how he closed his book, speaking in the third person:

And thus desperately challenged, the young man's conscience threw off once and for all the yoke of his "dedication," and as respectfully as he could, without parade or remonstrance, he took a human being's privilege to fashion his inner life for himself.[5]

175

Their relationship was permanently severed. How did it all come about? Darwin's *Origin of Species* fell into the hands of young Gosse, and that was the beginning. The more he thought of it and wrestled with it, he concluded that if need be, he was willing to forfeit everything—including fellowship with God and with his family. If there was no home for the heart in any ultimate sense, why should there be one in any temporal sense? With Darwin's volume in hand, Edmund forged a purpose that had no compass but one of his own making.

This true story serves as a real but reflective throwback to what happened in the garden as God created it. The heart of the question was raised: Has God really spoken? When Adam and Eve questioned the authority of God, the allurement placed before them was that they could become as God, defining good and evil. What the tempter did not tell them was that good and evil as defined by God are rooted in His character, and there is nothing contradictory in God. Good and evil as defined by fallen humanity are born out of a spirit of rebellion that results in the disintegration of life. Can any reasonable person not see the difference as it has been played out in human history?

We live amid the devastation of the three sanctities: worship, relationship, and stewardship. Charles Darwin himself feared that the philosophical ramifications of natural selection had dire entailments. "Nature red in tooth and claw" was not just a poet's description, but the reality of a rebellion from a transcendent moral law. The mockery and ridicule in the Scopes trial was not the mockery of an intellectual over a lunatic. It was the mockery of the voice of man over the voice of God.

In the first garden, God spoke, and humanity denied that He had. Humanism was born, and man became the source of meaning.

ROCKS AND HUNGER

Now we come to the second garden, and here a strange twist is added. The question in this setting was not so much whether God had, in fact, spoken, but whether what He said could be contoured into something other than what He meant. The setting was ideal for distortion because it was not so much a garden as it was a desert. Gardens can seduce one by the beauty of the surroundings, delighting in the aesthetic while denouncing the moral. By contrast, deserts can generate mirages so that what is actually unreal and imaginary looks real. In the first, the deception is that of the will; in the second, the disorientation is that of the mind. The very paradigm is shifted, and truth is at the mercy of the imagination.

Jesus was hungry and physically weak, and the tempter stormed Him with a series of taunts. One of those gibes thrown was, "Jump, and see if Your Father will honor His word." Every temptation was fused with the same challenge: "Why don't You do this Your own way and prove Your autonomy?"

What, then, is the twist? In Eden, the question was one of the text: Did God actually speak? Here, it is one of context: Change the meaning of the text, and you play God. While in the first setting humanism was born, in the second, religion without truth was born—a form of polytheism, many gods, or pantheism, in which individuality is exalted to divinity. The irony here is that though Jesus was divine, He could not lay claim to His power without forfeiting His mission.

The inability to think in context is so manifest in the moral conflicts that we live with today. Every major moral battle we fight is either because we deny the text or because we justify the contrary by appealing to a different context. By the change of a word or by justification of some other kind, nothing is essentially good or evil anymore.

Something far-reaching comes to birth as a result. Common sense tells us that we cannot live without a moral law. But how does one generate a moral law if God has not spoken? The only answer is to arrange a morality of one's own design that, though mystical and transcendent, is attainable by one's own efforts. This way we appeal to our spiritual bent and at the same time incorporate our self at the center. If we can be good without God but retain a religiosity, we win both the secular and the sacred.

The New Age philosophies came in order to satisfy this demand. What better way to apply an economic theory of supply and demand than to manufacture a religion that is in limitless supply and can be tailored to fit one's personal demand? A personalized religion with an impersonal God—that's what it is. This kind of religion by its nature has an immense capacity to reflect the pragmatic, a chameleon's dream. In the desert, the temptation was not to invent a naturalistic explanation as much as it was to reinterpret the revelation by massaging the context.

No religions have done more to prove the reality of this temptation than Hinduism and Buddhism. With repeated effort, noted scholars and practitioners have tried to shade the truths of Christianity and make them resemble their own world-views. Verses such as, "The kingdom of God is in you," or "I and My Father are One" are used to sustain pantheism. Some of the most renowned Hindu philosophers have strained to make this point and tell us there is no difference. Any reading of the context in which these statements in Scripture were made shows clearly the illicit use of the texts by those who seek to distort them.

This reasoning is in violation of both logic and theism. What begins with a subtle departure from the truth by the allurement of self-deification ultimately results in the deification of everyone and everything. Such a world would be destroyed by powers of conflict because every power would claim autonomy. That is why Hinduism's epics are full of war and killing as an integral part of being gods and goddesses. Animal features emerge on the divine, the stories behind them leaving one utterly puzzled. And into the mix of polytheism and pantheism, other divinities are added—rivers, wind, and fire. The world of god-making had begun.

The Christian Scriptures are dramatically different. When God sent the plagues upon Egypt in the Old Testament, they were designed to show that He alone was supreme over the objects that they had deified (rivers, planets, creatures, magic, and so on) and that there was no other like Him. Nature, humanity, and every other entity or quantity is distinct from God. We cannot try to eliminate that distinction with impunity. From pantheism to the worship of nature, the temptation of the desert is still with us today, to have religion without God.

Rejecting the text of God in the first garden paved the way for humanism, and rejecting His context in the second led to polytheism or pantheism— many gods or self-deification.

THE GARDEN OF PAIN

The third garden is the point on which I wish to truly focus because, by any standard of measurement, here the Christian faith offers an answer for which no other system even pretends to find a substitute.

Having withstood the test in which He was challenged to go His own way, in this garden Jesus now kneels at the most desolate moment of His mission. It was to accomplish this mission that He resisted the urge to invoke the supernatural as an easy way out.

All the Gospel writers place Him at Gethsemane when the betrayal by Judas took place. Matthew in particular gives us an extensive look at the anguish of Jesus in those moments preceding His arrest. That garden has become synonymous with loneliness, sorrow, pain, and death. The events that took place during those hours had to be a source of great embarrassment to the disciples when they were happening and an even greater humiliation when they reported it after the fact. They do not flatter themselves here, and the reason they do not is because they had never expected to see Him or themselves in this time of horror. This was not what they had "come to see." How could the Son of God be in such anguish and in the throes of death? Was not death itself the greatest enemy to be conquered? How could it conquer the Author of life?

Once they understood the purpose and the means of His death, it became the riveting truth of the gospel they preached with unshakable conviction. The apostle Paul said, "We preach Christ crucified . . . Christ the power of God and the wisdom of God" (1 Cor. 1:23–24). He went on to add, "I resolved to know nothing while I was with you except Jesus Christ and him crucified" (1 Cor. 2:2).

What is the cross all about? How can that which the Greeks considered foolishness and over which the Jews stumbled (see 1 Cor. 1:21) be described as the power of God? To this day, it does not sound like a work of power to any kingdom builder. Pascal once referred to humanity as the glory and the shame of the universe. In the cross, we see why that is an appropriate description.

COMING CLOSE TO THE CROSS

Theologian Martin Hengel has written an extraordinary book called *Crucifixion: The Ancient World and the Folly of the Cross*. Hengel takes the reader through the grim and historic details of all that crucifixion meant and implied, and in particular, the crucifixion of Jesus. In his summary at the end he makes several points. I will present just a few of them.

> Crucifixion was a political and military punishment, and while the Persians and Carthaginians inflicted it upon high officials, the Romans used it on the lower classes—slaves, violent criminals, and unruly elements in society.
>
> Crucifying an individual satisfied principally a lust for revenge and brought great sadistic pleasure. It was the triumph of the state.
>
> By displaying the victim naked, at a prominent place, crucifixion represented the uttermost of humiliation.
>
> Often, the victim was never buried, so that wild beasts could feed on the carcass.[6]

Think about it. If death in itself is a "defeat," how much more a death in which politics, revenge, and power inflict their mark on the crucified one. These are institutions and attitudes with which we measure influence. To the disciples, principally Jewish, this punishment signified the loss of everything. Anger, power, pride, and cruelty were victorious over the One who claimed to be God.

Millennia later, we see the symbol of the cross on necklaces and on church steeples so often that we have no concept of what it meant and accomplished. In fact, if it were truly expounded upon, we would take offense at the preacher. Hengel helps us in his concluding remarks:

> It is impossible to dissociate talk of the atoning death of Jesus or the blood of Jesus from this "word of the cross." The spearhead cannot be broken off the spear. Rather, the complex of the death of Jesus is . . . that . . . Jesus did not die a gentle death like Socrates, with his cup of hemlock, much less passing on "old and

full of years" like the patriarchs of the Old Testament. Rather, he died like a slave or a common criminal, in torment, on the tree of shame. . . . Jesus did not die just any death; he was "given up for us all" on the cross, in a cruel and a contemptible way. Reflection on the harsh reality of crucifixion in antiquity may help us overcome the acute loss of reality which is to be found so often in present theology and preaching.[7]

I might add, "The acute loss of reality which is to be found so often today, both in preaching and in hearing." We do not seem to have the capacity to reflectively hear anymore, even if it were preached.

The first and foremost reality is that suffering and death are not only enemies of life, but a means of reminding us of life's twin realities, love and hate. Here, the love and hate did not just happen. The paths were chosen. Those who hurt Him hated Him. Those who hated Him, He loved. Those who killed Him wanted to be rid of Him. By allowing Himself to be killed, He made it possible for them to live. The crucifixion of Jesus was the embodied expression of rebellion against God. His desolation was a profound attempt to break apart the very being of God, in the Holy Trinity.

But here is the point. He did not die as a martyr for a cause, as others have done; nor was He just nonviolent so that the enemy would surrender through public outcry, as still others have done. He did not even die because He was willing to pay the price that someone else would live. *He came to lay down His life so that the very ones who killed Him, who represented all of us, could be forgiven because of the price that He paid in the hell of a world that does not recognize His voice.* Those who had rejected the text and manipulated the context of His Word saw and heard what God incarnate disclosed of reality. Every feeling they experienced, every state of mind, every utterance was the opposite of what Jesus felt, did, and said. His counterperspective stands in brilliant and sharp contrast, even as He invited them on the basis of that death to come to Him for forgiveness, because He longed to reach out to them.

In *Crime and Punishment,* Dostoevsky writes these lines of God's invitation:

Then Christ will say to us, "Come you as well, Come drunkards, come weaklings, come forth ye children of shame. . . ." And the wise men and those of understanding will say: "O Lord, why do you receive these men?" And he will say, "This is why I receive them, O ye of understanding, that not one of them believed himself to be worthy of this." And he will hold out his hands to us and we shall fall down before him . . . and we shall weep . . . and we shall understand all things! . . . Lord, thy kingdom come.[8]

Henry Nouwen, whose short life was characterized by a deep commitment to Jesus Christ, tells of a very moving personal experience. Nouwen, as some might not know, was a distinguished scholar, having taught at the University of Notre Dame and at Harvard University. He gave it all up to work with the mentally retarded at a center in Toronto. In his book *The Return of the Prodigal Son* he brings to life one of Rembrandt's paintings.

He had been profoundly affected by Rembrandt's depiction of the prodigal son returning to the waiting father, in whose arms he was clasped. Nouwen journeyed to see the original painting and admitted to being apprehensive, lest the work be less than what his imagination suggested. This is how he words the impact, after sitting in front of the painting for four hours:

And so there I was; facing the painting that had been on my mind and in my heart for nearly three years. I was stunned by its majestic beauty. Its size, larger than life; its abundant reds, browns, and yellows; its shadowy recess and bright foreground, but most of all the light-enveloped embrace of father and son surrounded by four mysterious bystanders, all of this gripped me with an intensity far beyond my anticipation. There had been moments in which I had wondered whether the real painting might disappoint me. The opposite was true. Its grandeur and splendor made everything recede into the background and held me completely captivated.

Rembrandt's embrace remained imprinted on my soul far more profoundly than any temporary expression of emotional support. It has brought me into touch with something within me that lies far beyond the ups and downs of life, something that represents the ongoing yearning of the human spirit, the yearning for a final return, an unambiguous sense of safety, a lasting home.[9]

Those closing lines strike deep into my own soul—"An unambiguous sense of safety, a lasting home." I have lived half of my life out of a suitcase, sometimes seeing this world more from thirty-seven thousand feet in the air rather than on terra firma. I have to check and recheck where I have left my passport and wallet and all the other things that form the luggage of life on the road. I lock my suitcases each time I leave the hotel room and twirl the combination lock. There are visas from places near and far stamped in my passport. Border officers or guards have carried out their routines dozens of times in my life. I walk ever conscious of being on foreign soil, with an over-the-shoulder awareness. Oh! for an unambiguous sense of safety in a lasting home. It is the reality of the cross cut deeply into my soul that brings comfort of a final home that awaits me. I can identify with the songwriter who wrote,

> O Love that wilt not let me go,
> I rest my weary soul in Thee;
> I give Thee back the life I owe,
> That in Thine ocean depths its flow
> May richer fuller be.
>
> O Cross that liftest up my head,
> I dare not ask to fly from Thee;
> I lay in dust life's glory dead,
> And from the ground there blossoms red
> Life that shall endless be.[10]

When the missionary John Paton arrived in the New Hebrides in the mid-1800s, he began translation on the New Testament. First, he had to reduce their language to writing. He worked with his young helper to come up with the vocabulary. He did not know how to illustrate the word *believe*. Finally, when he leaned completely on a chair in such a way that his whole weight was on it, the concept of trust emerged. John 3:16 now reads in their Bible, "For God so loved the world, that He gave His one and only Son, that whoever throws his whole weight on Him, will not perish but have eternal life."

Such is the procurement of the cross. A form of Christianity that goes by that name but loses sight of the cross is not Christian. A "religious" person that thinks nature and the cross portend no difference understands neither. His cross is the hill from which our gardens are addressed. His was a crown of thorns. His voice rings above the sounds of hate and torture and death, "Father forgive them, for they know not what they do."

This carries us beyond the text and the context to the contest—whose way? God's way or ours? The Garden of Gethsemane pointed Jesus to the cross.

THE LAST GARDEN

From the Garden of Gethsemane, which preceded the Cross of Calvary, we move now to the final garden. After Jesus was crucified, two men came and asked Pilate for permission to take His body down from the cross and entomb Him. They were men who, when Jesus was alive, were afraid to follow Him openly. One was Joseph of Arimathea, whom the Bible describes as a secret follower. The other was a teacher who had earlier come to Jesus at night so that he would not be seen in His company. His name was Nicodemus.

Nicodemus and Joseph brought a sack of myrrh and aloes and, along with spices and strips of cloth, they wrapped Jesus' body in keeping with Jewish custom. But His enemies were nervous. They went to Pilate and asked to have a guard placed around the tomb because they feared the body would be stolen by His disciples who would then claim that He had risen from the dead, just as He had declared He would.

This I find startling. Utterly startling! Jesus' enemies evidently knew what Jesus meant better than His own followers did. The disciples were hiding in fear of being arrested and sharing in Jesus' fate. But His enemies evidently understood that Jesus had said that He would rise again from the dead after three days. Often, those who reject the message have greater fears that there might be a haunting truth to it than those who claim to believe it. They took extra precautions to guard against it. However, they could not permanently fight off God. This is how the Scriptures describe the closing moments of this part of the story:

At the place where Jesus was crucified, there was a garden, and in the garden a new tomb, in which no one had ever been laid. . . . They laid Jesus there.

Early on the first day of the week, while it was still dark, Mary Magdalene went to the tomb and saw that the stone had been removed from the entrance. So she came running to Simon Peter and the other disciple, the one Jesus loved, and said, "They have taken the Lord out of the tomb, and we don't know where they have put him!"

So Peter and the other disciple started for the tomb. Both were running, but the other disciple outran Peter and reached the tomb first. He bent over and looked in at the strips of linen lying there but did not go in.

Then Simon Peter, who was behind him, arrived and went into the tomb. He saw the strips of linen lying there, as well as the burial cloth that had been around Jesus' head. The cloth was folded up by itself, separate from the linen.

Finally the other disciple, who had reached the tomb first, also went inside. He saw and believed. (They still did not understand from Scripture that Jesus had to rise from the dead.)

Then the disciples went back to their homes, but Mary stood outside the tomb crying. As she wept, she bent over to look into the tomb and saw two angels in white, seated where Jesus' body had been. . . . They asked her, "Woman, why are you crying?"

"They have taken my Lord away," she said, "and I don't know where they have put him." At this, she turned around and saw Jesus standing there, but she did not realize that it was Jesus.

"Woman," he said, "why are you crying? Who is it you are looking for?"

Thinking he was the gardener, she said, "Sir, if you have carried him away, tell me where you have put him, and I will get him."

Jesus said to her, "Mary." (John 19:41–42; 20:1–16)

What a moment that was—a moment that spanned the breadth of the four gardens. From the text in the garden, to the context in the desert; from the contest in the Garden of Gethsemane, to the contrast, indeed, the culmination, in the garden where they laid Him. He was Lord of the universe, yet He called this simple woman by her name. Everything suddenly bloomed with meaning. The story of life was now seen through the eyes of her risen Lord. It is no wonder that she reached out just to touch Him. God is personal, God is relational, and God sees in an eternal sense. The victory was that of Jesus over those who would silence Him, then and for centuries after. He not only spoke, He also called them by their names. That is the difference in our world of anger, hate, and rancor. Name-calling is the symptom of our breakdown. How can we fully enter into the wonder and exultation that must have now pulsated through the very beings of those who loved Him and followed Him and whose names He called so tenderly?

I was reading recently the following words of a historian as he described the day the Second World War ended.

Men wept, unable to restrain themselves. . . . Feelings pent up and damned behind the mounting walls of five successive torturing, introverted years, had to erupt. They welled up like gushing springs, they overflowed, they burst their banks, they tumbled unhindered and uncontrolled. Frenchmen with tears streaming down their faces kissed each other on both cheeks—the salute of brothers. They kissed the GI, they kissed everyone within range. The storm of emotion burst. Home and country beckoned, loved ones were waiting . . . loved ones . . . were calling across the gulf of absent years. Man was at his finest amidst the grandeur of this moment of liberation. A noble symphony arranged by the Great Composer had reached its thunderous finale and, as the last triumphal chord swelled into the hymn of Nations, man looked into the face of his Creator turned towards him, a vision of tenderness, mirrored for an instant by the purity of his own unrepressed torrent of joy and thankfulness. At such a moment, mountains move at the behest of man, he has such power in the sight of God.[11]

Only one who fought that war can truly understand what these words mean. A battleground had suddenly turned into a celebration of life, when mountains moved, flowers bloomed, weapons were put away, and the sound of loved ones' voices could be heard once more.

Only one who has known the bondage and enslavement of sin and the emptiness it brings can fully fathom the liberation of the cross and the glory of the resurrection—to hear His voice again. No wonder the world of Christian thought is so adorned with a wealth of music. They are the sounds of finding that there is more than just a garden.

When Jesus speaks and says, "I am the way the truth and the life," He claims what no other did. When He says, "My sheep listen to My voice; I know them, and they follow Me. I give them eternal life, and they shall never perish; no one can snatch them out of My hand," He speaks as no other does. The Bible says that though God has spoken to us through the prophets and the apostles, His climactic expression is in the person of His Son, Jesus Christ (see Heb. 1:1–2).

In the second chapter of the Book of Philippians, the apostle Paul says this of Jesus:

> Who, being in very nature God, did not consider equality with God something to be grasped, but made himself nothing, taking the very nature of a servant, being made in human likeness. And being found in appearance as a man, he humbled himself and became obedient to death—even death on a cross! Therefore God exalted him to the highest place and gave him the name that is above every name, that at the name of Jesus every knee should bow, in heaven and on earth and under the earth, and every tongue confess that Jesus Christ is Lord, to the glory of God the Father. (vv. 6–11)

This Jesus called Mary by name and asked her, "Why are you crying? What are you looking for?"

Author Ken Gire tells this lovely story. A little girl who lived at the edge of a forest wandered off one day into the woods and thought she would explore all the dark secrets of the forest. The farther she wandered, the denser it became, till she lost her bearings and could not find her way back. As darkness descended, fear gripped her, and all her screams and sobs only wearied her till she fell asleep in the woods. Friends, family, and volunteers combed the area and gave up in the thick of night. Early the next morning, as her father began his search afresh, he suddenly caught a glimpse of his little girl lying on a rock and, calling her by name, ran as fast as he could. She was startled awake and threw her arms out to him. Wrapped in his tight embrace, she repeated over and over, "Daddy, I found you!"[12]

Mary discovered the most startling truth of all when she came looking for the body of Jesus. She did not realize that the person she had found was the One who had risen and that He had come looking for her.

Perhaps if our naturalists would stop looking only for a gardener, they might be surprised at who they would find, or should I say, at who finds them. They might actually hear Him call them by name also and might truly understand the gardens and the deserts of this world for the first time.

He is not dead. He is alive in the best sense of the term. The celebration has begun.

NOTES

Chapter 1: Climbing a Massive Wall

1. W. E. H. Lecky, *A History of European Morals from Augustus to Charlemagne*, II (London: Longmans Green & Co., 1869). Quoted by F. F. Bruce in *Jesus, Lord and Savior* (Downers Grove, Ill.: InterVarsity Press, 1986), 15.

2. Sir Walter Scott, "Patriotism: Innominatus," *The Oxford Book of English Verse 1250–1900* (Oxford: The Clarendon Press, 1924), as cited in Bartleby Collection of Columbia University, http://www.bartleby.com/101/547.html.

3. The speaker on that occasion was Rev. Sam Wolgemuth, president of Youth for Christ International. Mr. Wolgemuth's son, Robert, published my first book in 1991, *A Shattered Visage: The Real Face of Atheism* (Nashville: Wolgemuth & Hyatt). Since that night, Sam Wolgemuth has become a treasured and revered friend, a spiritual father—something I had never envisioned as one of hundreds sitting and listening to a preacher on a warm night in Delhi. He, too, remembers the evening. He recalls getting little response as only one person had come forward in that large auditorium. As it turned out, I was that one.

4. Charles Wesley, "And Can It Be," *Hymns of the Christian Life* (Harrisburg, Pa.: Christian Publications, 1978), 104.

Chapter 2: Addressing a Heavenly Home

1. C. S. Lewis, quoted in Elisabeth Elliot, *Discipline: The Glad Surrender* (Old Tappan, N.J.: Fleming H. Revell Co, 1960), 62.

2. Christopher Hitchens, quoted in Carla C. Engelbrecht, "Hitchens' talk controversial sparks debate," *Campus Times News* (University of Rochester), on-line edition, 13 November 1997, www.ct.rochester.edu.

3. This event is recorded as *Al-Miraj,* in Surah 17.1. It is very important to note that this one verse in the Koran, on which they base Mohammed's heavenly journey, doesn't actually specify whether this journey was literal or visionary. Interpreters are on opposite sides of what this night journey actually meant. Not the least of their challenges is that Mohammed's wife said he was by her side the whole night and never left her physically. Also of consternation to Muslim scholars is that a very similar episode exists in Zoroaster's legend of a heavenly journey, which predates Islam. Textual critics continue to battle over whether this story was borrowed by Islam.

4. Used by personal permission of Larry King.

5. Islam from the beginning was primarily predisposed toward one particular people. There is very little doubt that in its inception, Islam was a geopolitical reaction to the other groups around them. Even those sympathetic to Islam, such as Ali Dashti, the noted Iranian journalist, comment that the greatest miracle in Islam is that it gave Mohammed's followers an identity, something they had lacked as various warring tribal groups. The very language of the Koran is restrictive. To claim that Mohammed's only miracle was the Koran and then to state that one cannot recognize the miracle unless one knows the language makes a miracle anything but universal. How can a "prophet to the world" be so narrowly restricted to a language group? The Koran, it is said, is only inspired in the original language—no other language can bear the miracle. The narrowness of its ethnic appeal cannot be ignored.

6. G. K. Chesterton, "The House of Christmas," from Robert Knille, ed., *As I Was Saying* (Grand Rapids: William B. Eerdmans, 1985), 304–5.

Chapter 3: The Anatomy of Faith and the Quest for Reason

1. Thomas Nagel, *The Last Word* (New York: Oxford University Press, 1997), 130.

2. Stephen Neill, quoted in J. Oswald Sanders, *Spiritual Leadership* (Chicago: Moody Press, 1994), 15.

3. Matthew Parris, "The Rage of Reason," *(London) Times*, 22 May 1999, 22.

4. David Hume, *On Human Nature and the Understanding*, Anthony Flew, ed. (New York: Collier Books, 1962), 163.

5. Lewis Thomas, quoted by Henry Brand and Philip Yancey, *Fearfully and Wonderfully Made* (Grand Rapids: Zondervan, 1980), 25.

6. Chandra Wickramasinghe, quoted by Norman Geisler, A. F. Brooke, and Mark J. Keosh, *The Creator in the Courtroom* (Milford, Mich.: Mott Media, 1982), 149.

7. Francis Crick, *Life Itself* (New York: Simon and Schuster, 1981), 88.

8. Deepak Chopra, *The Seven Spiritual Laws of Success* (San Rafael, Calif.: Amber Allen Publishing, 1994), 68–69.

9. Quoted in David Grossman, "Trained to Kill," *Christianity Today*, 10 August 1998, 7.

Chapter 4: A Taste for the Soul

1. Elizabeth Barrett Browning, "Aurora Leigh," quoted in Ken Gire, *Windows of the Soul* (Grand Rapids: Zondervan, 1996), 39.

2. Ravi Zacharias, *Cries of the Heart* (Nashville: W Publishing Group, 1998), 221.

3. Jon Krakauer, *Into Thin Air* (New York: Villard Books, 1996), 187–88.

4. David A. Brown, *A Guide to Religions* (London: SPCK, 1975), 148.

5. Douglas Coupland, *Life After God* (New York: Pocket Books, 1994), 338.

6. Chopra, *The Seven Spiritual Laws of Success*, 3.

7. Ibid., 98.

8. Ibid., 102.

9. This is also the very reason, I might add, that there came an upheaval in Hindu thinking. Later philosophers repudiated this notion of God being impersonal, and a flurry of teaching emerged in subsequent Hindu thought that led to the worship of personal gods. The Gita forms the most popular of the Hindu scriptures and is rife with songs of worship and praise directed toward a personal god.

10. See Radhakrishnan in his *Hindu View of Life* (New Delhi, India: Indus, 1993), and Pandit Nehru in his comment on Hinduism, quoted in Brown, *A Guide to Religions*, 63.

11. Paul Waitman Hoon, *The Integrity of Worship* (Nashville: Abingdon Press, 1971), 164.

12. Mary A. Lathbury and Alexander Groves, "Break Thou the Bread of Life," *Hymns of the Christian Life*, 411.

Chapter 5: Is God the Source of My Suffering?

1. Used by permission of Mark Triplett.

2. Peter Kreeft, *Making Sense Out of Suffering* (Ann Arbor, Mich.: Servant Books, 1986), 51.

3. David Hume, *Dialogues Concerning Natural Religion, Part 10,* Henry D. Aiken, ed. (New York: Hafner Publishing Co., 1963), 64.

4. J. L. Mackie, quoted by J. P. Moreland, "Reflections on Meaning in Life without God," *The Trinity Journal,* 9 NS (1984): 14.

5. Richard Dawkins, *Out of Eden* (New York: Basic Books, 1992), 133.

6. Richard Dawkins, "Viruses of the Mind," 1992 Voltaire Lecture (London: British Humanist Association, 1993), 9.

7. G. K. Chesterton, *Orthodoxy* (Garden City, N.Y.: Doubleday, 1959), 41.

8. Jean Paul Sartre, *Being and Nothingness* (New York: Pocket Books, 1984), 478.

9. From Angutarra Nikaya, 7.5, quoted in *Guide to the Tipitaka* (Bangkok: White Lotus Company, Ltd., 1993), 97.

10. John McCutcheon, "Christmas in the Trenches," Lyrics and music by John McCutcheon/Appalsongs (ASCAP), 1984.

11. Robertson McQuilkin, *A Promise Kept* (Wheaton, Ill.: Tyndale House Publishers, Inc., 1998), 18–19.

12. Ibid., 85.

13. Coupland, *Life After God*, 359.

14. Alvin Plantinga, "A Christian Life Partly Lived" in Kelly James Clark, ed., *Philosophers Who Believe* (Downers Grove, Ill.: InterVarsity Press, 1993), 73.

15. Philip Hallie, *Lest Innocent Blood Be Shed* (Philadelpia: Harper & Row, 1979), 2, cited by Eleonore Stump in her essay "The Mirror of Evil" in Thomas V. Morris, ed., *God and the Philosophers* (New York: Oxford University Press, 1994), 244.

16. Ibid., 241–42.

17. Stump, "The Mirror of Evil," 240, 242.

18. Malcolm Muggeridge, *A Twentieth Century Testimony* (Nashville: Thomas Nelson, 1978), 72.

19. Elie Wiesel, quoted in Dennis Ngien, "The God Who Suffers," *Christianity Today*, 3 February 1997, 40.

Chapter 6: When God Was Silent

1. Quoted in Henry Parry Liddon, *Liddon's Bampton Lectures 1866* (London: Rivingtons, 1869), 148.

2. Fyodor Dostoevsky, *The Brothers Karamazov* (Garden City, N.Y.: International Collectors Library), Chapter 5: "The Grand Inquisitor."

3. C. S. Lewis, *The Lion, the Witch and the Wardrobe* (New York: Collier Books), 159–60.

4. Hafiz Ghulan Sarwar, *Muhammad: The Holy Prophet* (Lahore, Pakistan: Sh. Muhammad Ashraf, 1969), 195.

5. For those interested in following up on the most recent challenges, I

recommend reading the January 1999 issue of *Atlantic Monthly,* which contains a fascinating article on Koranic studies: "What Is the Koran," by Toby Lester, 43–56.

6. M. K. Gandhi, *Pathway to God,* compiled by M. S. Deshpande (Ahmedabad: Navajivan Publishing House, 1971), 8, 9, 23. See also M. K. Gandhi, *In Search of the Supreme,* vol. 2 (Ahmedabad: Navajivan Publishing House, 1961), 265ff.

7. Christopher Isherwood, ed., *Vedanta for Modern Man* (New York: New American Library, 1972), 246.

8. Robert Bolt, *A Man for All Seasons* (Toronto: Irwin Publishing, 1963), 82.

Chapter 7: Is There a Gardener?

1. Anthony Flew, "Theology and Falsification," in John Hick, ed., *The Existence of God* (New York: Collier Books, 1964), 225.

2. John Frame, *"God and Biblical Language: Transcendence and Immanence"* in J. W. Montgomery (Ed.), *God's Inerrant Word* (Minneapolis: Bethany Fellowship), 171.

3. William Hamilton, quoted in Matt Ridley, "Why Should Males Exist?" *US News and World Report,* 18 August 1997 http://www.usnews.com/usnews/issue/970818/18male.htm.

4. Edmund Gosse, *Father and Son* (New York: Penguin Books, 1907, 1989), 249–51.

5. Ibid., 16–17.

6. Martin Hengel, *Crucifixion: The Ancient World and the Folly of the Cross* (Philadelphia: Fortress Press, 1977), 86–88.

7. Hengel, *Crucifixion,* 89–90.

8. Fyodor Dostoevsky, *Crime and Punishment* (New York: Bantam Books, 1987), 20.

9. Henri Nouwen, quoted in Gire, *Windows of the Soul,* 85.

10. George Matheson, "O Love, That Wilt Not Me Go," *Hymns of the Christian Life*, 181.

11. P. R. Reid, *The Latter Days at Colditz* (London: Hodder and Stoughton, 1952), 226–27.

12. Gire, *Windows of the Soul*, 215.

DELIVER US
FROM EVIL

To Sarah, Naomi, and Nathan,
whose lives have been enriched by
many cultures,
but whose hearts belong to God.

The ideas that shaped our culture were great and worthy. The principal goal was to reconcile liberty with law. But in the last century our culture has undergone incredible changes and challenged the ideas that once shaped and guided us. The result has been the collapse of law, the eradication of the spirit, and the unleashing of evil.

The response of the Christian calling for a return to morality is a scream in the dark, because morality has no self-sustaining light. It is a vacuous term left at the mercy of our passions.

Only in the defense and authority of the Word can morality be anchored, evil understood, and the soul restored.

Contents

⌘

Foreword

PICTURE THIS:

A vast, teeming sea of people stretching as far as the eye can see, boiling, agitated. Most are wearing Walkman headsets and the latest fashions; every person has the most recent issue of *USA Today* in one hand and a television remote control in the other. Some are quite educated, but still lost. Some are lost, but don't care. All are shouting, chanting, bumping into each other as each tries to march in his own direction, spouting a favorite truism. There is no right or wrong, so no one feels ashamed; all opinions are equal, so no one is allowed to think; religious convictions are private, so they are meaningless in any discussion. It's like a massive tabloid talk show gone berserk.

But there is one figure out there that isn't moving, like a reef standing dry above the crashing surf. The man is dark-skinned and gentle-eyed with a crown of white hair, and he is speaking firmly, steadily, in measured tones to whomever will listen. It's easy to pass him by: he has no traveling band, no loud PA system, no stage smoke or lights, no premium giveaways or easy goodies from God.

All he has is wisdom—the kind you have to sit still to receive; the kind you must take in small bites and chew slowly.

But if you truly wish to know, he'll tell you how this unruly mob got this way, and suggest the way to find peace and direction again.

He'll even show you where the solid rocks are in this ocean so you can stand steady above the tossing waves.

I happen to appreciate his boldly standing there, giving his lectures, writing his books, teaching, debating, getting bumped and jostled like the rest of us but standing steady nevertheless. The media don't provide disclaimers, the politicians don't come with subtitles, opposing opinions don't list their ingredients on the package. But he's been digging into these things for years and he's ready to help us do the same.

People often ask me where I get my ideas and what books I read. Well, I read novels to learn from the styles and techniques of other fiction writers, but to gain wisdom and insight into our times, I turn often to those who have already hacked a trail through the jungle of ideas: people like C.S. Lewis, Francis Schaeffer, Josh McDowell, and someone I've just recently discovered, Ravi Zacharias.

In *Deliver Us from Evil* this brilliant thinker writes on a subject that has been the primary theme of my novels: the mystery of evil. Though he was hard at work on his calling long before I even started mine, and though he paints with a different brush stroke, many of you already know about him and his work. For the newcomers like myself, I can only say welcome and congratulations on your find. The Bible says "a gray head is found in the way of wisdom," and I can affirm that his hair is far whiter than mine.

Frank E. Peretti

Acknowledgments

WINSTON CHURCHILL described the writing of a book in metaphors ranging from "a monster" to "a master." While those images attend as deadlines stare one in the face, a book is more than anything else the documentation of a thought life on a specific subject. In that sense an author alone knows how much he or she is indebted to others. To list all whose writings and ideas I have interacted with is impossible. But those whose immediate effort has made the transference from thought to script possible are more readily and easily acknowledged. They too are many.

I would like to thank my research assistant, Danielle DuRant, for being a determined and dedicated "seeker of sources." She has helped me track down numerous thoughts once read but in need of retrieval. My assistant, Nancy Bevers, is always able and willing to pull loose ends together as the project nears completion. The staff at Word Incorporated are a writer's delight. They do their end of the work with excellence and contagious courtesy. Kip Jordon and Joey Paul are dear friends. They have interacted with the material with heart and mind, beyond the call of duty. The editorial help from Jan Dennis and Sue Ann Jones is immensely valued, as is the project management by Laura Kendall. I must also mention that throughout this writing my colleagues led by Dan Glaze have been my best friends. They have encouraged me beyond measure and prayed that this book will meet a very specific need in a society so clearly at risk. So many others have stood alongside them to help keep me going.

Finally and most importantly my debt in this book is to my wife, Margie. If there is anyone else whose heart is interwoven with concern for content and effect as passionately as mine, it is hers. I thank her for the hours of work and patience. But neither of us could have afforded the time needed if it had not been sacrificially given to us by our three children. This book is rightfully dedicated to them.

All that is good in here reflects that which comes from the Author of Life. All that falls short is from yours truly.

Ravi K. Zacharias
Atlanta, 1996

Introduction:
Vandalized by Wickedness

IF THERE IS an image that mirrors the mind of the West today, it is strikingly reflected in Oscar Wilde's *The Picture of Dorian Gray*. This familiar story describes an exceptionally handsome young man so physically captivating that he drew the persistent and awe-stricken adulation of a great artist. The artist talked him into being the subject of a portrait, saying he had never seen a face more attractive and pure. When the painting was completed and presented to young Dorian he became so fixated and enraptured by his own looks that he wistfully expressed the longing to draw license from such beauty and to live any way he pleased, unfettered by any restraint. Any ensuing disfigurement from a dissolute life he hoped would mar only the picture, leaving him unblemished.

Like Faust of old, Dorian received his wish. His life of sensuality, indulgence, and even murder left his physical appearance completely untainted. Spurred on by the success of his undiscovered duplicity, he plummeted ever further into the depths of wickedness. One day, alone and pensive, he uncovered the portrait he had kept hidden for all those years, only to be numbed by the hideousness of the face, which bore the horror and scars of a life scandalously lived.

Besieged by the fear of being found out and of the incriminations the portrait would reveal, he buried it among the goods he kept stowed in his attic. But the pathetic charade came to an end one day when the artist himself laid eyes on it. Overcome with grief because of what he knew it meant, he confronted Dorian and implored him to turn his wasteful life around and seek God's forgiveness. "Does it not say somewhere," he pled, "'Come now let us reason together. Though your sins be as scarlet, they shall be as white as snow. Though they be red like crimson, they shall be as white as wool'?" In a fit of rage Dorian Gray grabbed a knife and killed the artist, silencing the voice.

The story reaches an emotional climax when, no longer able to stand the indictment of the picture, Dorian reached for the knife once more to destroy the portrait and remove the only visible reminder of his wicked life. The moment he thrust the blade into the canvas the portrait returned to its pristine beauty, and Dorian Gray himself lay stabbed to death on the floor. The ravages that had marred the picture now so disfigured his own countenance that he was unrecognizable to the servants who heard the scream of death and came rushing in to help.

The power of this book lies in its most central idea: Can an individual or a society live with complete disregard for a moral and spiritual center and not suffer from the wounds of wickedness? Can the soul of a people who have lived without restraint be left unravaged? Is there a point at which one must cry a halt to the passions and the whims of unbridled appetite and admit that enough is enough? Ironically, Oscar Wilde himself is renowned for his disdain of any moralizing. It was he who said that "form is content," "nothing succeeds like excess," and "nothing is good or bad, only charming or dull." He died at the age of forty-six, finding out that it was easier to live out his maverick philosophy in art than in life.

The book has a grave message for the West, so imbued with strength, so splendidly attractive, and so rich in resources. But here, too, the culture is living with philosophical risk, not pausing to uncover, even for a moment, the ramifications for the soul. One strongly suspects that in story after story that headline the news almost every day of the week there is betokened a deep disfigurement in the soul of a culture. Tragedies and atrocities are common fare, and in any corner coffee shop discussions can be heard of the latest horror or carnage to strike at our communities. Evil has taken on forms and concoctions that shock the world. Any catalog at the end of any given year tells a painful story of what is happening in our streets and homes and institutions.

But it will not do to just bemoan the reality or to condemn the evil. Much more is required of us as thinking people before we can get past the symptoms and diagnose how this has all come about. Behind an act is a thought or a belief, and those thoughts unleashed in anti-social behavior make the headlines. Yet seldom are these thoughts and beliefs scrutinized. When that is done we, like Oscar Wilde, may find out that though we may play with sinister ideas in our imaginations and artistic escapes, we cannot do the same with life. The ideas we now popularly espouse are reshaping our culture, redefining our destiny, and are at the heart of the rampant evil that we now witness. They are ideas, therefore, that must be seriously questioned or we will find ourselves in some remorse-filled future, wondering how it all happened. It is in order to thwart such a possibility—and even more to guard the soul from the vandalizing attacks of seemingly innocent ideas in our culture—that this book is written.

As we journey through the thinking that has shaped the present, we will highlight the shifts we have made along the way and the losses we have incurred. Losses that, if left unaddressed, cannot but make life unlivable. How did these losses come about? How, for example, does America today make decisions on the deepest questions of life if there is no single vision or consensus of spirit? The intent of this analysis is to wrestle with these questions as they have surfaced and affected not just America but all of the West. Here we will understand the real nature of a culture in the midst of a revolution, a culture plagued with what we now call the mystery of wickedness.

I have divided the material in this book into three sections, the first of which I have titled "The Moods of the Present." In this section the ideas and circumstances that spawned our present cultural struggle are underscored. The postmodern mind and contemporary passions are rigorously examined in the light of the moods they have engendered with such cultural force. Secular social theories bring with them inescapable entailments that are logically connected to the ideas themselves. If the idea is believed and lived out, the outcome is inevitable. A few decades ago Francis Schaeffer described our culture as one that had its feet planted firmly in midair. Things have changed since then. Our feet are now firmly planted on a field of ideas mined with explosive theories that have been proven to be devastating. Even uncertainty is preferable to wrongheaded confidence.

This first section of the book is the most difficult because of necessity it deals with the thinking in the formative stage of Western consciousness. This section will focus particularly upon the secular concepts that helped frame the present. We will delve into the traits that left their mark upon the birth of a nation. But as remote as some of the influences may seem at first, the argument is critical to our understanding. To borrow from the Dorian Gray analogy again, there was no single act that has led to the present disfigurement. The process was gradual as choices were made because of philosophies espoused. Gaining an understanding of our cultural journey will enable us to see how far we have come and how far off we have ended from where we first began. As theoretical and philosophical as these issues may seem, they are vitally important. Once this material is covered, we will break free to the inspirational and more engaging thrust of the subject. The answers can then be measured against this backdrop.

In the second section we will hear from "The Voices of the Past." These are voices that can be heard from across the centuries, voices of religious import that have conditioned Western culture possibly more than any others. There is an attempt today to silence some of these voices, but they too must be heard. "Those who cannot remember the past," said George Santayana, "are condemned to repeat it."[1] We will see from these first two sections that philosophy and religion have had their day. Tragically, in the hands of society's powerbrokers, both often exploited people, and neither could stem the tide of evil. For decades social theorists trumpeted the glories of the Renaissance and the Enlightenment. They made great boasts that those historic movements would be the salvation of mankind. Today that optimism has been blunted, and that anticipation has left admitted disappointment. If anything, postmodernism has mocked the promise once offered by modernity and called its bluff. But an even greater contempt is felt by some toward the voice of religion as it informs either education or law and particularly as it addresses morality. Here the disconcerting reality stands in clear view. History tells a sorry tale of the dismal failure of politicized religion and even of the masses who used and abused it to their own impoverishment. Evil was still at center stage. There are at once some sobering and actually thrilling lessons here. We must give ear to these truths.

Finally, we will examine the options available to us as a whole generation lives in the silence of apprehension and tears "The Face of the Future." To the subtle yet real forces that influence and even control our culture, there must be given due recognition and response. In an unprecedented fashion, events and atrocities are now confronting us with disorienting impact. With increasing frequency journal articles and scholarly writings voice the bedeviling question of unmitigated evil and cry for answers. Here we find the common ground of what threatens all of us. And from that common ground the answers will become clear and possibly inescapable. In the light of the past and the moods of the present we can help shape the face of the future. The potency of the answers calls for a response of the heart, mind, and soul and cannot be ignored. Neutrality on these issues is impossible.

A final note of caution as we begin: The focus of this study may seem to be on one particular nation, America, but do not be misled. The struggles addressed and the truths uncovered here apply not only to America but to the entire West and indeed, to our whole world. Whether one likes it or not, America today is, if not the quintessential embodiment of the Western rationalist tradition, certainly on the cutting edge of that mind-set and shares in the soul of postmodern Western civilization. Yet despite the aberrations that exist in her cultural conflict, there is also in her spirit a belief in the reasonableness of deliberation and a yearning for answers that address the soul. Therefore, though we are focusing on this one nation, let it be clear that the implications and applications of the truths are global. Even the so-called nonsecular and religiously dominated cultures of the world had better pay due heed to the truths we will uncover.

With wise choices, as we reason together there is the real possibility that a nation so great and a culture so generous—one that has given much to the world—can contend for good and be restored in her soul, and that her countenance may reveal a spiritual beauty of essence and not merely of style. Such restoration always begins with individuals, and such is my hope and prayer as these thoughts are penned.

The Moods of the Present

One

The Winds of Change

THERE IS AN ancient Eastern parable instructively titled "The Wealth Is Nearer to You Than You Think." It tells of a wealthy merchant who had undertaken a lengthy journey, carrying with him his most valuable jewels. Along the way, another traveler befriended him, making it look like a chance meeting but with the sole intent of laying his hands on those precious stones. At the end of each day when they arrived at a local inn they would share the room for the night. As was customary, each received his mat and pillow and also a wash basin with a towel for his nightly ablutions.

The merchant, somewhat suspicious of his newfound friend's real motives, devised a scheme to safeguard his valuables that was to leave his ill-intentioned companion completely befuddled. Before they turned in for the night, he would graciously offer the would-be thief the privilege of washing up first. As soon as the thief would leave the room, the rich man would take his bag full of precious stones and hastily hide it under the pillow of the thief. When the thief would return, the rich man would make his exit, taking his turn at cleaning

217

up. Awaiting this moment of opportunity, with predatorial glee the rogue would plunge into the rich man's belongings, rummaging through his bag, even ransacking in and under the rich man's pillow, feverishly searching for the precious stones. His frenzied and fruitless attempts at every stop left him utterly frustrated, and eventually he would lay his sleepless head on his pillow, angry at his failure to locate the treasure.

Finally, as it came time to part on their last day together, the rich man began his farewell pleasantries and, to the speechless astonishment of his companion, informed him that all along he had been painfully aware of his real motives. Then came the agony-inflicting revelation: "You poured all your energies into looking everywhere—except under your own pillow. The wealth was nearer to you than you realized."

This story, with all the markings of country wisdom, has a clear injunction that stirs the Eastern imagination by weaving a simple truth about life into a profound proverbial climax. But it is a parable with a wealth of wisdom to offer to the West as well, which appears at this time in its own cultural journey to be in search of an all-embracing value by which it can define itself. Surrounded by vociferous and confident secular theories on life's purpose and destiny, and becoming increasingly aware of radically different world-views from its own, there is a restlessness within and a frenetic search for some new idea that will assuage its impoverished spirit.

If a consortium of thinkers were to gather and give serious thought as to what defines the West in its primary pursuit, it would be impossible to find a consensus. At best, one might cynically observe that the essence of Western culture is its willingness to die for a higher standard of living. But that would be unfair, because in the midst of the ideational war the gnawing recognition that consistently emerges from social critics is that all is *not* well and that the world's malady has very little to do with any economic solutions. In such diagnoses is the concession that material gains alone have not quenched the deep-seated hunger of the soul, a hunger we share with all humanity.

AN UNFULFILLED SPIRIT IN A
MATERIALISTIC CULTURE

This sense that something is missing spiritually is exacerbated by the tacit admission that in and through our harried lives the culture in which we find ourselves is in turmoil. Among the elderly, a sense of fear overwhelmingly dominates their outlook while the young unblushingly confess to a sense of emptiness within. Those in their middle years often capture these twin agonies with a veiled apprehensiveness that bespeaks an uncertainty in an increasingly hostile world. But when one probes deeper into these felt realities what stands out is the lack of a clear cultural scaffolding on which to build one's values, or a distinctive identity from which a cultural ethos may be drawn. Culture has become like a dress code, varying with the time of the day and presence or absence of the elite. Such drastic variables have blurred the lines of demarcation within which we may navigate our lives.

In spiritual terms the only statement one can confidently make is that the West is engaged in a momentous battle, one in which it is risking its very soul.[1] No, it may not be as overt or as consciously sinister as Goethe's *Faust* or Wilde's *Dorian Gray*. But let us make no mistake about it: The ramifications are the same when the destiny of the soul is traded for the enthrallment of the moment. With the increasing awareness in the West of other cultures and religions, there is honest doubt about the adequacy of traditional answers on matters of the spirit, and many now believe we must instead search under "other cultural pillows" to find the real treasure.

Ironically, the search for a "soul-fulfilling idea" looms uppermost at the end of the greatest century of human progress, a century in which the West has decidedly played the lead. This irrepressible pursuit cannot easily be cast aside even though some in academia may wish it were possible. For although such terms as *progress* and *wealth* are common in the Western socioeconomic lexicon, the reality is that millions of people, though blessed by material abundance and dynamic options in life, still seek liberation from their personal enslavement to habits and from pursuits that have brought disintegration within and fragmentation without.

While we prowl and scavenge relentlessly through a variety of lifestyles in search of that all-fulfilling treasure, we seem to have forgotten that this hyperactive pursuit and empty-hearted feeling are not new to the human experience. The Bible, through the prophet Haggai, called upon the people of his day to take note of their indulgences, which were also attended by diminishing returns:

> Give careful thought to your ways. You have planted much, but have harvested little. You eat, but never have enough. You drink, but never have your fill. You put on clothes, but are not warm. You earn wages, only to put them in a purse with holes in it. (Hag. 1:5–6)

AN UNEASY AMERICA IN A NERVOUS WORLD

As old as the malady is, this existential bewilderment of the West has caught many by surprise because it has come at the end of this much heralded century of humanism's zenith. As knowledge in every field grew exponentially, the assumption was made that the loftiest dreams of the human spirit would finally be attained. Instead, those hopes have been dashed, and the answers that were sought after have become more remote than ever. Though the intellect has conquered new ground, the will is still plagued by old weaknesses, and the mind is incapable of either explaining the spirit's hungers or of taming the heart's passions. Honest seekers of truth have begun to feel as if they are being trampled underfoot from all directions, and they are having to buckle and stretch like artificial turf upon which intellectual games are being played out.

The world bears the scars of numerous wars and carries the grief of horrendous crimes committed at the whims of demagogues who stormed into history and bloodied it in the process. Political and social theories that were touted as advances for society begat criminal experiments that were justified by the promise of utopia but left in their wake the slaughter of millions. The cost exacted in human suffering has staggered the imagination. At the midpoint of this century, the sobering effects of the human frailty that brought about these global tragedies left political leadership around the world painfully aware of a crisis of the spirit. For a while, a concerted commitment was made to right the wrongs that lost sight of human worth and to bind humanity once again for the common good. The West began to do some serious soul-searching, and the years of rebuilding a broken world began, with America at the forefront.

But suddenly and turbulently in the decade of the 1960s a self-mutilating cultural upheaval burst upon the American scene that cut to the very core of the nation's soul. She was now engaged in a war of her own, searching for an identity by which she might define herself and a cultural soil from which she could sprout anew. The world was watching. Every standard of right and wrong was up for redefinition. For America nothing compares with the fallout this upheaval has brought.

What two world wars did to rudely awaken the world in general from its own apathetic slumber, the 1960s did to America, enshrouding her in a tense cultural struggle that has not yet left the national consciousness. The fires of internal conflict that burned within the hearts of the student world at that time, stoked by the fuel of a losing war effort, generated a cloud of cynicism that the winds of political change have not dissipated.

A NEW DIRECTION FOR AN OLD REBELLION

With haunting and ubiquitous force, the mood of that decade has resurfaced, laying claim to the nation itself. The death of Jerry Garcia of the Grateful Dead rock group prodded many of his followers to note that the spirit of the sixties is very much alive. This time-lapse effect sustained a long-held maxim that the books read and the philosophies imbibed in one's teens and twenties erupt with a delayed effect, exerting redoubled influence in one's middle years.

For America this has proven to be undeniably true. The Vietnam War came to an end and the Paris Peace Treaty was concluded, yet something vastly more important remained unresolved—the moral conflict that raged as radical ideas and social theories refashioned a culture. At that time many believed that this revolution could be contained because it was merely the student world—a subsection of the culture—that was in revolt against the system. One could draw some consolation from the security that at least theoretically there was a system, an establishment, that could deal with the revolt and stem the tide.

That was a costly miscalculation. We are presently witnessing a more radical agenda built upon the revolutionary zeal of three decades ago. Now, however, it is no longer students rebelling against the system; it is the system itself that is in revolt against the very ideas on which it was built. Listen to the haughty pronouncement of this long-awaited upheaval in the words of Middlebury College English professor Jay Parini:

> After the Vietnam War, a lot of us [antiwar graduate students] didn't just crawl back into our library cubicles; we stepped into academic positions. With the war over, our visibility was lost, and it seemed for awhile—to the unobservant—that we had disappeared. Now we have tenure, and the work of reshaping the universities has begun in earnest.[2]

AN APATHETIC POSTURE TO AN
AGGRESSIVE CULTURE

One leading academic has described this as a revolution from the top down. As bastions of intellectual strength have taken the lead, the conflict has come into the mainstream of culture with even deadlier force and now occupies center stage in our cultural struggle. The clash within the American mind in search of an identity is insightfully discussed by authors such as Dinesh D'Souza[3] in *Illiberal Education* and Myron Magnet[4] in *The Dream and the Nightmare*. But one wonders whether the popular mind is paying any heed to the troubling signs to which these authors are pointing. The old story about a student who was asked whether ignorance or apathy was worse and answered, "I don't know, and I don't care," is not humorous to anyone who knows the stakes in such a conflict.

There are terrifying analogies in the history of geopolitical conflict that speak to this common indifference to the reshaping power of society's gatekeepers. When Karl Marx, for example, was buried at London's Highgate Cemetery, only eleven people attended his graveside funeral. In his eulogy Friedrich Engels was more prophetic than the world then conceded when he spoke of the enduring potency of Marx's ideas. Who at that time would have believed what Marx's thought and philosophy would exact from our world? Who would have by the wildest stretch of imagination thought of a Mao Zedong or a Joseph Stalin who would harness that philosophy and plunder the soul of a people? Now, in the cultural revolt that is under way in America, the same apathy prevails. The assumption is made that the changes taking place are those of a people coming of age. The dire reality of a nation whose soul is endangered and whose youth live on the knife edge of irrational definitions of life is unaddressed.

Yet the proponents of this revolution have spoken of their vision. There is a clear call to uproot the sentinels of decency that line the past and to reconfigure the future without any points of reference. Magnet reminds us of this in his reference to Norman Mailer's prediction in the 1950s of "a new kind of man" who would enter the arena of ideational conflict:

> He was the hipster, who knew from the atom bomb and the Nazi concentration camps that societies and states were murderers, and that under the shadow of mass annihilation one should learn . . . to give up "the sophisticated inhibitions of civilization," to live in the moment, to follow the body and not the mind, "to divorce oneself from society," and "to follow the rebellious imperative of the self," to forget "the single mate, the solid family, and the respectable love life," to choose a life of "Saturday night kicks," especially orgasm and marijuana. For 1957, this was prophetic. It contained in a nutshell much of the self-liberation part of the cultural program of the sixties.[5]

For those who thought that the frisking and frolicking Gadarene herd of sinister ideas from the sixties had been drowned in the sea of the past, it is terribly daunting to hear of their sevenfold return to a house not properly cleansed. But there is incontrovertible reason for this, and it must be addressed.

The primary question has been raised: Has the West forged a new self-consciousness and disfigured its soul as a result? Has there been a wanton squandering, or forfeiture, of its spiritual wealth? Forfeiture, I say, because it is precisely that—the casting aside of what was once the source of our national life and the pervading influence in all relations and institutions. In this resulting maelstrom of conflicting ideas one may legitimately ask why this revolt has come about, against whom it has come, how it has come to be, and whether it is possible for us as a culture to find a stable road ahead. The issues are of supreme importance and must be addressed if we are to understand why our culture is at risk and how serious the implications are for every household and life.

A MAP FOR THE MIND IN THE MAZE
OF A CONFLICT

Thankfully there are answers and there is hope. To glibly sing the words from "America the Beautiful"—"Thine alabaster cities gleam undimmed by human tears"—is only to mock the hurts and torments of families living with brokenness and fear in our troubled cities, cities that merely reflect the larger hurt the nation is experiencing. But the unfolding lyrics—"Confirm thy soul in self-control, thy liberty in law"[6]—cause the emotions to swell with hope that the eyes of grief may be unblurred and that we might once again see our cities throb with the happy laughter of children unafraid.

It is time for us to reason together, because the issues are immense. But let us be absolutely sure that *reason* is not the same as *intellect*, or the brain. As the brain informs the body, the mind informs the soul. The distinction is important. And it is the mind that needs to be addressed if the soul is to be saved. The mind, unlike the brain, does not feed on isolated and fragmentary bits of information. It frames its response to both the intellectual and the existential challenge of knowing and living.

This whole controversy of the human mind transcending the human brain is not incidentally or accidentally at the forefront of academic debate today. That very quest reveals how deep the search for identity has gone. Ironically, this discussion recently intensified when the world's chess champion, Gary Kasparov, narrowly escaped defeat by a computer. With no humor intended, Kasparov said he had undertaken the computer challenge to preserve the dignity of humanity. If the world champion escaped defeat by the skin of his chess prowess, one must wonder what that would have said for us if an ordinary person had been mercilessly humiliated by the thinking machine.

But there is the clue. The computer does not feel mercy when inflicting loss or feel wonderful when enjoying the triumph of its victory. Information and data do not make a person. As humans, many senses coalesce in our daily lives. The mind-set by which we live blends together more than academic megabytes. The hurts and loves, the fears and aches, the dreams and nightmares we experience condition the way we look at reality. We speak of the wholeness of our beings because we cannot live with the absurdity of being reduced to sheer matter. The mind blends the values of our convictions with the thoughts of reality, and we respond with purpose and feeling. We are more than programmed chess players. We do not want to be pawns risked in ideational warfare. The glory of human experience transcends a game and defies scientific dissection. That glory lies in humanity's "soulishness." The cultural revolt that was spawned in educated minds proved that the brain can be well fed while the spirit is starved and that people are more than ideas.

The old adage still speaks: The world was made for the body, the body was made for the soul, and the soul was made for God. When that discovery is made and the soul is restored in a disfigured culture, we find the greatest treasure of all—and it is nearer to us than we realize.

Two

Dying Beliefs and Stillborn Hopes

TRUTH IS STRANGER than fiction, it is said, but as G. K. Chesterton has appropriately declared, that may well be because we have made fiction to suit ourselves. There is possibly a more disturbing reason for our estrangement from truth, particularly if that truth signifies a reality that is terrifying and unchangeable. Our inability to alter what is actual frustrates our grandiose delusions of being sovereign over everything. And that may be at the heart of why we find truth to be so strange. Remorse offers no relief to one seeking an escape from an irreversible situation. Any hope that the nightmarish present is just a dream or that it is erasable by merely wishing the opposite dissipates in the face of a stern, concrete reality.

Some years ago a friend shared just such a heartrending story—the truth of which seemed much stranger than fiction. To do full justice to the poignancy of the incident I must briefly describe the surroundings that occasioned my being privy to it. We were sitting in the parking lot of a historic building, a venue for gatherings of the gatekeepers of society. An air of sophistication surrounded all who entered. I was preoccupied with an address I was to deliver on the problem of the emptiness that stalks our younger generation, growing up in a time of such moral confusion. The arrival of a rather prominent individual prompted my host, a minister, to recount his story in very somber tones.

"There goes our federal prosecutor," he said, "a fine man I met under very tragic circumstances." As he labored through the details of their first contact, I knew this was not just another crisis in a minister's routine but an ineradicable scar on his pastoral heart.

He told me of a young couple he had married some years ago who had represented to him every ideal worth emulating. They embodied excellence to the youth of the church. Both were preparing to practice medicine and were on sizable merit scholarships. As he had driven away in his car after performing their wedding ceremony, my host had rehearsed in his mind the grand occasion it had been; in all his years of ministry he had not seen a more radiant couple. He thrilled at the prospect of all that lay ahead of them.

But then, like a shattered dream, only a few months into the marriage came a dreadful awakening. In the predawn hours of a wintry night the pastor's telephone rang, and a distraught voice begged him to come. The caller, the young man of such promise, kept stuttering the words, "I think I've killed her! I think I've killed her!" The minister hastily dressed and rushed over to the couple's home only to find the young woman lying lifeless in her bed and the young husband sobbing inconsolably at her side.

What had happened? What had brought about this tragedy? After a long time of prying and pleading, the story was finally uncovered. Some weeks earlier this young woman had discovered that she was pregnant. With years of study still ahead, neither of them had wanted to start a family so soon. This sudden turn of events unsettled all their plans, driving them desperately in search of a solution. They considered every option. Finally, words escaped her lips that she had never dreamed she would utter. "This is completely devastating," she said. "There is no other way but to abort this child if our careers are to survive."

The very suggestion opened a deep rift between them. They were both known on their campus for their outspoken conviction of the sanctity of the child's life in the womb. They fervently believed that each unborn child had a right all its own. Now, circumstances beyond their control had invaded their absolutes; "fate" had threatened their autonomy. Conviction clashed with ambition, and they agonized over a private decision they hoped would never be betrayed in public.

That is when she proposed her final solution. "Let's do this at home," she said. "You bring all the equipment we need to the apartment, and no one need ever know." As a young medical student, he felt this could be accomplished, and so they nervously laid meticulous plans for that fateful night. The young man was not yet fully trained in the administration of an anesthetic, and as he stumbled through the procedure he unwittingly gave her a much larger dose than he should have. His greatest fear became a ghastly deed, and he lost her. In the panicky moments that followed, with trembling hands and a cry of desperation he reached for the telephone and uttered those remorse-ridden words, "Pastor, please hurry and come to our apartment. I think I've killed her!"

ENCOMPASSED BY POSSIBILITIES

Anyone who has experienced the consequences of an act which no amount of human ingenuity can undo knows the horror of such a feeling. The most painful aspect of such a feeling is that it is a stark reminder of our finitude, which before the unchangeable consequence had thought itself omnipotent. It is not my intention to use this experience to validate one side or the other of the abortion debate. I only share it because in this nightmarish event, every individual and societal struggle that we as a civilization now face seems crystallized, and our institutions seem powerless to find a solution. For here, deeply held convictions collided at cross-purposes with career goals. Here, church and state met with equal dismay and sorrow. Here, private solutions sought escape from public castigation. Here, technology goaded a mind into a high-risk decision. Here, expediency compromised wisdom. And here, human sovereignty lay crushed by its own hands. In short, the confrontation between religious belief and a preferred lifestyle left a bloody trail.

This incident dramatically demonstrates that the moral options we face are more confounding than ever as technology, education, and cultural shifts have become powerful factors in our decision-making. At the same time we are all aware that the dilemmas we will increasingly face will not be restricted to the controversial matters of abortion or sexuality; nor will they be in the uncharted terrain of genetic engineering or euthanasia, nor, for that matter, even in the vastness of global issues such as violence, ethnic cleansing, or AIDS. Inexorably, our search for ever-increasing prosperity carries with it unprecedented entailments and costs as new technologies developed apart from moral considerations become available. These are undoubtedly monumental concerns, life-altering in their scope. But as divisive as they are, these issues are only the "above-ground" manifestations of a deep foundational shift in our culture, whose proud boast is self-determination and whose legitimizing license provides the very basis for our decision-making. If that foundation, which continues to shift under many strains, settles unevenly, the once stable infrastructure standing upon it will be imperiled, and a total collapse is only a matter of time.

Of one thing we can be certain: The range of our choices in life will be on the rise. Life has begun to resemble a smorgasbord where the entrees are laid before us in an alluring array, making us ever more gluttonous but with proportionately diminishing satisfaction. The cycle of imbibing and disgorging that characterizes gluttony is not just physical; it ultimately cuts deeply into the very spirit of our human experience. And if recognized too late, the symptoms of the bulimic spirit could destroy our very souls.

We must understand, therefore, that it is not just the range of choices that must bear study; the greatest scrutiny must be paid to *how* and *why* we make our individual and societal decisions. As a rule we are each prone to giving due attention to the specific decisions that confront us individually every day. We are also mindful of how those decisions bring about change. But the decisions are commonly based on reasons that themselves are not thought through. When those reasons are examined, they often prove to be unblushingly spurious and would result in chaos if everyone operated by the same principles. The implications of our choices carry over into what we call *lifestyles*. Individually they may seem to be insignificant, but when the mind-set of a whole culture is altered in accordance with those choices, the ramifications are staggering.

History is replete with examples of unscrutinized cultural trends that were uncritically accepted yet brought about dramatic changes of national import. Social analysts recognize that there has never been a time like our present, when such bold-faced positions are espoused and such carriers of change prevail. It is not sufficient to say, "This is just the way it is," when the intellectually curious demand the rationale for why it must be so. The appropriate response to Bertrand Russell's explanation of the universe—"It's just there"—is to remind him that the question is not one of the existence or nonexistence of the universe but of the "why" of its existence. And even more to the point, why do we even ask why it is there? The same applies to every culture. Our practices cannot be dismissed with a "just there" attitude. Cultures have a purpose, and in the whirlwind of possibilities that confront society, reason dictates that we find justification for the way we think and why we think, beyond chance existence.

ENDANGERED BY PROXIMITY

Few influences in life are as dominant—and as faltering—as the power of culture. There is implicitly in all of us a tacit surrender to its demands while we supposedly boast individuality and freedom of thought. That subtle entrapment by itself ought to alert us to the ambiguity of privilege and peril in being part of a drifting culture that carries us unaware into turbulent waters. This subsuming effect of culture is analogous to the heartbeat of a people. Let me illustrate how all-absorbing culture can be.

A medical doctor who is a friend of mine suffered a serious heart attack while still in his thirties. He described the pain of that event as different from any other pain he had ever felt. He had always experienced every prior injury or hurt, whether a broken arm or a sore knee, as a hurt to a part of his body. In some measure he could separate himself from the pain. "But during my heart attack," he said, "I was *in* the pain. There is no other way to describe it." The notion conveyed is instructive—that the very organ that should have been pumping life was instead disseminating pain.

I can think of no better analogy to describe the all-consuming hold of culture as it becomes the source of thinking and feeling in its members. So engulfing is this power that we cannot discuss the essential theme of our culture at its crossroads without being locked into it ourselves. We are *in* it, and we are hard pressed to find a fulcrum outside of it with which to leverage a shift.

IMPERILED BY IMMERSION

An old Chinese proverb says if you want to know what water is don't ask the fish. The fish does not know any other kind of life because it is submerged in the monotony and single vision of a watery existence. To the fish, no other existence is possible; hence, it can conceive of nothing by which to measure its own existence.

Similarly, it is important for those immersed in a culture to recognize that proximity does not necessarily guarantee an accurate perspective. Sometimes a culture can so imperceptibly absorb and transmit ideas into its consciousness that it is hard for those within it to be objective about the propriety of its practices when measured against a counter-perspective. In other words, if we want to know what America is like, the surest way to gain that understanding may not be to ask one who has been culturally American all his or her life.

Admitting this blind spot is not easy, though it plagues us all and breeds a subtle form of prejudice. I well recall my own struggle with cultural awareness in the early days of my relocation from one part of the world to another. I would become very agitated whenever I heard public speakers report on their impressions of recent trips they had taken to the land of my birth, because they often came back with reports of shocking and heartrending conditions. This troubled me greatly for it seemed exaggerated, embellished for the sake of effect, and far removed from life as I had experienced it, growing up in those very surroundings. The annoyance never abated until years later when I returned for a visit and was completely overcome by my own reactions to all that I saw and felt. I did not recall being overwhelmed by these same conditions when I had lived there. But now my responses seemed to echo in self-indicting fashion those I had heard described by eyes to whom it was foreign.

The same holds true for a westerner who has lived in the East and returns to the West years later. All of a sudden, definitions of wants and needs take on new points of reference. Priorities all become rearranged. Sometimes there is more justification in the surprise reaction of unfamiliarity than there is in the desensitization that comes from immersion. We all remember the old story of the frog that is gradually boiled to death. When placed in a cauldron of cold water that is gradually heated to boiling, the frog continues to swim in comfort, oblivious to what is happening. If, on the other hand, the same frog is dropped into boiling water, it immediately leaps out for its safety. The gradual change went unnoticed, accommodated beyond reason, while the drastic change met with self-preserving common sense.

Undeniably, being part of a culture brings about a level of comfort with the ways and means by which people live. But that familiarity does not guarantee sensitivity or objectivity. Proximity is not synonymous with understanding. Indeed, the very nearness we experience through modern technology may make us *more* vulnerable to distortion and victimization. The ideas and personalities the media thrust upon our imaginations subtly condition our consciousness in ways that even political totalitarianism cannot accomplish. We are unavoidably beguiled, in this so-called postmodern world, to an unprecedented degree. The constant bombardment of images shapes the perceptions of a whole generation and results in altered beliefs and lifestyles that make even the aberrant seem normal. The double-edged tragedy is not only that we are *in* such an environment but any warning that we are being molded possibly for the worse is contemptuously mocked as insane.

INFORMED BY UNDERSTANDING

Since every person is in the grasp of this cultural thrust, understanding what is happening to us as a civilization becomes critical or we risk a destiny of alarming possibilities. At any given time, minds are almost certainly at work at a feverish pace—penning modern-day versions of *Mein Kampf* or *Das Kapital*, plotting new worlds to conquer or old hates to avenge, conjuring new technologies to make our present attainments dissatisfying and obsolete. Some movie mogul somewhere is probably discussing a script that will tear away at any last vestige of reverence still residing in the human heart. Some new weapon may be in the works that could bring the world to its knees, at the mercy of a despot. And while all these possibilities loom, none of us knows what new diseases, atrocities, or tragedies await us at the turn of the next century.

Immersed in this mix of change and decay, can we at least understand the scope of the conflict? Can we appeal to our collective conscience while a few still remain who realize that there must be fences in life, else predators, with unrestrained and insatiable passions, will break down every wall of protection and relentlessly plunder everything we treasure?

Bearing in mind that we are not only *near* to this cultural explosion but are also, in fact, *in* it, the first step is that of diagnosis. What is it we are supposed to be near to and immersed in? The answer may at first seem to be protracted, but a simplistic approach for the sake of brevity only adds to the shallowness that is symptomatic of our crisis of thought. When a cultural mind-set has cut deeply into one's life, the correctives must also be deep.

After this step is completed we will not only understand the mystery of wickedness but we might well be jolted by the reality of the molding and manipulative power of culture over each of us. Only this depth of analysis will help us to understand why we make certain decisions or choose certain lifestyles. An awareness of the profound impact of culture can be a rude awakening but a necessary one. It not only reveals the rationality or irrationality of our reasons; it also exposes the inevitable consequences of the choices we make, consequences we might wish to escape but find to be unalterable.

EVICTING THE SACRED

One of the symptoms of modern and postmodern change is our large stock of new words, or certainly the new use of old words—terms such as *user-friendly, downsizing, multiculturalism, politically-correct, homophobic, postmodern, poststructuralism,* and *deconstruction.* If the cartographers of our time are working away furiously to draw up new maps as countries emerge and dissolve daily, our neologists (those who coin new words) are having a field day. One such word that we are all now accustomed to hearing repeatedly is *secular*, or *secularization*. Despite its familiarity, I suspect that many of us would find ourselves stumbling when asked to define what this word really means.

The word itself has a broad sweep and in differing contexts brings a different spin to the central idea. For our purposes we will concentrate on its social implications. Secularization is one of the most powerful conditioning influences in cultural formation today. Virtually every major decision that affects our mind-molding institutions—even in the highest offices of the land—is made on the basis of a secularized world-view. This factor, more than anything else, is the vantage point behind the emotionally charged debates that are at the forefront of Western life and, to varying degrees, of life in other parts of the world as well.

What does secularization really mean? With a touch of humor and an edge of sarcasm, the following lines summarize this new reigning world-view.

> First dentistry was painless.
> Then bicycles were chainless,
> Carriages were horseless,
> And many laws enforceless.
> Next cookery was fireless,
> Telegraphy was wireless,
> Cigars were nicotineless,
> And coffee caffeineless.
> Soon oranges were seedless,
> The putting green was weedless,
> The college boy was hatless,
> The proper diet fatless.
> New motor roads are dustless,
> The latest steel is rustless,
> Our tennis courts are sodless,
> Our new religion—godless.[1]

A secular world-view is admittedly and designedly the underlying impetus that presently propels Western culture. As the poem artfully reminds us, secularization assumes that this world—the material world—is all we have. To uncover and explain how this came about is a historian's challenge and a sociologist's occupation. The hard reality is that secularism is the philosophy of choice for American intellectual and political life. Any view that affirms the supernatural is, by definition, considered irrelevant or irrational. Secularism, or "saeculum," is implicitly "this worldly."

Peter Berger, the renowned sociologist and director of the Institute for the Study of Economic Culture at Boston University, defines secularization as "the process by which sectors of society and culture are removed from the domination of religious institutions and symbols." He expands on this in the following way:

> When we speak of society and institutions in modern western history, of course, secularization manifests itself in the evacuation by the Christian churches of areas previously under their control or influence as in the separation of Church and State   or in the emancipation of education from ecclesiastical authority. When we speak of culture and symbols, however, we imply that secularization is more than a social-structural process. It affects the totality of cultural life and of ideation, and may be observed in the decline of religious content in the arts, in philosophy, in literature and, most important of all, in the rise of science as an autonomous, thoroughly secular perspective on the world.[2]

Berger's choice of words is very interesting indeed, and the wide range that his lines encompass is of enormous importance. "The evacuation of the church" speaks of a fleeing body while "the emancipation of education" describes the liberation of the enshackled mind. All of the images stirred up are emotionally charged and are alluring as a study in themselves. Simply stated, secularism asserts that public life is to be conducted without reference to religion or to any notion of transcendence. This mood, as innocent and even as attractive as it seems in our modern day, has become the first step on the road to unmanageable evil. We will see that mood clearly as the idea is expounded. So let us get to the root of it, for here evil makes its entry through an innocent theory that moves so wrongheadedly.

GENTLE WORDS, HARSH REALITIES

Social analyst Os Guinness defines secularization as "the process by which religious ideas, institutions, and interpretations have lost their social significance." Herein lies both the heart and the will of the issue as crafted by the protagonists of secularism. Religious ideas have been knocked senseless in the social arena by the gladiators of the intellect. This is indeed stronger language than terms like *evacuation*. For some of the more aggressive secularists, the public humiliation and eradication of all religious belief would even be the goal. In the marketplace of ideas secularization claims to operate like free enterprise, with all points of view, even religious ones, vying equally for acceptance. In reality, however, religion has been systematically eliminated from public policy debates by an entrenched, highly secularized information elite.

The contention being made here—that this is not a mild-mannered drawing of the lines but, more accurately, a hostile takeover—is not even slightly overstated. Those who have carefully looked at our moral struggles universally acknowledge this philosophical attack upon the moorings of contemporary society. One has only to read the polemical overtones in the writings of Stephen J. Gould of Harvard, Richard Dawkins of Oxford, Carl Sagan of Cornell, and Eric T. Pengelley of the University of California at Davis to understand that the ridicule of a theistic framework is unblushingly overt. The success of secularization in keeping religious convictions out of the public arena is touted in vengeful terms. Science has vanquished theology. Reason has embarrassed faith.

As a test of this thesis, imagine with me the following scenario. A volatile moral issue that divides the nation is being discussed on prime-time television by a panel of experts. The panel is comprised of an educator, a philosopher, a civil libertarian, a politician, a lawyer, a journalist, and a minister. Who would be considered by the listening audience to be the most biased or "irrelevant" on the subject and therefore the least credible? Without a doubt, it would be the minister.

As much as one would seek to be conciliatory and work around this unfair bias, it is foolish to deny its existence. In academia, and even more so in the media, anyone in ministry today is more often than not ridiculed. To speak from a Christian perspective is frequently to become a target for abuse and hostility. The title "Reverend," especially if borne by a conservative, denotes anything but scholarship. Secularists, on the other hand, are assumed to be either well informed or transcendingly objective or both. They supposedly have no hidden agendas, no ulterior motive of making society conform to their repressive views. It is the religious who are bigoted and prejudiced and seek to crush the culture under their tyrannical heels.

When religious ideas are discussed, they are most often depicted as oppressive or antiquated. Seven decades after the Scopes trial, religionists who took part in that event are still the butt of the rationalists' ridicule. Those who believe in God as the author of the universe are dismissed as intellectual dinosaurs who have outlived their usefulness and ought graciously to cease to exist. They often find themselves the objects of witch hunts that seek to destroy belief in the sacred and portray religious belief as unwelcome and prejudicial. "Let us show God-talk for what it is," these militant secularists say, "full of ignorance and repression, signifying hate and intolerance." Not surprisingly, therefore, students entering college are very guarded about their religious beliefs for fear of being outcasts in the world of learning.

HOW DID WE GET HERE?

This is a radical inversion, is it not? Once it was the church that blazed new trails in education. Once the halls of learning were founded by religious leaders. Now, in a strange twist, secular powers charge that it is religious exploitation that has brought about our present situation; therefore it is payback time.

How this state of affairs came to be is important to understand. Let us look at it in two stages. We will first trace the evolution of secularism from being merely a voice among many vying for allegiance to becoming the reigning mind-set with the power to grant or ban the admissibility of all other views. In the second stage we will fully consider the ultimate destination of secularization in its logical outworking. The latter is felt by us in practical terms while the former—the analysis of the antecedents of the secularist mood—is unwittingly ignored as purely academic. To be fair and accurate, both aspects are important if one is to examine the subject and counter the situation with intelligence. The causes and results are with us today. To fully understand our situation and to appreciate the strengths and weaknesses of the secular perspective, we must examine both sides of the issue. Much may be learned from this social theory.

Our focus in this instance will be the secularization of America, because we see within this nation one of the high points of Western culture and the self-destructive downside that results if a secularized world-view becomes sovereign in matters of moral direction. We must come to grips with that ultimate end. It will not do to talk of evil as a result while ignoring its brain trust, the cause. Reality does not play mind games. What is more, if the mind is anesthetized in order to abort what comes to birth when wrong ideas are conceived in the womb of culture, the very life-giving force of the nation that nurtures that idea will die as well. When life is lost it does little good to cry out, "I think I've killed her!"

Three

The High Noon
of Promise

HOW DID the present American attitudes take form? Sociologists are careful to point out that the answer to that question will vary depending on one's philosophical starting point. If one thinks our contemporary cultural shift is all for the good, then the answer is arguably more pragmatic. If, on the other hand, the present is portrayed as all bad, then the answer is more philosophical. The truth is somewhere in the middle. For our purposes, therefore, we must approach this important subject of why we think the way we do on so many life-defining issues from at least three points of entry—the philosophical, the sociological, and most importantly, from the spiritual dimension. From these vantage points the pragmatic can be better understood.

Spanish scholar Julian Marias, who profoundly understood America even in its modern manifestations, once said:

> The United States is one of the great creations of history, like Rome or the Spanish Empire, realities which we enthusiastically study and understand today. . . . And the United States is being created before our very eyes, at an accelerated rate that allows us to observe it within our

lifetime, or even in less than a lifetime. . . . Is this not an intellectually exciting spectacle? Has there been a greater social and historical experiment available for man's contemplation in many centuries?[1]

He is right. How great and how exhilarating are the ideas embodied in this nation called the United States of America. Whatever else may be said of it, it is truly one of the most notable creations of history, born out of the amalgam of an enriching diversity. That is why millions come here to make it their home, aware, nonetheless, of its flaws and weaknesses. It is a dream in the eyes of the world's oppressed, and it was a dream in the making for its founding fathers. What, in the enfleshing of its vision, one may ask, was America "created" for? What provides this "intellectually exciting spectacle"?

The late Russell Kirk, the much-respected scholar, answered this question after years of research. As he brought his lengthy and well-argued case to an end in the closing pages of his book *The Roots of American Order*, he drew heavily from a lesser known American author, Orestes Brownson. (It should be added that Brownson's critically acclaimed book *The American Republic*, alongside his other writings, caused Lord Acton to remark that Brownson was probably the most penetrating American thinker of his day. That is a remarkable compliment, bearing in mind that he was a contemporary of writers like Melville, Emerson, and Hawthorne.) Blending his thoughts with those of Brownson, Kirk said:

> The United States was not brought into being to accomplish the work of socialism. For every living nation, Brownson wrote in *The American Republic*, "has an idea given it by providence to realize, and whose realization is its special work, mission, or destiny." The Jews were chosen to preserve traditions, and so that Messiah might arise; the Greeks were chosen for the realizing of art, science, and philosophy; the Romans were chosen for the developing of the state, law, and jurisprudence. And the Americans, too, have been appointed to a providential mission, continu-

ing the work of Greece and Rome, but accomplishing yet more. *The American Republic is to reconcile liberty with law.*[2]

Some will take issue with Kirk's invocation of a transcendent destiny assigned to America, implied by his words "appointed" and "chosen." However, the idea of a national "higher call" is not unique to the United States but has often been expressed by those from other nations. William Blake, for example, in his Romantic notions for England's destiny, said:

> And did those feet in ancient time
> Walk upon England's mountains green:
> And was the holy Lamb of God
> On England's pleasant pastures seen!
>
> I will not cease from Mental Flight,
> Nor shall my Sword sleep in my hand:
> Till we have built Jerusalem
> In England's green and pleasant Land.[3]

Mystics, or even visionaries, may be pardoned for invoking divine national purpose, because in a real sense nationhood needs its beacons and its paths to impart a sense of mission to its people. For America, in particular, her quest is poignantly defined in the noble but difficult pursuit of reconciling liberty with law. "Confirm thy soul with self-control, thy liberty with law" was not just poetic license. It was the vision. It was the dream. It was the central idea. It is not an accident of American history, therefore, that to this very day the nation is embroiled in debates over rights of privacy versus legislative authority. Morality, freedom, self-determination, happiness, sexuality, and security are all personal in their application. But nationally, they impinge upon the legislative role of government as it makes liberties possible for the protection of each and the benefit of all.

VISIONS OF POWER

The seemingly insurmountable struggle to reconcile liberty with law generated volumes of literature from eighteenth-century thinkers, whose writings provided the intellectual resource that positioned the individual as the peerless sovereign in the universal landscape. Their estimate of humanity's reasoning capacity formed the basis for their confident predictions of the future. But their hope that the light of reason could resolve every divisive issue was disappointed, for revolutions of a different nature were lurking in the shadows of the future for which reason alone would not be sufficient.

If the eighteenth century can be pictured as the intellectual looking in the mirror and becoming entranced by his or her own reflection like Narcissus of old, the nineteenth century by its end can be portrayed as one looking toward the horizon and being wooed by the mirage of the pragmatist. The encouraging smile of pragmatism—the philosophy of doing whatever works—beguiled many into opting for a world-view that in the long run simply doesn't work. The eighteenth century brought a confidence that exalted "rational man." The nineteenth century sounded the buzz and hum of machines that announced the arrival of "technical man." How could this combination of enlightened humanity and technical humanity have produced anything but the enfleshing of the age-old dream of utopia?

In retrospect, one would have thought that the bloodletting occasioned by the Indian mutiny in its revolt against the British (1857–1858), and India's attempt to shake off Western power, and the terrifying toll of the American Civil War (1861–1865), a raging conflict within a Western power, would have blunted the utopian hopes of the West. The reasonable response would have been to rethink humanity's self-confidence and narcissistic self-worship and to admit that the mind untamed by decency would imperil the process of law seeking to inform liberty. But the tug and attraction of the cerebral capacity with its inventive power overrode any philosophical caution that called for an examination of the person behind the machine. With blatant self-deception the assumption was made that mankind could be trusted with any instrument. Technological genius introduced an array of implements on civilization's field of dreams for the new games that would keep the imagination limitlessly entertained.

Undaunted, therefore, by the human toll in death and destruction that spelled caution, the Western dream was most dramatically expressed in the Great Exhibition of 1851. This exposition, for which the historic Crystal Palace was built in London, presaged the scientific triumphs that would define the march of the West into the future.

Hailing this occasion, the *Edinburgh Review* declared the accumulation of inventive genius under one roof as mankind's opportune moment: "to seize the living scroll of human progress, inscribed with every successive conquest of man's intellect." Historian John Warwick Montgomery insightfully draws attention to the most representative exhibit in the Crystal Palace, the model of a train that laid its own track. This curiosity symbolized the then existent mind-set, not just scientifically but philosophically, as mankind was on the move with built-in durability. In a very real sense a new road was being built to redefine the destination. This would be the classic "City of Man":

The train that laid its own track can be regarded as the arch-symbol of the 19th century mind: the horizontal equivalent of pulling oneself to heaven by one's own bootstraps. For a train to have any advantage over an ordinary conveyance, its tracks must be so firmly anchored— independent of the train—that the train can build up great speed while safely relying on their stability. A train that lays its own track and takes it up again would have no superiority over a vehicle not running on tracks at all, for its tracks would be no more solidly anchored than the train itself. This was the 19th century: trying to lay its own tracks through technological inventiveness, achieving only pseudo-stability, and blind to the crash that will inevitably destroy all individual and societal engineers who refuse to let Christ provide a stable track for their lives.[4]

The self-contained train was the metaphor of self-sufficient man. The built-in capacity of power and provision, of overpowering and undergirding, was the envisioned reality ahead. From that day to this, pragmatism has been the handmaiden of secularized living: "We can do it."

IDEAS OF CHANGE

While technology was blazing the trail for humanity with tools for the future, Charles Darwin was unveiling humanity's primordial past. Science, in fact, was elbowing its way into becoming the sole interpreter of the past and the sufficient hope for the future. As confidence in humanity's creative capacity was increasing, confidence in God's creative power was diminishing. In keeping with the metaphysical mood, therefore, Marxism, avowedly atheistic and politically repressive, was spawned at this time, dehumanizing millions in its wake. Paradoxically, while espousing atheism, Karl Marx in small measure understood the human capacity for a destructive self-centeredness. He worked furiously, therefore, to ensure that the worker not be lost in the whirlwind of technological gains. His ideology called for the employer and the employee to march together to their classless society. How pathetic was his utopian zeal, for it instead provided the philosophical womb that birthed some of history's most dastardly crimes.

The change in the cultural landscape was patently clear. The human mind was becoming the factory of cultural retooling, gaining its impetus from scientific theory, which worked itself into political theory and finally into our value systems. It was only a matter of time before social engineers would demand a rebuilding of the philosophical framework underlying national morality. Amid the victorious cheers of the new horizons within humanity's reach, the voice of God and the way of Christ were summarily discarded. The bright lights on the outside ignored the disfigurement and indeed, the darkening within. The tracks of technology prepared the way for the engines of reason and the shunting of the spirit. Destined for the secular city, those along for the ride courted the intellect while ignoring the longings of the heart. That mistake is deadly: Any cultural imperative that obstinately refuses to understand the human heart lives with an irrationality that breeds the monstrosities we have witnessed in this century.

This "seizing the living scroll of human progress," as the *Edinburgh Review* described it, locked step with the conquering march of science and left its mark on the American mind. Secularism as a sociopolitical theory—this worldliness—was taking shape, born from the fusion of brain and machine with disregard for the soul.

But this, interestingly enough, is only the recent past. Technological capacity was not the sole progenitor of the American mind. One can readily understand how and why such enthusiasm could take hold of human imagination. Inventive and pragmatic genius are recent attainments and accomplishments that can induce a sense of creative self-sufficiency. But for the West there had been a more distant past that should have tempered that philosophical hope. There were traits in her character and knowledge that harked back to a people who also had envisioned a glorious future. An understanding of that imprint provides an even more fascinating tale and reveals the grandeur and vulnerability of human intellect in its progressivistic march.

CONCEPTS OF OLD

Even prior to the great scientific accomplishments that have led to the present, the philosophical ideas that made these creations possible had already been imparted into America's national character. This is of extraordinary importance to note, because the mind-set that existed in the formative years of this nation provided the soil to nurture the ideas that, in turn, made modern technology possible. But if the mind-set that led to our discoveries has since changed drastically, then those very advancements that now provide our strengths become liabilities and can destroy their "creators," becoming in their hands the deadliest instruments of evil. The *soil* of the Western mind into which the seeds of scientific gains were sown made what was previously only a possibility an actuality for this generation. But now, secularism dangerously flirts with contaminating the moral soil that had helped sprout her gains. It is pivotal, therefore, for those of us who are the inheritors of this new world to come to terms with the "ancestral" traits that fathered this nation and to examine the soil that nurtured those ideas.

Kirk brings a wealth of fascinating information to bear on this discussion, arguing that there are at least four cities, or cultures, that have left their indelible marks upon the Western world in general and upon America in particular. The American mind, he rightly says, has resulted from the confluence of Athens, Rome, Jerusalem, and London.

The Greeks have given to us our philosophical categories; the Romans have given to us much in our legal categories; the Hebrews have provided a base for our moral categories; and the English have given us our very language and the principles of representative government. (One may add to England's bequest architecture, institutes of learning, and a wealth of other strengths.) Many who ignore this heritage do so, not so much out of willfulness, as from a chronic disinterest in history. A knowledge and appreciation of history is difficult for a culture so enthralled by the moment, a culture that shuns the discipline of a larger context in any study. Unfortunately this loss of historical interest has made the present difficult to address because the context of the past is imperative if we are to salvage the future.

I remember sitting next to a young man at the fiftieth anniversary celebration of a church. After enduring about fifteen minutes of "I remember when" speeches, he turned to me and muttered, "I hate all this nostalgia stuff." I paused and then whispered, "The only thing worse than nostalgia is amnesia."

The story is told of a Western diplomat a few years ago who found himself seated next to Chinese premier Chou Enlai. Unable to make much conversation with this disconcertingly quiet state leader, he finally said to Premier Chou, "What do you think of the French Revolution?" Chou paused for what seemed an interminable silence and then said, "It's too soon to tell." Such, I fear, is the diametric difference in perspective; the East finds a two-hundred-year span too short while the West finds fifty years too distant. How easy is it, then, for the modern reader to care for cultures of two millennia ago and recognize how definitive such a study can be for us? But the information gleaned can actually be stirring to the soul if it is studied well.

For the sake of a little self-knowledge, which is indispensable, let us take a cursory look at just one of the cultures that molded our early soul. Even a brief glance yields a challenging lesson. In Greece we may well see our own reflection. But while recognizing the classic grandeur of its legitimate glory, we must resist the temptation to be enamored too long by the image. For it was a glory that was ultimately dissipated by a colossal spiritual blind spot.

INFLUENCES THAT SHAPED US

"It's all Greek to me" is our common way of saying something is incomprehensible. Yet, if we look carefully at the roots of common English words, we will see how much we have gained from the Greeks, even in our conceptual framework. We speak of an elaborate argument, rich in words but impoverished in ideas, as mere *sophistry*—an ostentatious verbal display intended to impress and deceive. This comes from the Greek philosophers, the Sophists, who were known for their skill in argumentation that employed a fallacious use of logic.

Or, we speak today of *agoraphobia*, a fear of open spaces, which originates in a reference to the Greek open-air markets, called the Agora. We might talk of being *stoical* in the face of tragedy, meaning a grim endurance without emotional display. The Stoic philosophers held that wisdom lay in rising above passion and in unperturbed submission to the divine will.

Much has been written on the legendary splendor of Greece, and indeed the West owes an unpayable debt to this great civilization and culture that in its halcyon days knew tremendous glory, a glory that continues to inspire even through its ruins. Lord Byron eulogized her, "Fair Greece! Sad relic of departed worth! Immortal, though no more; though fallen, great!" Milton acclaimed Athens "the eye of Greece, mother of arts and eloquence." Johann Goethe extolled, "Of all the peoples the Greeks have dreamt the dreams of life best." Percy Bysshe Shelley lyricized, "'Let there be light!' said Liberty, and like the sunrise from the sea, Athens arose!" Dionysius Solomos, the nineteenth-century thinker, intoned, "Enclose in your soul Greece . . . and you shall feel every kind of grandeur." Modern historian Edith Hamilton surmised, "They [the Greeks] were the first westerners; the Spirit of the West, the modern spirit, is a Greek discovery, and the place of the Greeks is in the modern world." And Sir Henry Maine wrote in 1876, "Except the blind forces of nature, nothing moves in this world which is not Greek in its origin."

The Greeks came very close to conquering the whole world. But if their own writers of antiquity had penned the story of Greece, they might well have portrayed her glory and demise in microcosm through the person of Alexander the Great. It was said that even if he had conquered the world he would still not have attained contentment, for he was his own worst rival. A daring general in military warfare and a student of Aristotle, he made great gains in his attempt to unify the world under Greek thought, though he was not able to find unity in his own life.

And that represents the ultimate Greek tragedy. Today the fallen stones of its once legendary cities tell the tale of a former splendor; in reality the "great age" of Athens lasted less than fifty years.

While the Greek experience in politics and government was known and studied by many of America's founding fathers, it was more in the arts and philosophy that Greece was to leave its mark on America. The names of Socrates, Plato, and Aristotle are familiar to modern university students. Their concepts of virtue, Plato's *Republic*, Aristotle's *Ethics*, and Socratic maxims are woven into an understanding of Western philosophy.

But it is here that our attention ought to be really piqued, because in the American experience there was both a borrowing and a refusing of Greek culture. For example, the Greek concept of the Academy and her systematization of knowledge has helped to shape the study of the major disciplines in America. Ideas that originated in Greece were sifted via Rome through European medieval culture and carried from there into America. In fact, even predating that, so much of Hellenic thought had entered the world of New Testament times that the apostle Paul singularly addressed those issues in the Scriptures. Paul's teaching on the soul, on sin, and on the afterlife was done in such terminology that the Greeks would be hard-pressed to miss both the relevance of the Christian message to Greek thought as well as its contradistinction. Augustine's *The City of God* can never be fully appreciated without an understanding of Platonic teaching. The medieval church was heavily instructed in the works of Aristotle.

THE RELATIVISM THAT KILLED

But it is here that we must pause and ask why this glory was so short-lived. What brought about the ultimate ruin of this, the mother of the arts and invention? These questions have much to say to America in her struggle with wickedness today.

It was the Sophists who popularized Protagoras's phrase "Man is the measure of all things" and translated it to mean that individuals are not responsible to any transcendent moral authority for their actions. Aristotle had taught that the three principal reasons for knowledge were Truth, Morality, and Technique (technology), in that order—what is true, how to live, and the instrumental use that this knowledge could serve. The warning from philosophy is powerful. Kirk forthrightly describes the death knell that sounded the demise of this great nation.

> It was the clear relativism of the Sophists, not the mystical insights of Plato, nor Aristotle's aspiration after the Supreme Good, which dominated the thinking of the classical Greeks in their decadence. The failure of the Greeks to find an enduring popular religious sanction for the order of civilization had been a main cause of the collapse of the world of the polis.[5]

This may be the most important sociophilosophic pronouncement for America to learn. Even though scholars tire of hearing it, the truth of Alexis de Tocqueville's statement is hard to ignore. The famed French thinker repeatedly said it was America's religious bond, which was stronger than that of either Rome or Greece, that held her together.

Perhaps a very simple but poignant legend told of Alexander the Great illustrates the point. It is said that when he was dying at Babylon, Alexander crawled out of his tent on all fours at midnight, intending to drown himself in the Euphrates River. He hoped his body would be lost and that men would then believe that he was, in truth, immortal. But his attempt failed. His wife brought him back to die in his bed, and posterity would laugh at that attempt by one who conquered the world but lived under such a self-deluding and farcical notion.

Alexander could not accept his human limitations, and as he toyed with playing god he was dragged back to his chambers to die as a man, out of control. The Greeks had long believed that the very concept of human excellence could be pursued only if man's purpose was first known. Purpose and performance had to be tied together. But purpose had been lost, and technique and pleasure had replaced truth and morality. The pragmatic plague of "how to build" became more important than "how to be." Under the debris of the pillars and the stones is not just the story of a civilization destroyed by internecine wars but of a people who would not acknowledge the wretchedness and evil pent up within the human heart and the absolute necessity that man find a measure outside of himself. It was not long before preoccupation with a perfect body overtook the warning cry of an imperfect heart and soul.

America's scientists and artists need only to look back at Greece to realize what happens when technological genius and unbridled imagination become ends in themselves. Artistic liberty multiplied by technological capacity produces a modern-day Greece fashioned with American ingenuity. The old America had the mind to sift through these strengths and harness them. The new America finds itself without a point of reference. An extremely vocal and domineering influence in our culture, the arts are now energized with distributive power for global impact. On the part of some, art itself has become just a euphemism for deviance and discord, creating alternate realities in its path and perverting the popular imagination as it runs roughshod over every virtue. Purpose and performance have been severed, and performance is now judged in the free-fall zone of artistic vacuum, totally unsecured by the safety net of human essence. The cultural train that is laying its own tracks is derailing an entire nation, and the screams of the victims of the resulting evil call out for help.

THE DEFINITIVE DIFFERENCE

In its early days, though philosophically indebted to Greece, America also had a fundamental ideational difference. Greece's noblest philosophers merely nudged us in the direction of an ultimate mind to which we must look. But America did not stop there, for she knew what the autonomous heart could engender and what it needed from God Himself. The first line ever printed in North America was in the *New England Primer*, and it read, "In Adam's fall we sinned all." That man had fallen was at least given popular consent, some credence. The human heart was deemed to be in need of instruction in moral uprightness. There needed to be a renewing of the mind.

Today, however, such sentiment has been angrily and mockingly denounced in academia; laden down by our technology, we crawl to our halls of fame like Alexander, desperately wanting the world to believe that we, too, are immortal. How revealing it is that in the bloodiest century of history we deny human depravity. The relativism of ancient Greece has worked its way into modern America, though the Greek philosophers themselves, even in their day, warned that relativism would be suicidal. To her credit, early America knew that this was not merely a philosophical problem, as real as that was. This was a problem of the soul, and the heart of humanity was in need of redemption.

Today we have gone backward. We deny both the spiritual and the philosophical. And our end result will be the same as ancient Greece. The imprint of Greece is upon us and upon the new soil of American secularism. It is said of Greece that it is not that the people were abandoned by their gods because they had become so wicked but that they abandoned their gods because their gods had become too wicked. In our time, the gods of relativism who shape our ideas may well be in the same mold and worthy of abandonment if we are to avert the debacle that overtook the Greek soul.

A brief look at the philosophical influence of Greece clearly reveals at least one component of American culture. But even here, early America knew both her legitimate heritage and what she would not borrow. Centuries have passed, and as America has grown and waxed strong, the belief that was once rejected—that man is the measure of all things—is now espoused. The conviction that was once held—the fallen nature of men—is now rejected. And in every sense of the term, a major conflict for cultural control has begun to emerge. On the one hand there is the cry for liberty from the superintendency of law over private practice. On the other hand the same voices call upon the law to ban the assumptions of the Christian truths of the fall of man and of mankind's redemption. And the Christian, bewildered by this dramatic turn, sees the darkening horizon because of the encroaching deformity within the cultural soul. The call of the Supreme Artist, who created all things beautiful, is being mocked. Secularism has grabbed its philosophical knife to silence the Artist in the public square. But the memory of where the nation first began still haunts, and the evil being evidenced is painful. The heart and mind cry out in prayer.

> O God of earth and altar, bow down and hear our cry,
> Our earthly rulers falter, our people drift and die;
> The walls of gold entomb us, the swords of scorn divide,
> Take not thy thunder from us, but take away our pride.
> From all that terror teaches, from lies of tongue and pen,
> From all the easy speeches that comfort cruel men,
> From sale and profanation of honor and the sword,
> From sleep and from damnation, deliver us, good Lord.
> Tie in a living tether the prince and priest and thrall,
> Bind all our lives together, smite us and save us all;
> In ire and exultation, aflame with faith and free,
> Lift up a living nation, a single sword to thee.[6]

THE VISION IMPERILED

The despairing words of the poet Wordsworth as he saw England on the same slippery slope will translate well onto the American scene:

Milton! Thou shouldest be living at this hour.
England hath need of thee: She is a fen
Of stagnant waters: Altar, sword and pen,
Fireside, the heroic wealth of hall and bower
Have forfeited their ancient English dower
Of inward happiness. We are selfish men;
Oh! raise up. Return to us again;
And give us manners, virtue, freedom, power.[7]

As stated earlier, it has been common in history for nations to see themselves as a context in which the cities of men do battle with the City of God. And in that sense the conflict between *soulcraft* and *statecraft*[8] is not new. Keats has said the world is a "vale of soul-making." But in America it has reached unprecedented proportions because the whole drift into secularization has, by virtue of modern capacity, touched every area of life, from womb to tomb.

There are no signs of letup, and the philosophy now undergirding the interpretation of law implicitly denies the soul. The destiny-defining consequences have moved from a philosophical theory to a social reality from which we seek deliverance. It is that sociological understanding of the road to the present that next occupies our attention.

Four

The Storms of Conflict

STORIES HAVE a way of making the rounds, especially if they have a good punch line. One such story told and retold in India describes a rich man who sought to buy up an entire village. The man walked from house to house, offering a disproportionately large sum of money to each householder in exchange for his property. Delighted at the prospect of such a large profit, all readily entered into the sale except for one determined old man who owned a small shack right in the center of the village. No sum of money would change his mind, and he responded to each increment offered with the calm rejoinder, "I'm not interested in selling."

Frustrated, the rich man finally had to be content to buy the whole village except for this tiny piece of real estate in the middle. The old man relished his symbolic victory. Every time the rich man had a visitor in the village, the old man stepped out of his little hut and, wagging his bony finger, tauntingly declared, "If he tells you he owns this whole village, don't believe him; this part right here in the middle still belongs to me."

There is a sad, yet striking similarity in this story to the church and her solace when conceding the cultural dominance of secularism over what was once religious terrain. The analogy is even heightened, for the transference of dominion has not been just of land but also of ideas. Retreating from the world, many Christians seek cover inside their church buildings, wagging their fingers at the "secular owner-ship" of the social landscape and receiving petty satisfaction in saying, "This little part still belongs to us." This is the way the dust has settled after the storms of conflict and the winds of change have raged over which central ideas should govern our culture.

BETRAYING A TRUST

Certain differences surface from a study of the changing moods to-ward the Christian faith in Western countries where there has always been freedom to proclaim the gospel. But there are also some strik-ing similarities. The directional shift away from Christianity was set in motion in the eighteenth and nineteenth centuries as the process of secularization was unmistakably under way. The storms of moral and cultural controversy that have raged in the twentieth century, tearing away at the core of Western culture, find their progenitors in these earlier eras.

There is no dearth of analysis in the scholarly world to attempt an explanation of the whys and hows of these social changes. Any debate that arises lies in the allocation and degree of responsibility attributed to the various carriers of such changes. The world was changing not just in capacity but in speed, and shifts were under way in every arena.

Canadian historian David Marshall lists the conditions that gradu-ally made the social climate in Canada inhospitable to the Christian message. These conditioning influences are not restricted to Canada alone. They are true for much of the West. The increase in scientific knowledge and the philosophy that was smuggled in with it, the shifting focus of intellectual life in its "this worldly" expertise, the rise of a consumer culture, the emergence of an urban industrial society, and the struggle of the church to cope with a rapidly changing world—all of these factors energized a world moving at high speed.

With such multidimensional agents of change it would be presumptuous to single out one exclusive cause that altered the mind of a whole society. But Marshall does take a bold step to point the finger. His conclusion may come as a surprise to the Christian who has left this subject unstudied. A vision of the prophet Nathan standing before King David and saying, "You are the man!" certainly comes to mind when we encounter Marshall's daring charge. Alarmingly, it may also be justifiable.

Marshall lays a major portion of the blame for the slide into secularism at the door of the Christian clergy. It was from their ranks, he says, that the defection began. From their ranks came the call to congregations to abandon the notion of an authoritative Scripture and surrender the biblical perspective on life's deepest questions. This was the explosive force that would demolish any claim to Christian uniqueness.

The point that Marshall makes is too vital to hastily bypass. It is of paramount importance to note that intellectuals across history have played key roles in the uprooting of one idea and the planting of another. The establishment of new orthodoxies by the intellectual elite and the dismantling of others is not as formidable a task when the desired change propelled by scholars appeals to the common person's autonomy while enthroning the elite at the same time.

The perilous blunder that society so often makes when it surrenders such an empowerment to the few is to assume that intellectuals always arrive at cultural deductions by virtue of open minds and scholarly objectivity. Surprisingly, and often, these groups bring an agenda all their own, and their motivation is anything but pristine. Was it not Aldous Huxley who admitted that he wanted this world to not have meaning so that he was freed to pursue his own erotic and political pursuits? One of the great temptations to intellectuals is to assume that in grabbing the finger of their own discipline they have grabbed the fist of reality. Specializing in one field, some are able to exploit that knowledge to interpret every other discipline as well. Their motives are not value-free. We must beware of the vulnerability of the many to be shaped in their thinking by the few whose narrow expertise becomes life-defining to the mainstream.

Here, then, is the terrible disappointment to Christians. Betrayal came from their own educated ranks as some in leadership succumbed to and even joined forces with skeptics, giving strength to the tentacles of secularism to gradually choke out religious life. Secularizing voices among the clergy berated the conservative authorities in institutions for not giving free vent to those of a liberal stripe. Once that openness was granted and liberals had gained power, those same voices countered with greater bigotry to block out any conservative view. Since then, there has been made, at best, a patronizing provision for the conservative as a marginalized viewpoint.

Marshall's thesis, singling out the clergy, is disheartening and incomprehensible to those who cherish their sacred call to ministry as stewards of the Word of God. But those from within the church who called for a watered-down scriptural authority hailed the capitulation of the Christian message to contrary philosophies as the triumph of reality over religion. Conservative scholars for whom the Scriptures were absolute were left with the staggering task of their defense—a monumental responsibility with limited access.

FORSAKING A CALL

With a sharper thrust but from a different angle, Peter Berger moves beyond the role of the clergy in the secularization of the world to the role of Protestantism as a whole. He concludes that in their preoccupation with "other worldliness" and in their emphasis on redemption as "personal and individual," Protestants unwittingly abandoned the arena of *this world* itself, leaving it a vacated venue. The "New Jerusalem" became the place of focus for them, and *this* world was relinquished to secular causes and activity. In effect, with "angels" no longer in this world, the astronomer and, indeed, the astronaut could now interpret space and time.

Does Berger single out Protestantism for that unique and dubious role in distinction to the rest of Christendom? Yes, he does. In contrast to Catholics, who still retained the mystery, the magic, and the miracle woven into the fabric of the world order, Berger says Protestants stripped the material world to bare matter and separated it totally from the world to come. The winds of irreligion gained momentum, unencumbered by a spiritual presence. The keys of the kingdom had been handed over.

As fascinating and true as these factors may be, there is very little doubt that one major idea or theory was ultimately to become the hatpin in the heart of Christian thought—a hatpin stuck in the heart of Christendom and buttressed by the rear guard of other advancing secular ideas. By the middle of the nineteenth century, what became known as "higher," or "historical criticism"—with roots in Germany— began to gain wider acceptance and do severe damage to scriptural authority. Though acceptable as a discipline, negative higher criticism prejudicially reduced the Bible to mere literature and created doubts about the authorship and authenticity of certain books of the Bible, especially the Gospels. This theory, clearly tendentious by its users, swept through Europe and Great Britain and stormed the institutes of higher learning in North America with equal devastation. Ultimately, it drew the life blood from the church.

The church was already caught in the context of economic, social, and academic change. Now, into that frame of reference the text of Scripture was brought under judgment. Suspect, and positioned as a piece of literature to be dissected and dismembered at the hands of scholars with unhidden pretexts, the Scriptures were well on their way to being dismissed as nothing more than ethnic utopianism punctuated with altruistic pronouncements. By stripping the Bible of divine authorship, liberal scholarship made it just another piece of literature, open to attack and critique. Its definitive roles for faith and conduct were debunked, and its injunctions were de-legitimized. Many who were determined to pursue this agenda dared to remain in the ministry and function within the church, all the while reducing its reason for existence to myth. This was a Copernican revolution within the church, and the signature of God upon the Scriptures was deemed a forgery. It was no longer a God-authored book, but a man-concocted collection.

This was no longer theology—from God to us—but anthropology—about us and our thoughts toward God. In short, the author of the Scriptures was renamed. If Marshall and Berger are even close to being right in their deductions, it is truly lamentable that secularism may have entered into such dominance with the help of the church.

One cannot overstate how important a social factor this was in secularizing Western consciousness. Had there been only the advancement of scientific theorizing and the socioeconomic changes, skeptics would still not have been able to mount a sufficient attack upon so many treasured beliefs. It took this extra step, this dizzying punch delivered from within the church itself, this attack upon the very mind and heart of the Christian message, the Bible, to make possible secularism's total victory.

Accompanying this devastating attack upon the Scriptures came a scramble for power. Inaugural addresses at seminaries and universities became predictable—the conservatives protesting that the Scriptures were being plundered, and the liberals hailing the victory of learning over superstition. Not accidentally, therefore, as the decade of the sixties dawned and the culture began to convulse against authority, *Christian Century* published a poem by Thomas C. Arthur entitled, "Death of Another Salesman."

Sooner or later the preacher
Wakes up to the fact
That he can't save *everybody*.

He may even think
That after all,
There is such a division
As the Elect.

If he goes on thinking
He may come to realize
That the "Elect" are inclined
To agree with him.

If by some chance
He contemplates still further,
He may find
That *some* of the damned
Have a *point*.

Then he may wonder
If *anyone at all* can be saved!
He might even count himself
Among the great mass
of the Lost.

He will then flounder about,
Snatching at slivers of truth.
He may even discover
That he can't swim.[1]

At first blush one may not realize how pitiful such a plunder of the message of Christ is when accomplished at the hands of those to whom it was entrusted. Somehow, a slow bleed and loss of philosophical strength does not seem as real to people as a sudden amputation. One of Christendom's most revered buildings serves as a very painful illustration of how tragic such self-mutilation can be to the cause of Christ when the carriers of such division are within it. I refer to the Church of The Holy Sepulcher as it functions today in the city of Jerusalem. Let me quote the words of the English writer Arthur Leonard Griffith.

> At the center of the old city [Jerusalem] stands the Church of The Holy Sepulcher, reputedly on the sight of the original Calvary and the original Garden of The Resurrection. It stands, but only because ugly steel scaffolding permanently supports the walls inside and out. This church is one of the dirtiest, most depressing buildings in all Christendom. It should be torn dowr and rebuilt. This is not possible, however, because the Church of The Holy Sepulcher belongs jointly to the Abyssinians, Armenians, Copts, Greeks, Syrians and Roman Catholics, and their priests will hardly speak to one another, let alone cooperate in a joint enterprise of rebuilding. Each communion preserves its own separate chapel, and conducts its own ceremonies; and to make the situation ludicrous, the keys of the church have been entrusted to a family of Muslims who in order to answer the call of Allah five times daily, have turned the entrance into a Muslim Mosque. Nowhere in all the world can you find a more tragic symbol of the mutilation of Christ's body than the Church of The Holy Sepulcher in Jerusalem.[2]

The only difference between the Church of The Holy Sepulcher and the self-defacing influence of those who attacked scriptural authority in Western Christendom is that the keys of the kingdom were handed over to secular powers as the voice of God in the Scriptures was silenced by those to whom it was entrusted.

REDEFINING REALITY

Common to the voices of both the liberal clergy and those hostile to Christianity was their view of the supernatural. The shift from the sacred to the secular was undergirded by one fundamental idea that was foisted upon Western culture: The implicit denial of the miraculous or the supernatural to explain human essence or existence. It was clearly acknowledged by all its detractors that the Christian message incorporated many great ideas. But intrinsic to all Christian orthodoxy is the belief that the world did not come about because of natural causes or means. Both in its creation and in its sustenance a supernatural entity is recognized. The entire existence of Israel as a nation, says the Old Testament, is by virtue of God's intervening hand: "I carried you on eagles' wings and brought you to myself. . . . I am the LORD your God, who brought you out of Egypt" (Exod. 19:4; 20:1).

The whole prophetic message pointed to the coming of One who would bring personal and cosmic redemption. In the New Testament, Jesus, who was born of a virgin (a truth believed even by Muslims), punctuated His life and message with the dramatic and instructive use of the miraculous. From the restoration of sight to the blind to the regeneration of the human heart—all was the work of God. Jesus' death on the cross and His resurrection from the dead attested to the authority and purpose for which He had come. The church was instituted as the "bride of Christ" to reflect His splendor and await His return, in the meantime, "occupying" until He came. The Bible is God-breathed, and as such it is the revelation to man of the mind of God and of His absolute standard for our lives.

All of this belief was leveled by the new winds blowing, winds that made "Thus says the Lord" an impossibility. The Bible itself was in question, and the world was reconstituted as a "brand-new creation" assembled by the minds of men riding upon the engines of change, marketed by the genius of consumer demand and licensed by the institutions of the state. As a result, it is no longer only land that is secularized but life itself. Matter is under the spotlight; the soul is systematically disfigured in the attic of existence.

MOCKING THE SACRED

The sequence that followed became predictable. The open mocking of the sacred by the modern critic culminated a long process of desacralizing life itself. First the world was denuded of transcendence, then the Scriptures were rendered irrelevant, and finally humankind was made nothing more than matter. In the name of progress and of supposed sensitivity to other systems of thought, much has been done to bully the Christian believer. The ravages of a diminished view of Scripture have gained even greater momentum, to the point of complete absurdity.

Few instances better illustrate this than one of the recent translations of the Bible. Referring to the Oxford University Press's release of a "culturally sensitive" version of the Bible, the religious editor of *Newsweek* recently quipped that the King James Bible "never looked so good before." These are his poignant comments:

> Readers who find the Bible sexist, racist, elitist and insensitive to the physically challenged, take heart. Oxford University Press's new "inclusive language version" of the New Testament and Psalms has cleaned up God's act. In this version, God is no longer "Father" and Jesus is no longer "Son." The hierarchical title of "Lord" is excised as an archaic way to address God. Nor does God (male pronouns for the deity have been abolished) rule a "kingdom"; as the editors explain, the word has a "blatantly androcentric and patriarchal character." . . . Even God's metaphorical "right hand" has been amputated out of deference to the left-handed. Some examples:
>
> - In the majestic opening of John's Gospel, "the glory he has from the Father as the only Son of the Father" becomes "the glory as of a parent's only child." (John 1:14)
> - The Lord's prayer now begins like this: "Father-Mother, hallowed be your name. May your dominion come." (Luke 11:2)
> - Jesus's own self-understanding as God's only son is generalized to: "No one knows the Child except the Father-Mother; and no one knows the Father-Mother except the Child . . ." (Matthew 11:27)
> - Avoiding another traditional phrase, "Son of Man," the Oxford text reads: "Then they will see 'the Human One' coming in clouds with great power and glory." (Mark 13:26)

The editors do not claim that Jesus spoke in gender-neutral language. But they obviously think he should have. The changes they have made are not merely cosmetic. They represent a fundamental reinterpretation of what the New Testament says—and how it says it. The King James Bible never looked so good.[3]

Truly noteworthy about such blatant ridicule is that it seems reserved only for the Christian. One is tempted to ask whether Oxford University Press would have dared to tamper with or so implicitly demean the Koran in this way. This single-minded attack on Christianity in the name of relevance underscores secularism's primary target. This translation has been done supposedly to achieve relevance—in principle, such an effort shows no more respect for the relevance of the Scriptures than it does for the claims of the Scriptures. No, such relentless attack upon anything that has to do with the supernatural is the imprint of secularist dogmatism.[4] To the secularist, the Bible cannot be the Word of God, for to grant even that theoretical possibility would be an admission of the supernatural. That concession by the postmodern person sold out to a naturalistic view of reality would be tantamount to the surrender of his or her world-view of a voiceless universe.

If this were all that secularism demonstrated we could accept it as a process that began two centuries ago and has now led to our social theory. But if the goal at the inception of America was to reconcile liberty with law, then we have reached a devastating contradiction. For law cannot merely serve as a random set of rules without any objective point of reference. And for law to be effective it is equally necessary that a reaction to its violation must go beyond an objective framework to a felt subjective response within the individual to whom the law is making its appeal. In other words, it is not sufficient just to have a law "out there" for people to obey. There must be an inner urge, or hunger, to keep and honor that law because it is good. Secularism cannot accomplish this in the hearts and minds of people, because the mind it has created is a pragmatic one, and pragmatism will always find ways to circumvent and misuse the law rather than to revere it.

Secularism criminally fails to measure up even theoretically to the purpose for which the nation was founded. It has done away with a moral law and destroyed the sensitivity of an individual toward honoring that law. The evil we now witness is from the ash heap of destroyed sensitivities. How that desensitization was accomplished we will further uncover. But this we know: Law and liberty can never be reconciled when external and internal constraints are arbitrary. How drastic that failure is, for it leads to the incredible eradication of one of society's greatest needs, which we will now address. This is a failure no nation can afford.

Five

The Twilight of Decency

A VILLAGE MAN was making his first visit to a big city. As he came closer to the teeming metropolis he was quite overwhelmed by the cars he saw moving past him at high speeds. Never having seen a car before, he scratched his head in puzzlement, wondering what made them run and wishing he had one of his own. How much better life would be if one could move at such speed, he thought.

Just at that moment, he noticed a car sputtering and fuming and jerking as it came to a stop. He observed the driver walk away and come back several moments later with a can in his hand. His curiosity piqued, he watched intently as the driver poured something from the can into the opening on the side of the car. Promptly thereafter, the car started again and sped on its way.

As the car disappeared he suddenly spied the tin can the driver had used, lying on the side of the road. With sheer delight he picked it up and let out a triumphant shout, "Now all I need is the thing that moves."

If the poor man wagging his finger at the rich landowner and saying, "This part still belongs to me," represents the beleaguered Christian in a secularized culture, the villager holding the empty gasoline can in the belief that all he needs now is the car represents the half-baked theory of secularism. It just does not work.

Secularism is a social theory holding the tin can of technology. The engine of civility is still eluding it. The question clearly has to be raised: If the supernatural is irrational, what will the secularist use as a point of reference for rationality? Who does one call upon for guidance in life's choices? Whose voice shall we hear on these issues, or is each one to depend on his or her own inner voice?

THE STRIPTEASE OF SECULARISM

After the wind and after the earthquake there came to the prophet Elijah living in the ninth century before the birth of Christ the comfort and direction of the still, small voice. In our current storm of controversy the silence is terrifying. There is no longer any voice, no more revelation "from above." Not only has secularization brought us a silent universe with no voice from without, it has also brought us a silence from within as it has redefined the whole role of conscience. It has removed any possibility of an objective supernatural revelation and supplanted it with the so-called inner voice of reason. It was only a matter of time before there would be no way to differentiate between the inner voice of reason and the inner promptings of unreason. Let me sustain this argument, because now we will see not merely the theoretical incoherence of secularism and its primary carriers; we will see that it leads to a pragmatism that is unworkable and an evil that is devastating.

As I have previously stated, implicit to the secularized world-view is not just the marginalization of any religious idea but its complete eviction from public credence in informing social policy. If an idea or a belief is "religiously based," be it in a matter of sexuality or marriage or education or whatever, then by that very virtue it is deemed unsuitable for public usage.

A definitive example of this public expulsion of religious ideas can be seen from two historic incidents in the city of Toronto, Canada. In the 1880s the mayor of that city was William Howland. Howland's platform, as he campaigned for office, was one of concern for the city's moral degeneration. He pledged to work toward making it a decent city and ridding it of some of the public vices and trades that victimized its people. His bid was successful, and he left as his legacy the still-used qualifier to the city of Toronto, "Toronto the Good."

Ironically, nearly a century later a major moral issue again caused political debate between candidates running for the mayor's post in Toronto. The incumbent was inundated with pleas to reconsider his position on the issue. He staunchly resisted that pressure, stating that most of those who were troubled by his stand were religiously minded people who, he said, "were prejudiced on such matters," and therefore, he would disregard their counsel.

That sweeping generalization of a position on a soul-testing, divisive, moral issue, patently dismissed as wrong because it is held by people who are also religious, is the cold hand and despising stance of secular consciousness. It has a self-blinding glare as it censors the rationality of religion. And it is indicative of the blatancy of the secularist's prejudice.

In the 1970s a leading entrepreneur who peddled hard-core pornography was brought to trial in a southern city of the United States. Most intriguingly, in the process of jury selection one of the questions posed of potential jurors by the defense attorney was whether or not they were members of a church. An affirmative answer to that value-laden question generally disqualified any juror in the eyes of the defense because "religious people have a prejudice against pornography." One can imagine how long it took in the South to find a jury so "uninfected" by the church that it could be "objective" on the matter of hard-core pornography.

But this was not the lowest point of it all—and it is here that the brains behind secularization manipulate the mind in matters that threaten decency. During the process of the trial the defense attorney resorted to a clever, indeed, intimidating line of questioning that disoriented and confused any witnesses against his client. The strategy ran as follows.

"Have you ever been into an art gallery?"

"Yes," would come the answer.

"Have you ever paid to go into an art gallery?"

"Yes," the witness would say again.

"Have you ever paid to go into an art gallery where there were paintings by the great masters of art?"

"Yes," once more the witness would repeat.

"Have you ever paid to go into an art gallery where there were paintings of unclothed people by the great masters?"

"Yes, I have," would come the hesitant reply as the witness would suddenly recognize that the predator was ready for the kill and there was no place to flee.

"Could you tell this jury," the derisive voice would thunder forth, "why you call what you paid to go and see 'art,' yet what my client sells you brand 'pornography'?"

With wringing hands, a confused mind, and a stuttering voice some meager philosophical banter would ensue—but the trap had been sprung. One could be absolutely certain that the worst possible answer in that secular courtroom would have been for an aged woman with hat and gloves and a cross hanging from her neck to have said, "Well, the Bible says that the body is the temple of God. . . ." The defense attorney could have rested his case with no further comment.

How irrational. How repressive. How irrelevant to the secularized consciousness is the invocation of a religious belief when establishing social moral boundaries and imposing them upon the ever-shifting soil of "community standards." But we may well ask from which side the imposition and irrationality *really* comes.

THE INDIGNITY OF NATURALISM

As I pondered this approach and argumentation thrust upon witnesses, it was obvious to me that they had clearly been placed in an indefensible position, because one cannot defend the particulars of a moral choice without first defending the theory in general upon which that choice is made. Secularism, on the other hand, can defend any choice because it is never compelled to defend its first principles, which are basically reduced to an antireligious bias. But secularists do not take into account that on their own terms no position needs to be defended if a commitment to it is sufficient reason in itself. If it is believed that all moralizing is purely one's private view then ought not that view itself be kept private? The secularist never answers how he or she determines whether anything is wrong with anything except by sheer choice. Secular belief grants itself privileges that it does not equally distribute.

That prejudice notwithstanding, let us consider the ploy behind the questioning in that courtroom and the possibility of unbridled evil that is created by implication. Secular theory has its self-preserving bag of tricks. When debating on any moral issue, secular thinkers delight in introducing some aberrant situation for which only two evil options are possible and forcing the absolutist to choose between them. By forcing those extreme solutions, they extrapolate the false deduction that there must, therefore, be no general rules for life. Even here they fail, and it is important to establish the indefensible extent to which their own theory is driven.

This was precisely the strategy and goal that was used and set in the courtroom by the defense on the matter of pornography and art. This very issue of pornography as a vehicle for unrestrained sensuality may well be the tip of the iceberg. Behind it moves a massive force of value-denying and morality-mocking ideas trying to clear any inhibition in Western culture's path. An implicit dehumanization is taking place here as the waters of decency are muddied in the name of secular humanism. It is, therefore, imperative for us to unpack this particular issue of art and pornography and of the purported absence of a difference between the two. As we deal with this we will address far more than the question at hand; we will expose the evil to which secular theory is inexorably drawn.

The answers the Christian gives define the difference between these two world-views because this is one of the conflicts that is tearing away at Western culture. The war of ideas rages with agendas such as these. So let us respond to that attorney.

Two immediate thoughts came to mind as I read his approach. My first thought was of Michelangelo, who, when he began to paint unclothed people, was sternly challenged by his instructor, asking him why he wanted to do this. Caught off guard for a moment, Michelangelo replied, "I want to see man as God sees man."

The instructor's wry smile was followed by his stern rejoinder, "But you are not God."

There is a world of thought in that caution that warns artists to rethink the self-aggrandizement behind their aesthetic endeavors. Art does not have a sovereignty over morality but dares to assign to itself that privilege. Sinister minds, whether or not they are artistic, cannot whitewash evil by renaming it.

My second response came as I reflected on the irrationality of what was being implied by the lawyer, who forged a false analogy by failing to differentiate some substantial points of dissimilarity between art and pornography. I borrow from C. S. Lewis's thoughts expounded in his book *The Pilgrim's Regress*. The book itself is a fascinating allegory of Lewis's spiritual pilgrimage "past the city of Claptrap and the far-off marshes of deviant thinking to the glorious reason of Christianity." His journey to God took him from the "false simplicities" of modern thought to the "complex relations" of truth. The allegory bristles with imagination and delights the mind. In this illustration we will get to the heart of the problem.

In distinction to Bunyan's *Pilgrim's Progress*, Lewis calls his account

The Pilgrim's Regress because it was written in retrospect after he had embraced the person of Christ. This new-found relationship enabled him to understand and answer more convincingly why he had rejected all else along the way. At the midpoint of his allegorical journey, he reached a crisis point of decision between the way of the world and the way of Christ. The tug of Christ had become more pronounced and the mind of Christ supremely attractive as the ideas of the world looked more and more ludicrous. But he did not know how to expose the contrast that loomed larger each day while he was still in the iron clasp of the Spirit of the Age. Lewis personified this Spirit as one who dwelt in a cavernous mountain where those who lived by his thinking were kept in bondage to his will. All of the inhabitants in his prison were in chains, existing fearfully under his Neronian stare—hollow people, bereft of a soul. "Mind-forg'd manacles," as William Blake would have called it—mental handcuffing.

In one transcending moment, John (the name by which Lewis calls himself during this pilgrimage) got a glimpse of himself through the eyes of the Spirit of the Age and saw his real enslavement. It was here that he got his clue. He noticed that he was not seen by his oppressor as a person, nor were the others in his grasp. They were just physical substances—spongy lungs, cartilaginous windpipes, chemical compounds, and so on.

The point is an important one. In a purely naturalistic universe there is nothing to transcend matter—there is no soul or spirit because that would imply the supernatural. This dehumanizing "net worth" is all that secularism has left when life is seen through the eyes of the Spirit of the Age—a discomforting but defining realization indeed in this allegorical tale.

John began to feel the full weight of this degradation. He knew he was something more than how he was perceived by his tormentor. His moment of confrontation came in an unexpected discussion with the jailer, who represented the Spirit of the Age.

Their argument began when John remarked on the nourishment and tastiness of the milk he had just consumed. The jailer had been hoping for just such a comment so he could launch his personal attack on John. He responded that John's enjoyment of the milk was positively absurd, for milk was nothing more, he said, than one of the many secretions of a cow. It was no different from any of its other secretions. This crude approach of reducing everything that was consumed to some odious comparison became the jailer's stock response—meat was just this, or eggs were nothing more than that. So went the repulsive reductionism the jailer delighted in spitting forth. The harsh deception became unbearable to John, and he seized the moment to destroy the philosophy of Spirit of the Age. The reduction of things to nothing more than this or that was the very dehumanization it had thrust upon the people by reducing them to nothing more than cartilage and tissue. "With the light of reason" dawning upon him, John exploded: "You lie! You lie because you do not know the difference between what nature has meant for nourishment, and what nature has meant for garbage!" It was the irrepressible cry of the mind against the disfiguring lie of a naturalist's universe.

At that moment in the narrative Lewis is at his best in moral theory. He portrays the bold and statuesque person of Reason, riding in on a magnificent stallion and rescuing John, applauding his answer. And as Reason latched on to John's common sense and whisked him away, "she stabbed at the heart of the Spirit of the Age with a series of piercing questions." The grim countenance of that tyrant, imprisoned by his own materialistic mind-set, could give no answer. Brain power was not sufficient to explain what the mind and the heart instinctively understood, and the demolition of the naturalist's case began. Says Lewis:

> Reason set spurs in her stallion and it leaped up on to the giant's mossy knees and galloped up his foreleg, till she plunged her sword into his

heart. Then there was a noise and crumbling like a landslide and the huge carcass settled down: and the Spirit of the Age became what he had seemed to be at first, a sprawling hummock of rock.[1]

In bringing the mind and common sense to bear upon the mindlessness and senselessness of the Spirit of the Age, John knew the blow would be fatal to naturalism. If humanity is nothing more than its lowest common denominator, the very philosophy espoused by a valueless creature is valueless. The ideas we pursue can be classified in terms of worth only if human beings have an essential glory. And if there is that essential worth in humanity we cannot reduce it to worthless usage. This begins the rejoinder from reason and common sense in response to the one who sees no difference between art and pornography. Secularism strips humanity of decency because it strips it of common sense first by denuding the mind.

Where then does that lead us? Let us not lose sight of this titanic battle in society, because it hides the heart of our struggle. Granted, in some cases there is no difference between art and pornography, not because art is the same as pornography, but because some art is nothing more than pornography masquerading as aesthetics in the name of art. But here is the point. If an artist seeks to portray the unclothed human body as art while actually bringing to that rendering his or her own lustful and vile intentions, the unworthy motive of the artist cannot be denounced by the unthinking canvas. The canvas cannot come to the artist and say, "Stop." But by contrast, the undisguised purpose of pornography is erotic and seductive. One would like to hope that the unclad individual, used as such bait in the marketing of her flesh for the sensually insatiable, would raise her hands in embarrassment, saying, "Stop, please don't do this to me." But that does not happen. Such objections are not forthcoming because when secularism has spawned its offspring, it produces a loss of a sense of shame. There is no voice within to say, "No, this is wrong. Don't do this to yourself."

This pathetic, psychological, voiceless posture where shame is excised from our cultural intercourse, leaves behind a hell of possibilities and swings wide the door to evil in any and every form. This is the unworkable pragmatism of secular thinking. All attitudes and all behavior find avenues of unbridled expression, and no one reserves the right to say, "It is not enough to say you're sorry—you ought to *feel* sorry and ashamed of what you have done." Ah! But this is too much to ask of the postmodern mind where self-congratulation is the mood engendered by irreligious social policies.

Let us be certain: It is our philosophical commitment that ends up legitimizing shamelessness that puts an individual on the road to incorrigibility. The difference between criminals who try desperately to cover their faces when they are escorted into court and those who smile remorselessly as they strut into the courtroom is civilizations apart. The ones covering their faces or shedding a tear have at least a vestige of reachability. There is at least the hint of the possibility of change, because there is a point of reference for wrong, some shared meanings between the wrongdoer and society. For any corrective in behavior or for punitive measures to be effective there must be some point of hurt or undesired feeling within the one who has done wrong. Shame or remorse or society's disapproval is powerless today to induce a desire to change, because the ideas that shape our culture make shame a hangover of an antiquated religious world-view. How then is it possible to reconcile law with liberty when both the sense of right and the sensation of wrong have been eradicated?

THE GENESIS OF SHAME

Shame is to the moral health of a society what pain is to the body. It is the sense of shame that provides an indicator to the mind. There is a powerful analogy even from the physical world of the materialist. It comes to us from the scanner theory of cancer causation.[2] This theory propounds that an incurable cancer is not ultimately caused by the cancer itself as much as by a detection system that has broken down.

According to this hypothesis, healthy cells in the body routinely become cancerous. But built into the body is a system of detection and a mechanism that comes into play to identify the cancerous cells and destroy them before they take over. It is not the cancer but the breakdown of the detection system that proves fatal.

How pitiful is the condition we have reached if we smother that sense of shame that was part of society's scanner system to detect wrongdoing and deal with it. Is it any wonder that our news journals are filled with page after page of incidents that continually shock us and are steadily bleeding decency out of life's mainstream?

The loss of shame in a society is ultimately an attack upon all of civilization. Why is that so? Put succinctly, it is this. The man who molests a child and feels a sense of shame expresses that shame because he has denuded and defaced that one person. The person who commits this same act and feels no shame in effect denudes and defaces the whole world because he is thereby telling us that our self-respect and the sacredness of physical privacy are worthless. His loss of shame is an attack upon all of humanity, because shame was given to us as a guardian, not only of ourselves, but of our fellow human being.

In *The Great Divorce* C. S. Lewis drove home this point of sensitization toward evil with riveting force as one ghost in the netherworld says to another:

> Don't you remember on earth—there were things too hot to touch with your finger but you could drink them all right? Shame is like that. If you will accept it—if you will drink the cup to the bottom—you will find it very nourishing: but try to do anything else with it and it scalds.[3]

It can be carved into the national ethos that the loss of belief in the supernatural, which secularism implies, has led to an eradication of the sense of shame, which secularism cannot deal with. That may well have been the goal in the minds of some societal engineers, but let us be sure that it produces a completely different soil than the one that brought America to its greatness. The soil of shamelessness gives root to evil in its most violent forms. The unbearable reality of secularism's consequential loss of shame is that the ones we victimize by evil can even be the ones we claim to love.

To raise a child without shame is to raise one with no immune system against evil. This was the dastardliness of the crime when the son killed the father in Dostoevsky's *The Brothers Karamozov*. This is the crime we end up witnessing when family members kill their own offspring or their parents. To remove shame is to perpetuate evil even toward the ones we love.

The catalog of crimes within families and between friends is one of the most painful and incomprehensible. The evils we foist upon children at the hands of responsible adults are not crimes born of hate. They are passions unleashed and justified by a conscience bereft of shame or remorse. Any conversation with a police officer who investigates such criminality within families reveals horror stories that stun the mind. Almost every such officer I have met has said to me that if we were to know even a fraction of all that goes on in homes behind closed doors the knowledge would be heartbreaking. Shame is meant to protect the very ones we love. But our culture has killed it. With the name of God now unhallowed and His kingdom not welcome does it make any sense to cry, "Deliver us from evil"?

THE EXODUS OF LOVE

Through secularism, this mood of a society without shame now covers the land. We may analyze the carriers and progenitors that led to this state ad nauseum, but it all ultimately points back to the first three chapters of the Book of Genesis. The big question Adam and Eve were asked was, "Has God *really* said . . . ?" When they questioned the reality of His voice and supplanted it with their own authority, they made themselves the measure of all things. No sooner had that choice been made and God's voice overridden than the feelings of fear and shame overcame them, and they tried to cover themselves.

Shortly thereafter, the Voice from Without came to them again: "Adam, where are you?" God knew the answer to that, but it was an opportunity for them to recognize their transgression and to repent of it. God in His grace provided a covering for their sin.

Just one generation later when Cain murdered his brother Abel, the Voice from Without came again: "Cain, where is your brother Abel?"

Now there was no shame, no remorse. "Am I my brother's keeper?" thundered forth the response, bereft of shame. There was no covering this time. The divine pronouncement was unequivocal. "You will be a restless wanderer on the earth."[4] The silence would now be one of apprehension, of ever looking over his shoulder.

It was Luther of old who once cried out, "Bless us, oh Lord; yea, even curse us, but please be not silent." Secularization—the silencing of the supernatural—brings about an eerie silence. And there is little consolation for Christians inside their church walls to wag their fingers at a dominant landlord who owns everything else, even the conscience of a nation. There is even less consolation for secularists who own a small container in which to carry their gasoline but have no car in which to put it. Even if one were procured, the villager still has to be taught the rules of the road. There are other drivers on the highways. That is what pluralization is all about, to which we now turn. In that mood we see how evil comes through another innocent but misunderstood idea.

Six

With Deference for Difference

WHEN OUR SON was only four years old and we moved to a different city, he raised a question of my wife that brought rounds of laughter from the whole family and even prompted a wistful thought—how nice it would be if life did provide such a sequence of colors. Driving in the car one day, right out of the blue he turned to my wife (who is from Canada) and said, "Mummy, when do we turn black?"

Caught completely off guard she said, "I don't know what you mean."

"Well," sounded the pensive, albeit innocent, childish voice, "You are white, we are beige, and Daddy is brown—when do we turn black?"

In his young mind, magnificently untainted by years of biases and indoctrinations, he saw life as a time-released kaleidoscope of colors and apparently envisioned the possibility of each of us experiencing the joys and hurts of all.

I must confess that the thought crossed my mind as to why God did not do it that way. How much more understanding of each other we would be if each of us could live for a time from within another's world. However, I strongly suspect that even if that were possible, we would create reasons with which to justify our intolerance of others. For reasons of pride of race, place, grace, or face, human beings somehow make room for hate. In fact, when much of the world's agonies are uncovered they reveal the immense capacity of humanity for rejection and an undying search to find someone, or some class, toward whom to vent its anger. In this, of all the centuries, we have caused so much hurt to one another that it has made even the most optimistic of us sober-minded about the tenuous nature of human relationships. This chapter deals with the differences with which we all live and how the Christian faith responds to the social phenomenon we call *pluralization*, the second mood of our time.

A BODY OF DIVERSITY

After millennia of human existence and decades of efforts and laws to find unity amid diversity, we still live in a highly volatile mix of world-views and values. Upon every American coin we have the inscription "E Pluribus Unum"—out of the many, one; out of diversity, unity. This was to be the melting pot, but painfully and unfortunately the analogy too often resembles a simmering cauldron, precariously close to boiling over. Political convictions are very diverse and seem increasingly anger-ridden. The rhetoric used to challenge another view has become inseparable from the rhetoric used to attack another person. Consciously or otherwise the media generate feelings of affection or disaffection about people, and intelligent debate has been sacrificed at the altar of personalities.

As if political antagonisms were not enough to fragment us, religious intolerance has also raised its countenance in settings around the world. Added to this mix is the gender conflict, which in intensity is at an all-time high and is possibly the most sensitive issue on university campuses today. But most volatile of all is the disheartening constancy with which ethnic tensions have led to crimes on a global scale. Of all the struggles we face in living with our fellow human beings, here, it was assumed for some time, progress would have been made. Yet, just as the word *multiculturalism* gained common usage and propelled social change, *ethnocentrism* made a discomforting entry. In three short decades the plaintive cry for harmony in our increasingly diverse world has been silenced, drowned out by the militant screams of isolationism under the banner of celebrating distinctives.

There is a very thin line of difference between the legitimate pride of self-acceptance and an illegitimate self-exaltation that fosters superiority and alienation. It is in this context that our attention is drawn to the second mood of contemporary society, that of pluralization and a search for community and the evil it begets when it is misunderstood.

Very simply, pluralization is defined as the existence and availability of a number of world-views, each vying for the allegiance of individuals, with no single world-view dominant. It has been primarily in the last thirty years that the North American mind has had to make a popular appraisal of what the world believes and then respond culturally to such varying descriptions of reality. With the arrival of people like Maharishi Mahesh Yogi, for example, and the popularization of his Eastern meditation techniques, a whole new world of reflectiveness was introduced into the harried pace of the dynamic, economically driven lifestyle of the West.

The cultural revolution that began thirty years ago called for a rejection of the old and the embracing of the new. Paul Simon sang a dirge to the era that was being displaced and reviled a generation which paid homage to its neon gods. Pete Seeger castigated the materially minded who lived in "little boxes on the hillside, little boxes made of ticky-tacky, little boxes . . . all the same."[1] Carly Simon

traced this spiritual journey through the alluring streets of Cambridge
to the bucolic life in the country, only to conclude:

> Now you run a bookstore
> And you've taken on a wife,
> And wear patches on your elbows
> And you live an easy life.
> But are you finally satisfied?
> Is it what you were lookin' for?
> Or does it sneak up on you
> That there might be something more?[2]

But this was only a small sound bite amid the high-decibel discord
of many new voices. The soul of America was tested again as pluralism became a reality in the country's decision-making process. Once
again moral categories were not easy to establish, because what was
anathema to one culture was a blessing to another. Pluralism became
a vital force in the West because it came at a time when weariness
with mainstream religion provided justification for many to dabble in
other ways of thinking.

However, the change of cultural and philosophical mix took a
strange twist. These new ideas that were planted in the mind were no
longer just "visiting" ideas. Rather, the proponents of these ideas and
the pockets of new belief systems had begun to reside in the West
and, in fact, to audaciously demand not only a change in Western
thinking, but privileges that the West itself would never be granted in
foreign soil. By acceding to those demands, a new America was
forged—spiritually unsure of itself, bereft of cultural confidence, and
glorying in self-deprecation. It has become the "in thing" now to
"think foreign," or radically, and the outrageous thing to affirm Western strengths, or "think conservative." This shift is not just imaginary;
it is real. A journey into the past once again shows a fascinating trail.

THE SIGNS OF TENSION

In a sense, the present scene in America was prefigured at a conference on world religions held in Chicago in 1893. There, a notable and brilliant Indian religious scholar, Vivekananda, was to rattle the rafters and challenge the mind of the West with the thinking of the East as never before. As he extolled the glories of Hinduism and castigated the abuses of Christianity and Islam, the delegates to that conference were roused by his exposition and wooed by his pathos. His provocative address launched a full-scale attack on the "imperialist West," charging it with an attitude of dominance and superiority. His polemic accomplished his goal, and he may well have set the mood for all future religious interaction at the level of a world platform. Though his thoughts were strongly worded, they might have opened meaningful dialogue had he been more sensitive and had those responding been able to differentiate between fact and perception. But that was not to be. Some of his ideas and his accusations were unfortunate, and in fact, misleading. Here is what he said:

> We who come from the East have sat on the platform day after day and have been told in a patronizing way that we ought to accept Christianity because Christian nations are the most prosperous. We look about us and see England, the most prosperous Christian nation in the world, with her foot on the neck of 250,000,000 Asiatics. We look back into history and see that the prosperity of Christian Europe began with Spain. Spain's prosperity began with the invasion of Mexico. Christianity wins its prosperity by cutting the throats of its fellow men. At such a price the Hindu will not have prosperity. I have sat here today and I have heard the height of intolerance. I have heard the creeds of the Moslems applauded when today the Moslem sword is carrying destruction into India. Blood and sword are not for the Hindu, whose religion is based on the laws of love.[3]

His emotionally charged words encompassed all the elements that have come to represent Western uncertainty and self-recrimination and the deep-seated struggle with religious and ethnic pluralism. He gained a hearing by touching the raw nerve of racial tension; he intermixed his content with his own religion's affinity for science in general and evolutionary theory in particular; he lauded the appealing side of pantheistic tolerance and created a caricature of Christianity that was easy to attack. In essence, he combined all the issues that were dividing people—the unequal yoking of nations, the historical baggage of Christianity's abuses, and the readiness of uncritical minds to absorb contradictory belief systems. His thoughts and ideas were to open the doors of universities across the country, and a century later this inaccurate use of religious history and thought still prevails in religious discourse.

However, much of what he said, though clearly tendentious, in fact revealed a perception that was real and passionately held by detractors of the Christian faith and by critics of Western culture. We must understand that these notions and predispositions are precisely what make up the collision course on which we now seem to be headed. A mixture of truth and error can be deadly when combined with passion and power. The pluralization of the West, therefore, is a phenomenon worthy of serious attention in order to harness the strength of cross-cultural interaction and thwart the evil that threatens both the present and future generations.

THE FEATURES CHANGE

With most historical drifts, the factors of influence come from many directions, and the pluralism that has reconstituted America is no exception. The reshaping elements have come from at least three sides—ethnic, political, and religious. Each of these bring a strength but also present a warning that our thinking on these issues must be very clear. If the ideas and their ramifications are not properly thought through, the danger is immense.

According to census figures released in May 1992, during the 1980s the United States admitted 8.6 million immigrants. Within the context of this century, that number is more than in any other decade since 1910. These figures tell a significant tale because they represent half of the total number of immigrants worldwide. In other words, of all those involved in cross-national transplanting and relocating during the 1980s, 50 percent of them headed to America. It is impossible to ignore the attraction that this country holds for people the world over. A very interesting sub-statistic is also thought-provoking. Eleven percent of these immigrants to the United States during that period, i.e., more than three-quarters of a million people, specified their destination as Los Angeles.

I well remember speaking at a convocation on ethnic America in the early years of that decade and being both humored and informed by the comments of the opening speaker. He was much beloved by the multicultural audience, who responded to his introductory comments with roars of laughter when he quipped, "Where else but in Los Angeles can you find a fast-food outlet where a Korean is selling kosher tacos?" Indeed, pluralism is a reality, not just in food, but in our thinking. By the end of the decade, the City of Angels boasted a population in which 40 percent were foreign born and in which nearly 50 percent spoke a language at home other than English. That alone ought to have spelled caution, because language goes beyond syntax and grammar. Language frames a reality and structures the context out of which one relates. When a person from one culture complains that the statement he or she made loses something in the translation, it is not because the words are limited; it is because the experience brought and the sentiment provoked will not be the same in another language.

Ironically, the very timing of the release of these burgeoning statistics that describe a growing disparity could not have been more indicative of the unease that was lying below the surface. Just two weeks prior to this, America had experienced the most violent urban riot in its history. Fifty-one people were killed, and $750 million in property damage was inflicted[4] in Los Angeles in the anarchy that resulted from the acquittal of four white policemen charged with the assault of a black traffic offender, Rodney King. It is this mix, this low combustion point, this unease and apprehension, that prompted sociologists years ago to speak of the "Los Angelization of the West."

In other words, pluralization does not always provide a haven, and the stakes can be high when people are forced or prepared to risk everything. The romantic predispositions and sentimental notions of idealized relationships notwithstanding, such ambition and anticipation must be weighed against the harsh realities of the costs that are exacted when several world-views collide.

An ancient Indian proverb says, "Whatever you are overflowing with will spill out when you are bumped." It conjures up the picture of a village woman carrying an urn on her head filled to the brim with water or milk. Unexpectedly, some careless youth comes running errantly across her path, causing her to suddenly stop, and resulting in a spill of whatever she was carrying. The point of this proverb is that one's reactions may be a truer test of character than one's actions. Actions, though sometimes impressive, can be premeditated and designed to deceive, but *re*actions come from the overflow of the heart and are impulsive. And here it is that the melting pot shows itself to be, in reality, a boiling cauldron—in the turbulent issues that rock our communities. The well-moderated speeches of politicians and the platitudes of reformers may sound cool, calm, and promising, but the point of ignition is low in our streets and neighborhoods and makes the promised hopes tenuous.

Why is this so? The reason is the hidden assumption in pluralism that is often the same assumption as in secularism—the idea of relativism. Moral choices are assumed to be relative to the person's predisposition. It is unpopular to assert that even the melting process requires a medium in which a desirable mix can occur. In the final analysis, the perennial addition of ingredients requires something insoluble to contain it. The old problem of the universal solvent holds true—where do you store it?

POLITICS OF CULTURE

It would be a relatively easy task to manage the situation were it only a matter of balancing the numbers added to the cultural mainstream each year. This would be true in any country. But like all very critical issues the answers are not as simple as a single corrective. The ideas that are represented must be dealt with and sensibly discussed. The intermix goes far beyond just a cross-cultural issue. Let us now examine the three principal sources of pluralism today.

The lead article in the July 10, 1995, issue of *U.S. News and World Report*, was titled "Divided We Stand." From that mainly political perspective, the writers identified seven different voting mind-sets. Each of the "species" was further defined by a television character who was representative of its values. I must confess that, not desiring to spend my life in front of a television, many of these mascots were unrecognizable to me, but the assumption may be made that to most of our "educated by vision" group, this would not be a problem. The seven types of voters were: (1) the populist traditionalist, as represented by Roseanne's husband, Dan; (2) the stewards, represented by Thurston Howell; (3) the dowagers, represented by the "Golden Girls"; (4) liberal activists, represented by Murphy Brown; (5) conservative activists, represented by Alex P. Keaton; (6) ethnic conservatives, represented by Louise Jefferson/Edith Bunker; and (7) agnostics, represented by "Frasier." The writers were also careful to point out that there was a "don't know" category, but did not elucidate how the "don't know's" differed from the agnostics.

In each of these categories the political perspectives are deeply felt, and the convictions of "how to govern" are very diverse. If diversity of governance were all that divided the group it would be understandable. However, when anger is vented in disagreements, it is very disconcerting. One need only reflect on the vilification that took place when the conservative Vice-President Dan Quayle questioned the ethical implications of a Murphy Brown-type lifestyle. It was as though centuries of hatred was unleashed as a result, and the ideological clashing of swords cut deeply.

Political differences have taken such a turn because, to the pluralistically minded in a secular culture where shame has already been excised, the power to create and enforce moral relativism has been placed into the hands of government. Political power is a strange place to entrust morality because proverbially politics is not synonymous with moral uprightness. The very institution that is distrusted by most has now become the shaper of the soul. Aesop of old had innumerable stories on what lay ahead for such credulity.

RELIGION SEEKING REPRESENTATION

A further alteration in America's cultural landscape has come about with the drastic shift in religious commitment. In a subsection of his fine work *Culture Wars*, James Davison Hunter has given us a remarkable study and pointed out the changing mix here, as well. The Catholic component, for example, has played a fluctuating role in the American ethos by virtue of its numerical status. In the 1830s, 600,000 Catholics arrived in America. In the 1840s, that number rose to 1,700,000. In the 1850s, there were 2,600,000 Catholic immigrants, and hence, the shift within a century from a Protestant predominance previous to 1830 to a swiftly changing tide. In the 1790s Catholics comprised 1 percent of the total population. In the 1920s that changed to 17 percent of the population, and by the mid-1980s nearly 29 percent of the population of the United States was Catholic.[5]

The Jewish scene is quite different, moving from comprising one-tenth of 1 percent of the population in the 1830s to forming 3 percent by the 1920s. Writing in the 1950s, Will Herberg pointed out that American culture had become a roughly comparable blend of Protestant, Catholic, and Jew.[6]

This is a vitally important point to note. In spite of economic rivalries and even hostilities between these three religious groups, in spite of prejudices and several points of tension, in broad strokes there was nevertheless a biblical theism common to all on the questions of origin and destiny. God was understood as being personal, morality had a bearing on reality, and accountability to a higher law was implicit to all moral demands. Even natural law, i.e., nature's "order," was considered to be part of the revealed truth from the Creator.

But this intermix was to face a foundational struggle from a social theory coming from a new direction. As has already been described, secularism, the offspring of the Enlightenment that exalted reason, inevitably brought about not only the dethronement of God but also demanded a radical redirection away from issues of the soul to an exclusive focus on "this worldliness."

With a philosophy diametrically opposite of secularism, Islam has recently begun to make a serious impact both globally and in America. In the 1930s there was only one mosque in the United States and fewer than twenty thousand Muslims. By the late 1980s there were over six hundred mosques, and more than four million Muslims inhabited the country. This very real presence of Islam may well be a positive thing in the long run if calmness and courtesy can prevail, because for the first time in centuries of history we have the possibility of meaningful interaction with one another. The Christian will be compelled to better understand what he or she believes and to know how to defend that belief.

But what America's secular-minded social engineers need to constantly remember is that Islam defines history from a transcendent perspective with temporal application. Consequently, Islam seeks to translate the law of Allah, derived from the Koran, into the law of this land. To some in Islam's ranks that vision alone justifies all actions. Transcendent leverage is given to present upheavals and laws. This view of social theory is radically different from a secular, this-worldly perspective of life's purpose.

The attraction of Islam to the "disenfranchised" in many countries, especially in the United States, is that Islam is more than a religion; it is, in fact, a geopolitical theory. The gains Islam has made in the black community are indicative of its appeal to those dissatisfied with the establishment. The conversion of Cassius Clay into Muhammed Ali was symbolic and well represented by Ali's poetic fervor. He said something to the effect that he wanted "no pie in the sky by and by when I die, but I want my castle on the ground while I'm around." This combination of discontent and geopolitical intent have a tremendous bearing on the pluralization of American values and ideals, a situation that is equally true in Great Britain. Secularism and Islam by definition are on an ideological collision course.[7]

The influx of Eastern pantheistic religions, i.e., Hinduism, Buddhism, and Zen, introduced another dimension and further reconfigured the Western world. The more popular forms of these ideas, often called New Age teachings, are also well known and have made inroads into the business community by offering meditational techniques to increase professional performance. If a Christian were to refuse an invitation to participate in Eastern meditation on the basis of his or her own faith, the followers of the guru would smilingly counter with, "Oh, but you can do it during your lunch hour." Such is the dichotomy enjoined and the possibility offered by pluralism.

Beneath the surface congeniality, however, this diversity and these deeply felt religious distinctives bring with them a challenge of monumental proportions.

VULNERABILITY OUT OF STRENGTH

There is again one fundamental difference from the early mix of people in America, in contrast to the present drastic change. When discussing America's dream in the making with diversity as its strength, no quotation is more familiar to the student of ethnic confluence than the one by French immigrant and loyalist Michel Guillaume Jean de Crevecoeur in his essay, "What Is an American?" His statement has recently come under fire from some as being biased. While that criticism may be worthy of serious note, it is important not to bypass the reasoning behind his praise of America, for that oversight misses the logic of what de Crevecoeur said:

> He is an American who leaving behind him all his ancient prejudices and manners, receives new ones from the new mode of life he has embraced, the new government he obeys, and the new rank he holds. The American is a new man, who acts upon principles. . . . Here individuals of all races are melted into a new race of men.[8]

If this statement is descriptive of a willing predisposition when adopting a new homeland, that is, to leave behind ancient prejudices and melt into a new race, then the modern influx of world-views makes the dream very elusive. The points of tension are too many and, for most, are nonnegotiable. More is brought in today than is left behind.

These factors of culture, politics, and religion, all struggling in increasing proportions for unfettered expression, have made North America an intensely and voluntarily pluralistic society. This is not merely a changing face; it is a reconstituted mind. When demographics such as the shifting proportions of old age to youth and the increasing power of youth in the economy are factored in, the resulting changes are only further complicated. The commercialization of Christianity—where feeling has replaced thinking—has played no small part in this process, either.

In short, pluralism with all its strengths and hazards makes this tail end of the twentieth century one of enormous possibility but also one of gigantic risk. The great glory and strength of pluralism is that it compels the holder of any belief to measure its truthfulness against alternative interpretations. The great hazard of pluralism is the faulty deduction, in the name of tolerance, that all beliefs can be equally true. It is ultimately truth, not popularity or rights, that determines destiny.

It has been correctly stated that religion is the essence of culture while culture is the dress of religion. The intermix in our society today leaves one completely apprehensive as to what will become of the essence of the West. Will it be the nakedness of secularism, or will it be the garb of some belief that is at its core inimical to the fundamental beliefs that framed the West? Will our inability to get along unleash an evil with which none can live? Or can pluralism be harnessed in its strengths and minimized in its vulnerability?

SEEKING THE ETERNAL

For the Christian, before addressing the fundamental philosophical fallacy that pluralism courts, there are at least three vitally important principles that should condition every response.

First, it is imperative that the Christian learn to differentiate in his or her own beliefs between *opinion* and *conviction*. An opinion is merely a preference in a continuum of options. A person may prefer one color to another or one style to another. A conviction, on the other hand, is rooted in the conscience and cannot be changed without changing that which essentially defines the person. In a pluralistic culture, an opinion should not be given the same passion as the weight of a conviction. And every conviction held must be done so with the clear and required teaching of Scripture. Once these differences are made in a Christian's mind then a very important logical consequence follows: Every conviction that is held should be undergirded by love.

Without the undergirding of love, the possessor of any conviction becomes obnoxious, and the dogma believed becomes repulsive to the one who disagrees with it. The early church also lived in an intensely pluralistic culture in which it had to deliver an exclusivistic message, but the believers were distinguished and recognized by their love. Our Lord Himself proclaimed truth in exclusive terms, terms in which there was no compromise, but He demonstrated that truth by the embodiment of a perfect love. Being possessed of a conviction is a necessary part of following God, but doing so with love and patience are the necessary handmaidens.

Second, pluralism will ever be the reality by which societies are constituted, be they in political theory or religious conviction. The alternative—totalitarianism—is deplorable and terrifying. The danger for the Christian is not that pluralism exists on the outside; rather, it is the deadly effect of relativism that has taken hold of the Christian mind. The life of one who follows Christ must have the clear ring of truth to it rather than conveying a surrender in the name of pluralism to the relativism of the age.

Third, Christ never sought to establish His kingdom here on earth. He set His eyes determinedly on the cross, in full recognition that only there could a heart ever be broken and mended in order to live as a healer in a broken world. Yes, He engaged His counterparts in incisive dialogue, and He wept for them. Indeed, He knelt beside His own beloved city of Jerusalem and prayed with deep anguish for her. But He never, ever intimated that the city could be changed merely by a tougher legal system, as important as that might have been. He sought to change the hearts of men and women by the renewing of their minds through the work of the Holy Spirit. That kind of work is slower but more definite. That kind of power is moral and spiritual, and in the long run outdoes brute force and hate.

The words of Malcolm Muggeridge come to mind and encourage the heart that our struggles are not new and that our confidence can remain unshaken:

> The world's way of responding to intimations of decay is to engage equally in idiot hopes and idiot despair. On the one hand some new policy or discovery is confidently expected to put everything to rights: a new fuel, a new drug, détente, world government. On the other, some disaster is as confidently expected to prove our undoing. Capitalism will break down. Fuel will run out. Plutonium will lay us low. Atomic waste will kill us off. Overpopulation will suffocate us, or alternatively, a declining birth rate will put us more surely at the mercy of our enemies.
>
> In Christian terms, such hopes and fears are equally beside the point. As Christians we know that in this world we have no continuing city, that crowns roll in the dust and that every earthly kingdom must sometime flounder. We acknowledge a King men did not crown and cannot dethrone, and we are citizens of a city of God they did not build and cannot destroy. Thus, the apostle Paul wrote to the Christians in Rome, living in a society as depraved and dissolute as our own. Paul exhorted them to be steadfast, unmovable, always abounding in God's work, to concern themselves with the things that are unseen, for the things which are seen are temporal but the things which are not seen are eternal. It was in the breakdown of Rome that Christendom was born. Now in the breakdown of Christendom there are the same requirements and the same possibilities to eschew the fantasy of a disintegrating world, and seek the reality of what is not seen and eternal, the reality of Christ.[9]

To that cultural breakdown and the exposure of one fundamental danger in misunderstanding pluralism we now give our attention. This study will help in the important discovery that it is not color that informs our ideas but our ideas that color our world.

Seven

The Flickering Flame of Reason

THE ASSUMPTION that all ideas are equally true is false. Philosophically it is very easy to demonstrate that falsity. Any society, however sincere, that believes in the equality of all ideas will pave the way for the loss of good ones. What *is* true, however, is that most people are guided in life by a handful of ideas, and therefore it is all the more important that there be a way of measuring why one idea is chosen over another. This is the issue at the heart and soul of Western pluralism; on what basis have we surrendered ourselves to the ideas that govern our culture?

One of the symptoms of a society that has lost its ability to think critically is that intricate issues are dealt with in a simplistic manner. The uncritical adherence to simple platitudes uttered by the masses is proof of this and demonstrates a failure to take into consideration the complexities that lie beneath the surface of our impassioned slogans.

For example, we speak of freedom as if it were a virtue only when it is devoid of all restraint and absolute in and of itself. As cherished as that ideal may be, failure to understand the ramifications of that

kind of freedom in a culturally diverse society brings tyrannies a thousand times worse. Freedom can be destroyed, not just by its retraction,
but also by its abuse.

Pluralism is precisely that kind of a challenge, for beneath the
simple goal of peaceful coexistence lies a web of disparate concerns.
It is an ever-present temptation in free societies to latch on to one or
two good concepts while failing to recognize that those ideas presup-
pose other indispensable conditions. Underestimating the complexities beneath our oft-quoted platitudes undermines the foundation on
which the truisms stand.

In his brilliant book *Bridge on the River Kwai*, Pierre Boulle gives
us a memorable account of how self-destructive a simple albeit great
idea can be whose complexities are not appreciated. Told against the
historic backdrop of the Second World War, Japanese-held prisoners
of war were put to work to build a bridge that would link the Japanese
rail system all the way to Burma and pour more firepower into that
theater of warfare. Building that bridge was a vital step in ensuring
Japan's military success.

The bridge could obviously be devastating to Allied efforts. Adding insult to injury, the prisoners of war ordered to carry out this
project were, in effect, erecting a structure for the defeat of their own
homelands. Naturally, the commander met with staunch resistance
from the highest-ranking British prisoner, Colonel Nicholsen. But
his resistance was for a completely different reason than one would
have expected. Nicholsen agreed to organize the project but only
under the Geneva Convention Pact, which demanded that officers
not be forced to do manual labor. This simple but "honor-saving"
insistence became the focal point of a contest of wills between the
Japanese commander and the British colonel. The commander was
determined to subdue Nicholsen's will in this matter, and he employed severe punitive measures to break down the British officer's
stubbornness—starvation, solitary confinement, torture, and all the
deprivations of personal dignity.

Finally, the Japanese commander recognized that by pursuing this personal battle of his he was running out of time to complete the bridge. At the risk of his own humiliation he granted Nicholsen his demand, with Nicholsen's guarantee that the bridge would be ready in time. Nicholsen put his genius and his fellow prisoners of war to work. He developed a passion for excellence and wanted to make this the best bridge ever built. He gave attention to every detail so that the Japanese forces could transport all of their heavy equipment with safety. In fact, Nicholsen became so obsessed with proving British engineering brilliance that he even changed the site of the bridge to make it sturdier and more easily protected from "enemy sighting."

The soldiers and officers under Nicholsen's authority were completely confounded. Why would Nicholsen want to construct an edifice of such perfection that would only enhance the enemy's capacity to destroy their homelands? They wondered if he had gone mad in his zeal for protecting a lesser idea, the dignity of officers, at the cost of a greater love, the safety of his country.

The story gains incredible intrigue as, unknown to him, a group of officers around him devised a plan to blow up the bridge just as the first Japanese train transporting its military might would pass over it. These two goals working at cross-purposes with each other occupy the last moments of the story. As Nicholsen raced against time to complete his bridge for the enemy in the name of British ingenuity and within the "nonnegotiable" proviso of the Geneva Convention, an undercover group from within the ranks was making plans to blow it up.

With the bridge completed, Nicholsen proudly marched across its expanse, flushed with pride, checking every beam while underneath the bridge the wiring was being set in place that would destroy it as the train approached. Melodramatically and predictably during this, his final inspection, Nicholsen detected some strange cables in the pillars and rushed to see what was happening. Suddenly realizing that sabotage was under way, he engaged in a hand-to-hand struggle with these "subversives" in the ranks. At the critical moment he staggered and fell wounded onto the lever that detonated the explosives and himself destroyed the bridge at the very moment the train was crossing over. His last words were somewhat intentionally ambiguous—"What have I done?"

This is a classic illustration of a man who got lost in a sublime principle in which he won a small personal battle but lost sight of the bigger war. And to add to the irony, his adversary was willing to lose a personal battle in order to win the bigger war. How fraught with danger are principles we repeat to ourselves, especially if they come in the garb of philanthropy or altruism.

Pluralism and diversity are such principles, attractive to all of us. But if they are left without other informing factors and parameters, they can serve the cause of inimical forces to destroy the very commitments that gave us the possibility of the freedom in diversity we so cherish. The evil generated by the destruction of those commitments crushes the very ones who nobly defended an uncritically pursued principle. Let us take a brief look at both the simplicity and complexity of multicultural existence to understand the ramifications.

DEFINING THE STRUGGLE

"Culture," said sociologist Daniel Bell, "is the effort to provide a coherent set of answers to the existentialist situations that confront all human beings in the passage of their lives." This simple definition is very refreshing and free from the long list of qualifiers that some scholars use in defining culture. The search is for coherence in the existentialist situations, that is, situations with which we all are confronted—from what we cherish to what we abhor, from how we live to how we die, from what is sacred to what is profane, from how we feel to how we react. Culture is the glue that holds our common values together. At first blush this may seem self-evident if we are seeking to live with each other, for we all know that there must be a shared commonality. But often at life's most painful intersections this does not happen because the points of contact between us are not casual but intense. The closer a home is to its neighbor the greater the possibility of conflict between the two.

I recall once being at a dinner for the ambassadors to the United Nations. I had already been alerted that the seating was unalterable and as fixed as the laws of the Medes and Persians. There were to be no changes because some ambassadors had come with the categorical condition that they not be placed at the same table as the representative of a nation hostile to them. As the evening progressed, I dared to ask one of the ambassadors at our table what hope he held for the United Nations. He made a very politically noncommittal statement and then said, "The good news is that we are talking to each other; the bad news is that we don't talk the same language." Somewhat puzzled, I asked, "Don't you use interpreters?" He looked even more befuddled than I was and then added, "Oh no, no, no, you don't understand. Of course we use the same language. Where we differ is in the contrary meanings we choose to assign to the same word. When I say 'peace,' I mean 'peace—no guns.' When he says 'peace'"—he pointed to another ambassador from a neighboring country, fortunately sitting tables away— "he means that I should remove my guns while he keeps his guns pointed directly at me."

This is just a small indication of the massive barrier that pluralism brings, even when the goal is reconciliation. For the Westerner, secularization may provide the steam for running the engine of culture, but in a pluralistic society the tracks are pulled up and different ones are laid down. Living under the illusion that we are safe because of assumed parameters, we only bring hazard to our journey together. At their core, cultures operate in a given situation in ways that are fundamentally opposed to each other, each culture guarding its own past prejudices and convictions.

THE LIGHTER SIDE

For those who have ever seen Indian movies, the illustration I share now will be well understood. India is the largest movie-producing nation in the world, and to grow up in India is to grow up in a culture where anything on the screen always brings a crowd. But romance on the screen was, at the time I was growing up, very typical. Since kissing was not permitted by the cultural ethos, romantic encounters routinely consisted of a "boy meets girl" scenario that ended with starry-eyed expressions, each chasing the other, generally in a treed lot while melodramatic music added to the atmosphere. It is best described as grownups playing peekaboo in a jungle. Just as the pursuer and the pursued would meet and the long-awaited moment of embrace would finally come, the scene would suddenly change, and the audience would applaud. An Indian comedian who wrote a question-and-answer column in a national film magazine was once asked, "What is the difference between love on the Western screen and love on the Indian screen?" His answer was in one word: "Trees."

In the existential questions of our lives and in the struggles of our minds, the trees that separate the worlds of culture are numerous. In fact, the same comedian sang a famous song that, translated, says, "My shoes are Japanese, my trousers are English, my hat is Russian, but my heart is Indian." Need it be added that it is the heart that beats out life's passions? Pluralism is ultimately a contest, not only of the intellect, but of the mind and heart. And sometimes those heartfelt passions can bring terror.

THE DARKER REALITY

In 1983 William J. Winslade, codirector of the UCLA program in medicine, law, and human values, and Judith Ross, lecturer in the department of psychiatry, wrote a book titled *The Insanity Plea*. In this book, seven major criminal cases were considered to show the effects of "psychologizing" criminal behavior in Western culture to the point that brutal acts of murder can be overridden by invoking cultural and psychological contingencies.

One of the cases in this compendium is called "The Kiss of Death." It gives a sad and heartrending account of the murder of a nineteen-year-old Berkeley student named Tanya Tarasoff. She was a promising student of Russian descent, born in Shanghai, with dreams of a future in America. All who knew her described her as outgoing, carefree, and flirtatious. Consistent with her personality and with no serious intentions, she befriended a young man from Asia, who was, for his part, quite enamored by her. Coming from a radically different system of values, he mistook her playful hugs and kisses on festive occasions for romance. He became obsessed by the desire to marry her and finally proposed to her. When she lightheartedly turned him down, he reacted with dismay. That bitter disappointment festered into scorn when he interpreted her flippant rejection of his proposal as a personal humiliation. To him, it was an affront to his honor and to the decency of his intent.

Gradually overcome by depression, he stepped on the path to murder. That dreadful deed accomplished, like a schizophrenic he convulsed with despair as he saw her stabbed body at his feet, dead at his own hands. Shocked and dazed, he reached for the telephone to call the police and confessed to what he had done.

Although an insanity plea is what got him off, his attorney buttressed his cause by underscoring the effect of two cultures on a collision course. As drastic and deadly as this illustration may be, the relationship may well have been fraught with misunderstanding right from the start because each gave a different meaning to the same behavior. And here is the point: If our misunderstandings are multiplied across numerous cultures and prejudices, the points of variance only increase as pluralism then exposes its sharp edges. There are no shared meanings of the past and no common mind-set—our lives have converged for economic reasons, our allegiances to the past are diverse. Suddenly people worlds apart in their values are neighbors in search of common ground.

To this one might legitimately counter that if the shared meanings of the past are an indispensable component in culture, should not the conflicts exist only in one generation and be moot in the next one? Though one might wish it were so, this is precisely where cultural roots are long and strong. Religion is just one aspect of culture. In some cultures the way one relates to society is so ingrained that centuries will not eradicate it. If the constant turmoil in the Middle East has proven anything, it is how we transfer grudges and prejudices for generations.

THE ROOTS OF DIFFERENCE

Paul Tillich, the noted liberal theologian, spoke of three kinds of cultures as they relate to religious knowledge. The names he assigned to them are distracting and the ideas seem unwieldy. But the concepts underlying those categories are very accurate. He speaks of cultures that are heteronomous, theonomous, and autonomous.

He defines a *heteronomous* culture as one where forms and laws of thinking and acting are directed by an authority outside of the individual. The authority is provided by an ecclesiastical body or a political structure. Islam and Roman Catholicism provide appropriate examples of heteronomy in religious history. In Islam, particularly in the Shiite sect, the religious figure of the Imam is given such status of interpretational authority that he reaches the level of an infallible voice. For the Shiite, the authority of the Imam or the authority of the habits and customs of their prophet Mohammed for the Sunni provides outside and "dictatorial" authority for the life of the Muslim. To that authority the Muslim must submit—that is the very meaning of the word *Islam*.

In the political arena Marxism, or any form of dictatorship, provides an example of a heteronomous culture. Here again the authority is outside the level of the mainstream of life and is imposed upon it.

Theonomous culture, on the other hand, is one where the authority from without and the intuition from within each individual life are synonymous. Hinduism provides a classic and rare example. The parameters of belief are so wide that any aberration or contradiction is seen only as either temporary or apparent. Ultimately, it is held that the roads of all beliefs will converge and there is no reason to deem one road more truthful than any other. The only wrong move, they say, would be to switch roads, or "convert," for that would imply a dichotomy of truth and error that is not essential to reality itself. The mainstream of India's culture, with all of its diversities, maintains this belief that truth is intuitive and that the moral law (Karma) determines the reincarnational cycle. This is not imposed from without. It is believed that both the circularity of life and the moral imperative are intuitive to all of humanity.

It is very difficult to meaningfully argue against such a position, because the Hindu responds that sooner or later the disagreeing individual will arrive at the higher level of knowledge and agree.[1]

Finally, there is the *autonomous* culture. Here every individual is self-determining and independent of authority. Morality imposed from without is resisted, and intuition as grounds for belief is optional. In short, autonomous cultures deny any moral authority and shrug their shoulders at intuition. The word *autos* means "self," and *nomos* means "law." North American culture and much of the West lives with autonomy at the core of its values.

To sum up Tillich's categories: Heteronomy argues for a "different" law that comes from without; theonomy argues for "God's law" that is intuitively within ("god" being defined differently by pantheism than the Christian would define God); and autonomy argues for "self-law" as the only law. The question then arises: Can an autonomous culture absorb theonomous and heteronomous cultures and still remain autonomous? The answer to that is no, not without the compromise of major assumptions.

It is this unwillingness of the West to see the fundamental differences that makes the situation so perilous. Daniel Yankelovich described a cultural revolution as that which makes a decisive break with the shared meanings of the past, particularly those that relate to the deepest questions of the purpose and nature of human life. Western culture and Eastern culture are built upon diametrically opposed foundational beliefs of what brings life meaning. And we must recognize this if we are to relate meaningfully and to understand one another. The deepest questions of life elicit opposite answers. The question is, how do we bridge them? To assume that we have common parameters on the most basic questions is to delude ourselves.

I am reminded of the humorous anecdote of a nervous flier aboard a turbulent flight. As the woman's discomfort continued, the flight attendant tried every conceivable way to ease the mind of this passenger and to assure her the plane could take an extraordinary amount of pounding and still be safe. Noticing, however, that her agitation was unabated, the attendant decided to ask for the pilot's help.

A member of the cockpit crew came into the cabin and, taking the hand of the distraught traveler, he said, "Madam, as you look outside the right window, do you see a light blinking?"

"Yes," she said nervously.

"As you look outside the left window, do you see a light blinking?"

"I do," she murmured.

"As long as we stay between those two lights," the crew member said, "we are safe."

He returned her sweaty palm to her with the reminder that each time she felt impending death she should look to the right and to the left and remind herself that the blinking lights meant they were on the right track.

Like the train that laid its own track, this assurance was an illusory one, for obviously the aircraft could plummet headlong with its lights still blinking on either side. The path pluralization provides is equally unconfirming of safety, for the lights are not a path at all but are locked into the performance of the aircraft itself. Its safety is dependent upon itself.

THE FATAL FLAW

Pluralization offers much in the way of variety, and the enrichment we bring to one another is incalculable. But when pluralism breeds a doctrine of relativism the cost has been too great. The abandonment of some necessary transcultural parameters has given way to the absence of reason in the contemplation of life's deepest questions. The end result is a cultural amalgam that will be unstable in its journey. That instability is now represented in the loss of reason. If the loss of shame was the child of secularization, the loss of reason is the child of pluralization.

This may be the key indicator to why there is such a sense of alienation in this so-called Generation X. Over half a century ago, G. K. Chesterton saw this coming

> The new rebel is a skeptic and will not entirely trust anything. He has no loyalty; therefore, he can never be really a revolutionist. And the fact that he doubts everything really gets in his way when he wants to denounce anything. For all denunciation implies a moral doctrine of some kind and the modern revolutionist doubts not only the institution he denounces, but the doctrine by which he denounces it. Thus, he writes one book complaining that imperial oppression insults the purity of women, and then he writes another book, a novel, in which he insults it himself. He curses the Sultan because Christian girls lose their virginity, and then curses Mrs. Grundy because they keep it. As a politician he will cry out that war is a waste of life, and then as a philosopher that all life is a waste of time. A Russian pessimist will denounce a policeman for killing a peasant, and then prove by the highest philosophical principles that the peasant ought to have killed himself. A man denounces marriage as a lie and then denounces aristocratic profligates for treating

it as a lie. He calls a flag a bauble and then blames the oppressors of
Poland or Ireland because they take away that bauble. The man of this
school goes first to a political meeting, where he complains that savages
are treated as if they were beasts. Then he takes his hat and umbrella and
goes on to a scientific meeting where he proves that they practically are
beasts. In short, the modern revolutionist, being an infinite skeptic, is
always engaged in undermining his own mind. In his book on politics he
attacks men for trampling on morality, and in his book on ethics
he attacks morality for trampling on men. Therefore the modern man
in revolt has become practically useless for all purposes of revolt.
By rebelling against everything he has lost his right to rebel against
anything.[2]

It is this undermining of our own mines that most represents the
collapse of reason. The schizophrenia with which we lived just a few
years ago was revealed by two front-page stories that ran at the same
time. One described a professional basketball player who tragically
had been diagnosed with AIDS; he conceded that he had lived a fla-
grantly promiscuous lifestyle. He was, nevertheless, hailed as a hero.
At the same time another renowned individual was nominated as a
justice for the Supreme Court. His nightmare began when allegations
were made that ten years earlier he had used some rather lewd or
sexually motivated language toward a colleague, who was also a
friend. This judicial nominee was publicly humiliated for these al-
leged remarks that by implication deemed him unfit for the office.
One, a self-defined philanderer, was hailed as a hero; the other, because of unproved charges of questionable language, was labeled a
villain.

Whether one should be vilified and another exalted is not the
point. The point is that these opposite conditions of exaltation and
humiliation did not come from a single standard. The machinations
behind the scenes and the viciousness unleashed to derail the judge's
nomination bred an evil even more heinous than the one it was trying to counter. Once again we were a culture schizophrenically staring into the face of our own wickedness.

THE IRRATIONAL ENTAILMENTS

The same soul-searching debate gnaws away at the conscience of the nation on the issue of abortion, pulling us apart. This contradiction was illustrated when I participated in an open-line talk program at one of America's fine and renowned universities.

The host of the program was a confessed, mix-it-up-type atheist. From the moment the telephone lines were opened, the callers vented their hostility, unblushingly using slurs and epithets. Finally, in a surprising call, a woman who had become quite outraged brought up the issue of abortion, which had not been one of the subjects under discussion even by extrapolation. Yet she raised it and charged that Christians used the issue of abortion as a smoke screen for their ultimate goal of controlling society. Her whole point of emphasis, on which she wanted a comment from me, was that the freedom to abort was her moral right. Although the main subject we had been originally discussing was the existence of God, I decided to respond to her challenge.

It was interesting, I pointed out, that on virtually every campus where I debated the issue of God's existence, some individual challenged God's goodness by pointing out all the evil in this world, especially the gratuitous evil that seems purely the result of a whim. "A plane crashes, and thirty die while twenty live . . . what sort of God is that? If God is good, why does He arbitrarily allow some to live and destine others to die?" The implication was, of course, that since God is so arbitrary in His actions He must be evil.

"My question to you, madam, is this," I said. "When you arrogate the right to yourself to choose who may live in your womb and who may die, you call it your moral right. But when God exercises the same right, you call Him evil. Can you explain that contradiction to me?" The response was nothing but anger and verbal frustration on the other end of the line. It was the torment of contradiction desperately seeking escape. We apply our beliefs selectively and judge by different standards. This is the sad result of living with flagrant contradiction that exacts a heavy toll, ultimately breeding justification of even the most irrational opinions and actions.

Think, for example, of the rationale behind the defense of abortion. The comment is often made that we do not know when life begins and therefore may abort at will. How irrational can that argument get? If my two-year-old son were missing on a friend's farm, would I go plunging a pitchfork into haystacks looking for him, because I do not know whether he is lost in a haystack? The death of reason has resulted in such loss of the sanctity of life because pluralism has bred irrationality, which is the steppingstone to the unconscionable. It is the equivalent of plunging the pitchfork into the womb because we do not know if life is there.

One of my clearest childhood memories is of being on a busy street and watching a crowd convulsing in laughter. It soon became apparent what the amusement was all about. An insane man, completely naked, was carrying on in the most senseless and irrational way. A heartless crowd had gathered and passers-by were dismounting from their bicycles to join this farce in action. The convulsive laughter continued until a policeman came and hauled the madman away to clothe him and admit him into an asylum. Even as a young person, I felt remorse at that pitiful sight, not just for the man who was insane, but for the unreasonableness of the ones enjoying his derangement.

What we laugh at and what we weep for has much to say about our rationality. One look at the current fare from our entertainment world ought to give us pause about where our reason has gone. What is more, when academia joins in and belittles reason itself and tells us that the laws of logic no longer apply to reality, then we are doubly denuded, for there is no one to rescue us.

AN INSATIABLE APPETITE

If we seek coherent answers for our culture, then we had better realize that the contradictions with which we live reveal a deep cultural incoherence. Yankelovich brilliantly points out this deadly contradiction that ushered in the eighties. He presents, among other results, the case study of a couple he calls Abby and Mark. They were a typical upper-middle-class couple, climbing the ladder of wealth and power. But with all their gaining and getting, there was an internal ruptur-ing and bleeding. Their malady Yankelovich sums up well in a run-on sentence where "and" is the key word:

> If you feel it is imperative to fill all your needs, and if these needs are contradictory or in conflict with those of others or simply unfillable, then frustration inevitably follows. To Abby and to Mark as well, self-fulfillment means having a career *and* marriage *and* children *and* sexual freedom *and* autonomy *and* being liberal *and* having money *and* choos-ing non-conformity *and* insisting on social justice *and* enjoying city life *and* country living *and* simplicity *and* graciousness *and* reading *and* good friends, *and* on *and* on.[3]

Yankelovich adds:

> The individual is not truly fulfilled by becoming even more autonomous. Indeed, to move too far in this direction is to risk psychosis—the ulti-mate form of "autonomy."[4]

And then this postscript from him:

> The injunction that to find one's self one must lose oneself contains a truth any seeker of self-fulfillment needs to grasp.[5]

Yankelovich, of course, neither tells us how one loses oneself, nor to what. For that only Christ has the answer. But certainly we ought to see the unattainability of contradictory goals. Internal emotional estrangement and the loss of reason are connected. This is a mood that dominates in our time and is symptomatic of the mind games we play with no rules. The *ands* in Yankelovich's essay demonstrate a grim reminder that sometimes there is only an "either/or" to life's decisions, not a "both/and."

There is a reason why the law of noncontradiction is called the law of either/or. The eradication of that difference may seem to be paying deference to all sides, but in reality it signals the death of all. Shakespeare put this well:

> Take but degree away, untune that string,
> And hark what discord follows! Each thing meets
> In mere oppugnancy. The bounded waters
> Should lift their bosoms higher than the shores
> And make a sop of all this solid globe;
> Strength should be lord of imbecility,
> And the rude son should strike his father dead;
> Force should be right; or rather, right and wrong
> (Between whose endless jar justice resides)
> Should lose their names, and so should justice too.
> Then everything includes itself in power,
> Power into will, will into appetite;
> And appetite, an universal wolf,
> So doubly seconded with will and power,
> Must make perforce an universal prey,
> And last eat up himself.[6]

There must be a common string by which we tune. There must be a boundary to the waters if the whole world is to not turn soggy. There has to be a system of justice. If that does not happen strength of body will determine right and wrong. Children can strike their parents dead; our voracious appetite for power will ultimately devour ourselves. We are already seeing some of this happen. Yet there is nothing so vulgar left in our present cultural experience for which some professor cannot be found somewhere to justify it. Reason has died.

THE CONTINUING SEARCH

Can we accommodate just anything without spoiling everything? Can we believe any idea without belittling every idea? Can we enjoy love without respect for its demands? Can we claim coherence when we live with contradiction? Can we nurture the soul when we feed only the flesh? The late Richard Weaver, one-time professor of English at the University of Chicago, rightly said that if we attach more significance to feeling than to thinking, we shall soon, by a simple extension, attach more significance to wanting than to deserving.

We looked at secularism and saw how the evil it generated could end up victimizing even the ones we love. When pluralization finds no answer amid our differences to the questions of culture, evil is unleashed particularly upon those whom we do not claim to love and, indeed, end up hating. This is an important point to note. Evil toward those we identify with is born out of the first mood. Evil toward those we differ from comes by way of the second mood. Every victim of hatred and prejudice lives with that irrepressible cry within, "Deliver us from evil." To whom shall we turn? Where should we go to find answers to such pain and evil?

In God's framework we are all created equal, made in His image; yet our ideas collide, each vying for superiority over the other. Pluralization and secularization are unable to provide the philosophical base with which to pattern coherence. As we will see later, only in the created order, in recognition of God's design for people and ideas, can this conflict be resolved.

In the end, with all due deference for differences, the mind knows it cannot be indifferent to truth. Where then does one go to find truth? A secularized world and pluralized culture tell us to find it at home — and leave it there. But doing so opens the door to an evil even more seductive. That now takes us to the third mood in a disintegrating culture.

Eight

The Disoriented Self

SOMEONE HAS SAID that old age is signaled when everything you hear reminds you of something else. But that tendency comes all too early in life for it to be labeled as a sign of old age. Life affords us the privilege of making connections and finding relationships, not only with people, but also with ideas. And sometimes the most exhilarating conversation takes place when one name or one event, shared between two individuals, unlocks a storehouse of memories and a wealth of emotions. I have not been able to recall where I first heard the following story, but I do recollect it as being true.

Some years ago a person in Christian ministry from the United States happened to be visiting Romania. It was during the bitterest days of the Cold War. As he trudged slowly through a rather busy but beleaguered section of town, bundled up against the biting cold, he was aware of the somber, grim faces of the people hurriedly brushing past him. Suddenly, as if in a different world, a man walked by, his ragged, coarse coat wrapped tightly around him, a woolen scarf thrown around his neck, and a warm cap pulled tightly over his scalp, whistling a melody to his heart's content. The veteran Christian worker was caught completely by surprise, for the melody was that of a grand but not too common Christian hymn, "The Great Physician now is here, the sympathizing Jesus." Shocked to hear it on a busy Romanian street, he picked up his pace to match strides with the cheerful whistler. He was aware that he might be under observation, so, not wanting to put the Romanian at risk, he cautiously walked alongside of him and softly whistled the tune with him.

The Romanian stopped, looked, and excitedly spouted forth a barrage of words in his own tongue, his face beaming. Immediately he knew that the words meant nothing to this stranger, separated as they were by the barrier of language. As if by instinct, simultaneously they both pointed to the heavens, laid their hands on their chests, and clasped one another in an emotional embrace. Not a word was spoken, but two worlds were joined as they bade each other good-bye and went their separate ways, still whistling the same tune. In one memorable moment eternity's resources knit together two spirits, bridging two worlds, because of identical life-transforming experiences—the mending of their lives by the touch of "the Great Physician." Everything else that separated them, culture, language, political experience, and myriad other differences were set aside, for they were united by a deeper love and a transcending truth.

How stirring such an experience is, demonstrating the breadth of commonality a shared spiritual commitment brings. This deep bond born out of a relationship to Christ is possible because it reveals the most treasured pursuit of each life, and a kinship that shares the fatherhood of God. Though they had never met before, these two men knew the deepest value of the other and, on that basis, could embrace as brothers. They were linked by eternal commitments. The American visitor could not have dreamed then that the day would come when the church of Christ in Romania would play such a pivotal role in displacing a murderous and ruthless dictator. Nor could he have foreseen, by contrast, a day when the dictates of government in

America would make the naming of Christ in the public arena a risky proposition. Though Romania has proven that seventy years of a brutal atheistic regime could not eradicate spiritual hunger by relegating it to privacy, here in America we are making a fresh attempt to privatize religious belief in the hope, at least of some, to silence it.

The dramatic change in direction toward spiritual issues taken by the two contrasting ideologies of totalitarian government and democracy may be the most astonishing reversal of the twentieth century. And the confounding silence of the powers in place who leave the subject undiscussed and ignore its drastic ramifications is even more mystifying. The wildest speculator could not have predicted that religious ideas would be brought into the open for discussion in what were once Marxist countries, while in democracies the same ideas would be held, for all practical purposes, under house arrest.

A STRANGE AMPUTATION

This *privatization* of religion is the basis of the third mood in modern America, a mood that has brought a deep rift within its own culture. The concept is somewhat difficult to explain in simple terms though it is enjoined upon us all, with Christians receiving unequal victimization.

Privatization may be defined as the socially required and legally enforced separation of our private lives and our public personas; in effect, privatization mandates that issues of ultimate meaning be relegated to our private spheres. Obviously, one who disavows any transcendent meaning, or one for whom the concept of meaning itself is meaningless, is comfortably compliant with this injunction. But for the Christian, this amputation from one's deepest convictions on life's most basic questions is a mutilation of that which only makes sense when it is kept whole.

This secular handcuffing of Christianity has caused anguish-ridden confrontations in the public square. Not only are we each marching to a different drummer, finding no commonality to harmonize life, but a concerted effort is made at the same time to ensure that any public expression of the basic Christian message is silenced. The extent to which Christian conviction is muzzled reaches new and bizarre dimensions each succeeding year. One must now walk through shopping centers at Christmas and listen to bowdlerized carols from which the name of Christ has been deliberately removed so that the celebratory mood of some shoppers is not offended. Powerful voices have even demanded that the calendar be changed from the historic delineation of B.C. and A.D. because such religious intimations intrude upon our newly fashioned Western world. Is this secularization all over again? Not quite. But certainly it is its philosophical handmaiden.

While secularization has cleansed the public arena of religious ideas, privatization insists that though one may choose to believe whatever one wants to it must be kept private. This is the social phenomenon of privatization that magnanimously gives with one hand and militantly takes away with the other—and is then mystified that this benevolence is not appreciated.

This allowance for private belief supposedly distinguished democracy from totalitarianism, where one's personal belief is dictated. But in effect the same public outcome results; life's deepest quests and most cherished values are sequestered. Every thinking person knows that to imprison a sacred belief within the private realm is ultimately to fracture, if not to kill, the belief. One could no more sever belief from public expression and still live spiritually fulfilled than one could remove the heart from the body and bid the blood flow. The separation kills the life in the body. Such is the impact on privatized spirituality.

A well-known musical composition may serve to illustrate this point. Even the uninitiated into the world of great classical music have heard of Schubert's "Unfinished Symphony." But what is not common knowledge is that to the ears of the novice the composition sounds like a finished work. In fact, if Schubert had not composed it as a symphony it would not need to be called "Unfinished." A symphony by definition must have four movements, but this has only two, hence the designation, the "Unfinished Symphony." The death of the composer left the last two movements undone, and the aficionado may only now imagine how grand and climactic, how magnificent and inspiring, the completed work might have been.

This is precisely what privatization in the West has done to Christianity. The Author of creation never intended the fundamental principles of right and wrong, justice and injustice, love and hate, peace and war, wealth and poverty, sexuality and promiscuity, profit and loss, freedom and tyranny, to be aborted at midpoint or to be fluid ideas at the mercy of a changing intellectual, political, or cultural elite. Yet, ironically, this very strength of Christianity, which allows such attacks upon its truths, lends itself to such abuse, just as the very strength of democracy makes it vulnerable to destructive forces within. There are other religions that will not stand for such public abuse and will respond with unbridled violence if such suppression is demanded. The glory and the gentleness of the Christian faith makes it vulnerable to such a siege of the soul, but the greater loss is that of a culture that moves resultantly from harmony to discord. The culture that so mangles the soul will never rise to the grand crescendo written into the human heart by the Author of life.

Commitment to God most certainly has its private expression, but it implicitly directs all of life. Spiritual reality is not just a sentinel from 5:00 to 11:00 P.M. behind closed doors. Privatization with disregard for coherence forces this dichotomy. In the name of nonoffensiveness, religion is privatized and relegated to the home, while in the name of freedom all kinds of indecencies and abandonments are made public. How ironic that sexuality and nudity, which are meant to be private, are now fare for public consumption while spiritual convictions, which are meant to strengthen public polity, are now for private expression only.

This rupture has had very significant effects on the place of religion in public life and on life itself as it is lived in the West. The notion is emphatically conveyed that moral beliefs are only private preferences, and therefore all beliefs are equally valid. Also promulgated is the pathetic and false notion that what people do in private ought not in any way to impinge upon public office and empowerment. By implication, the language of religious belief has been reduced to purely emotional talk, superstitious inclination not worthy of academic recognition or acceptable in public discourse. As a result, people have been left fragmented and alienated within society and within themselves.

Secularization left society without shame and with no point of reference for decency, and pluralization left society without reason and with no point of reference for rationality. Privatization—born from the union of the other two—has left people without meaning and with no point of reference for life's coherence. The greatest victim of evil so engendered is the self. We no longer know who we are as people.

It would be impossible in a brief treatment to cover the necessary ground to fully consider all of these implications. So let us examine at least two reasons why we know that privatization is a false premise. It is easily demonstrated that private belief separated from public practice is philosophically contradictory and pragmatically unworkable. Since privatization deals with the practical thrust of secularization, rather than resorting to a formal argument I would like to present its existential impact upon leadership and upon those of us in life's mainstream. This will demonstrate the all-important counterpoint that spiritual truth brings an unbreachable connection to life, which no law on earth can ultimately sever.

A PAGE OUT OF HISTORY

We know that the premise of privatization is flawed because who we are in public *is* determined by what we have learned and cherished in private. The role of the home is ineradicably etched into the mind of every individual. We have all heard the popular saying, "The hand that rocks the cradle rules the world." History has demonstrated this to be profoundly true.

A page out of Abraham Lincoln's life brings a thrilling story to light. When Lincoln was seventeen years old, he sang a song with a tender message at his sister's wedding.

> The woman was not taken
>   From Adam's feet we see;
> So he must not abuse her
>   The meaning seems to be.

> The woman was not taken
>   From Adam's head, we know;
> To show she must not rule him—
>   "Tis evidently so.

> The woman she was taken
>   From under Adam's arm;
> So she must be protected
>   From injuries and harm.[1]

How Lincoln first came across these thoughts put to song is a strong demonstration of a life that bore the fruit of early instruction. Rather than trying to present it in my words, let me do so in the words of the great English essayist F. W. Boreham:

The quaint verses as anyone with half an eye can see, are merely Matthew Henry turned into rhyme. But what did Abraham Lincoln at seventeen know of Matthew Henry? Yet one remembers an incident described by Judge Herndon—a thing that happened some years before Abraham Lincoln's birth. A camp meeting had been in progress for several days. Religious fervor ran at fever heat. Gathered in complete accord, the company awaited with awed intensity the falling of the celestial fire. Suddenly the camp was stirred. Something extraordinary had happened. The kneeling multitude sprang to its feet and broke into shouts which rang through the primeval shades. A young man who had been absorbed in prayer, began leaping, dancing, and shouting. Simultaneously, a young woman sprang forward, her hat falling to the ground, her hair tumbling about her shoulders in graceful braids, her eyes fixed heavenwards, her lips vocal with strange, unearthly song. Her rapture increased until, grasping the hand of the young man, they blended their voices in ecstatic melody. These two, Thomas Lincoln and Nancy Hanks were married a week later, and became the parents of the great president.[2]

Boreham explains that the preacher at those meetings, Peter Cartwright, and others with him were very familiar with the biblical commentaries of the devout English preacher Matthew Henry and often quoted from his writings. Following the trail from Henry to Cartwright to Hanks to Lincoln, Boreham could not resist this postscript: "It is interesting to know that at that formative stage of his epoch-making career, the noblest of the American presidents was sitting at the feet of our English Puritan."[3]

I do not believe for a moment that Boreham has stretched his point, because the faith of Lincoln's mother is well known, and his love for her is proverbial. Though he was only nine years old when she died, her last words to him were to admonish him to be faithful to his heavenly Father.

One cannot help but wonder what would have happened to the United States if a man of Lincoln's character had not been president at her most painful time of internal strife as brother fought against brother. The nation was in the grips of her most defining days. As blood flowed and dark days beclouded the horizon, the leadership of the land was in the hands of this great man. Who Lincoln was in private is what made him what he was in public. We are all familiar with his famed Gettysburg Address, but we would also do well to see him with his face in his hands before God, pleading with Him to save the nation.

History is replete with the instances of leaders prostrated before God when their nation faced its most critical moments. As the spires of Russia burned under the scorching hand of Napoleon's armies the czar was on his face before God in St. Petersburg, praying for the nation. As Ferdinand Marcos's helicopter gunships hovered over a small band of eight hundred soldiers who had called for him to step down from his dictatorship, this paltry group of soldiers were having read to them the words of Psalm 91: "He who dwells in the shelter of the Most High will rest in the shadow of the Almighty." Such, indeed, are the moments that try men's souls, and if the soul of the one leading the nation has been marred, wholeness is lost at the grassroots, and malevolence sprouts from the polluted soil of culture. Evil then reigns supreme.

No one realizes this need for the strength of a nation's soul more deeply than honest, sensitive politicians. They know just how impossible is the task of leading a nation, especially at a time of crisis when passions run deep, tempers run high, and brute force is unleashed. I recall a veteran congressman telling me that Washington is the loneliest city in the world. Each day he is pulled in different directions on someone else's whim, and in each instance his deepest personal convictions are tested. Privatization may seem fair and objective at face value. But it is a mindless philosophy that assumes that one's private beliefs have nothing to do with public office. Does it make sense to entrust those who are immoral in private with the power to determine the nation's moral issues and, indeed, its destiny? One of the most dangerous and terrifying trends in America today is the disregard for character as a central necessity in a leader's credentials. The duplicitous soul of a leader can only make a nation more sophisticated in evil.

The time has come to give careful attention to whether public life and private behavior can indeed be severed with impunity. Perhaps in the short run gains in single issues may be made, but in the long stretch this thinking will destroy the soul of the culture. If those who are empowered with public trust impeach their own character in private, it *does* matter, and it ought to matter. One can no more reconcile immorality in private with a call to public integrity than one can reconcile being a racist in private with being unprejudiced in public.

WHEN LIFE DOES NOT CONNECT

Of all the scandals that feed the public appetite, the one most delightedly pounced upon by some in the media is the scandal of a minister who has betrayed his trust. A politician may lead a double life; a lawyer may shamelessly abuse the legal process; a professor of ethics may lead the most unethical life; a doctor can make killing his or her profession. But when a minister crosses over the line of propriety even slightly, the relativists mercilessly pour down the anger of an absolutist's judgment.

But if religion *is* only a private matter, why must it invade the public office of the preacher? The charge of hypocrisy is the unintended compliment that vice pays to virtue. Even the defender of privatization knows that the essence of life cannot be conveniently portioned out to some particularities of living; it must apply to all of existence, whether one is a politician or a preacher.

Many years ago Arthur Miller wrote a play called "The Death of a Salesman." The whole plot was undisguisedly intended to reveal America's cultural reality behind the drama. It was the story of a man named Willy Loman, whose whole life was a masquerade. He feigned success in business, pretended faithfulness to his wife, and crafted an image of himself before his children as a man who had all the wealth and contacts that were needed to bring every material dream within their reach. But the charade came to a sudden stop when his son, Biff, discovered the private failure and infidelities of his father's life. In bitter disappointment he agonized over the lies on which his father's entire life was built. Finally, on a fateful night when Willy Loman could take the discovery of his deceit-ridden life no more, he stormed into his car and drove recklessly into a suicidal collision, graphically portraying the reality of his own inner self-destruction. The postscript tearfully muttered by Biff said it all: "Dad did not ever know who he really was."

That is the disintegration of a double life. It breeds a schizophrenia. No one applauds when he or she has been victimized by someone else's duplicity. In this implicit condemnation lies the first point of consideration for all of us immersed in Western culture. Does Western culture know anymore what it is at its core? Do we as individuals know who we are? We all hunger for meaning and judge other lives according to their coherence. Where there is no coherence, there is no meaning. We look for coherence between law and life. We look for coherence between word and deed. We look for coherence between promises and fulfillments. We look for coherence between love and trust. In short, there is a longing to find a connectedness in life.

Cultures seek coherent answers within themselves because without coherence in community there is evil in the home and on the streets. And there is no coherence in our communities because there is no coherence in our individual lives. We cannot put into living what we do not have in life. We cannot give to others what we do not have ourselves or know where to find. In denying this generation the viability and the reasonableness of the Christian faith we have tossed away the only resource we had. We now find ourselves with nothing of the spirit to offer, only the material. That spiritual hunger must be fed or our culture will slide deeper and deeper into concoctions of evil that no civilization ever thought possible.

THE POSTSCRIPT OF THE CENTURY

As we close this section let us see how far we have traveled. Secularization led us to a loss of shame, pluralization to a loss of reason, and privatization to a loss of meaning. We noted that when secularization has bred its loss of shame it will generate evil even against those we love. Pluralization in turn has given birth to the loss of reason, generating evil toward those whom we choose to hate. Privatization kills meaning and gives rise to evil against ourselves because the alienation within mutilates the soul. No event in recent memory better encapsulates this threefold evil with which we now live than the trial of the football icon O. J. Simpson, charged with the murder of his estranged wife, one whom he claimed to love. The emotionally laden trial that gave opportunity for every trick in the book ultimately led to his acquittal. He was found not guilty by the introduction of ideas that fostered hate in our ethnically diverse culture.

But the ultimate irrationality has to be the statement made by one of his attorneys, Robert Shapiro, in his interview with television talk-show host Larry King. When Shapiro was asked by King what he personally felt about his client's guilt or innocence, he answered, "It does not matter what I think. . . . What I believe is something that really is of no importance, and I will tell you why. That's a moral judgment. And I can't make moral judgments. I can make professional judgments."[4]

Does Shapiro need to be told that the decision to make only a professional judgment rather than a moral judgment is itself a moral judgment? One must wonder whether such heartless cruelty would pass off as magnanimity if he sat where the parents of Nicole Brown Simpson sat or if it were his own son or daughter who had been murdered. Ah! But privatization has done its work in his mind. He lives under the illusion that his disconnected belief is a medal of professional excellence, failing to realize the conscience-destroying lie to which he has sold himself.

Let us take careful note. Evil does not come only in the garb of a masked murderer. In its most cunning and destructive form, it comes as an idea dressed in sophisticated attire, rationalized by these prophets of the wind. Nothing is more perverse than the idea that where murder is concerned truth and morality do not matter. But privatization reared its lying countenance in the philosophy espoused by the defense in the trial of the century. The trial may have been more than that. It is the prime example in this century of a culture that has killed shame, reason, and meaning. The evil begotten by these losses has victimized the ones we love, the ones we hate, and ultimately ourselves.

The last expression of Prime Minister Konoye of Japan, who committed suicide after his role in the Second World War, is a fitting reminder. On his night table was Oscar Wilde's *De Profundis.* The words he had underlined read, "As terrible as it was what I had done to others, nothing was more terrible than what I had done to myself."

The cultural revolution began in the sixties, and the children of that generation are now crying out for help and for answers. Who will deliver them from evil? The revolutionaries of the sixties told us then in their art that their private lives were eroding. One has only to read the lyrics of the culture in revolt to hear what they were saying. It was in the sixties that Justin Hayward and the Moody Blues sang:

> Why do we never get an answer
>   when we're knocking at the door
>   with a thousand million questions
>   about hate and death and war?

> 'Cause when we stop and look around us
>   there is nothing that we need
>   in a world of persecution
>   that is whirling in its greed.

Why do we never get an answer
when we're knocking on the door?

With perceptive power the chorus states the innermost quest:

I'm looking for someone to change my life.
I'm looking for a miracle in my life.[5]

Like Oscar Wilde, that generation found it easier to live in its art. Those of this generation have carried that alienation one step beyond. They even find it difficult to live in their art. The art of this generation has reached hideous proportions of violence and hate that are then transferred into life itself. Even within the artistic world voices are crying, "Stop!" Can we hear their cry for deliverance?

No one admits to this alienation more candidly than our young. Some years ago, a pastor handed me a piece of paper on which was written a poem. He had just returned from visiting a troubled teenager who had attended some meetings his church had hosted. Arriving at the young man's home the pastor had discovered that the teenager had committed suicide and left this note behind for the pastor to read:

Lost in a world of darkness
   without a guiding light,
Seeking a friend to help
   my struggling, failing plight.
Now all of you good people
   just go on passing by,
Leaving me with nothing
   but this lonely will to die.

Somewhere in this lonely world
   of sorrow and of woe
There's a place for me to hide,
   but where I do not know;

For no matter where I go
   I never will escape
The devil's reaching, clutching hands,
   or the drink of fermented grape.

So out of my grief and anguish
   Perhaps some wandering boy will see,
Long after I have left this world,
   And build his own life, strong and good and free.

The quest to escape from reality has revealed that there is no place to hide. The journey of our culture has now reached its destination, a destination it never intended. A society without a point of reference for shame, reason, and meaning has very little to offer to a generation in search of *strength* with which to live, *goodness* by which to live, and *freedom* in which to live. These were the very failures that felled the Greco-Roman world.

Western culture now faces the same possibilities. We have made a decisive break with the past and have changed the soil of culture which nourished the seeds of progress. That soil is now being reconstituted, and one of the principle features of the change is the removal of boundary lines between the sacred and the profane. When that happens we court an even greater danger. Any time a decisive break is made with the past the ramifications are profoundly serious.

But the question arises, do we turn the keys of the kingdom over to religious authorities then? The Bible has much to say about changing the rules of culture in midstream and about the peril of religion that has no truth. The Hebrew world more specifically addressed the questions of national survival in transcendent terms and came to some shocking conclusions. Therefore, let us bend our ears to what the Bible has to say about culture and meaning. The Scriptures resound with lessons from history for a nation's character and for personal coherence. The truths from these voices of the past are fascinating.

Part 2

The Voices of the Past

Nine

Establishing Boundaries

THE ONLY THING more startling than a tap on the shoulder in the dark is a voice that shatters the eerie silence. And if that voice happens to be of someone who is dead, then the jolt is even more terrifying. Just such an ominous encounter was narrated to me at a home I was visiting. Understandably, it had an unnerving effect upon the one who had experienced it.

I had been invited for dinner during a conference at which I was speaking, and although he was cordial when I arrived, my host seemed notably uneasy in my presence. The conversation throughout the meal was noticeably strained, and I was quite aware of the frequent, piercing glances in my direction. After dinner, he asked if we could stroll in his backyard and talk awhile. And minutes into our conversation alone, the mystery unraveled.

While still attending college his son had been tragically killed in a car accident. "For a long time I was not able to get over my son's death," he said. "There had been many things going on in his mind that I wished we had been able to talk about. I agonized for months over the opportunities forever lost."

One day, his story continued, as he was driving on a business trip he decided to play some of his son's favorite music on tape, hoping somehow to reach back into his son's life. In what had to be a shock to him, suddenly, in the middle of the tape, his son's voice spoke as clearly as if he were sitting in the back seat of the car. The grieving father was caught completely by surprise.

The voice, of course, was on the tape itself. As the father pieced it together he discovered that a few weeks before the fatal accident, his son had made a serious commitment to Christ during some meetings at his college at which I had the privilege of speaking. So deep an impact had been made in his heart that he had returned home and recorded on tape what this commitment meant to him. It was an expression of his spiritual journey, and the mention of my name on that recording had since prompted the father to extend his dinner invitation. First, he wanted to say thank you for the role God had given me in the life of his son whom I did not even know, and second, he wanted me to know how therapeutic it had been for him to hear this voice that had passed from his life. How consoling a voice can be, especially if it is a voice we long to hear, speaking of things so profound and personal.

But there is only one voice that has that capacity to speak on matters of ultimate reality, and that is the voice of God. The Bible reminds us that God has spoken to us in numerous ways. Not only has He spoken in the written Word and in the consummate expression of His own Son, but also in the steady unfolding of the drama of history. In fact, His voice is also heard in periods that seem to be silent or in ways that seem unpretentious. We mistakenly limit God's involvement in our lives to the spectacular or the sudden. In the coinage of current aphorisms, we have ascribed only the destructive (such as hurricanes, earthquakes, and tornadoes) to "acts of God" and have missed the gracious voice that has beckoned humanity since the days of our creation. It may well be that His care and keeping are most powerfully demonstrated during those times in the life of an individual or nation when everything seems to be ordinary.

The avenue upon which we will focus now as we give ear to the voices of the past is the arena of history through which He has spoken with such inescapable force. How we read and understand history sets the parameters by which we glean the lessons it so repeatedly offers. For this reason some of the brightest minds and most influential thinkers in every century have sought to define what history is all about. In so doing they offer a key to unlock the past and shape the future, for after all, the present is the conduit that transforms the future into the past. As we probe into the past we will get a glimpse of evil's long reach and of God's shaping of the soul even through it.

THE IMPORTANCE ESTABLISHED

Karl Marx defined history in terms of economic power and its distribution between the owner and the worker. The philosopher Hegel, on the other hand, said that to lay hold of the interpretive key to history one needed to grasp not the blend of economic power as much as the interplay between the ideas that are woven through the historical process. To him, each principal idea spawns its opposite, and in the synthesizing of these opposites the historical drift finds its direction. Philosophies of history abound, and our present century has seen both the enrichment and the cost-exacting ramifications of how it is defined.

There have been others, of course, varying from the profound to the cynical, who have had their say on the subject. In the genre of the most maverick pronouncement, Henry Ford's oft-quoted quip, "History is bunk," battles for the lead. But far more radical is the statement, unfortunately more reflective of contemporary attitudes, "The past does not affect me; rather, I affect the past."

Amid the verbiage of conflicting theories, the warning words of the Romantic poet Samuel Taylor Coleridge stand out with common sense and have a ring of truth, unimpeachable even by the cynic: "If men could learn from history, what lessons it might teach us! But passion and party blind our eyes, and the light which experience gives is a lantern on the stern which shines only on the waves behind us."[1] This over-the-shoulder look at the stern lights the path we have already traversed and instructs us in some of the most important lessons so that we might avoid repeating the mistakes.

Something of cardinal importance must be added lest we reduce the world of events and biographies to an impersonal tale of one inexorable sequence of cause and effect. Behind this theater of reality is a God who is not only involved in the macrocosmic move of people, powers, and ideas but is intensely involved in each and every individual life. That is why giving ear to the voices of the past is not just a theoretical pursuit. G. K. Chesterton astutely observed, "The whole difference between construction and creation is exactly this: that a thing constructed can only be loved after it is constructed, but a thing created is loved before it exists."[2]

If history is seen as a construct of the human mind, then it is ours to love or to hate or even to ignore. But if it is seen as the arena of the Creator's self-disclosure and His love for His creation, then we can be absolutely sure of His purpose and goodwill as He works in and through His creation, indeed, a creation He loved before it even came to be. By doing so we may see the underlying truth that in the final analysis history is "His story." If we miss His story, evil will ever remain a mystery and good will ever remain at the mercy of cultural drift.

This portion of our study will take us into another time and place in history, both to look at our lives from His perspective and to gain a glimpse of what it is that God has tried to communicate repeatedly and pleadingly to preserve the purpose of our being. Only in understanding the Author of life can we cling to that which is good and be delivered from that which is evil. There is no better place to look than in the record of His story.

History understood this way is the arena in which God unfolds His truth, with the hearts of men and women as the locus in which He attempts His work. This is the fundamental difference in the definition of history that separates a secular view from a spiritual one. To the rugged materialist we just happen to be here, clothed apes, a blip on the radar screen of time, a cosmic accident. But to the Christian our existence is by the designed will of our heavenly Father who is ever in control of the universal scene. Each of us is here at this specific time within the compass of His sovereign will.

Admittedly, this is also one of the most tested beliefs for the Christian, for if we were to pause long enough to think of all the tragedies and atrocities of a single day, how easy would it be to cast all our care upon Him and know that He is in charge? Yet it is that consolation of His love for this world that enables us to see the bigger picture and not be brainwashed by isolated sound bites. That is why the role of history is so important to understand.

The cities of mankind tell a fascinating story of the reach of this God and of the resistance of the human will to Him, of the longing in the heart of God for our well-being, and of the schemes of the human heart that spell destruction. Today, if one were to travel through some of the historic cities that once displayed such splendor, the piles of rubble would speak from the past. God intended it to be so. These piles of rubble call to mind a scene from Jesus' life as He entered the city of Jerusalem from the Mount of Olives, riding on a colt, while the people irresistibly cried out to Him with shouts of praise. The annoyed Pharisees called on Jesus to order them to be silent, but Jesus replied that if they were to keep silent the very stones would cry out. The context in which He spoke these words is a worthy reminder. He warned them, first of all, to be ready for the spectacle of desecrated sanctuaries and demolished buildings that would posthumously tell the tale of their humiliation at the hands of an enemy. But He went on to underscore that the reason for this forth-coming debacle was their inability to recognize "the time of their visi-tation."

If the voice of God is unrecognized in its timely utterance, timeless reminders carved in stone will remain, haunting generations to come. But also implicit in Jesus' sobering reminder was the possibility of a brighter tomorrow for a nation that had "ears to hear" and would heed His call. To them would ensue a greater consolation, the prom-ise of the recovery of righteousness and of peace—those deathless handmaidens of godliness. Such consolation is greater than the voice of one on a tape that breaks the silence from the backseat of a car. For when God speaks and beckons, the eternal has intersected with the moment, not merely to explain the past, but to instill an anticipation for the future as it is guided by the comforting hand of the One who holds it.

Let us therefore take a walk through the galleries of the past that not only show us the hall of fame but also the hall of shame. The stones and the personalities will tell us the story with buttress-ing eloquence. These galleries will present us with both script and deed, with the dominant role of leadership and the gullibility of the people, with the national choices made and the resultant drift of his-tory, and with the failings of political power and the seduction of religious power. Through it all we may catch a glimpse of the strong feet of the "Hound of Heaven" pursuing the swift feet of human resistance.

The picture unfolds with clarity, and one can be overcome by the story His imprints tell. The challenge before us in such a journey will be to thwart the constant temptation to cynicism, a cynicism that leads one to wonder if the human mind is incorrigibly plagued by the belligerence of an unteachable spirit. But we will thrill to discover that just as hope may begin to fade, there will come some incredible surprises to remind the incurable pessimist that His story has not only its grim reminders, but its climactic interventions, too.

THE STONES THAT SPEAK

Percy Bysshe Shelley penned a memorable poem called "Ozymandias":

> I met a traveler from an antique land
> Who said: Two vast and trunkless legs of stone
> Stand in the desert . . . Near them on the sand,
> Half sunk, a shattered visage lies, whose frown,
> And wrinkled lip, and sneer of cold command,
> Tell that the sculptor well those passions read
> Which yet survive, stamped on these lifeless things,
> The hand that mocked them, and the heart that fed:
> And on the pedestal these words appear:
> "My name is Ozymandias, king of kings:
> Look on my works, ye Mighty, and despair!"
> Nothing beside remains. Round the decay
> Of that colossal wreck, boundless and bare
> The lone and level sands stretch far away.[3]

No part of the world offers more to the archaeologist's spade than the Middle East. Whether it be the crestfallen countenance of an ancient monarch or the faint markings upon a sacred altar in a buried commune, the wealth of information is shoveled out in spadefuls, delighting the mind as a banquet for the hungry. For our purposes, I would like to look at two very influential leaders in the Old Testament and focus on their times, their choices, and their legacies. I have deliberately chosen to focus on these periods because their times, like ours, experienced radical shifts—sometimes soaring with spiritual exuberance and at other times plummeting with reckless indulgence. The lessons of failure and success are often writ large.

The span of time this covers is the seventh century before Christ. Within this century the extremes to which the nation of Judah swung were so radical that had anyone fallen asleep between the reigns of Hezekiah and Josiah they would have assumed that the nation was basking in a century-old high noon of spiritual glory. But the reality is that the hiatus of over half a century between these two reigns brought Judah to her darkest days, days of benighted spirits and self-inflicted wounds that were mortal without being immediate. Those wounds are the most insidious and ultimately destructive, because continued survival lulls the leadership into a false security that disregards the slow bleed.

During this period the people were led by one of the most radical and destructive of all monarchs, Manasseh. That this one king, sandwiched between two of the most historic reformations in Judah, could undo during his single reign all the good that had been accomplished and would be accomplished, is a potent reminder that *any nation at any time—however spiritually alive—is always potentially only a generation away from paganism and mind-defying evil.* One can never sit back on past successes and assume a sustained strength for the future. Every generation must win its own victory.

> Once to every man and nation
> Comes the moment to decide,
> In the strife of truth with falsehood,
> For the good or evil side;
> Some great cause, God's new Messiah,
> Offering each the bloom or blight,
> And the choice goes by forever
> 'Twixt that darkness and that light.[4]

To every generation there comes that defining moment, and if it is squandered, the chain of events is long and painful. This is Western culture's hour of decision.

Ten

Pulling Down the Fences

GERMAN THEOLOGIAN Emil Brunner made the curious suggestion that Adolf Hitler should be posthumously given an honorary
doctor of theology degree because he awakened Europe to her Christian heritage by showing her what the world would be like without
Christianity. Brunner's sarcastic pronouncement would apply in the
same measure to the individual who now draws our attention, for
through him we shall see the hell that is unleashed when spiritual
truths are renounced.

With the death of Hezekiah a new and devastating day dawned
upon Judah as the leadership abandoned God and set the tone for the
people to frolic in unfettered restraint. Although on the surface the
nation mourned the loss of their great king Hezekiah, their periodic
invocation of his name and his legacy was primarily a charade, for
very quickly and drastically the spiritual climate was set back by a
generation. That reversal was brought about by the single-handed
determination of Manasseh, the son of Hezekiah. Old Testament

writers and commentators are united in describing this as one of the darkest periods in Judah's history.

If there is one word that comes close to summarizing the effects of Manasseh's reign, which tragically was also the longest one in Judah, it would be *pitiful*, for by the time he was through both he and those who had become his victims were to be pitied. They knew they were on a path to complete destruction, and though Manasseh himself belatedly recognized the evil he had wrought and tried desperately to stop the degenerative process he had started, he found out that it is easier to destroy a nation than to rebuild it. Leading a people into evil has always been an easier process than shaping a people for goodness.

John Adams, the second president of the United States and a principal negotiator to end the American War of Independence, said, "Facts are stubborn things; and whatever may be our wishes, our inclinations, or the dictates of our passions, they cannot alter the state of facts and evidence."[1]

The facts of Manasseh's reign leave us puzzled. Yet similar bents toward unmitigated evil have been relentlessly and stubbornly repeated in history, with punishing force. Malcolm Muggeridge's cynical comment, "All new news is old news happening to new people,"[2] is perennially true.

Manasseh made three specifically defined decisions that altered Judah's course and drove her to the same tragic fate that had already overtaken the Northern Kingdom. The first and most radical choice he made was to lead a reaction against his father's spiritual reforms. Manasseh was very young when he took the reigns of government, and his childish vulnerability merits our sympathy. Old Testament scholar Alfred Edersheim has described the hazards of juvenile limitation when thrust into extraordinary power, "before thought could have tempered willfulness, or experience set bounds to impulse."[3]

But the policies Manasseh pursued and the choices he made were carried out not only in the seedling years of his adolescence; they were also wantonly made in the full flower of manhood. He was consumed with a passion to break the hold of God's law upon the people. Chesterton has said that there are many angles at which you can fall, but only one angle at which you can stand straight; Manasseh was going to test all the angles.

In four painfully blunt verses, the Scriptures tell us the course he charted:

> He did evil in the eyes of the LORD, following the detestable practices of the nations the LORD had driven out before the Israelites. He rebuilt the high places his father Hezekiah had destroyed; he also erected altars to Baal and made an Asherah pole, as Ahab king of Israel had done. He bowed down to all the starry hosts and worshiped them. He built altars in the temple of the LORD of which the LORD had said, "In Jerusalem I will put my Name." In both courts of the temple of the LORD, he built altars to all the starry hosts. He sacrificed his own son in the fire, practiced sorcery and divination, and consulted mediums and spiritists. He did much evil in the eyes of the LORD provoking him to anger. (2 Kings 21:2–6)

Leading the reaction against his father's reformation, Manasseh set a personal example. It has been rightly said that before any fence is removed, one should always pause long enough to find out why it was placed there in the first place. The moral law God gave to Moses at Mount Sinai was just that. It not only revealed the nature of God and His purpose for His creation, it also served as a boundary line for the people, a line that could not be crossed with impunity.

There is no creative impulse or end result in life that provides for limitless possibilities without some parameters. In the fragile path of living, where relationships intersect and passions collide, God in His wisdom has provided fences, walls, and boundaries for our well-being, that we might not stray into terrain that destroys the very essence for which we were made. And it is these fences and walls that are coming down today with thundering force.

The social libertarian may find great ecstasy in the sound of their falling, but it may well be the very death knell of the one for whose protection the barriers were built. One of the most aberrant breeds in the American political scene these days is the one who gleefully describes himself or herself as a fiscal conservative but a social liberal. That is just another way of saying that people must live within their means financially, but can die beyond their means socially.

TRACING THE MOMENT OF CHANGE

In 1993, *Forbes* commemorated its seventy-fifth anniversary by asking eleven distinguished writers and thinkers around the world to contribute an article addressing the befuddling contradiction of the West, which, although it has so much materially is nevertheless a place where millions live lives of quiet desperation. The distinguished writers included Nobel laureates like Saul Bellow, prolific novelists like John Updike, and others of stellar credentials. Of all the wisdom presented in their preachments, the most insightful analysis may have been offered by journalist Peggy Noonan. In her article, alluringly titled "You'd Cry Too If It Happened to You," she presents this powerful illustration:

> We have all had a moment when all of a sudden we looked around and thought: The world is changing, I am seeing it change. This is for me the moment when the new America began! I was at a graduation ceremony at a public high school in New Jersey. It was 1971 or 1972. One by one a stream of black robed students walked across the stage and received their diplomas. And a pretty young girl with red hair, big under her graduation gown, walked up to receive hers. The auditorium stood and applauded. I looked at my sister. "She's going to have a baby."
>
> The girl was eight months pregnant and had the courage to go through with her pregnancy and take her finals and finish school despite society's disapproval.
>
> But society wasn't disapproving. It was applauding. Applause is a right and generous response for a young girl with grit and heart. And yet in the sound of that applause I heard a wall falling, a thousand year wall, a

wall of sanctions that said: We as a society do not approve of teenaged unwed motherhood because it is not good for the child, not good for the mother and not good for us.

The old America had a delicate sense of the difference between the general ("We disapprove") and the particular ("Let's go help her"). We had the moral self-confidence to sustain the paradox, to sustain the distance between "official" disapproval and "unofficial" succor. The old America would not have applauded the girl in the big graduation gown, but some of its individuals would have helped her not only materially, but with some measure of emotional support. We don't do that so much anymore. For all our tolerance and talk we don't show much love to what used to be called "girls in trouble." As we've gotten more open-minded we've gotten more closed-hearted.

Message to society: What you applaud, you encourage. And: Watch out what you celebrate.[4]

Peggy Noonan dealt with a harsh reality in a gentle way and warned of the delicate balance that is needed in many indelicate issues. But this very balance is shaken when fences are removed because straying becomes impossible when there is no line to differentiate between the safe and the perilous. In an unbelievable and shocking turn of events we have moved from speaking out against certain moral choices to being pressured by political enforcement and the so-called tolerant cultural elite not only to accept what was once disapproved of, but to celebrate it. Allowance for people to determine their own moral destinies has been supplanted by the demand that even that which may be repugnant or offensive to one's moral sensitivities must be acclaimed and glorified.

New experiments are made in education and entertainment that endanger the lives of impressionable children, and any voice of concern that is raised is promptly dismissed as reactionary. How many riots and suicides and broken lives is it going to take before we will give up this illusion that we can enter any zone of imagination and feed any image or idea into young minds, trusting them to their own good judgment in their selections?

Os Guinness said it best: "'Just say no' has become America's most urgent slogan when 'Why not?' has become America's most publicly unanswerable question."[5] It does not require a sophisticated moral sense to predict the outcome whenever a society pretends there are no fences. Common sense alone alerts us to the dangers.

The repudiation of the God worshiped by one's parents is a daring step and ought to be thought through carefully, because the family's worship is the scaffolding of the morality the children espouse; it helps them, with that priority, to structure their lives. This is not by any means to state that all belief, right or wrong, must be retained from generation to generation. No. It is possible that a world of error can be transmitted uncritically across the ages. But rather, this is only to affirm that whenever such a fundamental change is made, it ought to be sober-mindedly taken in full recognition of what is being uprooted and of what is being put in its place.

The terrifying reality of our current social scene with its unprecedented violence, ravaging drug addiction, and the painful specter of AIDS, is that we ought to at least pause long enough to ask whether the repudiations we have made in the past generation coupled with the current celebrating of a boundaryless existence have a direct bearing on the present tragedies.

Every now and then, especially when new crime statistics are released or when electioneering rhetoric heats up or some horrible story of a mangled life hits the press, speeches pour forth urging us to teach our children moral principles again. Few indicators of the paucity of our moral resources are more mind-staggering than a recent bestseller that was nothing more than a compilation of old stories of moral rectitude. The book sold on a massive scale, beyond the publisher's greatest expectations, with purchasers lining up at the cash register like starving peasants queuing up for bread in a famine-stricken country. That response does instill some hope, but it is going to take more than that. Just to call people back to morality, without saying why they should be moral or what morality is at its core is only another form of pragmatism. We know the fences have fallen, and we see marauding bands invading terrain that does not belong to them, and once again the cry goes out, "Deliver us from evil."

THE DEADLY DESTRUCTION

The second step Manasseh took was predictable. When any belief is expelled, one is not left with a position of neutrality. Any time a world-view is evicted, it will be replaced by another. Manasseh's next move was to accelerate the development of heathenism, and here he led the way in the most heinous practice of all—child sacrifice.

Today, to walk down into the Valley of Hinnom outside of Jerusalem brings a surge of emotion when the description is read of what took place there. Biblical scholar Cunningham Geikie describes Manasseh's dastardly practice:

> The hideous image of Moloch, the god of the Ammonites, once more rose in the valley of Hinnom, and Manasseh himself led the way in consecrating his own children, not to Jehovah, but to the grisly idol, or as the phrase ran, making him pass through the fire to the god; as if the flames, burning away the earthly impure body, let the freed soul pass through them, cleansed from all taint of earth, to unite with the godhead. . . . Human sacrifice became common at the "high places of Tophet" in the valley of Hinnom; the stately central mound, on which the idol towered aloft, rising deep and large in the midst.
>
> Night time seems to have been the special time for these awful immolations. The yells of the children bound to the altars, or rolling into the fire from the brazen arms of the idol; the shouts and hymns of the frantic crowd; and the wild tumult of drums and shrill instruments, by which the cries of the victims were sought to be drowned, rose in discordance over the city; forming, with the whole scene, visible from the walls by the glow of the furnaces and flames, such an ideal of transcendent horror, that the name of the valley became, and still continues, in the form of Gehenna, the usual word for hell.[6]

One can only imagine what all this meant to the destruction of the people's mind-set. When the king himself led the way and the sounds of burning infants were repeatedly heard echoing in the valley, it is little wonder that they called the location "hell."

Picture the scene of this unbelievable time in history. A long procession led by the king and his bodyguard followed by the thronging masses makes its way to the Valley of Hinnom. Filling the last ranks were parents holding tiny little children who were completely unaware of the fate that awaited them minutes away. In the affectionate embrace of their mothers they were oblivious to the agony through which they would be put by these same arms as they would be rolled into the flames from the arms of the idol. Think of young pregnant women watching this wondering, *Is this what I am carrying my child for?* Think of the young teenagers observing this, hearing the screams of their brothers and sisters and thinking, *Is this what life is about?* How incredible that such a scorching form of paganism could, at the whim and power of a leader who pulled out the fences of decency, replace the nobility of a righteous people.

Removing the good never stops with just that step. Defiance of that sort is not a momentary outburst on a single issue. Rebellion that sees no sanctity in life's essence is a constant state of mind bespeaking a heart that will never be satisfied. Just as a blackmailer can never have enough, so also a rebellious heart will never feel that it has enough autonomy. Leadership that caters to the rebellious will find in them an insatiable demand for more. Thus, in Manasseh's hell-born schemes, once he had begun the downward slide he could not stop, for autonomy becomes addictive.

There is an irresistible footnote to the Valley of Hinnom. As one stands in the valley and looks upward, the view encompasses what is called the Mount of Offense. It was so called because that is where Solomon housed his harem. There is an inextricable connection between the Mount of Offense and the Valley of Hinnom. The heart fueled by promiscuity will someday fall into the burning arms of an idol that devours our offspring.

Manasseh took a third and final step. There were voices crying out for a halt to what he was doing. One such voice was that of Isaiah the prophet, who paid for his protests with his life. Manasseh instituted a bitter persecution of the prophets, thinking that by silencing them he was doing the politically expedient thing. He did not even bother to look over the historical landscape and learn that he could never succeed in eradicating true spiritual passion by persecuting it. False and superficial beliefs can be stifled by law or power, but those etched into the conscience or soul cannot be obliterated by decree. Somewhere, at some time, they will resurface in public. The words of James Russell Lowell are enduringly true.

> Truth forever on the scaffold,
> Wrong forever on the throne,
> But the scaffold sways the future
> And behind the dim unknown
> Standeth God within the shadows,
> Keeping watch, Keeping watch above His own.[7]

The very prophet that Manasseh killed, Isaiah, was the one who told us more of the Messiah's triumph through suffering and of the everlasting nature of God's kingdom than any other prophetic voice. But for then, with these three deliberate steps, Manasseh changed his country.

This chapter in Judah's experience has some life-affecting lessons to offer to us. First, it proves one of the most repeated lessons in history: *It is possible for one person to lead millions of people into untold evil.* C. S. Lewis pointed out years ago that "man's conquest of nature" was nothing more than the wresting of power by some to control others with the instruments of nature. And for centuries politics has dabbled in the deadly game of social engineering. The whole point of state-controlled education is that it gives to the government the power to shape the souls and write on the fresh slates of young hearts. This empowerment is the most important trust given to elected officers, and to assume that they accept that responsibility from a posture of neutrality is to live under the most destructive illusion. To elect one to the highest level of leadership, therefore, is to put into his or her hands the possibility and opportunity of shaping a nation's conscience.

A few years ago I took part in a discussion with seven military generals at the Center for Geo-political Strategy in Moscow. The imposing structure stands eight stories above ground and descends four stories below ground. As one enters, the ceiling of the welcoming hall towers high above while the massive and highly decorated pictures of all the famous Russian generals throughout history line the walls. Staring into the faces of men like Peter the Great and Mikhail Kutuzov, who led the Russian forces against Napoleon, it is impossible not to feel dwarfed in the historical hall of fame of a superpower nation.

Yet, as we talked about the greatest needs of the hour for the world as a whole, one of the most meaningful moments came, reducing us all to silence, when one of the generals, with an icy stare of hard reality said, "We know what war can do, and we have great fear of it." As we prepared to leave, all seven generals lined up to bid us good-bye.

Then each of them, softened by the hours of interaction, took my wife's hand and kissed it. Finally the chief of staff said to me, "Mr. Zacharias, I believe that what you have said about our need for God is true. But after seventy years of believing a lie it is very hard to change." What a monumental testimony to the power of a handful of individuals seven decades ago who changed the soul of a nation.

I could not help thinking of all that has been done to the Russian people, who are so gifted and capable, by some of their own leaders, and in particular, by Joseph Stalin. During his reign of terror he obliterated fifteen million of his own people. It defies every imagination. Think of his counterpart in Germany, Adolf Hitler, who provoked the bloodiest, most unnecessary, most disruptive war in history and changed the pattern of the world irremediably. Just one person's influence. With that thought, consider the means we now have within our reach by which one person can change history again. If that does not alarm us to the potential consequences when fences have been pulled down, I do not know what will.

THE GULLIBILITY THAT MAKES IT POSSIBLE

The second lesson from Manasseh's life is that *one person is able to lead millions into untold evil only because the nation has ceased to think clearly.* That has been extensively true in the past and is even more pathetically so in the present.

Some years ago ABC news-anchor Ted Koppel delivered the commencement address at Duke University. He daringly challenged the members of the graduating class to hark back to the Ten Commandments and find their moral compass again. In the middle of his talk he made a very pointed reference to America's diminishing capacity to think, glaringly reflected in the heroes our nation creates. (He also, with embarrassment, conceded that his own medium of professional involvement—television—was the principal culprit in producing an unthinking generation.)

In citing Mr. Koppel it is not my intention to cast any aspersion upon the specific person to whom he referred: She herself bears no indictment here, but the unthinking sycophants who swoon at her success strain credulity. To make his point, Koppel coined a new word—"Vannatized"—and then went on to talk about the Vannatization of America, referring to the popularity of game-show assistant Vanna White. Ms. White has done a masterful job, said

Koppel, of turning letters of the alphabet when they light up. She looks utterly enthralled to be doing it, creating such an aura about her in this cerebrally minimal activity that it has brought her a cultic following of national proportions. Her published autobiography sold so quickly it went into a second edition. I repeat, as I echo Koppel's concern, that this befuddling phenomenon says nothing of her. It must not be easy to look so perfectly contented and fulfilled by a feat that does not make much demand on the mind. But how utterly incredible that an activity as minuscule as that should make one a national figure to be adulated—if the pun may be pardoned.

This does say, however, that there are millions out there for whom thinking would indeed be a challenge. And that is why it is possible for one person to lead millions into busy lives with inactive minds. Listen to the horrendous illogic that sounds forth from the gatekeepers of our culture when they try to make a case against the sacred. The argumentative capacity of talk-show hosts who make moral pronouncements against morality is exceeded only by a pathetic inability to build a sound argument. The move from unsubstantiated premises to invalid deductions consistently color their faulty thinking, and what is more, the same fallacies get transmitted to uncritical hearers. Assertions claiming truth frequently go uncorroborated, and the arguments that are built show a complete disregard of validity. One can only shake one's head in disbelief and marvel at how mushy our thinking has become. The science and art of critical thinking have been humiliated in a generation that thinks with its eyes.

THE CRIME THAT FOLLOWED

The greatest lesson Manasseh's life teaches is not just the capacity for one to lead the many nor the incapacity of the many who follow the one. The greatest lesson is that *the ultimate test of any civilization is what we do with our children.*

When the soul of a nation is scarred, its children are part of the loss. Interestingly enough every culture today claims, in theory, to place the highest value on its love of its children. Some time ago when one Middle Eastern leader was asked when the fighting in that part of the world would stop, she answered, "When they love their children more than they hate us." I have little doubt that the opposing side would say the same. There is a profound expression of values in that statement. In our own prisons those whose crime was committed against a child are kept in protective custody to protect them from the anger of other prisoners. Even criminals draw a line. In any course on ethics, the bottom-line illustration is still, "Is it all right to torture babies?" rhetorically stated, of course, and always eliciting a thunderous "Of course not!" In a bizarre way, even in Manasseh's time child sacrifice revealed that the child was of greatest value, and therefore it was offered up to idols of their own making.

Some years ago, I was preaching in a small town in Australia. Sitting close to the front was a woman with two young children. She was somewhat unkempt and bedraggled in her appearance and quite hostile in her expression. Sitting next to her, her little boy fought back tears throughout the entire evening. There was a constant disturbance from their direction with sporadic whispering and threatening gestures from her to the children.

At the end of the service she asked if she could see me alone for a few minutes. She told me she was a convinced Marxist and hated religion with a passion. But because of a promise she had made to a friend, she had come to church that night. Her decision was made on the spur of the moment, and she literally dragged her hastily dressed children into the car. As she sped along through the traffic her son tried to get her attention, but she angrily screamed at him to be quiet. He persisted in trying to get her to just look at him, so she turned around and backhanded him across the mouth, drawing blood, then continued to ignore his sobs and pleas.

Halfway through my message I evidently made a comment about

the hardening or tenderizing role that parents play in their children's lives. Just at that time she caught sight of her son's feet and noticed he was wearing his sister's shoes. She looked at him with bewilderment and asked him why he was not wearing his own. And that is when her private world came apart. She could bottle up her tears no longer as he stuttered out that this was what he had been trying to draw to her attention the whole evening. In her haste, she had grabbed the wrong pair of shoes, and without giving him a chance to tell her they were not his shoes but his sister's, she flung them into the backseat, instructing him to put them on.

The woman herself cried like a child as she talked, acknowledging that her own life was not manageable anymore. Then she muttered, "Dear God, what am I doing to my children?" It became the glorious night that she turned her life over to Christ, and as she walked out into the darkness, she paused to wipe her son's face and left clasping one child in each hand.

The application to our own culture is obvious, is it not? What is it we live for, and what, in that pursuit, are we doing to our own children? One look at the world we are giving to them spells horror. The statistics speak for themselves: In the last fifty years, 149 major wars have been fought, killing twenty-three million people. This figure is double the number of victims of war in the nineteenth century and seven times more than the eighteenth century. The principal victims, of course, are children. In the last decade alone two million children have been killed, four to five million have been disabled, and twelve million have been left homeless. One million have been orphaned or separated from their parents, and ten million have been psychologically traumatized while millions of them have suffered in civil wars such as that in Angola for thirty years, Afghanistan for seventeen years, Sri Lanka for eleven years, and Somalia for seven years.

A whole generation has grown up not knowing a day of peace. In Somalia, for example, more than half of all the children under age five who were alive on January 1, 1992, were dead due to violence by

December 31 of that year. The vortex of violence in which the children are trapped becomes even more horrific when we realize how many of them are now involved in the front lines themselves—literally hundreds of thousands.[8]

Can anyone read these statistics without being overcome? What a price civilization is paying. The statistics in America may be different because we are not engaged in civil war. But we are certainly involved in a moral war that is even more insidious, for it ravages the souls of our children. Greater than the violence in our inner cities is the violation of decency within a child's heart perpetrated by adults. When reason has no point of reference in society the next generation will embody the logic of unreason.

The questions haunt us: What are we doing to our children when we tell them there are no moral boundaries? When we ridicule sacred things? When we leave them vulnerable to any philosophy of life that comes around? When we walk out on marital commitments and leave them defenseless in a predatorial world? What have we done? We have sacrificed them as we have gambled away the sacred and left them to be vandalized by the evil that is present at every stage of life. We have a role in delivering them from evil. But we do havoc to their souls when we tell them there are no fences in life or when we laugh at the proclamation of God's Word. Need one even belabor their victimization in child pornography today? Or recount that scores of children in the inner cities are planning their own funerals at age eight or nine because they do not expect to live to see their teen years? Intellectual capacity can help us to do the surveys and print out the statistics, but only the mind that is disciplined with ultimate values can find answers to these horrible realities. These are questions of the soul.

Some time ago, as I walked into my son's room to kiss him good night, I found him in bed with tears running down the side of his face. I asked him what the matter was. He tried to shrug it off, but at my persistence he finally said, "I am just sorry to be growing out of my childhood so soon. I have enjoyed it so much." What a statement to be made by a fourteen-year-old on the heels of a wonderful week-end we had spent together as a family. Contrast these words with the words of a fourteen-year-old from Bosnia, a young lad named Dinja:

> So many people have been killed fighting for justice. But what justice? Do they know what they are fighting for, who they are fighting? The weather is growing very cold now. No longer can you hear the singing of the birds, only the sound of children crying for a lost mother or father, a brother or sister. We are children without a country and without hope.[9]

Children want to be valued, but they also want to know the reason for that value, and there is no surer way to instill value into them than to impart to them that they are a gift from God. They are not objects to be gambled away by spilling them into the destructive arms of the spirit of the age, arms that have been fashioned by the intellect at the cost of the mind and soul.

These are the lessons the seventh century B.C. taught Judah. And in a most incredible turn of events, Manasseh himself fell on his face before God and repented. But by then a whole generation had been lost. It was literally the hell of a delayed conversion, for his victims lay strewn in his path. Personal rescue at the cost of national disaster was little consolation to him and has a lesson all its own.

By removing the fences he let in a flood of evil ideas. Today with maverick zeal we debunk the absolute. Can we pause long enough to think of what we are doing? Hear, for example, the words of noted scholar Arthur Schlesinger as he touts the brazenness of a society that is gladly and confidently taking such risks.

In 1989 Schlesinger was asked to speak at the induction of the president of Brown University. As he presented his challenge, his target was obvious—"the mystic prophets of the absolute":

> The mystic prophets of the absolute cannot save us. Sustained by our history and traditions, we must save ourselves, at whatever risk of heresy or blasphemy. We can find solace in the memorable representation of the human struggle against the absolute in the finest scene in the great-

est of American novels. I refer of course to the scene when Huckleberry Finn decides that the "plain hand of Providence" requires him to tell Miss Watson where her runaway slave Jim is to be found. Huck writes his letter of betrayal to Miss Watson and feels "all washed clean of sin for the first time I had ever felt so in my life, and I knowed I could pray now." He sits there for a while thinking "how good it was all this happened so, and how near I come to being lost and going to hell."

Then Huck begins to think about Jim and the rush of the great river and the talking and the singing and the laughing and friendship. "Then I happened to look around and see that paper. . . . I took it up, and held it in my hand. I was a-trembling because I'd got to decide, forever, betwixt two things, and I knowed it. I studied a minute, sort of holding my breath, and then says to myself: 'All right, then, I'll go to hell'—and tore it up."

That, if I may say so, is what America is all about.[10]

How frighteningly candid. How pathetically wrongheaded. But before we dismantle all the fences of moral absolutes, we would do well to listen to the voice from history, the voice of Manasseh. He speaks to our darkness from the vantage of having made a similar speech in his time. Thankfully, Manasseh's was not the last chapter in Judah's history.

Eleven

Restoring the Soul

I LISTENED ON ONE occasion to an informative and impassioned talk on the condition of our large cities around the world. The content ranged from population sizes, criminal activity, social conflicts— all the way down to sewer systems or the lack thereof. As the information quotient was rising something inside me kept crying out, "I agree, I agree, please stop! Just tell us what to do about all of this." The conclusion, when it came in the form of an anecdote, has since provided me with a unit of measurement for an anticlimax.

The speaker related that during the Second World War the British navy was frustrated by the threat of Germany's elusive submarines and was desperate to find a way to spot them before it was too late. A plan was finally offered by one for whom practicality had no value. He suggested that all they would need to do would be to "boil the ocean." He explained, "Once you bring the ocean to a boil, the submarines will be forced to surface. Then we can knock 'em off, one after the other."

"But how does one boil the ocean?" shouted an irritated questioner.

"I don't know," came the reply. "I have just given you the idea; now it is up to you to implement it."

With that quip and a broad smile upon his face, the speaker at our conference sat down. Thankfully, he did not intend to leave the question unaddressed; he was only biding his time to give us an opportunity to reflect on the magnitude of the problem he had presented.

More often than not, cynical solutions are commonplace with so monumental a problem. Such is the problem of wickedness confronting the world. The challenge lies in finding the solution. The Scriptures give us extraordinary insight into this subject of our soul-struggle in a disintegrating culture. Very quickly we notice how God deals with the issue.

Human beings have a limitless capacity to raise the question of the problem of evil as we see it outside of ourselves, but a disproportionate willingness to raise the question of evil within us. I once sat on the top floor of a huge corporate building owned by one of the biggest construction tycoons in this country. Our entire conversation revolved around his question of so much evil in this world and a seemingly silent God. Suddenly interrupting the conversation, a friend of mine said to him, "Since evil seems to trouble you so much, I would be curious to know what you have done about the evil you see within you." There was a red-faced silence.

I have never defended the existence of God at a university campus without being asked about this question of evil in the world. Yet on only one occasion have I been asked how to cope with the evil within. This dichotomy alone gives us a clue as to where it is that God begins to frame the problem and propose a profound answer. As we come to terms with God's response, we will soon detect how it is possible to withstand the most destructive influences of culture and steady the soul in the turbulence of colliding world-views.

The answer will be presented in three phases. First we will see how it has been addressed in the past, so that we may apply it to the present. In the next chapter we will attempt to unravel the mystery of wickedness, and then in the final chapter we will get a glimpse of the power and presence of God even in the darkest manifestations of evil. Such a confrontation seems inevitable as we look at the face of the future.

The man who led Israel to her greatest spiritual recovery, on the heels of Manasseh's evil-ridden reign, was young King Josiah. The Old Testament historian pays him the supreme tribute when he says, "Neither before nor after Josiah was there a king like him who turned to the Lord as he did—with all his heart and with all his soul and with all his strength, in accordance with all the Law of Moses."[1] The four "alls" pretty much tell it all—all his heart, all his soul, all his strength, in response to all the Law of God.

Josiah was only eight years old when he was crowned king. A gentle, but determined little boy, he was to mature into God's ideal of manhood. At age sixteen he passionately sought the mind of God by which to direct his own life. At twenty he realized how Manasseh had turned back the clock Hezekiah had set for the nation's spiritual recovery, and he made his primary goal the restoring of the national soul. His first step was to remove the idols and degrading altars the people had re-erected. Then, at age twenty-six, taking another page from Hezekiah's life, he began the cleansing of the temple, recognizing that its physical disrepair and displaced vision were symptomatic of a lost commitment in the hands of those to whom the people had entrusted their souls.

What a precedent was set by this young leader, eager in his own heart to bring his nation back in tune with the heart and mind of God. His first challenge, therefore, was to those who were in spiritual leadership. That alone tells us what his priority was. Today's leaders are more prone to relish the opportunity to speak before business and financial powerbrokers, making economic concerns of supreme importance. They repeat the seductive blunder of assuming that material comfort will set the nation on a prosperous course. When was the last time a politician up for election called upon the spiritual leadership of the nation to take their calling seriously and lead by example? How heart-stirring it would be for a people and for the youth in particular to see a political leader who cared more for being right than for being elected. Only as those who honor their call before God with responsibility are encouraged and supported will a people turn in similar inclination of spirit with concern for their souls.

By taking these historically proven steps—challenging the false gods of his time and issuing a plea for righteousness to the temple leaders—Josiah stumbled into the most surprising discovery of all. He found the Book of the Law, buried beneath the debris of a neglected temple. How unthinkable this is—that in the midst of the grand edifice whose sole reason for being was the worship of the living God and whose trust was the teaching of the oracles of God, the Word that was central to those purposes was lost under the clutter of ecclesiastical politics. This discovery was providential for Josiah, because there would have been no way for him to usher in a spiritual revival without a keen understanding of the very character of God. For that he needed God's self-disclosure—the Book of Books.

This is the basis on which every nation must structure itself if it is both to understand evil and to deal with it. If a nation does not believe that God has spoken, then all moral points of reference, individually and corporately, become vacuous, and evil will only confound the mind. If, on the other hand, the Scriptures are tested and proven to be what they claim to be, then the soul thrills at the possibility of the grandest freedom of all—deliverance from evil and restoration to unblemished beauty. History has supplied the light upon the stern, and God's Word provides not merely the interpretation of the past but the illumination for our present and the promise for the future.

To this very day when a British sovereign is crowned, as the Bible is placed in his or her hands the words are uttered, "This book is the most valuable thing the world affords." Some years ago, Margaret Thatcher, then British prime minister, did take the example of Josiah when, addressing the Scottish General Assembly of the Church of Scotland, she said to the delegates:

> The truths of the Judaic-Christian tradition are infinitely precious, not only, as I believe, because they are true, but also because they provide the moral impulse which alone can lead to that peace in the true meaning of the word for which we all long. . . . There is little hope for democracy if the hearts of men and women in democratic societies cannot be touched by a call to something greater than themselves. Political structures, state institutions, collective ideals are not enough. We parliamentarians can legislate for the rule of law. You, the Church, can teach the life of faith.[2]

In 1823 Daniel Webster said:

> If truth be not diffused, error will be; if God and His Word are not known and received, the devil and his works will gain the ascendancy; if the evangelical volume does not reach every hamlet, the pages of a corrupt and licentious literature will; if the power of the Gospel is not felt throughout the length and breadth of the land, anarchy and misrule, degradation and misery, corruption and darkness will reign without mitigation or end.[3]

Obviously this presupposes that the Bible is the Word of God. In Appendix A of this book that defense is presented, but we will consider its implication now.

THE GREATEST TREASURE

Few are better equipped to speak on the value of the truth and the place of Scripture than those who have seen the most despotic and tyrannical forms of power or who have been victimized by a culture overtaken by unmitigated evil. Many years ago in Lebanon, I was introduced to a family that was still reeling from the shock of recovered wealth when all seemed hopeless. The way it had come about brought tears and laughter as I heard the story.

Sami, a dear friend of mine, played the hero's role in this touching story. One of Sami's great characteristics was fearlessness. One day he was driving with his wife along a highway on the outskirts of Beirut when he suddenly saw a large suitcase lying on the side of the road. Most people would not only have driven past it, they would have probably picked up speed, almost certain that it was booby-trapped. But not Sami. G. K. Chesterton has defined courage as getting away from death by continually coming within an inch of it. That is a perfect description of Sami.

Much against his wife's pleas, he stopped, walked over to the suitcase, and began to feel its contours.

"Sami," she insisted, "leave it alone and let's go."

She may as well have been talking to a blade of grass. Triumphantly, he shouted back to her, "Joy! I think it is full of something!"

Hardly thrilled by that piece of information Joy called to him once more to come away. But Sami was convinced that somebody had lost it. So, much to his wife's utter anguish, he brought it back to the car and took it home.

To make a fascinating story short, when he opened it, he found every inch of space within crammed with money. It was certainly not the kind of experience that would cause one to moan in despair, "Why me, Lord?" Fortunately, there was also an address and telephone number inside, and after repeated attempts at phoning, someone finally answered. Sami asked for the person by name, and when, in a doleful voice, the man identified himself, Sami asked him, "Sir, have you lost something?"

Taken aback, the man paused and then said, "Have you found it?"

The rest of the story was basically that of a frenzied effort on the part of the man to make arrangements to retrieve his suitcase, which he had lost en route to the boat he was to catch as he was attempting to leave the country.

I was in Sami's home when the owner of the suitcase brought his family to meet, in flesh and blood, a man with a soul in a disintegrating society. Beirut was once called the pearl of the Middle East. Its beauty was both proverbial and historic. Yet in the tangled web of human greed and ideological heartlessness it is a city now where piles of rubble have taken the place of majestic buildings and ancient edifices. In this war-torn suburb a family was dumbfounded to see a life that had not been destroyed by the evil around it.

As they sat in Sami's living room, completely overwhelmed, Sami said gently, "You think you have recovered your treasure. Let me tell you how passing a treasure this is. With the fragile state of our country, this could become completely worthless overnight. Let me give you the greatest and the most enduring treasure you can ever have."

He handed them a copy of the Bible. It was a memorable moment as they held it in their hands. Was this real? Was this the Word of God? Was this indeed the greatest treasure on earth, a light to their feet and a lamp to their path? That was my last glimpse of Beirut, in Sami's home, before I myself set sail for Cyprus the same night, leaving behind a country in physical ruins. But I had witnessed the courage of a man who sought things that are eternal amid the ruins of human wickedness. In his heart he enclosed the city of God in stark contrast to the cities of men.

Indeed, the Bible is not just the trust of monarchs, nor is it just the standard for a nation's conscience. It is the definitive reality of life's purpose, from God's mind to ours. The "Book of the Law" mirrors the soul as it was intended to be. It reveals the sacredness of our words to each other—engendering trust. It holds us to the sanctity of our marital vows—enriching the splendor of love. It preserves the essential dignity of every human being—elevating the beauty of relationships. It bequeaths to us the sacredness of time—enjoining the sanctity of both work and rest. It commands us to respect the property of others—breaking the stranglehold of fear. It guards our essential purpose—energizing us by the coalescence of worship. It is the Mind of God. It is the Law of God. This is not a bondage to rules; this spells deliverance from evil. This was not meant for us to hate;

this was made for us to love. For this we were made: that we might know the mind of God and let that mind dwell in us. This is the Word that calls us to reason together with God so that the evil within us may stir us more than the evil around us. It is only in that sequence that the soul of an individual and the soul of a nation can be recovered.

This is the treasure Josiah gave back to his people—and it is the greatest contribution of the Hebrews to young America as well. Let us be absolutely certain of this. It was not the Code of Hammurabi that touched America's conscience. Nor was it the intent or content of the Koran. By no stretch of imagination was it the pantheistic framework of Eastern mysticism. America's soul was indubitably formed in keeping with the basic assumptions and injunctions of this, the moral law of the Hebrews, which gave her a vision of history's linear thrust whereby she was to reconcile liberty with law.

Let us get beyond the debate as to how orthodox or heterodox the founding fathers were. What is already beyond debate is that the fundamental precepts by which they wanted to govern could only have been possible within a biblical framework, not that of any other major religious system. But in our time the light of the ancient and time-tested blueprint of the soul that Josiah recovered has once again been smothered at the whim of an autonomous culture. The imprints of Athens, Rome, and London are still upon us. But the all-important endowment of Jerusalem has been tossed to the winds.

THE PUREST PURSUIT

Second, Josiah led the people by personal confession and restored to them the beauty and purity of worship. G. K. Chesterton astutely asserted that nothing sublimely artistic has ever arisen out of mere art, any more than anything essentially reasonable has ever arisen out of pure reason. There must always be a rich moral soil for any great aesthetic growth.[4]

Josiah knew that the road back was to put the Law of God into the hands of the people, but maintaining the nation's moral strength required the priority of worship. In this he has once again left an example that political leadership would be wise to follow. Moral convictions rooted in God's nature and in the worship of God are intrinsically related. To be moral for morality's sake becomes a form of self-worship. When the moral law of God is the blueprint for life then the worship that follows shows reverence to the God in whose being that law is revealed. That is the worship that builds strength against evil and triumphs over the fragile will. Nothing involves a greater discipline of the mind than the coherence that worship brings. Who or what a person worships provides the rationale for his or her behavior.

Apart from this moral soil in which people have a reverence for life, the best of minds get channeled in the wrong direction. The concept of moral necessity seems to elude some contemporary intellectuals who brand all moral talk senseless or relative. In reality, all talk outside of a moral context is vacuous. Here we immediately see the first point of variance between the moods of the present and a voice from the past. The debunking of morality by the secularists of our day makes it impossible for either the arts or the sciences to achieve their rightful grandeur. Only in the fertile soil of moral goodness can they truly flourish. And where moral goodness and spiritual hunger are mocked, any harnessing of the strengths of these disciplines is fraught with danger and, indeed, can be cause for fear.

Moral discourse without reverence for life itself is meaningless, and reverence is at the heart of worship. That is why, in one sense, the opposite of *sacred* is not *secular* but *profane*, which literally means "outside the temple." Secularism seeks to establish a cultural base for life apart from the temple, rendering life inside the temple unworthy of serious intellectual respect. The lesson from history is that sanctity within the temple ultimately defines life outside the temple, and without the former, life becomes profane. Just as reverence is at the heart of worship, profanity is at the heart of evil.

This lesson must be driven home because it explains the foundational difference from those who argue for morality without the need for God. Where there is no reverence there cannot be morality, and where there is no God there is no reverence. A world bereft of reverence breeds the very malady now bemoaned by secular intellectuals who seem mystified by what plagues them. Carl Sagan's recent writings are a classic example when he laments the fact that modern day scientists have lost their sense of wonder. Sagan does not seem to grasp the point that they are being more consistent than he is. When the universe is stripped away from a Creator, how long can brute facts enthrall the mind? Ideas have an expiration date for thrills; only the glory of a person is inexhaustible. Wonder can be thrillingly sustained when each new discovery points to the Creator. Without the Creator the means overtakes the end, and wonder dies. Worship is the culmination and continuance of a relationship with a person, not the celebration of an idea.

The same applies to human sexuality. If the sanctity of sexuality is lost, intimacy loses meaning and becomes mere self-gratification. The most demeaning comment ever made on the way sex has been profaned came from an actor who said his relationships have one prerequisite—"If you do not ask me for my name, I will not ask you for yours." The evil contained in such disregard for a person's essential value cannot be denied. Ultimately it is the person behind the relationship that provokes wonder because of the divine image stamped upon the human personality. If the person is a means to an end, then the greater has been destroyed by the lesser. Women who have been betrayed time and time again voice the sense of utter rejection they feel when the means has overtaken the end.

In one of his proverbs Solomon said, "The path of the righteous is like the first gleam of dawn, shining ever brighter till the full light of day" (Prov. 4:18). The only way righteousness can get brighter is when it is based on a relationship and not just on a set of guidelines.

It has been said that society prepares the crime and the criminal commits it. Similarly, genuine worship creates the soil in which society flourishes, and in that soil can be planted a people of peace. Josiah left that soil for his people. When the Law of God was returned to the people and worship was restored, three very direct transformations took place.

One may legitimately argue that this singular vision is possible only in a theocracy, a government that recognizes God as its head—which is what Israel was. That is a correct observation. But we had dare not miss the larger point and the more pertinent lesson of history. What was it that made it possible for a people to turn their backs upon a culture immersed in evil and make a heartfelt change for the good? It was the belief that God had spoken and that life is at its core sacred. Without those two beliefs no society can stem the tide of evil. The place to begin, therefore, is in the individual life. *The soul of a nation is changed one person at a time.* The method may seem slow, but the transformation then occurs with integrity and respect, and the end result is thorough. As we will see, several profound consequences followed from Josiah's two simple steps.

THE CONSOLATION OF THE HEART

First and foremost, the people once again lived with *a sense of safety.* They no longer needed to live in fear of one another or of what might befall them at night in their homes or on their streets. Jewish philosopher Dennis Prager interestingly sustained the connection between reading God's Word and the mitigation of fear when he asked listeners of his radio program the following question: If you were stranded on a lonely road in Los Angeles in the dead of night with your head under the hood of your car, and suddenly you heard the sound of footsteps and turned to see ten burly men walking toward you, would it or would it not make a difference to you if you knew they were coming out of a Bible study? Every caller who responded laughed and granted the deduction.

There are few things our generation longs for more than the confidence to be unafraid of each other. Being a victim is also a state of mind based on the reality that threatens. The billions of dollars we spend on alarm systems, theft-reduction devices, crime-fighting agencies, and weapons with which to defend ourselves tell a pathetic tale of the role fear plays in all of our lives. How glorious it would be to be free from this terrifying reality. That freedom from fear can only come when people love the Law of God and worship Him with reverence. It will not make a perfect world, but it does give our culture a foothold from which to respond to the dangers that lurk.

The evil all around us has cast a net of fear, and we now live perpetually looking over the shoulder. How can life not exact a heavy toll when such stress attends? The conviction of safety is the blessing of a culture at peace with God. Thomas Merton said that man is not at peace with his fellow man because he is not at peace with himself. He is not at peace with himself because he is not at peace with God.

Nearly ten thousand delegates attended the historic Conference for Itinerant Evangelists in Amsterdam hosted by Billy Graham in 1986. At that time, according to a United Nations statistical summary, it was among the largest representation of nations ever gathered. One of the most thrilling stories shared from the pulpit was by a renowned Korean speaker, Billy Kim.

Dr. Kim told of an American soldier hiding in a bunker during a skirmish in the Korean War. When his commander ordered him to scramble closer to the front lines and rescue some of his fallen mates, the soldier nodded his head, took a covert glance at his watch, stalled till his commanding officer was out of sight, and simply made no move. Several minutes went by, and a colleague reminded him of his assignment to rescue those who had fallen. Again he looked at his watch and delayed. Finally, he leaped out of the bunker and fearlessly began the arduous and risky process of carrying his compatriots to safety. At the end of the day when the guns were silent, a friend asked him why he kept looking at his watch when under orders to move. The soldier threw his head back, fighting off the tears, and said, "I was afraid—afraid because I knew I was not ready to die. I lingered for the moment when I knew my fear would be overcome—remembering that at a certain time every hour my mother had said she would pray for me. As soon as that minute struck I knew I was under the shelter of her prayers, and that no matter what awaited me, I could face it."

Who would have imagined that a grown man with so much fire power behind him would find a greater confidence in his mother's prayers? During life's most trying moments there is great comfort in the prayers of one whose life is lived under the shadow of the Almighty. Every time before my wife leaves with me on a trip she agrees on a time with our children when she will be praying for them. That promise has always met with a mutual commitment and obvious gratitude.

When I first heard this story from Billy Kim my mind wandered back to when I was in Vietnam, speaking at a service attended by several American airmen. They were in full uniform, some on alert for missions that were imminent and dangerous. I had already been told that most of them would probably not return. I will never forget that scene as long as I live. The closing hymn resounded throughout the room as these predominantly male voices sang from the depths of the emotions that welled up from within them:

> When Peace like a river attendeth my way,
> When sorrows like sea billows roll,
> Whatever my lot, Thou hast taught me to say:
> It is well! It is well with my soul!

But let us not miss the reason for this peace, stated by the songwriter:

> My sin! Oh the bliss of this glorious thought,
> My sin not in part but the whole:

Is nailed to the cross and I bear it no more
Praise the Lord, Praise the Lord, oh my soul.[5]

Freedom to have peace without begins with the freedom from wickedness within.

General Norman Schwarzkopf of Gulf War fame gathered the largest military arsenal ever assembled in history under his command. Yet, he said that even in the final seconds before the Stealth Bombers began their mission to fire the opening shots of the war and attempt to disable enemy radar, he himself was in prayer with his Bible beside him.

War is a wake-up call to where the real power lies and to what real peace means. In the war of ideas that rages today and amid the restlessness that seems endemic to the national mind-set, we can offer no greater peace than what Josiah gave to his people. The Bible says it with succinct promise: "You will keep in perfect peace him whose mind is steadfast, because he trusts in you" (Isa. 26:3).

THE EMPOWERMENT OF THE WILL

The second benefit of restoring the Law of God was that it gave the people *the power to change*. Our enslavements and indulgences have not only developed into more distasteful appetites; they have also taken from us the power to change. Many confess a craving to change but find themselves helpless and powerless to do so. In refreshing contrast God's Word promises that very power to make the changes we know are right.

Centuries after Josiah, history offers a great illustration of this capacity of God's Word to change lives. One of the most glorious tributes ever paid to the power of the gospel is in the impact it had in the ancient city of Corinth, a little stretch of land that became symbolic of all that was debased and immoral. It is the miracle of the gospel that a church even existed there. Of the twenty-seven books in the New Testament, two of Paul's epistles were addressed to this small city with an international reach.

Historians tell us that Corinth was a city destined for greatness. Strategically located, she took most of the traffic between the north and the south of Greece, and from the east to the west of the Mediterranean. Riches came her way from many directions: balsam from Arabia, carpets from Babylon, slaves from Phrygia, and dates from Phoenicia. However, it was not so much her material wealth that made her a byword among the nations as it was her impoverished spirit. If you had wanted to defame someone as profligate and unfaithful, you would call him or her a "Corinthian." What was it that spoke of her immorality? That story is visible today even in her rubble.

Atop a hill just on Corinth's outskirts sit the remains of the temple of Aphrodite. Aphrodite was thought to be a goddess who, living in continual infidelity to her husband, symbolized promiscuity. Finally he was able to set a trap for her that revealed her wretchedness to all. In Greek mythology we are told that when she was thus exposed, she fled, covering her face in shame. But out of her illicit relationships were born two children, Eros and Phobos, from which we derive the words *eroticism* and *fear* —one an insatiable appetite, the other a paralyzing emotion. How articulate is the past, once again, in its stones and in its lessons.

The temple of Aphrodite housed a thousand prostitutes who descended into the streets of Corinth at night to market themselves to the Corinthian passions. This was Corinth. This was her lewd worship. It is quite an experience to stand there today and remember what the apostle Paul said to the Corinthians when he first arrived. He had just come from Athens, where he had dealt with the questions of the intellect. Here in Corinth, he dealt with the passions of the body. For both, it was the mind that needed renewal. In delineating Corinth's catalog of vices, he graciously added the words, "And as such were some of you." The gospel had changed many a Corinthian, and we can now so clearly understand why it was to them he penned his greatest treatise on the purity of love. Those words stand etched in marble in Corinth to remind the tourist of Paul's text on God's love, which had such transforming power in a context so debauched by erotic love:

> Love is patient, love is kind. It does not envy, it does not boast, it is not proud. It is not rude, it is not self-seeking, it is not easily angered, it keeps no record of wrongs. Love does not delight in evil but rejoices with the truth. It always protects, always trusts, always hopes, always perseveres.
>
> Love never fails. . . .
>
> Now these three remain: faith, hope and love. But the greatest of these is love. (1 Cor. 13:4–7, 13)

How gentle was his touch, how relevant his subject. It was to these very Corinthians, so dead in their sins, that he wrote one of his greatest chapters on the resurrection of Christ. It was to these same Corinthians that he signed off, "with the grace of Christ, the love of God, and the fellowship of the Holy Spirit"—words that spoke of their newfound salvation, their new impetus in worship, and their new bond with each other. That very transforming power of a new love and new desires, God still gives today.

Many years ago when I was speaking in Boston, at the end of a particular message, one of the first persons to respond to the gospel invitation was a young woman. I saw her kneel down and be counseled by one of the pastors on staff. When he had finished, he brought her to meet me and handed me the card she had filled out expressing her desired commitment to Christ. In a complete shock to me, I noticed that under the section marked "profession" she had filled out "prostitute." My expression must have betrayed my surprise, for as I looked at her, she said, "It is true. And I am sorry. In fact, I was on my way to the street I walk every night, feeling so dirty inside but so helpless. I just saw the sign outside this church, saying you were talking on the theme of a new life. I wanted it so badly. God has spoken to me tonight, sir. I leave this place a new woman." In this one life, think of the evil that was stemmed from that night on.

That is the power of God multiplied across centuries in changed lives, lives in which God has brought that difference through His Word. This is the deliverance from evil that begins with the self and not with the philosophical attack upon a disembodied idea of external evil. Is this all just an escapist's haven? Absolutely not. G. K. Chesterton said the problem with Christianity is not that it has been tried and found wanting but that it has been found difficult and left untried. And the change the Word brings is not just a psychological one. The change is that of the mind as it grasps the truth and is not swayed by a mere feeling but by the deliverance deep within.

THE TRIUMPH OF THE MIND

The Word brings not only peace and power but also the third result of Josiah's discovery, which was that it *delivered them from the tyranny of the immediate.* Life can take twists and turns that at times make the best of us despondent as we see the wicked triumph and wonder if there is any purpose to righteousness. We easily become handcuffed by the here and now, or we cry "surrender" to the latest threat voiced by some new ideologue on the cultural landscape. How often we lose heart and hope because of a battle lost to a destructive policy. Despite the importance of these things, our discouragement over bad laws and policies should always be balanced by the larger context of where history has been and where it will inexorably go.

In a shocking turn of events, Josiah was to exemplify the truth that there is more to reality than just one's temporary successes or failures. In something that must have daunted their spiritual march forward, the people saw Josiah's life violently and ruthlessly cut short. They had not envisioned this end to a life so beautifully lived. Where was God in all of this? Where was God? Right in control, teaching them the most difficult of all lessons, that in the ebb and flow of history, pain and disappointment are real. Our moral sensitivity causes us to feel those sharp edges. But the way to victory is in the trust we continue to place in Him who is sovereign over history.

This very principle was embodied in the way Jesus dealt with the wickedness of His time. Author George MacDonald says this of Christ's method of changing society in the face of evil:

> Instead of crushing the power of evil by divine force; instead of compelling justice and destroying the wicked; instead of making peace on earth by the rule of a perfect prince; instead of gathering the children of Jerusalem under His wings—whether they would or would not, and saving them from the horrors that anguished His prophetic soul—He let evil work its will while He lived; He contented Himself with the slow unencouraging ways of help essential; making men good; casting out, not merely controlling Satan. . . . Throughout His life on earth, He resisted every impulse to work more rapidly for a lower good—strong, perhaps, when He saw old age and innocence and righteousness trodden under foot.

MacDonald adds, "To love righteousness is to make it grow, not to avenge it."[6]

Josiah's recovery of the Book of the Law built this kind of righteousness, revived the soul of his people, and gave them God's blueprint for the soul of mankind.

As we witness this drift through history from the Hezekiahs to the Manassehs to the Josiahs of every age, the voices of the past tell us much. Whether it be through the limited philosophy of Greece or in the religious failure of Jerusalem. Whether it be through the tarnished splendor of Rome or the long-set sun of the British Empire, America had better pay heed to these words of Malcolm Muggeridge:

> We look back upon history and what do we see? Empires rising and falling. Revolutions and counter-revolutions. Wealth accumulated

and wealth disbursed. Shakespeare has spoken of the rise and fall of great ones that ebb and flow with the moon. I look back upon my own fellow countrymen, once upon a time dominating a quarter of the world, most of them convinced in the words of what is still a popular song that the God who made them mighty shall make them mightier yet. I've heard a crazed, cracked Austrian announce to the world the establishment of a Reich that would last a thousand years. I've seen a murderous Georgian brigand in the Kremlin, acclaimed by the intellectual elite of the world as wiser than Solomon, more humane than Marcus Aurelius, more enlightened than Ashoka. I have seen America wealthier and more powerful than the rest of the world put together, so that had the American people so desired they could have outdone a Caesar, or an Alexander in the range and scale of their conquests. All in one lifetime. All in one lifetime. All gone. Gone with the wind. England, now part of a tiny island off the coast of Europe, threatened with dismemberment and even bankruptcy. Hitler and Mussolini dead, remembered only in infamy. Stalin, a forbidden name in the regime he helped found and dominated for some three decades. America, haunted by fears of running out of those precious fluids that keep her motorways roaring and the smog settling, with troubled memories of a disastrous campaign in Vietnam and the victory of the Don Quixotes of the media, as they charged the windmills of Watergate. All in one lifetime. All gone.[7]

Muggeridge then brilliantly adds that behind the debris of these solemn supermen and self-styled imperial diplomatists stands the gigantic figure of One because of whom, by whom, in whom, and through whom alone mankind may still find peace: The person of Jesus Christ, He who was the fulfillment of the Law and the object of worship.

Josiah could only show his people the Book. That Book pointed to a Person. The written law could only serve as a mirror and a guide, but Jesus has come to offer us the cleansing of the soul, to define for us the good, to give true freedom by revealing the truth for life's greatest questions, and to grant humanity the strength by which to live. Only by responding to that offer may the soul be steadied and evil understood for what it really is. This now commands our attention.

Part 3

The Face of the Future

Twelve

The Unmasking of Evil

IN 1993 THE *New York Times Magazine* ran a lead article entitled "The Devil in Long Island." It was a resident's evocative cry, wondering if Long Island was uniquely plagued with some kind of behavioral virus breaking out into an epidemic of horrors unthinkable a generation ago. The assemblage of crimes and victims, of eccentricities and bizarre happenings all under one suburban roof, was truly unnerving: The brutal killings of spouses, the pitiful torture of little Katie Beers, the militant irreverence of Howard Stern, the indulgences of Joey Buttafuoco. Adding intrigue to the long list of those whose lives spun them into the vortex of tabloid delights were Jessica Hahn for her role in the PTL scandal and Walter Hudson. Though not exactly a household name, Hudson needed a casket almost the size of a house for his twelve-hundred-pound body, which was lowered into the ground with the help of a crane. What is it about Long Island, questioned the writer, that endlessly provides grist for the tabloid mill?

The metaphor best suited for Long Island's woes, the author Ron Rosenbaum suggested, was a story that gained international attention—the garbage-laden Islip barge that futilely sought some-place to disgorge its refuse. No one would take it.

> As someone who grew up within the boundaries of Islip Township, watch-ing weeks of coverage of this epic odyssey of humiliation and rejection, I found it hard not to identify with the brave little barge as it was turned away from landfill after landfill all down the Atlantic coast and across the Gulf of Mexico, North Carolina, Florida, Alabama, Mississippi, Louisiana, Texas—all turned it away; then Mexico, Belize and the Baha-mas: No one would take Long Island's garbage! It was hard not to feel that what was being enacted was a metaphor, a dramatization of the disdain mainland culture had for Long Island itself.[1]

But here the writer anticipates with sermonic power the self-immunizing mockery of the reader and warns of the contagion:

> Long Island, after all, was supposed to be the future *before* the future. We always had a head start on the life cycle of suburban baby-boom culture because we were the first-born burbs of the baby boom; a burbland created almost all at once, very fast and almost ex-nihilo, right after the war, a self-contained social organism. An organism whose socio-biological clock started ticking a little earlier than subsequent burbs, and whose shrill alarms now seem to signal that it has raced through its mature stage and is now rocketing headlong into the social-organism equivalent of senile dementia.
>
> And so the America that laughs at Long Island's Satanist Demolition Derby, the America that looks down on Long Island as something alien, some exotic, carnivalesque pageant separable from its mainstream be-cause it's separate from the mainland, may have to think again. May have to learn to say of this unruly island what Prospero said of the unruly Caliban at the close of "The Tempest": "This thing of darkness I ac-knowledge mine."
>
> Because when America laughs at Long Island, it's laughing in the face of its own onrushing future.[2]

Is Rosenbaum right? Is this strip of land with its pockets of perversion only a microcosm of what awaits the rest of the country and possibly the world? It may well be the single issue that calls us all to a common concern.

THE MYSTERY OF EVIL

What will be the face of the future? Futurists dabbling in technology or science delight in the limitless terrain for their speculation. Hardly a week goes by without someone pontificating about the speeds at which we will be flying and the new contraptions we will be using.

Caught up in all these thrilling and, indeed, incredible possibilities, we human beings cavalierly ignore the one element that has plagued us through history but has escalated in this century more than in any other—our chronic bent toward destruction. No incident illustrates this oversight better than the slaughter we have witnessed in Bosnia after the fall of the Berlin Wall. I doubt if there was even one writer anywhere who would have hailed the collapse of the Soviet Union and at the same time envisioned the resultant Bosnian carnage. A catastrophic blind spot that prepared freedom for the people failed to prepare the people for freedom.

The degree of lawlessness and the vulnerability with which we all live was underscored for me in two incidents, minutes apart, on the streets of Moscow. In the first, as we casually walked at midmorning to an engagement, suddenly and without warning, a roving band of gypsies moved to overpower us and ransack our pockets. As we frantically tried to ward them off one member of our group was knocked to the ground. But not one passer-by stopped to help us. While being robbed and possibly injured, to watch yourself becoming a victim, unaided by onlookers, is one of the loneliest feelings in life.

The second incident occurred minutes later, right outside that great symbol of capitalism—McDonald's golden arches—as a crazy, shirtless individual in the biting cold of winter came running along

the sidewalk brandishing a huge butcher knife and threatening anyone in his path. He stopped within inches of me and just stared, eyeball to eyeball. The experience was terrifying but again was made even
worse as an indifferent crowd did not even bother to notice. Life was
too complicated to come to a visitor's aid.

What a drastic change has come upon a nation once so strong in
the eyes of the world. Now there is a powerlessness from within as
social disintegration has left the masses apprehensive of the
newfound freedom for which they had dreamed and hoped for so
long. Little wonder that the gentleman in the military heavily
intoned, "We have no hope to give our young people. They have a
purposeless existence. Can you help us?"

The tragedy is not that of Long Island or Moscow. We are compelled to ask the same questions of the world at large, and how we
answer will ultimately configure the face of the future. First, how do
we respond to what we now call the mystery of wickedness? Every
institution seems powerless to stem the drift into more and more
radically evil behavior. Measured against this grim reality the answer
to this question may well become the acid test of the viability of any
social theory. As the face of evil becomes more hideous and ruthless,
the face of the future becomes more fearsome and dreaded. Yet for
the gospel message this may be the most significant moment in history, for the message of Christ provides the only supernatural hope of
a changed heart and life.

In the plethora of recent books that reveal an unprecedented interest in angels, the average person may miss the fact that some of the
most sophisticated treatments are now being given to this mystery of
evil. Our society is so surrounded by such strange manifestations that
the question of evil can no longer be avoided. In a self-fulfilling prophecy written two years after the article just referred to, Ron Rosenbaum
shifted the locus of violence from Long Island to the nation as a
whole.[3] His treatment of the subject matter may be one of the most
articulate. Yet, by his own admission, in the volume of his analysis he

offers no hope, and what began as a mystery ends as a greater mystery.

For my part, I would like to follow the trail he has opened and try to unveil some of this painful reality. To simplify a complex subject, I would like to present three clues that lead to answers to the mystery of wickedness. As previously stated, this provides the middle ground for the secular and sacred to think together.

IT DOESN'T MAKE SENSE

As one reads Rosenbaum's 1995 article titled "Staring into the Heart of Darkness: Evil Is Back," one is numbed to realize that this is not some distant jungle existence being described. This is Long Island. This is America—her disfigured soul uncovered. The title of the article was prompted by a series of heart-wrenching crimes that victimize those of every age but particularly children and the elderly. This article high-lighted not just the catalog of crimes but the brutality and savagery that attended them. What is more, the most pernicious aspect of the discussion was the relational tie of the criminals to their victims.

Who can explain Susan Smith heartlessly drowning her two young children, supposedly to perpetuate an ill-fated love affair? Who can explain the animalistic cannibalism of Jeffrey Dahmer? Who can explain the cold-hearted murder of their parents by Lyle and Erik Menendez? Who can explain the brutal beating and killing of a little two-year-old boy at the hands of a ten-year-old and a twelve-year-old in Liverpool, England? Who can explain the dreadful crimes against at least two teenage girls in St. Catharines, Ontario, when Paul Bernardo tortured, raped, and mutilated them while the sister of one of the victims watched and videotaped it for their later viewing plea-sure? Who can explain the honor-roll killings in Fullerton, Califor-nia, when a handful of Ivy League-bound students bludgeoned one of their classmates to death and then calmly left for a New Year's Eve party? And who can explain the ripping open of a woman's body to wrench the child from her womb and kidnap it? The list seems to be endless and sickening.

How will we give an answer for this? Are we going to stand by and watch our children read of these atrocities and then not talk to them about it until only the most horrendous of crimes will even shock them anymore? I should hope not! It is obvious that answers based on the assumptions of secularism can neither explain nor solve this malady.

In his search for an explanation, Rosenbaum talked to a host of people from scholars and politicians to media personalities. After watching talk-show host Maury Povich interview some contract killers, he contacted Povich, pointing out that "talk shows like Maury's have become the American equivalent of the Athenian agora, where citizens, sophists, and philosophers bat around questions of behavior. They can be barometers of public feeling on questions of good and evil."[4]

Rosenbaum called Mr. Povich to ask him if he had a readout on his audience's perspective on such criminality. Povich had a shocking answer. He said that until recently people excused such criminal acts as child abuse by blaming psychological preconditioners. However, he said, it seemed to him that people were no longer buying these self-exonerating theories as they once had. And he could even pinpoint the moment of change: *When Lyle reloaded.*

What did he mean by that? He was referring to Lyle Menendez, who, having emptied his shotgun into his parents, watched his mother crawl in her own blood as she begged him to spare her life. Instead, he went out of the room, reloaded his gun, and came back to calmly finish her off. That, said Povich, was the turning point for most viewers of his program. They knew this defied reason.

But then his audience was subjected to the next shock. In observing the players behind the violent scenes, viewers began to wonder about the callous and relentless greed that surfaced on the part of those who capitalized on crime. They were completely dumbfounded when they became aware of the money that was being made by op-portunists who were marketing Jeffrey Dahmer trading cards and other gimmick-laden products.

Viewers were now visibly angered. Until then they had been will-ing to concede the possibility that negative factors in a life could con-tribute to a man or woman going so wrong. But they were outraged by the thought of ordinary human beings heartlessly capitalizing on such bloodthirsty criminal acts. How can it be, they thought, that a civilization could sink so low? They knew with certainty that psycho-logical theory could not explain this dressed-up side of evil. It may be time to tear off the mask and find out what hideousness lies behind the adornment. This may be the face that beckons us to look at the inordinate evil of the human heart.

Here we cautiously pick up our first clue. The question of wicked-ness widens beyond these few names and popular talk shows. Evil is not just where blood has been spilled. Evil is in the self-absorbed human heart.

IT CANNOT BE ENDURED

This world was dramatically changed after the Second World War. What happened then and what we are doing now only intensifies the question of evil. Perhaps one incident will help us put this into sharper focus. During a recent visit to the Holocaust Museum in Jerusalem, I once again felt the stark horror of the human capacity for evil. But one little activity going on in the back room of the museum drew my attention to the reality behind the exhibits. I watched as young people were riveted, evidently for hours, to the video footage of Adolf Eichmann's trial. Having read detailed accounts of that trial, I, too, stood back for a few moments, watching the expressions on those young faces as the grim details unfolded.

As I watched them I could not help thinking of the outcome of that trial. After all the evidence had been mustered, thousands upon thousands of documents compiled, and Eichmann found guilty, his closing speech summed up the unconscionableness of it all. He had sloganeered his way through the entire trial as the dreadful evidence mounted. Now, moments before his execution, he did the same. This is one journalist's description, as Eichmann walked to his death:

> Adolf Eichmann went to the gallows with great dignity. He had asked for a bottle of red wine and had drunk half of it. He refused the help of the Protestant minister, the Reverend William Hull, who offered to read the Bible with him: he had only two more hours to live, and therefore "No time to waste." He walked the fifty yards from his cell to the execution chamber calm and erect, with his hands bound behind him. When the guards tied his ankles and knees, he asked them to loosen the bonds, so that he could stand straight. "I don't need that," he said when the black hood was offered him. He was in complete command of himself, nay, he was more: he was completely himself. Nothing could have demonstrated this more convincingly than the grotesque silliness of his last words. He began by stating emphatically that he was a Gottgläubiger, to express in common Nazi fashion that he was no Christian and did not believe in life after death. He then proceeded: "After a short while, gentlemen, we shall all meet again. Such is the fate of all men. Long live Germany, long live Argentina, long live Austria. I shall not forget them." In the face of death, he had found the cliché, used in funeral oratory. Under the gallows, his memory played him the last trick; he was "elated" and he forgot that this was his own funeral. It was as though in those last minutes he was summing up the lesson that this long course in human wickedness had taught us—the lesson of the fearsome, *word-and-thought-defying banality of evil*.[5]

Eichmann's last words give us a glimpse into his soul, a soul that was truly wretched. In a very real sense he had not, in fact, forgotten that it was his own funeral; he had just so trivialized evil and made death and destruction so banal that his own funeral was also a frivolous thing. Such is the dire end when the soul makes light of evil. How much more so if a whole culture were to echo that soulless indifference! But that is the danger if we do not define evil in its weighty terms. This has to be the common existential starting ground in a society where secular theory conflicts with the Christian faith. Both despise the violence, and the clues must lead us to a common conclusion.

The mystery of wickedness begins to unravel, does it not? In the first instance we saw the unacceptability of foisting all blame on pre-conditioning psychological factors. Now we see the complete unacceptability of trivializing evil. That is our second joint step. We move to the third.

IT MUST BE DEFINED

A modern-day equivalent to this Eichmann malady is found in a recent movie, *Pulp Fiction*, which I have not seen, nor do I intend to see. But I have heard one scene from it discussed more often than any other. Judging by their comments, most critics, very few excepted, have missed the point. At one place in the story two of the lead characters, Vincent and Jules, are en route to commit a multiple contract murder. As they cruise through Los Angeles, laughing and carefree, they indulge in small talk, discussing what hamburgers and quarter-pounders with cheese are called in France. "Royale with cheese," they chuckle and joke. "Is it because they go by the metric system that they have different names?" asks one of the other. This is the giddy, nothing-serious-please theme of their conversation. The average movie-goer leaves the movie with a singular impression—how could they be indulging in small talk when they were about to commit such a dreadful crime?[6]

The point is sorely missed. This is not small talk. This is philosophical brainwashing taking place between the two, hitting at the heart of the absolute, insinuating with life-defining implication and application that what we name things is all relative to culture. There is no point of reference. Words are nothing more than culture and convention, conferring different sounds to the same thing. An act or a thing itself has no intrinsic value. *We* decide what to call it. The metric system to one is irrelevant in the imperial system of another. A quarter-pounder with cheese to one is "royale with cheese" to another. "Killing the undefended" to one is "affirming the superior race" to another.

Do we get the point? A shameful act of murder can be trivialized if we rebaptize it "getting even." We can sloganeer our way to the gallows because we may see ourselves as martyrs for autonomous definitions. Bemoaning the banality of evil in Eichmann's disposition, Hannah Arent reminds us that his words were "word-and-thought-defying." Eichmann would have retorted in "*Pulp Fiction* philosophy" that deeds and thoughts are nothing more than word creations.

The farce of that twist on reality is inescapable. Life is not as random as the definition we choose to give it. Words are not puffs of air. We cannot rename wickedness and consider it solved. There is an irrepressible voice, and it is the voice of the soul, which says evil cannot be trivialized. This is what the gospel message is about. This is what the cross is all about. Failing to recognize this has disfigured the soul of America.

Is there a reality that exists outside of mere language, and must our language not then conform to reality? There is a point to the opening verse of John, "In the beginning was the Word." That Word defined reality and the Word of God reminds us time and time again that the heart of man is desperately wicked and that only God is big enough to change it. If we refuse to act on this knowledge, we perfectly fit the description Jesus gave, saying, "If then the light within you is darkness, how great is that darkness!" (Matt. 6:23). On the common ground of acknowledging the mystery of wickedness and on the common conviction that we must know the truth, we find the answer again presented with such force in the Scriptures. Other explanations are no longer convincing.

UNVEILING THE MYSTERY

In summarizing these clues and expressions of evil, we can begin to define what wickedness is. The first component of wickedness is that it is a *fact* of our existence. But wickedness can only be defined in relation to the purpose for which we were created and on the basis of the character of the Creator. Wickedness does not depend on the whims and fancies of a given culture at a given moment. The deviance is always in the context of why God has made us in the first place. If the purpose for life is not known then wickedness can never be defined. This is the reason that all ethical theorizing runs aground if no consensus can be gained on our essence and purpose.

Secondly wickedness has within it the component of *feeling*. Which of us could stand back and read the Susan Smith story and not be aghast at the thought of a mother drowning her own children to pursue a private love affair? In this dimension we come to grips with the agony of evil. The most effective way I can sustain this all-important point is to borrow a very pertinent illustration from C. S. Lewis.

In his book *The Abolition of Man*, the first chapter is entitled "Men Without Chests." No, the title has nothing to do with an Arnold Schwarzenegger build or the lack thereof but with a profound warning of where society is headed if our educational theories fail in teaching children about right and wrong. Lewis tells of a book he had read. Not being one to attack another person or even to respond to any criticism when he was criticized, Lewis called the book "The Green Book" and referred to its authors as Gaius and Titius. The book is about teaching children how to think about morality.

In their second chapter, Gaius and Titius quote the well-known story of Coleridge at the waterfall, describing the response of two tourists to that spectacular sight. Coleridge reported that one called it sublime, and the other called it pretty—and Coleridge echoed the first tourist's judgment as the right one. But here Gaius and Titius go to great lengths to challenge Coleridge by saying that a waterfall is not sublime; the tourist was merely describing his *feelings*, which were sublime, because sublimity, they contend, does not exist as a reality outside of feeling.

Lewis is stirred by this bizarre notion of Gaius and Titius and mounts a tremendous counterpoint. He says there is no way feelings could be thus dismissed as glandular or just plain reaction that says nothing about reality. If anything, the sight of a gigantic waterfall renders a sense of smallness and humbleness in the viewer at seeing something so massive, beautiful, powerful, and spectacular. One's feelings are no more merely sublime feelings than calling one contemptible would mean that I have contemptible feelings.

Lewis goes to great length to explain that goodness and badness have corresponding realities and are not merely physiological conditions. Some things thrill because they ought to. Some things hurt because they must. Some relationships ought to inspire and do. Witnessing a brutal murder must cause us to shudder. Watching a beautiful child chuckling in its mother's arms is delightful.

But alas! What have we done to ourselves? We have told a generation that science is real and therefore the human brain is real. We have told them that food is real and therefore our stomachs are real. But we have told them that good and bad do not exist and therefore our emotions have nothing to do with reality. In effect we have produced a generation of "men with brains and men with stomachs. Men with no heart. Men without chests." Now as we witness wickedness at its worst we wonder how the criminal could be so heartless. "In a sort of ghastly simplicity we remove the organ and demand the function. We make men without chests and expect of them virtue and enterprise. We laugh at honor and are shocked to find traitors in our midst. We castrate and bid the geldings be fruitful."[7]

The failure of the perpetrator of wickedness to feel emotion is the result of a society that has trained itself not to feel guilty when wrong is committed.[8]

In biblical terms, encountering wickedness must of necessity engender a feeling of brokenness for both the perpetrator and the victim of the deed. That is why after his sin David compared his inner state to that of a man with broken bones aching within him. "When I kept silent, my bones wasted away through my groaning all day long. For day and night your hand was heavy upon me; my strength was sapped as in the heat of summer. Then I acknowledged my sin to you . . . and you forgave the guilt of my sin" (Ps. 32:3–5). In keeping with the comfort of forgiveness, that psalm begins with "Blessed [happy] is the man whose sin [is forgiven]." One can see in this soul-wrenching prayer why David is called a man after God's own heart. God has given us emotions that conform to reality. Let us be sure that emotion is not in itself a judgment upon reality. In that sense the emotions are alogical. But certainly they must conform to reason and obey it.

At a recent meeting I was addressing in Hong Kong, a businessman stood up and proposed that all values were just contrived and had no bearing on ultimate reality. After I answered his question, I invited him to come and have a personal talk on the subject. He took me up on the offer, and with a crowd of people straining their necks to listen in on the conversation, I said to him that by inference one could assume that he denied that any act was intrinsically evil.

"That is a correct inference," he said.

Hardly believing the hole he had dug for himself, I asked him the obvious. "Suppose I were to take a newborn baby, bring it to this platform, and proceed with a sharp sword to mutilate that child. Are you saying to me that there is nothing actually wrong or evil in that deed?"

To the stunned expressions of those listening in he shrugged and shifted and then said, "I may not like it, but I cannot call it morally wrong."

There was only one thing left to say. "How incongruous it is, even by your own philosophy, that while denying the fact of evil you are unable to completely shake off the feeling . . . for even you, sir, said you would not like it. An understatement I hope." The conversation suddenly took a dramatic turn on how one can know ultimate reality, because he had mangled his own.

This brings us to the third component of wickedness, and that is the *face* of evil. God never describes wickedness as a vaporous idea or appends it to a nameless, faceless throng. Evil is always personal, and the one who acts wickedly is responsible. In these three components of wickedness—the fact, the feeling, and the face—we can readily see why secular society calls it a mystery. With a philosophy of life that has removed objective moral standards and lost any purpose for existence, there is no fact. With a philosophy of life that has severed emotion from value, there is no feeling. With a philosophy of life that does not want anyone to take responsibility for anything but passes the blame onto someone or something else, there is no face. Wickedness that is fact-less, feeling-less, and face-less will ever remain a mystery.

God's Word makes no such blunder. The mystery is removed when we see wickedness as God sees it and when we see ourselves as God sees us. Evil is real. Feelings must conform to what is real. Personal responsibility is indispensable in dealing with the perpetrators of evil.

THE GROUNDING OF REALITY

Now contrast the bewildering unfeeling and unthinking bravado of Eichmann, going to the gallows trivializing evil, with the thoughts of Dietrich Bonhoeffer, going to his death because he took a daring stand against Hitler. Listen to the words of Bonhoeffer on the nature of good and evil and on the only source for right definitions. He penned these words after he, too, had witnessed the most blatant forms of wickedness renamed under the banner of nationalism:

> The great masquerade of evil has played havoc with all our ethical concepts. For evil to appear disguised as light, charity, historical necessity, or social justice is quite bewildering to anyone brought up on our

traditional ethical concepts, while for the Christian who bases his life on the Bible it merely confirms the fundamental wickedness of evil.

The *"reasonable"* people's failure is obvious. With the best intentions and a naive lack of realism, they think that with a little reason they can bend back into position the framework that has got out of joint. In their lack of vision they want to do justice to all sides, and so the conflicting forces wear them down with nothing achieved. Disappointed by the world's unreasonableness, they see themselves condemned to ineffectiveness; they step aside in resignation or collapse before the stronger party.

Still more pathetic is the total collapse of moral *fanaticism*. The fanatic thinks that his single-minded principles qualify him to do battle with the powers of evil; but like a bull he rushes at the red cloak instead of the person who is holding it; he exhausts himself and is beaten. He gets entangled in non-essentials and falls into the trap set by cleverer people.

Then there is the man with a *conscience*, who fights single-handed against heavy odds in situations that call for a decision. But the scale of the conflicts in which he has to choose—with no advice or support except from his own conscience—tears him to pieces. Evil approaches him in so many respectable and seductive disguises that his conscience becomes nervous and vacillating, till at last he contents himself with a salved instead of a clear conscience, so that he lies to his own conscience in order to avoid despair; for a man whose only support is his conscience can never realize that a bad conscience may be stronger and more wholesome than a deluded one.

From the perplexingly large number of possible decisions, the way of *duty* seems to be the sure way out. Here, what is commanded is accepted as what is most certain, and the responsibility for it rests on the commander, not on the person commanded. But no one who confines himself to the limits of duty ever goes so far as to venture, on his sole responsibility, to act in the only way that makes it possible to score a direct hit on evil and defeat it. The man of duty will in the end have to do his duty by the devil too.

As to the man who asserts his complete *freedom* to stand foursquare to the world, who values the necessary deed more highly than an unspoilt conscience or reputation, who is ready to sacrifice a barren principle for a fruitful compromise, or the barren wisdom of a middle course for a fruitful radicalism—let him beware lest his freedom should bring him down. He will assent to what is bad so as to ward off something worse, and in doing so he will no longer be able to realize that the worse, which he wants to avoid, might be better. Here we have the raw material of tragedy.

Here and there people flee from public altercation into the sanctuary of *private* virtuousness. But anyone who does this must shut his mouth and his eyes to the injustice around him. Only at the cost of self-deception can he keep himself pure from the contamination arising from responsible action. In spite of all that he does, what he leaves undone will rob him of his peace of mind. He will either go to pieces because of this disquiet, or become the most hypocritical of Pharisees.

Who stands fast? Only the man whose final standard is not his reason, his principles, his conscience, his freedom, or his virtue, but who is ready to sacrifice all this when he is called to obedient and responsible action in faith and exclusive allegiance to God—the responsible man, who tries to make his whole life an answer to the question and call of God. Where are these responsible people?[9]

This is a clarion call to the West, which has seen so much bloodshed. We can only stand our ground, not on the shifting theories of human ingenuity, but on the blueprint of the Creator. When we see our hearts as God sees them, we find His strength, not only to understand good and evil, but to act on it. The one who resists this truth has nowhere to turn.

Thirteen

The God Who Is Near

THE GRANDEUR of the gospel strikes deep into the soul of wickedness because it offers not merely an analysis of the condition nor just the strength to do what is right; it goes to our innermost being, where the work of God changes what we want to do. This is not an ethical system calling us to civility. This is the transforming work of the grace of God, who then deigns to call us His children.

Charles Wesley said it well:

> Long my imprisoned spirit lay
> Fastbound in sin and nature's night;
> Thine eye diffused the quickening ray.
> I woke, the dungeon flamed with light;
> My chains fell off, my heart was free;
> I rose, went forth, and followed thee.[1]

This transformation can only take place when evil is fully faced for what it truly is and the soul is bought back from under its control.

Only One was capable and willing to pay the price—the Lord Jesus Christ.

HIS TRANSFORMING POWER

Joseph Damien was a missionary in the nineteenth century who ministered to people with leprosy on the island of Molokai, Hawaii. Those suffering grew to love him and revered the sacrificial life he lived out before them. But even he did not know the price he would pay. One morning before he was to lead them in their daily worship, he was pouring some hot water into a cup when the water swirled out and fell onto his bare foot. It took him a moment to realize that he had not felt any sensation. Gripped by the sudden fear of what this could mean, he poured more boiling water on the same spot. No feeling whatsoever.

Damien immediately knew what had happened. As he walked tearfully to deliver his sermon, no one at first noticed the difference in his opening line. He normally began every sermon with, "My fellow believers." But this morning he began with, "My fellow lepers."

In a greater measure Jesus came into this world knowing what it would cost Him. He bore in His pure being the marks of evil, that we might be made pure. "For this I came into the world," He said (John 18:37).

R. S. Thomas poignantly captured the significance of Jesus' sacrifice to accomplish our redemption in his poem, "The Coming."

> And God held in His hand
> A small globe. Look, He said.
> The son looked. Far off,
> As through water, He saw
> A scorched land of fierce
> Colour. The light burned

There; crusted buildings
Cast their shadows; a bright
Serpent, a river
Uncoiled itself, radiant
With slime.

          On a bare
Hill, a bare tree saddened
The sky. Many people
Held out their thin arms
To it, as though waiting
For a vanished April
To return to its crossed
Boughs. The son watched
Them. Let me go there, he said.[2]

The gospel points to the person of Christ who went to the cross, not just to transform the Jeffrey Dahmers and the money-grabbers behind the scenes, but to renew even those whose self-righteousness blinds them to their own need. It was not just the prodigal in the far-off country who squandered the love of the father; the older brother lost out as well, though he was so close to the father's love. The treasure is within reach of America—the treasure of her recovered soul.

HIS PERSONAL INVITATION

How a culture responds to the cross will determine its face for the future, for the cross alone can transform the heart. But a second question arises: How is it possible to live in a world that will ever swing between extremes, possibly finding newer and more expeditious ways of multiplying evil? Just as the Word of God is definitive in explaining the human heart, that same Word must connect our lives through turbulent times—times past and times to come.

The Word was the instrument Jesus used to counter evil in His own wilderness experience. As Satan taunted Jesus and tried to persuade Him to compromise the greatest good for a seemingly innocent moment of self-glorifying power, Jesus responded to every distortion of the good with the simple words: "Be gone. It is written." This confidence in God's Word not only instructs us in our battles against wickedness but puts into perspective the short-lived emotional impact of even the greatest victories. Only the written Word transcends every experience, good and bad.

The writers of the Scriptures are very clear on this. I turn to one of the greatest experiences ever vouchsafed to the human eye, the transfiguration of Jesus. The three disciples who were with Him saw His countenance glow as His face shone like the sun and His clothes became as white as light. They saw Moses and Elijah descend from the heavens and talk to Jesus. They heard a voice from heaven as the voice of God Himself testified, "This is My Son; listen to Him." The three disciples fell on their faces, and when they had gathered their composure, Peter predictably beseeched Jesus that they ought to stay there forever and not go down to the city again. But Jesus unhesitatingly reminded him that there was work to be done and that the glorious experience was no substitute for the reality that surrounded them till the eternal reality would come.

We must bear in mind this mountaintop experience of Peter's if we are to understand the depth of the truth he stated when he himself referred back to this high point in his life. He says this in his letter to fellow Christians.

> We did not follow cleverly invented stories when we told you about the power and coming of our Lord Jesus Christ, but we were eyewitnesses of his majesty. For he received honor and glory from God the Father when the voice came to him from the Majestic Glory, saying, "This is my Son, whom I love; with him I am well pleased." We ourselves heard this voice that came from heaven when we were with him on the sacred mountain.

[But] we have the word of the prophets made more certain, and you will do well to pay attention to it, as to a light shining in a dark place, until the day dawns and the morning star rises in your hearts. Above all, you must understand that no prophecy of Scripture came about by the prophet's own interpretation. For prophecy never had its origin in the will of man, but men spoke from God as they were carried along by the Holy Spirit. (2 Pet. 1:16–21)

This is a most remarkable passage. What Peter is saying here in the context of the exhilaration of being present at the transfiguration is that every experience, however enthralling, must ultimately be seen as temporary. Only the Word of God exceeds the message of the moment and transcends all time. Christians live dangerously when experience is the final authority. The skeptics knew what they were doing when they attacked the Bible because they knew experience alone could easily be explained away, sometimes even by the one who lived the experience. If the critic can reduce all of Christianity to a "religious experience" unverifiable by any other means, then we are confined to a privatized belief with no objective authority left to defend. By being preoccupied with mountaintop experiences or being overcome by the face of evil, the Christian robs himself or herself of the greater treasure of the Word of God "made more certain."

Does this negate the value of experience? Absolutely not. It merely puts into perspective how every experience must point beyond itself to that by which it can be measured. This transtemporal certitude of the Word will carry us through the roller-coaster journey of human fickleness and experiential limitation. Our confidence is in His sovereignty over our nations and over history. But even beyond that we know that His care is personal even in the most turbulent times.

This Word reminds us that there is only one Eternal City. As the barbarians scaled the walls of his beloved city, Augustine wept and penned *The City of God*. No, Rome was not the eternal city. As Athens sowed the seeds of its own destruction, Socrates chose to drink the hemlock rather than give up his pursuit of the virtuous. In

England Wordsworth wept for the return of Milton to address the loss of England's heroic character. Jesus wept at the sight of His beloved city and said, "If you . . . had only known on this day what would bring you peace—but now it is hidden from your eyes" (Luke 19:42).

Rome, Athens, and Jerusalem have all lost their ancient glory. Today our alabaster cities have become tarnished, and with eyes dimmed by tears we cry, "Deliver us from evil." But that deliverance can come only if we respond to the Creator's loving invitation:

> Come to me, all you who are weary and burdened, and I will give you rest. Take my yoke upon you and learn from me, for I am gentle and humble in heart, and you will find rest for your souls. (Matt. 11:28–29)

> > Come, all you who are thirsty,
> >   come to the waters;
> > and you who have no money,
> >   come, buy and eat! . . .
> > Why spend money on what is not bread,
> >   and your labor on what does not satisfy?
> > Listen, listen to me and eat what is good,
> >   and your soul will delight in the richest of fare.
> > Give ear and come to me;
> >   hear me, that your soul may live. (Isa. 55:1–3)

If we can say, with King David, "As the deer pants for streams of water, so my soul pants for you, O God," our deliverance is at hand.

HIS IMMEASURABLE GRACE

As I bring this book to a close, let us look back over the long journey we have come through. In contrast to the secularizing influences that have disoriented our culture, we return to the precious truth of God's revelation. Throughout history the Word of God has remained firm; it rises up to outlive its pallbearers. The following story probably stirs my own confidence in God's sovereignty and the power of His Word through troubled times more than any other I know. The circumstances and the particulars are overwhelming.

During my ministry in Vietnam in 1971, one of my interpreters who traveled with me was Hien Pham, an energetic, devoted young Christian who had worked very closely as a translator with the American military forces, purely as a civilian, with no official or military responsibilities. He just knew English so well that he was able to be of immense help to them in their linguistic struggles.

By virtue of that same strength he also worked with the missionaries. He and I traveled the length of the country and became very close friends before I bade him good-bye when I left Vietnam to return home. We were both very young, and neither of us knew if our paths would cross again. Within four years Vietnam fell, and Hien's fate was unknown.

Seventeen years later, in 1988, I received a surprise telephone call that began with, "Brother Ravi?" Immediately I recognized Hien's voice. We got caught up with our pleasantries, then I asked him how he had managed to get out of Vietnam and come to the United States. I was not prepared for the story I was about to hear.

Shortly after Vietnam fell to the Communists, Hien was arrested. Accused of aiding and abetting the Americans he was in and out of prison for several years. During one long jail term, the sole purpose of his jailers was to indoctrinate him against the West—and especially against democratic ideals and the Christian faith. He was cut off from reading anything in English and restricted to communist propaganda in French or Vietnamese. This daily overdose of the writings of Marx and Engels began to take its toll on him. One of the books he was given to read pictured the communist man as a bird in the ironclad cage of capitalism, throwing itself against the bars of "capitalist oppression" and bloodying itself in the process. Yet still it continued to struggle in its quest for freedom.

Hien began to buckle under the onslaught. *Maybe*, he thought, I *have* been lied to. Maybe God does *not* exist. Maybe my whole life *has* been governed by lies. Maybe the West *has* deceived me. The more he thought, the more he moved toward a decision. Finally, he made up his mind. He determined that when he awakened the next day, he would not pray anymore or ever think of his Christian faith again.

The next morning, he was assigned to clean the latrines of the prison. It was the most dreaded chore, shunned by everyone, and so with much distress he began the awful task. As he cleaned out a tin can filled to overflowing with toilet paper, his eye caught what he thought was English printed on one piece of paper. He hurriedly washed it off and slipped it into his hip pocket, planning to read it at night. Not having seen anything in English for such a long time, he anxiously waited for a free moment. Under his mosquito net that night after his roommates had fallen asleep, he pulled out a small flashlight and shining it on the damp piece of paper he read at the top corner, "Romans, Chapter 8." Literally trembling with shock, he began to read:

> And we know that in all things God works for the good of those who love him, who have been called according to his purpose. . . .
>
> What, then, shall we say in response to this? If God is for us, who can be against us? He who did not spare his own Son, but gave him up for us all—how will he not also, along with him, graciously give us all things? . . .
>
> . . . Who shall separate us from the love of Christ? Shall trouble or hardship or persecution or famine or nakedness or danger or sword? . . . No, in all these things we are more than conquerors through him who loved us. For I am convinced that neither death nor life, neither angels nor demons, neither the present nor the future, nor any powers, neither height nor depth, nor anything else in all creation, will be able to separate us from the love of God that is in Christ Jesus our Lord. (Rom. 8:28, 31, 32, 35, 37–39)

Hien wept. He knew his Bible, and he had not seen one for so long. Not only that, he knew there was not a more relevant passage of conviction and strength for one on the verge of surrendering to the threat of evil. He cried out to God, asking for forgiveness, for this was to have been the first day in years that he had determined not to pray. Evidently the Lord had other plans.

The next day, Hien asked the camp commander if he could clean the latrine again. He continued with this chore on a regular basis, because he had discovered that some official in the camp was using a Bible as toilet paper. Each day Hien picked up a portion of Scripture, cleaned it off, and added it to his nightly devotional reading. In this way he retrieved a significant portion of the Bible.

The day came when, through an equally providential set of circumstances, Hien was released. He promptly began to make plans to escape from the country. After several unsuccessful attempts he began again to build a boat in secret. About fifty-three other people planned to escape with him, and Hien was taking the lead. All was going according to plan until a short while before the date of their departure when four Vietcong knocked on Hien's door. When he opened it, they accosted him and said they had heard he was trying to escape. "Is it true?" they demanded. Hien immediately denied it and went on to distract them with some concocted story to explain his activities. Apparently convinced, they reluctantly left.

Hien was relieved but very disappointed with himself. "Here I go again, Lord, trying to manipulate my own destiny, too unteachable in my spirit to really believe that You can lead me past any obstacle." He made a promise to God, fervently hoping that the Lord would not take him up on it. He prayed that if the Vietcong were to come back again, he would tell them the truth. Resting in the comfort of that impossibility, he was thoroughly shaken when only a few hours before they were to set sail the four men stood at his door once more. "We have our sources, and we know you are trying to escape. Is it true?" Hien resignedly gave his answer, "Yes, I am, with fifty-three others. Are you going to imprison me again?" There was a pronounced pause. And then they leaned forward and whispered, "No. We want to escape with you!"

In an utterly incredible escape plan, all fifty-eight of them found themselves on the high seas, suddenly engulfed by a violent storm. Hien fell with his face in his hands, crying out to God, "Did You bring us here to die?"

As he concluded his story, he said, "Brother Ravi, if it were not for the sailing ability of those four Vietcong, we would not have made it." They arrived safely in Thailand, and years later Hien arrived on American soil where today he is a businessman—forever grateful for America and praying that she would open her heart as a nation to Christ.

The famed poet William Cowper wrote:

> God moves in a mysterious way
> His wonders to perform;
> He plants His footsteps in the sea,
> And rides upon the storm.
>
> His purposes will ripen fast,
> Unfolding every hour:
> The bud may have a bitter taste,
> But sweet will be the flower.
>
> Blind unbelief is sure to err,
> And scan His works in vain:
> God is His own interpreter,
> And He will make it plain.[3]

How marvelous is the grace of God who has proven again and again that His Word brings light to a dark place, and who can take the wrath of men to bring praise to His name. The artist who spoke to Dorian Gray was right. The Bible does say, "Come now, let us reason together. Though your sins are like scarlet, they shall be as white as snow; though they are red as crimson, they shall be like wool" (Isa. 1:18). Killing the artist is but to kill the voice of reason.

WHAT A MOMENT; WHAT A POSSIBILITY

That is the invitation to the great country of America and to every nation and culture of the world. Churchill once said something to the effect that Americans would always do the right thing . . . after trying everything else first. There are some glorious signs on the horizon. Businessmen and women are responding in large numbers today to the gospel. There are home Bible studies in the tens of thousands. Young people in schools and universities are openly talking about spiritual matters. Many churches in Canada, the United Kingdom, and America are beginning to sense renewal. Our prayer can be concerted and confident. One can only imagine the impact the world over when the threatened soul of Western culture finds the light of Christ and is transformed by His life.

The words uttered by the frightened American cringing under God's judgment in Hermann Hagedorn's *The Bomb That Fell Over America* are most appropriate:

> Me, Lord? . . . How odd! I'm sure you must be mistaken.
> There's nothing the matter with *me*.
> It's the other fellow that's the trouble, a hundred and thirty-
> five million of him.
>
>   . . . . .
>
> The Lord said not a word . . .
> I felt a Hand on my collar, a hand that made me remember
> The woodshed and the shingle, and the glint in a father's eye.
>
>   . . . . .
>
> The Lord bent down over me as a mother bends over a baby.
> "You are a child," said the Lord, "and
> My heart is sick with your childness.
> But you have a soul, and I've found you just never can tell.
> If I could get by your ego, and somehow crack open your
>   nucleus—
> Something might happen . . . And there is a world at stake.[4]

Appendix A

The Ineradicable Word

AT THE 1995 Mayoral Prayer Breakfast in Washington, D.C., ten-year-old Ashley Danielle Oubré, delivered a memorable speech that brought the audience to its feet in two standing ovations. The brief but mind-stirring text follows.

Good morning, Mayor Barry, platform guests, ladies, and gentlemen. I appreciate this opportunity to speak to the leadership of the greatest city in the world on behalf of the children. I wondered what I would say to you when I was first asked if I would make a presentation. Being young limits the experience you have in most areas, but not as being a child.

Jesus said, "Unless you become like a child you cannot enter the kingdom." When I think about my friends, who are all young people like myself, many things come to mind.

If you would like to be a child in God's kingdom, I will share some of what we think about and do.

Children play together, have lots of fun, and sometimes fight, but the very next day we make up and play again. Wouldn't it be wonderful if mothers and fathers, sisters and brothers, neighbors and our leaders would be more that way? It hurts us when we see you fighting and not making up.

When you tell us something, we believe it, and we don't ask many questions. We have faith and trust in you until we grow up and find it's really not that way with adults. I think you tell us Bible stories because we are children. The Bible stories do us a lot of good, but you don't tell each other Bible stories. Are they only good for children?

You teach us that when we have a problem, we should talk it out with others and with Jesus. You say that we should pray about it and keep our hearts right for Jesus. You say that Jesus can solve all of our problems, both big and small. But we notice, when people get older and have problems, they are embarrassed to talk like that among themselves. We wonder if you really mean it, or is Jesus only for kids? I am still young enough to believe that Jesus knows how to solve my problems, the problems of the city, and of the world. I hope I never grow old enough to stop believing and that you all become like children in search of God's kingdom.

Thank you very much for listening to me. God bless you all![1]

The easiest response by a skeptic, even to such innocence, would be to dismiss this as childish simplicity at best, wandering in uncharted terrain and eliciting sentimental applause. But let us be clear of the adult-sized ramifications of this child's questions. Is the Bible merely a fanciful storybook, distorting reality? Or is it fantastically true, challenging the intellect against its escapist illusions? Is there truth for all of us within its pages, or is it only for those with superstitious and unsuspecting minds? Is this indeed the Word from God to us, or is it the fraudulent work of a few claiming divine superintendency?[2]

There is absolutely no doubt that the Christian message stands or falls upon the authenticity or spuriousness of the Bible. Believing it to be God's Word, millions across history have staked their lives upon it; destiny-defining trust has been placed in it; graveside hope has been based upon it; extraordinary good has been spread because of it; the charters of nations have been built upon it; others with equal intensity have sought to expel it; yet wrongheaded zeal has caused untold evil in its name. There is no book in history that has been so studied, so used, and so abused as the Holy Bible. How life-inspiring it would be to many more if only they could be indubitably certain of its truth. Can we muster the courage to face up to its claims of divine authorship?

Many routes could be taken in the defense of the uniqueness and authority of the Bible. The age-old approach would be to test its accuracy by measuring the authenticity of the present text of the Scriptures against the earliest extant documents. In such a venture scholars examine the text of Scripture as they would examine any document, investigating such things as authorship, date, historical reliability, and acceptability at the time of writing. This approach is obviously foundational because if these matters cannot be verified all else must stand on a leap of faith.

In addition, the supernatural nature of the content is important to consider, for example, miraculous claims such as fulfilled prophecies and the ultimate assertion of Christ's divinity and power in His resurrection from the dead. Still other buttressing factors—such as the sheer volume of early manuscripts, which is unmatched by any other writing of such antiquity—make the evidentiary basis quite overwhelming. When the archaeological and philosophical defenses are added to these arguments, a very powerful case can and has been made for trusting the Bible to be what it claims to be.

Instead of dealing with the question in the traditional way, because much is already available in that genre, my present response focuses on the authority of the Bible in the existential struggles of life, particularly as we cope with evil.

THE PERFECT ENDORSEMENT

First and foremost, the Bible is the only book in the world that points to a life perfectly lived amidst the grim realities and alluring forces of human existence. Pore over the countless pages written across time, and it becomes quickly evident that the founders of various religions or cults fall short in their own lives, not only when measured against the supreme standard of the Law of God, but even when measured by the standards they themselves have espoused. Biographical sketches of some who today have a following in the millions should only make one wonder how lives so poorly and immorally lived could be so revered.

In contrast to all of them, the life of Christ stands supreme and impeccable. The recognition of this uniqueness in the person of Christ has been readily expressed by some of history's greatest scholars, both those who are avowedly Christian and those distinctly non-Christian. (An example of the latter would be the historian W. E. H. Lecky who, in *A History of European Morals from Augustus to Charlemagne II*, granted the impact of Christ as unequaled in word and deed.)

So incredible is this unblemished life that, in an effort to make his own defeated aspirations seem normal, the noted intellectual Nikos Kazantzakis, in his novel *The Last Temptation of Christ*, tried desperately to construct a Christ who succumbed to the impulse of sensuality. Kazantzakis failed in his pathetic bid because he robbed himself of the life-changing truth that it was Christ's purity that made His empowering grace possible, not the indulgence Kazantzakis tried to fabricate.

How grand is a life so perfectly lived, a life that resisted every enticement of lust, greed, and power even in its most seductive forms. Pontius Pilate, the power seeker, said of Him, "I find no fault in this man." The convicted criminal hanging by Him said of Jesus, "This man has done nothing amiss." The religious leaders who saw Him as a threat to their demagoguery mounted the farcical charge that He was healing on the Sabbath and therefore He was ceremonially vile.

Is it any wonder that even the outcasts of society clamored for His spotless presence and that a devout though rich man like Joseph of Arimathea offered a tomb for His burial? A learned man like

Nicodemus sought Him out because he saw in Him a wisdom beyond anyone he had ever known. He whose dwelling was in the heavenlies attracted even those whose lives were marred and scarred by every pollution of the earth.

This One who lived with such perfection pointed to the authority of the Word when He said, "The Scripture cannot be broken." He spoke of the eternality of the Word when He said, "Heaven and earth shall pass away, but my words will never pass away." He pointed to the centrality of the Word when the Devil tried to tempt Him in the subtlest form of evil—to use His power for self-aggrandizement rather than for the honor of God. The Word reflected the character of God. That reflection was merely propositional in the Scriptures, but it was lived out in the life of Jesus. What good would the Law have been if its very author could not demonstrate its purity?

At the 1994 Presidential Prayer Breakfast in Washington, D.C., Mother Teresa delivered a soul-searching address in which she touched upon the sensitive theme of abortion. When a reporter afterword asked President Clinton what he thought of her remarks he simply stated, "It is very hard to argue against a life so well lived." If the life of Mother Teresa is considered a life so well lived, what should be said about the greater life of the One worshiped by her and by millions of others? We would do well to listen to His seal and verdict on the written Word.

One may, of course, ask whether the argument is not circular. We believe the Bible because Jesus affirms it to be true. We believe Jesus because the Bible says He is the Truth. The question is a fair one. But this is where the Bible stands uniquely among other religious books claiming divine authorship.

The Bible is a book whose facts can be tested outside of itself. The historical, geographical, archaeological, and prophetic data can be verified from outside the Scriptures. When sixty-six books covering a two-thousand-year span and written by approximately thirty-seven authors coalesce with such singularity, purpose, and empirical verifiability, the argument can hardly be considered circular. An honest investigation of such intricate convergences actually bespeaks a very profound moral and historical sense, dating back over four thousand years. The Bible is more than a book pointing to itself. Its attestations are multifaceted.

THE WIDE APPEAL

The second aspect of scriptural authority is revealed in its intellectual breadth. From the beginning to the end the narrative is rich in simplicity, so that even a child can grasp the truth of its stories. Yet it is so profound in its exposition of great theological themes that it has challenged the best of thinking minds and inspired the greatest of artistic genius. The stories are varied enough to apply to the king who hosted a feast; to the politician who sought the best seat in the banquet; to the athlete who ran a race; to the soldier who went to war; to the widow who lacked any income; to the shepherd who lost his sheep; to the father of a wayward son; to the fisherman who cast his nets; to the needy who longed for acceptance. In rich parable, illustration, and action Jesus spoke so that both the child and the rabbi craned their necks to hear Him.

It is very possible to miss just how meaningful is this truth. By contrast, in the religious books of another tradition a profound understanding of one particular language is necessary to even recognize the so-called miracle of the book. In the tradition of yet another, there is debate as to who is even qualified to interpret it, necessitating the birthright of a particular station in life to do so. These terribly restricting impositions do not apply to the understanding of the Scriptures. In fact, Jesus reprimanded His disciples when they discouraged children from coming to Him while fawning over those who were society's favored sons and daughters. Till this very day stories both from the Old Testament and the New Testament, such as

Solomon settling the dispute between two women who claimed to be the mother of the same child and the father waiting for the prodigal son to return, are told to eager minds, whether old or young.

It all makes sense. Why would a God who cares so particularly for the weak and disenfranchised of this world make it difficult for them to understand Him? In the middle of one of His sternest warnings to an unrepentant generation, Jesus said, "I praise you, Father, Lord of heaven and earth, because you have hidden these things from the wise and learned, and revealed them to little children. Yes, Father, for this was your good pleasure" (Matt. 11:25, 26). It is not accidental that in the darkest days of slavery in America the spirituals rang with simplicity and splendor, beckoning the slaves to steal their hearts away to Jesus or to think of that great crossing over one day into freedom and the Promised Land. Educated or uneducated, adult or child, bond or free—the Word has always been within the reach of all.

There is an important point to be made here lest a greater truth be missed. These are not just simple anecdotes or illustrations that Jesus used, not communication ploys to weave some fanciful tale. These stories, interwoven with the truths of history that narrate the very birth, life, death, and resurrection of Christ, address the existential struggle in the human heart for deliverance from the reality of evil. This method reinforces for us that the Scriptures are not inspired just in content, but also in form. Author Eugene Peterson comments on this.

Storytelling creates a world of presuppositions, assumptions and relations into which we enter. Stories invite us into a world other than ourselves, and if they are good and true stories, a world larger than ourselves. . . . The minute we abandon the story, we reduce the reality to the dimensions of our minds and feelings and experience. . . . This is in contrast to the ancient preference for myth-making, which more or less turns us into spectators of the supernatural. It is also in contrast to the modern preference for moral philosophy which puts us in charge of our own salvation. "Gospel story" is a verbal way of accounting for reality that, like the incarnation that is its subject, is simultaneously divine and human. It reveals, that is, it shows us something we could never come up with on our own by observation or experiment or guess, and at the same time it engages, it brings us into the action as recipients and participants but without dumping the responsibility on us for making it turn out right.[3]

Peterson goes on to point out how this form delivers us from both extremes, the one of becoming frivolous spectators always pining to be entertained by another story, the other of being anxious moralists, taking on the burdens of the world. In short, the story is more than just an illustration. It shoulders the truth of reality.

Have these not been the same extremes to which the modern mind has succumbed in facing evil? On the one hand we read story after story in the front page and succumb to becoming spectators in a journalists' arena. On the other hand we hear myriad moral philosophers offering yet another theory to address the scourge of crime. In the Scriptures there is a wholesomeness in the connecting of all of life, protecting us from a sense of entertainment when the reality should hurt and from pessimism when the hope is real. In other words, the headline story of a mother who kills her children is not lost to God in the weight of world politics and global issues. He who took pains to tell us of the sick son of a Roman soldier or of the man without sight who stationed himself at the temple in search of a cure must hurt with the things that break the heart of the individual, and He bends low not only to lift up the cause of the victim but to offer help to the victimizer.

Some of us may recall a particular author upon whom the death sentence was pronounced for "blasphemy and irreverence" shown to his religious heritage and his "holy book." Clearly the work was very disrespectful and mocking of a belief that millions held sacred. But by equal measure one must wonder about the irrationality of calling for a death sentence upon the writer. When a representative of that religion was asked on national television how such a sentence could be pronounced in disregard for the individual's right, the answer was definitive of the philosophy. "In our belief," he said, "the individual is dispensable; the cause must go on."

Here then is the cardinal difference. Jesus left the ninety-nine to search for the one, because the individual does matter. When we lose sight of people to pursue our own personal gain or when we devalue the individual in the name of cosmic priorities, we forget this truth and approach the core of evil. The Bible tells us that God knows even when a sparrow falls to the ground, that He adorns the lilies of the field, and that the very hairs of our heads are numbered. That is the degree to which His care is personal.

Jesus said, "Consider the ravens: They do not sow or reap, they have no storeroom or barn; yet God feeds them. And how much more valuable are you than birds! . . . Consider how the lilies grow. They do not labor or spin. Yet I tell you, not even Solomon in all his splendor was dressed like one of these. If that is how God clothes the grass of the field, which is here today, and tomorrow is thrown into the fire, how much more will he clothe you, O you of little faith!" (Luke 12:24, 27–28). By contrast He reminds us that "the nations are like a drop in a bucket; . . . he weighs the islands as though they were fine dust" (Isa. 40:15). The end of history will reveal the hollowness of national pursuit and the eternal value of each and every individual. History is His story told in individual hearts.

ENCOMPASSING THE WORLD

There is a third aspect of God's unique revelation in the Scriptures, the transcultural nature of His Truth. The Bible is neither Eastern nor Western but applicable to every culture, because the truth of life's purpose must always transcend any cultural shortsightedness. The imagery with which Jesus speaks so clearly addresses the Eastern mind. The parable of the ten women with their lamps waiting for the bridegroom to arrive engenders a wealth of sentiments to the Eastern reader. Anyone who has spent any time in the East can immediately envision the bridal procession, instruments playing and the accompanying throng rejoicing, making its way with the groom to the home of the bride. The whole picture is Eastern to this very day.

On the other hand, there is a touch here and there of the impact of Christ that would today be more readily identified in the West than in the East. He talks, for example, of the tyranny of the employer who lords it over the one who serves him, and He says true character is not to be found in commanding or suppressing other people but in serving one another. This reality of the dignity of labor is far more manifest in the West than it is in the East.

The impact of the gospel cannot be gainsaid on this matter. The disregard for essential human worth and the slavish pandering that is inflicted upon so much of humankind in parts of the world where the servant is considered to be inferior as a person is a terrible scourge upon people. Who we are should always be prior to what we do. Even the atheist Bertrand Russell admitted that it was debatable whether the method espoused by Mahatma Gandhi in calling for independence from the British would have succeeded except that it appealed to the conscience of a nation that had been influenced by the gospel. Today in Gandhi's ashram in the city of Ahmedabad in central India, Russell's quotation greets each visitor. How transculturally noteworthy that, in a predominantly Hindu nation, a quote by an atheist testifies to the impact of Christ upon nations both East and West, enjoining respect toward every human being.

Only in biblical terms do we see how God is able to humble each of us without humiliating us and to elevate all of us without flattering any of us. The West today lives off the capital of the Christian faith without realizing it. The work ethic of the West and the belief in the dignity of labor are biblically based. And the same equality applies in matters of race and gender, two turbulent conflicts of our time.

Peter Kreeft, professor of philosophy at Boston College, elaborates on this marvelous truth of equality that retains a difference. He demonstrates that in God's economy there is an egalitarianism in people but an elitism in ideas. By that he means the equality of all humanity but the inequality of ideas. While human beings are equal, ideas are not. By contrast, in the world's way of doing things we have created an elitism among people and an egalitarianism of ideas: We have made some people superior to others and rendered all ideas equal. The end result has been the exploitation of people and the death of truth. And that is why we have an epidemic of evil that denudes people but fights for ideas.

TRANSFORMING THE SOUL

One final argument for the authority of the Scriptures that I present is the power of this book to touch the spirit by focusing on the holiness of God rather than mandating a set of do's and don'ts as if that were at the heart of spirituality. Jesus has clearly pointed out where the root of wickedness lies.

> You have heard that it was said to the people long ago, "Do not murder, and anyone who murders will be subject to judgment." But I tell you that anyone who is angry with his brother will be subject to judgment. . . .

> Therefore, if you are offering your gift at the altar and there remember that your brother has something against you, leave your gift there in front of the altar. First go and be reconciled to your brother; then come and offer your gift.

> Settle matters quickly with your adversary. (Matt. 5:21–24)

In the same manner Jesus proceeds with the issue of lust. It was not the act of adultery alone that He spoke against, but dwelling on lustful thoughts from which adultery sprang. Does this not then address issues like pornography and violence, where thoughts sow the seeds of evil? In a similar manner He addresses the sanctity of the word, that our yes should mean yes without having to pile oath upon oath. He speaks to the terrible and unstoppable bent to exact personal revenge upon every wrong of the past. Finally Jesus climaxes that segment of His teaching by telling us that love is at the heart of all relationships and that without love, hate and anger will rule. Jesus gets to the heart—not to a set of rules that can be observed while the heart still rebels.

By setting the problem in its root form rather than in its flowering, Jesus directs us then to the holiness of God, the glimpse we need to touch our spirits. All the rules in the world cannot change a heart or make a person righteous. Only as the spirit is touched by the Spirit of God does the soul rise in worship and true goodness flow.

One of the greatest masterpieces of music composition, if not the greatest, is the work of George Frideric Handel simply called *Messiah*. Prior to its composition Handel had not been successful as a musician and had retired from much professional activity by the age of fifty-six. Then, in a remarkable series of events, a friend presented him with a libretto based on the life of Christ, the entire script of which was Scripture. Handel shut himself in his room on Brook Street in London. In twenty-four days, breathtakingly absorbed in this composition and hardly eating or drinking, Handel completed the work all the way to its orchestration. He was a man in the grip of profound inspiration. Later, as he groped for words to describe what he had experienced, he quoted Saint Paul, saying, "Whether I was in the body or out of my body when I wrote it I know not."[4] Handel's servant testified that on one occasion when he walked into the room to plead with him to eat, he saw Handel with tears streaming down his face saying, "I did think I did see all Heaven before me, and the great God Himself."[5]

When *Messiah* was staged in London, as the notes of the Hallelujah Chorus rang out—"King of Kings and Lord of Lords. . . . And

He shall reign forever and ever"—the king of England, drawn irresistibly, stood to his feet, and the audience followed as one.

Listen to how one writer sums up the impact of *Messiah*:

> Handel personally conducted more than thirty performances of *Messiah*, many of these concerts were for the benefit of the hurting and the needy. "*Messiah* has fed the hungry, clothed the naked, fostered the orphan. . . ." Another wrote, "Perhaps the works of no other composer have so largely contributed to the relief of human suffering." Still another said, "*Messiah's* music has done more to convince thousands of mankind that there is a God about us than all the theological works ever written."[6]

Even if overstated, the point is well taken. The work was based entirely on Scripture. The focus was on the person of Christ. The spirit of a man was enraptured by the holiness of God. A king rose spontaneously to his feet. The people followed his example. The first performance was a charitable benefit to raise money to free 142 people from prison who could not pay their debts. In the prison of suffering and evil within which the whole world now lives, the same Messiah offers us deliverance.

Young Ashley Oubré, is right. Her future, Western civilization's future, and indeed, the world's future, will depend on the answer to her question. Will we restore to the Bible its rightful authority or leave it for young minds till they can grow into our evil-ridden world? Only that which is ineradicable and true can counter that which must be eradicated and false. This preeminent role against the false ideas that are the root cause of evil is that of the Scriptures.

The Inextinguishable Light

IN THE FIRST SECTION of this book I commented that the basis upon which secularism attacked religious knowledge would ultimately destroy not just belief in God but belief in the very concept of truth itself. That is the deduction I will presently sustain. If this conflict is not resolved, nothing else will matter, for nothing will make sense. On this issue the two foundations of secularism and Christianity differ. Once this is settled, the answers we seek may be found

THE COLLAPSE OF A CATEGORY

The much-heralded belief of the postmodern West is that skepticism on ultimate matters is the law by which we must live. Truth as a category in relation to metaphysical issues no longer exists. All is relative. This surrender of truth is the hallmark of our culture's greatest crisis and makes the culture war so deadly, restricting meaningful dialogue on questions of the soul.

Winston Churchill once said that the most valuable thing in the world is the truth. So valuable is it, said he, that it needs to be constantly protected by a bodyguard of lies. Churchill made that remark in the context of intelligence and counterintelligence efforts during the Second World War. This assertion from that great statesman was probably the only pronouncement on which he and his nemesis, Adolf Hitler, agreed.

Unfortunately, the propagation of lies is not restricted to conventional military warfare—it has also been the most insidious weapon in the war of ideas. And what is more, the practice of lying, according to surveys, is at epidemic proportions—assuming, of course, that those surveyed told the truth!

All that aside, as valuable a commodity as it is and as indispensable as it is to meaningful existence, truth is possibly the most violated concept in our world. This is more so now than ever before in history. The lies that punctuate business transactions, the lies by which trusted relationships have been destroyed—these we are aware of. The greater tragedy is not just that we live with a proliferation of lies but that this is probably the first time, certainly in Western civilization, that society at large does not believe in the existence of absolute truth.

Such radical step toward moral and metaphysical skepticism, which asserts the very impossibility of knowing the laws by which our individual lives must be governed, is the single greatest indicator of our postmodern mind. What is most surprising is that a posture of disbelief in truth is not restricted to the liberal element; instead, truth as a category has been jettisoned by many at all levels of society, even among conservatives.

According to a study reported by George Barna in 1991, 67 percent of the U.S. population did not believe in absolute truth. In 1994, that figure rose to 75 percent. In 1991, 52 percent of evangelicals did not believe in absolute truth. In 1994, that figure rose to 62 percent. The difference between saying there is no such thing as the truth and living as if truth does not matter is a small one, and the consequences for both are catastrophic.

THE PERNICIOUSNESS OF ITS EFFECT

Several decades ago Malcolm Muggeridge warned of this spiritual plague coming upon the West, branding it her ultimate death wish. In his autobiography he beckoned humanity to beware of this, the most destructive of all trends—the death of truth. This is how he worded it:

> Yet even so, truth is very beautiful: more so I consider than justice—today's pursuit which easily puts on a false face. In the nearly seven decades I have lived through, the world has overflowed with bloodshed and explosions whose dust has never had time to settle before others have erupted. All in purportedly just causes. . . . The lies on behalf of which our wars have been fought and our peace treaties concluded! The lies of revolution and of counter-revolution! The lies of advertising, of news, of salesmanship, of politics! The lies of the priest in his pulpit, the professor at his podium, the journalist at his typewriter! The lie stuck like a fishbone in the throat of the microphone, the hand-held lies of the prowling cameraman! Ignazio Silone told me once how when he was a member of the Old Comintern, some stratagem was under discussion, and a delegate, a newcomer who had never attended before, made the extraordinary observation that if such and such a statement were to be made, it wouldn't be true. There was a moment of dazed silence, and then everyone began to laugh. They laughed and laughed till tears ran down their cheeks, and the Kremlin walls began to shake. The same laughter echoes in every Council chamber and cabinet room. Wherever two or more are gathered to exercise authority, it is truth that has died, not God.[1]

The most disconcerting aspect of this attitude toward truth is that anyone who holds to the possibility of truth is categorized as one who merely "believes" that truth exists. The implication is that because truth does not exist, what is held to be true is only a belief and is therefore not a rationally admissible fact. At the same time, those who dismiss truth can end up believing anything at all, and any belief that is contemptuous of truth is considered plausible for that reason alone. This is the raw nerve of postmodern existence, and unless we establish the possibility and the necessity of truth and of how one arrives at the truth, any belief system can be mocked at will or offhandedly dismissed as cultural.

For the Christian this is where the battle must be fought, for no world-view suffers more from the loss of truth than the Christian one. Strangely, as has been noted, other religions are culturally protected; no one had dare make light of an Eastern religious belief. The Christian faith, however, is free game for ridicule and analysis by social critics and is afforded no protection from hate or hostility by our so-called multicultural society. In a culture where truth no longer exists, the very cardinal statement of Jesus, "I am the way and the truth and the life," becomes meaningless. And unless truth as a category is defended every commitment that is made because of a commitment to Christ Himself will be deemed a "mere belief" and differentiated from fact, thereby making it unworthy of intellectual assent.

THE DAWNING OF AN ERA

Scholars who deal in social theory and cultural shifts tell us that the modern world as we know it spanned the two hundred years from 1789 to 1989—from the storming of the Bastille in France, which signaled the beginning of the French Revolution, to the dismantling of the Berlin Wall, which symbolized the collapse of communism. That brought the modern era to an end and ushered in the postmodern world. But the breakdown of both these edifices of human construction, with all the tyranny they represented, is meager compared to the breakdown now facing the West, a breakdown heartily sanctioned by the free Western societies now basking under the banner of the postmodern mind. In the modern world reason reigned supreme, and it was envisioned that rational man would hold all things together. Now, *postmodernism* has become the buzzword in academia, the word by which all things have fallen apart, for reason itself is banished as a dinosaur in humanity's evolutionary climb, and truth is considered extinct.

The modern world had emphasized purpose and design. The postmodern world emphasizes randomness and chance. The modern world sought stability in values. The postmodern world sees values as transient and relative. The modern world saw reason as the means and meaning as the end. The postmodern world glories in unreason and celebrates meaninglessness. The modern world pursued a synthesis of all disciplines in its search to find the unity of truth. The postmodern world focuses on deconstruction and extols the marvel of contradiction. In short, the very purpose of the university, which was to find unity in diversity, is now in contradiction to its own name, and students are graduating unable to bridge the disciplines and proudly boasting a skepticism that one can be sure of anything.

This is the one monumental difference between the modern and the postmodern mind. In the modern pursuit, even though there was an inhospitable climate toward spiritual truths, debate was nevertheless possible because information was still subject to induction and deduction. Calm spirits could prevail to allow facts a place in dialogue. In the postmodernist mentality the purpose of dialogue or debate is not for truth but only for feeling, and as passion has taken over, facts are given no legitimacy. The result is hate-filled shouting matches.

If any progress is to be made amid the shifting sands of cultural change it is imperative that we understand where any meaningful dialogue can begin. Too much is at stake, and too many lives will be hurt or lost if we are unable to agree even on the starting point.

This is not to imply that a moral consensus can be reached purely by arriving at the truth. Not by any means. But it does assert that at least in theory we can determine whether a statement that is made about reality is true or false. If even that is denied, then no judgment on any statement is possible. That state of affairs is rationally inadmissable and existentially unlivable.

THE SEDUCTION OF A LIE

We recall Aristotle's reminder that truth is primary, from which morality and technique flow. In our time, technology is supreme, morality is mocked, and truth has been eradicated. But thankfully, all is not lost, for at least postmodernism has unwittingly awakened society to the realization that truth, morality, and meaning are connected. If the first goes, there is nothing on which to base the other two. On every side society feels this colossal breakdown, and a stirring is taking place deep within the national conscience that when truth has been lost, the results are devastating. Nowhere has this been felt more than among those who think in the area of morality and ethics within the legal system and by our young people whose lives reflect the turmoil and emptiness within.

Consequently, many are aroused from their stupor, a stupor that the modern mind created when it trumpeted that rational man could arrive at his Utopia without God's absolutes. In fact, so drastic has been the realization that our purpose on earth is inextricably bound to our behavior that some scholars are reluctantly admitting that the teaching of the Bible provided a logical basis for goodness and that with the abandonment of the Judeo-Christian ethic, the basis for morality is gone. So how do such antagonists to the gospel message then deal with this need for a foundational ethic?

The suggestions range from the absurd to the preposterous. Take, for example, one scholar who presented his thesis at a 1991 symposium of the American Association for the Advancement of Science in Washington, D.C. His basic argument began with the admission that a catastrophe has come upon us as a people. Philosopher Loyal Rue argued that science has made it impossible to believe any longer in the myths of the Bible, myths such as God giving the Ten Commandments and Jesus rising from the dead. But with the loss of these tenets, he said, we have lost the very underpinnings of moral theory that had provided a legitimate recognition of accountability and charity. We are left, therefore, with the unprecedented situation of needing to concoct a "noble lie" so powerful that it will furnish us with reasons to be good, even though those reasons in themselves will be untrue. This is how he worded it:

> The illusion must be so imaginative and so compelling that it can't be resisted. What I mean by the noble lie is one that deceives us, tricks us, compels us beyond self interest, beyond ego . . . that will deceive us into the view that our moral discourse must serve the interests not only of ourselves and each other, but those of the earth as well.[2]

One should rightly be incredulous at the extent to which some will wantonly and deliberately dupe themselves. But let us take a beneficent route, because here again, there is a tacit concession that a purpose to life and a sense of accountability to a higher moral law are inseparably connected to the justification of ethics. In effect, what is being said here is that without a transcendent order, ethics is unjustifiable, and without ethics, life is unlivable.

On all fronts, therefore, our existential realities are pointing us to the relationship between truth and life. And what reality has revealed to be joined together, let no man put asunder. In short, the greatest concern of our time should be the recovery of truth. It was not too long ago that in a survey among Canadian young people, the majority said their greatest longing in life was to find someone they could believe in. The question is, how do we arrive at the truth, principally the truth on which all other truths hang and by which life must be governed?

The irony of defining truth is that while in practice we all instinctively recognize it when we see it, we nevertheless ask whether it exists theoretically. Professor Dallas Willard, who teaches philosophy at the University of Southern California, asks this of our sensitivity to and estrangement from the truth. What would you think if you asked your ten-year-old, "Susie, did you eat the cookies on the counter?" and she placidly replied, "Mother, what is truth?" Thankfully, Susie may not have gained that evasive philosophical sophistication. But Pilate of old had, and he raised the question of Jesus, "What is truth?" Jesus answered him with a categorical response (see John 18:38). But before we turn to His answer, let us establish some definitions.

First, we know that relativism as a theory cannot be true. The Greek philosopher Protagoras was the one who said, "The human being is the measure of all things." By that he meant that each individual measured in terms for himself or herself the fact or nature of anything. He was disagreeing with Parmenides, who stated that what is, is; what is not, is not. Without getting too far afield it would be simplest to demonstrate the fairly obvious that Protagoras's relativism is self-defeating. Professor Allen Wood of Yale University states it succinctly:

> The problem arises as soon as Protagoras tries either to *assert* relativism or to *believe* it. To assert a proposition is to say that it is true (and its denial false). To believe a proposition is to believe it is true (and its denial false). Thus if Protagoras asserts relativism, then he asserts that relativism is true, and that those (such as Plato) who deny relativism say and believe something false. But relativism denies that anyone can say or believe anything false. Hence to be consistent Protagoras must concede that the denier of relativism says and believes something true. Consequently relativism is committed to saying that its own denial is true, and in this refutes itself.[3]

THE SCAFFOLDING OF CERTAINTY

Very simply stated, truth is the judgment expressed when we use the word "is." The verb "is" asserts something about reality to which the statement conforms. In other words, the statement "This is so" expresses a state of existence that is real and not dependent on someone's belief in it to make it true. The reality being represented is objective, universal, and transcendent. This is precisely the logic by which we operate and the logic by which we either make statements about reality or make denials about what is not real.

It is of supreme importance to know that, as Mortimer Adler has said:

> The logic of truth is the same for all exclusionary claims to truth. Any claims that are correctly judged to be true also imply that all judgments to the contrary are false. The proposition may be a theorem in mathematics, a scientific generalization, a conclusion of historic research, a philosophical principle, or an article of faith.[4]

This leads us to the definition of an *absolute*. An absolute is basically an unchanging point of reference by which all other changes are measured. Each discipline brings with it a handful of certainties by which others are developed. Those certainties, if assumed, must be previously demonstrated when used as absolutes. In contrast, relativism in ethics denounces absolutes and erects an indefensible system that leaves all morality at the mercy of individual whim. *Relativism* is, therefore, only another word for *anarchy*, and that is why truth itself becomes elusive when there is no longer a point of reference.

Where, then, may one begin? There are fundamentally four questions that every thinking human being must answer: the questions of origin, meaning, morality, and destiny. How did life come to be in the first place? To what purpose is my life? How may I choose between right and wrong? What happens to me when I die? When these questions are individually answered, the answers must be seen to correspond with reality. These answers are then collectively tested for coherence, that is, that they do not contradict each other. Answers that correspond with reality and fit into a coherent system provide the individual a world-view by which all of life's choices may then be made.

For the Christian, the starting point is God. *He* is the eternally existent one, the absolute, from whom we draw all definitions for life's purpose and destiny. This God does not expect us to come to Him in a vacuum. He has so framed this world and our minds that the laws of reason and logic we use lead us to the certainty of His being and assure us that we may know Him who is the source of all truth. At this point the argument is a bit rigorous, but it is vitally important. Philosopher Norman Geisler says, "In order of being God is first: but in order of knowing, logic leads us to all knowledge of God. God is the basis of all logic (in order of being), but logic is the basis of all knowledge of God (in order of knowing)."[5] If one finds this statement too rigid, let us present it in a softer version. The right process of reasoning must at some point be invoked in order to defend the reality and "knowability" of God.

THE STRUCTURE OF REASON

Here we run aground and face the first criticism from the skeptic: Are we not using logic with which to prove logic? The answer to that is straightforward. The logical system is built on four fundamental laws, laws that are impossible to argue against without at the same time proving them. For the sake of brevity, let me discuss just two of them.

First is the Law of Noncontradiction. This law affirms that no two contradictory statements can be both true and false at the same time in the same sense. To deny the Law of Noncontradiction is only to affirm it, for to say that the Law of Noncontradiction is not true is to assume that the denial is true and the law is not. But that is precisely what the law says—that two contradictory statements cannot both be true. There is no way to get around this.

The second foundational law is the Law of Rational Inference. By that we mean that inferences can be made from what is known to what is unknown. No one can prove any point without the Law of

Rational Inference. There are conclusions that may be legitimately drawn when statements are true and the argument containing those statements is valid.

Postmodern skeptics cannot tolerate the Law of Noncontradiction because of the rational inferences they draw from it—that truth does exist—but it is evident that they live by the implications of these laws. And what is more, one of the most fallacious ideas ever spawned in Western attitudes toward truth is the oft-repeated pronouncement that exclusionary claims to truth are a Western way of thinking. The East, it is implied, is all-inclusionary. This is patently false. Every religion, without exception, has some foundational beliefs that are categorically nonnegotiable and exclude everything to the contrary.

Truth by definition is exclusive. If truth were all-inclusive, nothing would be false. And if nothing were false, what would be the meaning of truth? Furthermore, if nothing were false, would it be true to say that everything is false? It quickly becomes evident that nonsense would follow. In short, therefore, truth boils down to two tests: Statements must correspond to reality, and any system of thought that is developed as a result must be coherent. The correspondence and coherence tests are applied by all of us in matters that affect us.

Therefore, when Jesus said, "I am the way and the truth and the life. No man comes to the father except through me," He was making a very reasonable statement by affirming truth's exclusivity. The question one may legitimately ask is whether He demonstrated that claim rather than just stating it.

THE BATTLEGROUND OF THE HEART

Let us see, now, how Jesus responded to Pilate's question. The conversation had begun with Pilate asking Jesus if, indeed, He was a king. The very surprising answer of Jesus was, "Is that your idea, or did others talk to you about me?" (John 18:34).

This is the first and most important step to understanding the nature of truth. In effect, Jesus was asking Pilate if this was a genuine question or purely an academic one. He was not merely checking on Pilate's sincerity. He was opening up Pilate's heart to himself to reveal to Pilate his unwillingness to deal with the implications of Jesus' answer. Intent in the pursuit of truth is prior to content or to the availability of it. Author George MacDonald once said, "To give truth to him who loves it not is only to give him more plentiful reasons for misinterpretation."[6] The love of truth and the willingness to submit to its demands is the first step.

But Jesus said something else that is even more extraordinary. After identifying His Lordship in a kingdom that was not of this world, He said, "Everyone on the side of truth *listens to me*" (John 18:37, italics mine). Jesus was not merely establishing the existence of truth but His pristine embodiment of it. He was *identical* to the truth. This meant that everything He said and did, and the life He lived in the flesh, represented that which was in keeping with ultimate reality. Therefore, to reject Him is to choose to govern oneself with a lie.

THE WORD AS TRUTH

Let me take this point further. In the beginning, when God created the heavens and the earth, He branded His creation "good." That word both defined reality and specified how we ought to live. Out of that relationship with God, all other relationships take their cue, including the use of language in defining the world. We read that Adam named the creatures. That naming was the work of man as sub-sovereign, defining reality in God's terms.

It was at this point that truth was tested. The temptation of Satan was the challenge to the first humans to take upon themselves the prerogative of God and redefine reality in their own terms. The lie entered, and truth was violated by rejecting the propositional revelation of God and contradicting His definitions of good and evil. By yielding to that temptation Adam and Eve "exchanged the truth of God for a lie" and chose to create their own realities. This, as God had warned, led to death and destruction.

It is noteworthy that when the tempter came to Jesus in the wilderness the temptation was the same, namely, to make His own terms for living. Jesus rejected this seduction by quoting the Word, i.e., the definitions of God. As mentioned earlier, it is interesting that Jesus quoted from the Book of Deuteronomy, which literally means the "second law." This was God's law reiterated to His people—not as heteronomy, with the state as the authority; not as an undefined theonomy, with intuition or culture as the authority; and not as autonomy with self as the authority. This was God's law as given in the beginning, and it represented the nature of reality as God had designed it. The opposite of Deuteronomy is autonomy, or self law. It is in this context that we must understand Jesus' statement that the truthfulness of one's intent is revealed by the response to Him, for He is the fulfillment of God's law and the expression of His truth.

THE EMPIRICAL DEMONSTRATION

God's answers to the four basic questions, however, are not just proven by the process of abstract reasoning but are also sustained by the rigors of experience. And in the reality of history, He has demonstrated empirically the living out of truth in the birth, life, death, and resurrection of His Son.

In short, the intimations of truth come in multisensory fashion. The Guardian of Reason leads us to check the correspondence of His word with reality and ascertain the coherence of the assertions. Our grand privilege is to know Him, to bring our lives into conformity with truth that leads us to that coherence within. He has said, "If you hold to my teaching, you are really my disciples. Then you will know the truth, and the truth will set you free" (John 8:31, 32). In a world increasingly enslaved by error and alienation, how wonderful to be freed by the truth to His peace. The Scriptures tell us that the enemy of our souls is the father of all lies. He will do anything to keep us from coming to the truth, because it is the most valuable thing in the world and leads us to the source of all truth, to God Himself.

SKEPTICISM'S SURRENDER

To all of this the skeptic might say that such conclusions may be drawn only if the God of the Bible exists. To that I heartily answer, *Absolutely!* And on numerous campuses around the world it has been my thrilling privilege to present a defense for the existence of God and for the authority of the Scriptures, unique in their splendor and convincing in the truth they proclaim. But let us not miss what the skeptic unwittingly surrenders by saying that all this could be true only if God exists. For, implicit in that concession is the application of the Law of Noncontradiction and the Law of Rational Inference, which exist only if truth exists. Truth, in turn, can exist only if there is an objective standard by which to measure it. That objective, unchanging absolute is God.

I heard a cute little story, growing up in India. It is the story of a little boy who had lots of pretty marbles. But he was constantly eyeing his sister's bagful of candy. One day he said to her, "If you give me all your candy, I'll give you all of my marbles." She gave it much thought and agreed to the trade. He took all her candy and went back to his room to get his marbles. But the more he eyed them the more reluctant he became to give them all up. So he hid the best of them under his pillow and took the rest to her. That night she slept soundly while he tossed and turned restlessly, unable to sleep and thinking, *I wonder if she gave me all the candy.*

I have often wondered, when I see our angry culture claiming that

God has not given us enough evidence, if it is not the veiled restlessness of lives lived in doubt because of their own duplicity. God calls us all to enjoy His glorious truth. We believe, but not because we need to in order to make us feel better. We believe because truth survives in the end and it is truth that must be believed. What is more, when we trust Him who is the source of all truth there is an enjoyment in life beyond any momentary pleasure a lie can give. The battle in our time is posed as one of the intellect in the assertion that truth is unknowable. But that may be only a veneer for the real battle, that of the heart.

Annotated Bibliography on the Bible

Comfort, Philip Wesley, ed. *The Origin of the Bible.* Wheaton, Ill.: Tyndale House, 1992. Noted biblical scholars address the inspiration, translation and manuscripts of the Old and New Testaments, as well as the development of the canon. F. F. Bruce, Carl Henry, and R. K. Harrison are among the contributing authors.

Geisler, Norman. *Christian Apologetics.* Grand Rapids, Mich.: Baker, 1976. The classic resource on various tests for truth (such as rationalism and agnosticism) and world-views. The final section of the book examines the historical reliability of the New Testament and the case for the authority and inspiration of the Bible.

Geisler, Norman, ed. *Inerrancy.* Grand Rapids, Mich.: Zondervan, 1979. This book is a compendium of the scholarly papers presented at the International Conference on Biblical Inerrancy in 1978. J. Barton Payne's chapter on "Higher Criticism and Biblical Inerrancy" is an excellent examination of higher criticism's presuppositions and its unscientific disregard for the scriptures under observation.

Geisler, Norman, and William E. Nix. *From God to Us: How We Got Our Bible.* Chicago: Moody, 1974. A basic but thorough primer on the Bible's origins, including consideration of manuscripts, textual criticism, and early translations. Especially insightful are their discussions of what qualifies a book's authenticity and of the development of the Old Testament canon.

Habermas, Gary R. *Ancient Evidence for the Life of Jesus: Historical Records of His Death and Resurrection.* Nashville: Thomas Nelson, 1984. The author addresses the many extrabiblical sources—both Christian and non-Christian—and archaeological evidence that offer information on the life, death, and resurrection of Jesus. The initial chapters on historical methodology present a philosophy of history (how one studies a particular event) and the procedure of historical investigation.

Montgomery, John Warwick, ed. *God's Inerrant Word: An International Symposium on the Trustworthiness of the Scriptures.* Minneapolis: Bethany, 1974. A compendium of the papers given at the Conference on the Inspiration and Authority of the Scriptures in 1973. Scholars offering research articles include theologians J. I. Packer and John Gerstner, and philosopher John Frame.

Moreland, J.P. *Scaling the Secular City: A Defense of Christianity.* Grand Rapids, Mich.: Baker, 1987. Moreland provides an astute critique of secularism and communicates the rationality of Christianity. His scholarship reveals secularism's inadequacy in offering the individual meaning to live and reasons for being moral. His second chapter on the historicity of the New Testament and the resurrection of Jesus are concisely yet persuasively presented.

Wilkins, Michael J., and J. P. Moreland, eds. *Jesus Under Fire: Modern Scholarship Reinvents the Historical Jesus.* Grand Rapids, Mich.: Zondervan, 1995. New Testament scholars and philosophers examine the claims and methodology of the Jesus Seminar and present a well-argued case for the orthodox understanding of Jesus. The criticism regarding exclusivism and pluralism is also countered.

Wright, N. T. *Who Was Jesus?* Grand Rapids, Mich.: Eerdmans, 1993. An English scholar responds to the latest controversial works on the life of Jesus by Barbara Thiering, John Shelby Spong, and others. Wright offers an excellent overview of the broad arguments of this debate.

Notes

INTRODUCTION

1   George Santayana, "The Life of Reason," *Who Said What When* (London: Bloomsbury Publishing, 1989), 211.

CHAPTER 1   *The Winds of Change*

1   I use the terms *soul* and *spirit* interchangeably here, not to provide a theological frame-work, but to refer to the essence of each and every person as not merely material in being and bound to earthliness but as fashioned by our Creator to think His thoughts after Him, to rise beyond the physical, and to understand the purpose of our being in this world.

2   Jay Parini, "Academic Conservatives Who Decry Politicization Show Staggering Naiveté about Their Own Biases," *Chronicle of Higher Education*, 7 December 1988, B-1.

3   Dinesh D'Souza is a research fellow at the American Enterprise Institute.

4   Myron Magnet is an editor of *Fortune* magazine and a fellow of the Manhattan Institute.

5   Norman Mailer, "The White Negro," 1957. Quoted by Myron Magnet in *The Dream and the Nightmare: The Sixties' Legacy to the Underclass* (New York: William Morrow, 1993), 35.

6   Katherine Lee Bates, "America the Beautiful."

CHAPTER 2   *Dying Beliefs and Stillborn Hopes*

1   Arthur Guiterman, "Gaily the Troubadour," from *Gaily the Troubadour* (New York: E.P. Dutton & Company, Inc., 1936).
2   Peter L. Berger, *The Sacred Canopy*, (New York: Doubleday, 1990) 107.

CHAPTER 3   *The High Noon of Promise*

1   Julian Marias, *America in the Fifties and Sixties*, edited by Aaron Rockland (University Park, Penna: Pennsylvania State University Press, 1972), 412.
2   Russell Kirk, *The Roots of American Order* (Malibu, Calif.: Pepperdine University Press, 1978), 467, emphasis mine.
3   William Blake, from "Milton," *The Portable Romantic Poets: Blake to Poe*, ed. William Auden and Norman Holmes Pearson (New York: Penguin, 1987), 24.
4   John Warwick Montgomery, *The Shaping of America* (Minneapolis: Bethany Fellowship, 1976), 73.
5   Russell Kirk, *The Roots of American Order*, 93–94.
6   G. K. Chesterton, "A Hymn," in *As I Was Saying*, ed. Robert Knille (Grand Rapids, Mich.: Eerdman's, 1984), 27. Set to the tune of "The Church's One Foundation." Used by permission of A.P. Watt Ltd, London, on behalf of the Royal Literary Fund.
7   William Wordsworth, "London 1802," *English Romantic Writers*, ed. David Perkins (New York, Chicago, San Francisco: Harcourt, Brace & World, 1967), 288.
8   George F. Will has written a book coining these words, titled *Statecraft as Soulcraft* (New York: Simon & Schuster, 1983).

CHAPTER 4   *The Storms of Conflict*

1   Thomas C. Arthur, "Death of Another Salesman," Copyright 1961 Christian Century Foundation. Reprinted by permission from the February 1, 1961 issue of the *Christian Century*.
2   Arthur Leonard Griffith, *God's Time and Ours* (New York: Abingdon Press, 1964), 83.
3   Kenneth L. Woodward, "Religion: God Gets the He-Ho," *Newsweek*, 11 September 1995, © 1955, Newsweek Inc. All rights reserved. Reprinted by permission.
4   Predictably, secularism as a social theory did not stop at merely attacking biblical truth; it has ended up attacking the notion of truth itself. Please see the discussion on this in Appendix B.

CHAPTER 5   *The Twilight of Decency*

1   C. S. Lewis, *The Pilgrim's Regress* (Glasgow: William Collins & Sons, Fount Paperbacks, 1933), 82–83.

●

2   Scanner theory is described by M. Scott Peck in *A World Waiting to Be Born* (New York: Bantam, 1993), 10.
3   C. S. Lewis, *The Great Divorce* (Glasgow: William Collins & Sons, 1946), 57.
4   See Gen. 4:9–12.

CHAPTER 6   *With Deference for Difference*

1   Malvina Reynolds, "Little Boxes," words and music by Malvina Reynolds © copyright 1962, Schroder Music Co. (ASCAP), Renewed 1990. Used by permission. All rights reserved.
2   Carly Simon, "Playing Possum." Copyright by C'est Music (ASCAP.) Used by permission.
3   Vivekananda, as reported by the *Chicago Tribune*, 20 September 1893, quoted by David L. Johnson, *A Reasoned Look at Asian Religions* (Minneapolis: Bethany, 1985), 106.
4   Jack Miles, "Black vs. Browns," *Atlantic Monthly*, October 1992, 41.
5   James Davison Hunter, *Culture Wars* (New York: Basic Books, 1991), 69–70.
6   Will Herberg, cited in Hunter, *Culture Wars*.
7   Although statistics show a rapid increase in the number of Muslims to the point of becoming the second largest religion in the world and in the United States by the year 2000, one should be careful how to read these numbers. For example, numerical computation for Islam cannot be considered to have been done with the same methodology as for the Christian community. In many Islamic countries it is illegal to convert from Islam to another faith, and where it is not illegal, it is certainly a life-threatening situation. This point is often forgotten by Muslims themselves when presenting their "growth." It would be fascinating to see what would happen if the compulsive hand of law and government in enforcing religion were removed. The whole teaching of Islam in its inception rested upon the creation of an identity of a people in contradistinction to Judaism and Christianity. A failure to understand the implications of all this leads to enormous misunderstandings when all religions are grouped together.
8   Michel Guillaume Jean de Crevecouer, quoted in Arthur Schlesinger, "The Disuniting of America," *American Educator*, Winter 1991, 14.
9   Malcolm Muggeridge, *The End of Christendom* (Grand Rapids, Mich.: Eerdmans, 1980), 52–53. Used by permission.

CHAPTER 7   *The Flickering Flame of Reason*

1   Pantheism, that strand of Hinduism that identifies God and nature as one, is ultimately handcuffed on the fundamental question of the origin and destiny of evil. If everything is divine, where does wickedness come from? As philosopher Norm Geisler says in his book *Christian Apologetics*, "The ship of pantheism is wrecked on the reef of evil" (Grand Rapids, Mich.: Baker, 1976), 189.
2   G. K. Chesterton, *Orthodoxy* (Garden City, N.Y.: Doubleday, 1959), 41.
3   Daniel Yankelovich, "New Rules in American Life: Searching for Self-fulfillment in a World Turned Upside Down," *Psychology Today*, April 1981, 36.

4   Ibid., 50.
5   Ibid.
6   Ulysses, in William Shakespeare's *Troilus and Cressida*, 3, 3, 120ff.

CHAPTER 8   *The Disoriented Self*

1   Quoted by F. W. Boreham in "An Epic of Concentration," *A Late Lark Singing* (London: Epworth Press, 1945), 128.
2   Ibid.
3   Ibid., 129.
4   Robert Shapiro, in a transcript of a CNN interview with Larry King, 2 April 1996, 5.
5   Justin Hayward, "Question," © copyright 1970 Tyler Music Ltd., London, England. Essex Music International, Inc., New York. Used by permission.

CHAPTER 9   *Establishing Boundaries*

1   Samuel Taylor Coleridge, quoted in *The International Dictionary of Thoughts*, comp. John P. Bradley, Leo F. Daniels, and Thomas C. Jones (Chicago: J. G. Ferguson, 1969), 362.
2   G. K. Chesterton, quoted in John Bartlett, *Bartlett's Familiar Quotations*, 14th ed. (Boston, Toronto: Little, Brown, 1968), 918.
3   Percy Bysshe Shelley, "Ozymandias," taken from *English Romantic Writers*, ed. David Perkins (New York, Chicago, San Francisco, Atlanta: Harcourt, Brace & World, 1967), 971.
4   James Russell Lowell, "Once to Every Man and Nation."

CHAPTER 10   *Pulling Down the Fences*

1   John Adams, *A Biography in His Own Words*, ed. James Bishop Peabody (New York: Newsweek, 1973), 121–22.
2   Malcolm Muggeridge in a verbal communication.
3   Alfred Edersheim, *Old Testament Bible History* (Wilmington, Dela.: Associated Publishers and Authors, n.d.), 556.
4   Peggy Noonan, "You'd Cry Too If It Happened to You," *FORBES*, 14 September, 1992, 69. Reprinted by permission of *FORBES* Magazine © Forbes Inc., 1992.
5   Os Guinness, *The American Hour* (New York: The Free Press, 1993), 29.
6   Cunningham Geikie, *Hours with the Bible: Manasseh to Zedekiah* (New York: John B. Alden, 1887), 25–26.
7   James Russell Lowell, "The Present Crisis."
8   The source of all these statistics is Carol Bellamy, executive director, United Nations Children's Fund, UNICEF, *The State of the World's Children* (published for UNICEF by Oxford University Press, 1996).
9   Quoted in Bellamy, *The State of the World's Children*, 1996.
10   Arthur Schlesinger Jr., "The Opening of the American Mind," *The New York Times Book Review*, July 23 1989, 27. Used by permission.

CHAPTER 11   *Restoring the Soul*

1   2 Kings 23:25
2   From Lady Margaret Thatcher's address to the Church of Scotland, 21 May 1988. Permission granted by the office of Baroness Thatcher, London.
3   Taken from a list of quotations on the back cover of a book.
4   G. K. Chesterton, "In Defense of Nonsense," 1911, quoted in Bartlett, *Bartlett's Familiar Quotations*, 918.
5   Horatio G. Spafford, "It Is Well With My Soul."
6   George MacDonald, *Life Essential: The Hope of the Gospel* (Wheaton, Ill.: Harold Shaw Publishers, 1974) quoted in Philip Yancy, *The Jesus I Never Knew* (Grand Rapids, Mich.: Zondervan, 1995), 77.
7   Malcolm Muggeridge, *The End of Christendom*, 49–50.

CHAPTER 12   *The Unmasking of Evil*

1   Ron Rosenbaum, "The Devil in Long Island," *New York Times Magazine*, 22 August 1993, 21–27, 36–38, 42–44.
2   Ibid., 44.
3   Ron Rosenbaum, "Staring into the Heart of Darkness: Evil Is Back," *New York Times Magazine*, 4 June 1995, 36–72.
4   Ibid., 41.
5   Hannah Arendt, *Eichmann in Jerusalem* (New York: Viking Penguin, 1977), 252, emphasis is mine.
6   The *Pulp Fiction* dialogue is from Ron Rosenbaum, "Staring into the Heart of Darkness: Evil Is Back," 44.
7   C. S. Lewis, *The Abolition of Man* (New York: Macmillan, 1947), 35.
8   This is not to deny some emotional disorders where there is emotional numbing, a psychological condition. This is only to state that a person who lives by the rule that all morality is only individual preference will ultimately breed either a heartless philosophy or a heartless life.
9   Reprinted with the permission of Simon & Schuster from *Letters and Papers from Prison:* revised, enlarged edition by Dietrich Bonhoeffer. Translated by Reginald Fuller, Frank Clark et al. Copyright © 1953, 1967, 1971 by SCM Press, Ltd.

CHAPTER 13   *The God Who Is Near*

1   Charles Wesley, "And Can It Be."
2   R. S. Thomas, "The Coming" *The Later Poems of R. S. Thomas, 1972–1982* (London: Macmillan, nd.) Used by permission of Paper Mac, London.
3   William Cowper, "God Moves in a Mysterious Way."
4   Hermann Hagedorn, *The Bomb That Fell on America*, new rev. ed. (New York: Association Press, 1950).

APPENDIX A *The Ineradicable Word*

1 Ashley Danielle Oubré. Used by permission.
2 An annotated bibliography dealing with this subject follows this Appendix. As demeaning as the comment may seem, it must be said that some recent attacks on the historicity of the New Testament by radical scholars from groups such as the Jesus Seminar are so prejudicial and bizarre that even noted liberal scholars have rejected their ill-founded deductions. Such absurdity notwithstanding, these attacks have nevertheless been responded to by conservative scholars. If the defense of the Scriptures were made on such sparse accumulation of evidence as that upon which these extreme views have been constructed, the proponents of those theories would have scornfully dismissed such defense as unworthy of any response. But a tabloid mentality prevails in these matters even in respected journals, and even the most aberrant thesis gains legitimacy when a doctoral degree after the author's name is placed in the byline. There is no other explanation for the credulity of such intellectuals other than that they want to believe the spurious and desire to be so duped.
3 Eugene H. Peterson, *Subversive Christianity* (Vancouver: Regent College Bookstore, 1994), 4–5.
4 Patrick Kavanaugh, *The Spiritual Lives of Great Composers* (Nashville: Sparrow Press, 1992), 5.
5 Hertha Pauli, *Handel and the Messiah Story* (New York: Meredith, 1968), 51.
6 Kavanaugh, 6.

APPENDIX B *The Inextinguishable Light*

1 Malcolm Muggeridge, *The Green Stick* (New York: William Morrow, 1973), 19.
2 George Cornell, "Religion and Ethics," *Houston Post*, 7 July 1991.
3 Professor Allen Wood, Cornell University philosophy class lecture notes, 1993.
4 Mortimer Adler, *Truth in Religion* (New York: Macmillan, 1990), 10.
5 Norman L. Geisler and Ronald M. Brooks, *Come, Let Us Reason* (Grand Rapids, Mich.: Baker, 1990), 17.
6 George MacDonald, *The Curate's Awakening* (Minneapolis: Bethany, 1985), 161.

Study Guide

CHAPTER ONE: THE WINDS OF CHANGE

1 Discuss the story told by Ravi Zacharias in this chapter of the thief searching for the jewels. How does this Eastern parable relate to America and the West today? What would you say is the primary pursuit of Western culture at this time?

2 Discuss the sense that something is missing spiritually in Western culture. What happens to a society when "the destiny of the soul is traded for the enthrallment of the moment"?

3 Is our modern cultural state new in the world's experience? What does the Bible have to say about it, particularly as it relates to the events in the book of Haggai?

4 Discuss how the radical student movements of the sixties have influenced America. What is your reaction to Ravi Zacharias' comment that "it is no longer the students rebelling against the system, it is the system itself that is in revolt against the very ideas on which it was built." What evidence for this statement can you find?

5 What are the differences between reason and intellect, the mind versus the brain? Discuss what makes up the "wholeness" of human beings and why education alone is not enough.

CHAPTER TWO: DYING BELIEFS AND STILLBORN HOPES

1 Discuss the confounding moral options we face today, where convictions may clash with "career goals," and religious belief clash with a "preferred lifestyle."

2 How are the foundations of our culture shifting? What may be the consequences of a major shift of this type? Why do you think more people don't see these shifts or raise an alarm?

3 Discuss secularization and the secular worldview that propels Western culture today. How is this "the first step on the road to unmanageable evil"?

4 Discuss the "philosophical attack upon the moorings of contemporary society." What is society's view of those who speak from a Christian perspective? What is its attitude toward religious ideas in general?

CHAPTER THREE: THE HIGH NOON OF PROMISE

1 What was America "created" for? What does the late scholar Russell Kirk, in his book *The Roots of American Order*, say our destiny will be?

2 Discuss pragmatism and the story of the train that laid its own track. How does this fit in with dreams of Utopia and narcissistic self-worship?

3 What four cities or cultures does Russell Kirk say have helped shape the American mind? Discuss what each has contributed to our cultural legacy.

4 Discuss the ancient Greek culture and its influence on this nation. What does Dr. Kirk say killed that great nation? According to Alexis de Tocqueville, what was the most important force holding America together?

5 Discuss the idea of "relativism" in ancient Greek and modern American culture. What belief did America once have which it now rejects?

CHAPTER FOUR: THE STORMS OF CONFLICT

1 Discuss the origins of the shift away from Christianity and toward secularization in Western culture. What conditions does Canadian historian David Marshall list as making a country inhospitable to the Christian message? Where does he place most of the blame?

2 What does Peter Berger say about the role of Protestants in the movement toward secularization? How did the "higher" or "historical" criticism damage scriptural authority? Do you believe this has had a damaging impact on American culture?

3 Discuss the paragraph on the Church of the Holy Sepulcher in Jerusalem. In what way is this a parable of Western Christianity today?

4 How has the secular view of the supernatural influenced Christian beliefs? Discuss how—in the name of "progress" and "sensitivity to other thought systems"— the Christian believer has been bullied and intimidated.

5 Discuss recent translations of the Bible, as in the example on page 52. Do you think politically correct versions help or hurt the cause of Christ? Do they help or hinder the American mission of reconciling liberty and law?

CHAPTER FIVE: THE TWILIGHT OF DECENCY

1 If secularization throws out God as the "irrational supernatural," what is man's point of reference? How does this redefine the role of conscience? How is the Christian voice being treated in the new world of secularism?

2   How do secularists defend their choices? What is their first principle? Discuss some of the tricks and strategies employed by those with a strictly secular world-view.

3   Discuss C. S. Lewis' thoughts from *The Pilgrim's Regress*. What insights does Lewis have to offer about the Spirit of the Age?

4   What does a loss of shame in a society do to a civilization? How does shame act as a guardian for ourselves and others? And how does a lack of shame lead to great evil?

5   Discuss the origins of secularism, according to the book of Genesis. What has secularization given us?

CHAPTER SIX: WITH DEFERENCE FOR DIFFERENCE

1   Discuss pluralism, multiculturalism, and ethnocentrism. What is the difference between self-acceptance and self-exaltation?

2   Discuss how the sixties radicals changed Western thinking. What did the "new America" believe? What became the "in thing" and the outrageous thing? How did the Indian scholar, Vivekananda, prefigure these changes in 1893?

3   Discuss the reshaping elements of pluralism and their dangers. How have the huge numbers of new immigrants changed our country? What are the implications when many citizens here speak a foreign language?

4   Discuss the drastic shift in American religious commitment from a predominantly Protestant society to a new influx of Catholic, and recently Islamic, Buddhist, Hindu, and New Age teachings. What is the strength of pluralism, and what is its great hazard?

5   What is the difference between opinion and conviction? How does love figure into this? Discuss the passage in this chapter by Malcolm Muggeridge.

CHAPTER SEVEN: THE FLICKERING FLAME OF REASON

1 "The assumption that all ideas are equally true is false." Why is one idea chosen over another? What is a symptom of a society that has lost its ability to think critically?

2 Discuss the book *Bridge on the River Kwai* by Pierre Boulle, regarding losing sight of the big picture by warring over lesser principles. How do pluralism, diversity, and freedom figure into this?

3 Discuss the meaning of "culture." What is the massive barrier that pluralism brings? Cultures operate in ways that are fundamentally opposed to each other. How do the stories of the Indian movies and the UCLA murder illustrate cultural differences?

4 Name and discuss Paul Tillich's three kinds of cultures as they relate to religious knowledge. Can our culture absorb all these and still remain autonomous? What costly doctrine does pluralism breed? Discuss examples of this in American today.

5 What is "the law of either/or"? What does the eradication of difference signal? Comment on Shakespeare (see page 100). Discuss Richard Weaver's statement on feelings. How have we, in America, elevated feelings above all?

CHAPTER EIGHT: THE DISORIENTED SELF

1 What may be the most astonishing reversal of the twentieth century? Discuss privatization of religion. What has this done to Christianity in the West? What has it done to public life?

2 How have secularization, pluralization, and privatization affected society? List two reasons why we know privatization is a false premise. Discuss how President Lincoln became the man he was. Can public and private behavior be severed?

3 Why is there no coherence in our communities? Discuss Arthur Miller's play *The Death of a Salesman* in this context.

4 Discuss how the trial of O. J. Simpson encapsulates the three-fold evils with which we now live. How does evil come to us through ideas?

5 Discuss the failures that felled the Graeco-Roman world. Do you see these aspects in Western culture today?

CHAPTER NINE: ESTABLISHING BOUNDARIES

1 What are some of the ways that God speaks to us? How does He speak to us through the arena of history?

2 Discuss God's love for His creation. What do you think of G. K. Chesterton's remark concerning this?

3 Read and discuss Shelley's poem "Ozymandias." What does this tell us about the importance of people and things in our world?

4 The time period of the seventh century before Christ had radical swings in the nation of Judah when it was led by the destructive king, Manasseh. What potent reminder does this history lesson have for us today?

CHAPTER TEN: PULLING DOWN THE FENCES

1 King Manasseh found it easier to destroy a nation than to re-build it. He made three decisions that altered Judah's course and led her to a tragic fate. What was the first and most radical choice he made?

2 What do the Scriptures say Manasseh did that provoked the Lord to anger? Why do you think he wanted to take down all the barriers his father and God had put up? Why do people want to do so today? What are the results?

3   Discuss the Peggy Noonan article in this chapter. People celebrate
    when each old rule is broken. Are we a better or happier society
    today with our modern "no rules" world?

4   When any belief is expelled, it will be replaced by another. What
    is the second step Manasseh took? What heinous practice did
    this lead to? Do we do anything similar today?

5   What is the third and final step Manasseh took? What could
    he have learned about this action if he had studied history
    beforehand?

6   Discuss the three profound lessons we can learn from
    Manasseh's life. What is the greatest lesson? Can people
    change dramatically? Discuss Manasseh's changed life and that
    of the Australian lady.

CHAPTER ELEVEN: RESTORING THE SOUL

1   The problem of evil seems so overwhelming that people don't
    know how to confront it. What should be their first step?

2   Nations can return to good. What historically proven steps did
    Josiah take to restore the nation of Judah? Discuss Daniel
    Webster's comment on a nation without God.

3   What was the treasure that Josiah gave back to his people?
    What is the greatest contribution of the Hebrews to the young
    American nation?

4   Discuss the importance of worship in maintaining the nation's
    moral strength. Why is reverence at the heart of worship? Dis-
    cuss the word "sacred" and its opposite "profane." How has the
    soul of a nation changed?

5   What are several important consequences that follow Josiah's two
    simple steps? What peace did Josiah offer his people? What peace
    did the airmen in Vietnam find in the hymn? (See Isaiah 26:3.)

6   Read and discuss the Malcolm Muggeridge piece in this chapter. Does it remind you of Shelley's poem in chapter nine? What is the answer that Muggeridge presents?

CHAPTER TWELVE: THE UNMASKING OF EVIL

1   Discuss the mindless evil acts that seem to occur constantly in America. Are things getting worse? What is your reaction to the author's statement, "Evil is in the self-absorbed human heart"?

2   What are the three steps in unraveling the mystery of wickedness? How are words redefined to justify acts of evil, as in the example from the movie "Pulp Fiction"? What does God say about this kind of overt redefinition of language?

3   What are the components of wickedness? How can it be defined? Discuss C. S. Lewis' book, *The Abolition of Man*. How does the author's encounter with the man in Hong Kong parallel Lewis' book?

4   Discuss the thoughts of Dietrich Bonhoffer as he goes to his death for his stand against Hitler? Who will answer his call for responsible people who answer the call of God?

CHAPTER THIRTEEN: THE GOD WHO IS NEAR

1   God is not calling on us just to act more civilly. What does He want of us?

2   What was the instrument Jesus used to counter evil in the wilderness? What did Peter say of "religious experiences"?

3   Read and discuss the experience of Hien Pham in the Vietnamese communist prison. Is there any place too far removed for God to reach? Discuss also William Cowper's poem from this chapter.

4   What is the invitation to America and all the world? Discuss
    some hopeful signs that God is still transforming lives and souls,
    even in the midst of great evil.

About the Author

RAVI ZACHARIAS, president of Atlanta-based Ravi Zacharias International Ministries, was born in India. He immigrated to Canada in 1966 and studied at Trinity Evangelical Divinity School in Deerfield, Illinois, and Cambridge University in England. The author of *A Shattered Visage: The Real Face of Atheism*, *Cries of the Heart*, and *Can Man Live Without God*, he has addressed the issue of God's existence in many university settings including Harvard and Princeton in the U.S., as well as several prominent universities around the world. He has lectured in more than fifty countries, and his weekly radio program, "Let My People Think," is broadcast on more than 550 stations around the world. He and his wife, Margie, are the parents of three children, Sarah, Naomi, and Nathan.

The Ravi Zacharias International Ministries Internet Web site is
http://www.rzim.com